Atlas of the
JEWISH WORLD

Editor Graham Speake
Art editor Andrew Lawson
Map editors Nicholas Harris, Zoë Goodwin
Text editor Robert Peberdy
Picture research Mel Cooper, Diana Morris, Lynda Poley, Linda Proud
Index Sandra Raphael
Design Adrian Hodgkins
Production Clive Sparling

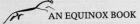 AN EQUINOX BOOK

Published in North America by Facts on File, Inc., 460 Park Avenue South, New York, N.Y. 10016

Copyright © Andromeda (Oxford) Ltd 1992
Reprinted 1984, 1986, 1988, 1989, 1992

Library of Congress Cataloging in Publication Data
de Lange, N. R. M. (Nicholas Robert Michael), 1944–
  Atlas of the Jewish world.
  Bibliography: p.
  Includes index.
  1. Jews—History. 2. Judaism—History. 3. Jews—Historical geography—Maps. I. Title.
DS117.D4   1984
909′.04924   84–10102
ISBN 0–87196–043–5

Origination by Alpha Reprographics, Harefield, Middlesex; Fotographics Ltd, London · Hong Kong; Lithocraft, Coventry

Maps drawn and originated by Lovell Johns Ltd, Oxford; Alan Mais, Hornchurch, Essex

Filmset by Keyspools Ltd, Golborne, Lancs, England

Printed in Spain by Heraclio Fournier SA, Vitoria

Frontispiece The Jewish world as represented by 19th-century drawings of traditional costume. From the left: a lady of Constantinople, a Smyrniote, a Jerusalem couple, a Moroccan, overleaf a Polish couple, an Indian pair, two Algerians, on p. 6 a Reform rabbi from Hamburg.

Atlas of the
JEWISH WORLD

by Nicholas de Lange

Facts On File®

CONTENTS

Special Features

List of Maps

CHRONOLOGICAL TABLE

	(1000 BCE)	300 BCE	CE 1	300	600	900
THE WEST		Beginning of western diaspora	Revolt 115–17	Beginning of Christian dominance	Forced baptisms Spread of Islamic rule	
ISRAEL	Kingdom of David and Solomon Assyrian and Babylonian conquests Persian rule	Macedonian conquest Hasmonean dynasty Roman conquest 63 Herod the Great 40–4	Roman rule First revolt 66–74 Second revolt 132–35	Revolt of Patricius 351	Persian rule 614–29 Arab conquest 634–40	Crusader rule
THE EAST	Babylonian exile Beginning of eastern diaspora	Parthian empire	Jewish rulers in Babylon and Adiabene	Sassanian empire Jewish rule in Himyar	Arab conquests Conversion of the Khazars	Settlements in India and China
RELIGIOUS DEVELOPMENTS	First Temple Second Temple	Greek influence	Rise of Rabbinism		Geonim Rise of Karaism	Influence of Islamic thought
CULTURAL HIGHLIGHTS	Biblical literature	Greek literature	The Mishnah	The Talmud		Arabic philosophy Hebrew poetry

The sacrifice of a ram from Mari, c. 2400 BCE.

IVDAEA

A coin proclaiming the Roman capture of Judaea in 63 BCE.

Moses expounds the Law: a Dura fresco of 245 CE.

The Ark of the Covenant: a 6th-century mosaic from Beth Shaan.

1200	1500	1600	1700	1800	1880	1930
Expulsions and massacres	Expulsion from Spain 1492 Ghettos and mellahs	Settlements in the New World Council of the Four Lands Chmielnicki massacres 1648–49		Partitions of Poland Russian Pale of Settlement Beginning of emancipation	Pogroms in Russia The great migrations Rise of antisemitism Rise of Zionism Emancipation in Russia 1917 Balfour Declaration 1917	Nazi persecution: the holocaust World Jewish Congress 1936

Solomon reads the Torah: a 13th-century French miniature.

A 16th-century Jew from Istanbul.

A Polish wooden synagogue.

The flag of the state of Israel.

Mamluk rule	Ottoman rule				Beginning of Zionist settlement	Jewish state 1948
					British Mandate 1920–48	
Mongol invasions	Ottoman empire Arrival of Spanish exiles				Rise of Arab nationalism Birobidzhan	Mass emigration
Kabbalah	Shulhan Arukh Lurianic Kabbalah	Shabbetai Zvi	Hasidism	Reform Orthodoxy	Conservative movement	Reconstructionism
	Beginning of Hebrew printing	Heyday of Amsterdam Jewry		*Wissenschaft des Judentums* Hebrew Enlightenment	Hebrew University 1925	Flowering of vernacular culture

The Jewish world today

areas of Jewish settlement

- dense
- other

places of Jewish settlement

- ⊙ major community
- ■ important community
- • isolated community

ITALY country with Jewish population

Equatorial scale 1:60 000 000

PREFACE

The story of the Jews is only one slim thread in the tangled skein of human history, but it is a story which reaches out far beyond the narrow confines of the Jewish people itself. The Jews have never been a large or powerful people, but they have found themselves repeatedly caught up in the most turbulent currents of history, and their story is fraught with adventures, mysteries and paradoxes. Today this involvement with history is only too visible, in the aftermath of the Nazi inferno and in a world uncomfortably dominated by events in the Middle East. The Jews have often appeared as the odd man out among the nations, and this has given rise to many misconceptions. The purpose of this book is to give an account, as plainly as possible, of the Jews: who they are, and how they have come to be where they are today.

I am not aware of any other atlas which has tried to do exactly this, and in the absence of a model I have had to devise my own, perhaps idiosyncratic, form of presentation. It may be helpful if I point out that the book is in three parts, each of which represents a different approach to the Jewish world. Part One approaches it through history, with the emphasis on the movements of population which have constituted the shifting foundation of Jewish existence, together with the political and social conditions which brought those movements into being and gave them their direction. Part Two is a series of very generalized essays on different aspects of the Jewish experience, which contrast the past with the present and cast a cautious look ahead to the future. Part Three is a guided tour through the Jewish communities of today's world. I have tried to give here not just dry facts and figures, but some assessment of the local conditions which make each community unique. The three parts are interdependent, but they can be read separately, and in any order.

Since this is first and foremost an atlas it is the maps that carry the main story. The rest, that is the written text, is merely commentary. Occasionally this commentary may take on a wistful or even a pessimistic tone. That is hardly surprising. The Jewish experience has not always been a happy one, as most Jewish readers will know only too well, and although we Jews have recently emerged from one of the darkest periods in our history there are still many causes for anxiety. Any assessment of the condition of Jewry today must be to some extent subjective. My own standpoint as a committed Jew is grounded in faith and optimism. But I have felt I should be doing a disservice to my readers if I tried to gloss over the very real doubts and disappointments which exist. Forty years ago the overall picture was incomparably gloomier

than it is today. But if on the material plane there is now more room for confidence, both spiritually and psychologically the outlook is far from bright. Whatever judgments I have made about the present state of Jewry are based on established facts and on my own experience of Jewish individuals and institutions. Not everyone, perhaps, will agree with them. I can only say that if my gloomier appraisals are proved false I shall be delighted.

The final choice of the illustrations has been in other hands than mine and I do not wish to comment on the selection, except to say that some of the very striking visual images make their own commentary on the state of the Jewish world, hardly requiring my written captions. It is often a subtle commentary, deriving its force from a contrast of past and present. But this is in accord with one of the major themes of the book.

I could never have written this book alone, and I should like to pay tribute here to the many people who have helped me. In the first place I ought to mention three departed teachers: Ignaz Maybaum, James Parkes and Cecil Roth. All three taught me, in their different ways, not only how to interpret the Jewish past but also how to live a better human life. They have all made specific contributions to the book, but more than this their memory was with me throughout the writing of it. I have also learned precious lessons from Alexander Scheiber, and I am grateful to him and to the staff of the Jewish Theological Seminary of Hungary for their kindness and hospitality to me in the course of my research. Peter Brown, who generously agreed to act as Advisory Editor, offered searching criticism and sound counsel. An inscrutable destiny brought us together in curious circumstances many years ago, and he might well be surprised to know how much he has given me since. I should also like to thank Susan Skilliter for her advice on everything Ottoman, particularly on illustrations, and many other friends and colleagues who have contributed snippets of information or useful suggestions (often perhaps unawares). I am grateful to Michael Neuberger for his readiness to lend me books or make good-humored comments as the occasion demanded. And I owe a special debt of thanks to Michael Stewart simply for being there at several moments when I needed him.

My deepest thanks are reserved for Patricia, who put up faithfully with the unwarrantable burden the writing of this book placed upon her life. I could not have finished it without her. I have written it for her and for our children, to tell them something about where we have all come from and what it means to be a Jew in today's world.

PART ONE
THE HISTORICAL BACKGROUND

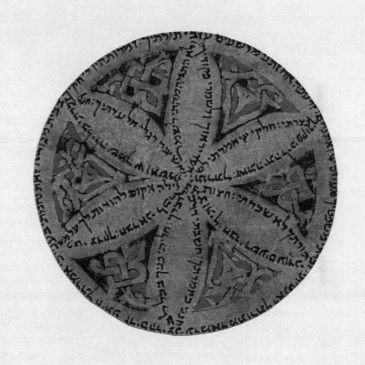

THE JEWS AND THEIR HISTORY

There is a mystery about the very existence of the Jews: a people dispersed through the countries of the world, without (until recently) a land of their own or a common language, and yet possessing a strong sense of unity and common identity. Jewish identity is an enigma even to Jews themselves, impossible to capture in a single phrase; the only way to approach it is through history. To be a Jew is not to assent to a particular creed, but ultimately to acknowledge an attachment to a past. Individual Jews are connected to one another in the way that the leaves of a wide-spreading tree are connected to one another: some leaves clustering close together or brought into momentary contact by the passing winds, others located far away, yet all similar in kind and linked by a complex structure of branches ramifying outwards or crossing in an apparently haphazard way, but all attached to the same trunk, through which they draw their nourishment from the invisible roots. A Jew in Philadelphia or Frankfurt may have little in common, on the face of it, with a Jew in Kiev or Casablanca, in Tel Aviv or Tashkent. The only thing that unites them all is a feeling, however faint or unformulated, that they share the same origins, perhaps the same historic destiny which might, almost at random, have placed the one here and the other there.

The Jews are a small, scattered people. With one exception they are a tiny minority of the population of every country where they live, and the majority of Jews almost everywhere are immigrants or the children or grandchildren of immigrants. To understand the contemporary Jewish world it is therefore essential to know something of the upheavals of the past hundred years. But the story must be traced further back than that. A hundred years ago the Jewish communities were somewhat less widely scattered, somewhat longer established. But the differences are only relative. Dispersion, migration, minority status are characteristic features of a long history stretching back 2000 years and more. And it is not only the superficial, external aspects of Jewish history which need to be studied against this long perspective but the subjective, internal world of the Jewish mind. Jews everywhere are acutely conscious of their long history and of the unhappy and often tragic vicissitudes that the people have undergone. Events occurring today, and Jewish responses to them, are profoundly influenced by the experience of the Jewish past and by the marks it has left on the collective Jewish psyche. In the foreground of the Jewish consciousness stand the recent epoch-making events of the Nazi holocaust and the establishment of the Jewish state of Israel. But these events themselves cannot be explained entirely in terms of modern European history. The holocaust was the culmination of centuries of isolation and hatred of Jews in Germany and other Christian countries. The establishment of Israel was, for many Jews, the realization of (in the words of the national anthem) "the two-thousand-year-old hope—to be a free people in our own land." Even the basic, complicated questions of Jewish identity—loyalty to the scattered people or full citizenship in the modern state, the sense of being a religious or an ethnic minority, the divisions and conflicts which exist within each Jewish community—need to be perceived against the background of Jewish history.

The shaping of Jewish history: evidence and interpretation

Where to start the story is a vexed question. Jews (like Christians) trace their own history back to biblical times. The Jewish historian Josephus, at the end of the 1st century CE, already stresses the antiquity of the Jewish people, and he refers his readers to the Bible as the authentic record of the history of the people back to the beginning of time. The Bible is certainly an important document of Jewish history. It presents an account of the origin of the people of Israel and of its development from a single family to a mighty kingdom and then, after a period of national defeat and exile, to a restored commonwealth in the old capital of Jerusalem. The biblical story already contains most of the ingredients of later history: migration and minority status, oppression and recovery, national aspirations and the sense of a moral mission to the world. These biblical themes have exerted a powerful influence, if not on the shaping of Jewish history, at least on the interpretation that has been put on events by generations of Jews down to our own time.

Any attempt to understand the Jews and Judaism must give a prominent place to the Hebrew Bible. But the Bible, at least in its older portions, is not a historical record. It sets forth an interpretation of earlier events, a blend of legend, poetry and propaganda, a formative myth of national origins which conceals at least as much as it reveals. We lack the means to test its historical statements, and the actual facts and their chronology are a matter of complex controversy. Archaeology and the records of neighboring peoples certainly help to fill out the story and to correct or confirm some details, but the picture still remains obscure and fragmentary.

It is only after the arrival of the Greeks on the stage of Jewish history that we have the means to recreate a fuller picture of the course of events, with their nuances and implications, their causes and their repercussions on a wider scene. It was a peculiar achievement of the Greeks to take seriously the objective study of history and the need to establish an accurate chronology. This had been done long before the Jews became part of the Greek world, and in time the Jews themselves caught the habit. Several Greek historical works written by Jews survive, of which the last and greatest is Josephus' *Jewish Archaeology* or *The Antiquities of the Jews*, together with his account of the first war against the Romans (*History of the Jewish War*). It is a measure of their significance that after the death of

Right Archaeological discoveries have added immeasurably to our knowledge and understanding of the past. Among the most sensational finds are the written documents recovered from remote caves dotting the desert hills which run down to the shores of the Dead Sea. One haul of texts brings the revolt of bar Kosiba to astonishing life. Another opens a window on a previously almost unknown Jewish sect, probably dating back to Hasmonean times. Texts of the latter group were found in these caves in Wadi Qumran, in close proximity to the remains of a settlement which may have belonged to the sect. These discoveries have answered some old questions, but they have posed many new ones, about Jewish political and social history, languages and literature, and religious ideas.

wealth and influence, but (with a few marginal exceptions) they were never the masters of their own destiny, and they were always vulnerable to changes in the political climate and threatened by the hatred of religious fanatics and hostile populations. Graetz was actually an optimist: he believed in progress, and in the inherent power for good of human conscience and reason. Even he had to recognize, however, in his later editions the rising tide of political antisemitism, and events since his time seem to have confirmed dramatically the insecurity of the Jewish condition. The bright moments in the medieval period were few and short-lived, and they do not counterbalance the misery which was the usual lot of ordinary Jews under Christian or Muslim rule or the horrors of massacre and expulsion which were inflicted not once or twice but repeatedly on Jews in Christian Europe. The oppression and hatred of the middle ages have left a wound on the Jewish psyche which is still far from being healed.

The profound crisis of the modern era

It was only in the 18th century that demands for an improvement in the status of the Jews were first taken seriously by governments and rulers. The ensuing reforms benefited only a minority of Jews, and they hardly affected the great centers of Jewish population in eastern Europe and the Muslim world. They tended to strengthen the forces of reaction, which gave birth to a new, secular and politically organized form of antisemitism. And they also provoked uncertainty and division among Jews themselves. While some Jews eagerly espoused the struggle for human rights, others pointed to the danger of assimilation, and turned their backs on the opportunities of the new age. Jewish religion, and in fact Jewish identity too, underwent a profound crisis, which still continues.

Meanwhile economic hardships and political oppression in eastern Europe and Muslim countries led to large-scale emigration to the industrial west and to the pioneering countries of the southern hemisphere resulting in the dissolution of traditional patterns of Jewish life and faith. There were more positive aspects to this troubled period, among them the gradual raising of the standards of living and cultural life of large numbers of Jews, and the emergence of various proposals among Jews themselves for ending the anomalies and injustices of Jewish existence. (The struggle for political emancipation and integration had been initiated and largely waged by non-Jews.) Organizations were also set up to assist emigrants and to develop resettlement programs, to relieve poverty and prevent exploitation of immigrant labor, to combat antisemitism, improve educational standards, and to safeguard and further the civil rights of Jews. These organizations achieved an enormous amount in a relatively short time. Some of them continue their good work, since the need for their services sadly persists.

The new political movements and welfare organizations were, however, powerless to ward off the most savage and crushing manifestation of inhumanity the Jewish people has ever experienced, the Nazi holocaust. Between the Nazi rise to power in 1933 and the defeat of Germany in 1945 a considerable majority of Europe's 10 million Jews

Josephus we are once again plunged into relative gloom, illuminated only by archaeological discoveries and occasional information in non-Greek or non-Jewish sources. But what remains is enough to illustrate the conditions of Jewish life in all their complexity, from different viewpoints and in various places. One feature which emerges is the relative "normality" of Jewish life, as compared with that of other similar peoples at the time and as compared with the "abnormality" of Jewish life during the subsequent period of Christian and Muslim dominance. At the same time we are able to read in the words of Jews themselves about their preoccupations and perplexities in the face of a changing world, their complaints and their ambitions.

The ensuing period is something of a dark age, in two senses: information is lacking, or at best patchy, and the course of events is somber and often tragic. The story of the Jewish middle ages, from the emergence of Christianity to the 18th-century Enlightenment, makes depressing and at times horrific reading. It is a period of *apartheid* and oppression, religious coercion and physical violence, in which the Jewish communities were virtually powerless to defend themselves. Many of them were destroyed or uprooted, and the survival of the rest seems little short of miraculous.

The 19th-century Jewish historian Heinrich Graetz was criticized for writing Jewish history as a catalog of woes. It was pointed out that there were periods of relative security and even of prosperity and cultural flowering. Even if Graetz's account is highly colored, it is clear that the status of the Jews almost everywhere was one of dependence and inferiority. Sometimes they were protected or encouraged, and some individual Jews achieved great

Left The formal opening of the Hebrew University in Jerusalem, on 1 April 1925: a painting by Leopold Pilichowski (1869–1933). Lord Balfour is speaking, and seated behind him on the rostrum are the Sephardi and Ashkenazi chief rabbis of Palestine, General Allenby, the High Commissioner Sir Herbert Samuel, Dr Chaim Weizmann, and the Chief Rabbi of the British Empire, Dr Joseph Hertz. The artist himself can be seen at work in the foreground.

were killed or made homeless, some six million of them ruthlessly put to death as part of a systematic policy of extermination. It is hard to contemplate or comprehend a destruction on this scale. Beyond the human loss (well over a third of all the Jews in the world), the catastrophe destroyed a whole civilization, or rather two whole civilizations: the Yiddish-speaking Jewry of Poland and eastern Europe with its flourishing communal life and its celebrated talmudic academies, and the German-speaking Jewry of Germany and central Europe with its splendid synagogues and seminaries and its extraordinary record of scientific, humanitarian and cultural contributions to western life. It also posed a challenge to hopes of progress grounded in enlightenment and understanding, and of the normalization of Jewish existence, and to traditional religious faith and national self-confidence. Forty years later the questions posed by the holocaust are still far from being answered. Meanwhile, partly as an outcome of the disaster, a Jewish state has been established in part of the old land of Israel, and this in turn has raised further questions about the nature of Jewish identity and destiny and about the relationship between Jews and non-Jews, not only in the Middle East but everywhere. Small wonder if today's Jews seem bewildered and confused, or if the Jewish world seems to be in a state of transition.

The renewal of Jewish history

Amid the confusion and change the appeal of history has become stronger rather than weaker. The study of the past seems to offer some hope of certainty or understanding. Jewish historiography is itself a recent development—or rather it has been resumed from the no less anguished times in which Josephus wrote. Jews of the middle ages apparently had no need of history: they lived their Judaism and the choices facing them were few and simple. It was only after the Enlightenment that Jews again began to study and write their own history. The early 19th century, a period of disillusionment with traditional Judaism, witnessed the birth of a new academic discipline which takes its name from the *Zeitschrift für die Wissenschaft des Judentums* ("Journal for the Study of Judaism"), founded by Leopold Zunz in 1822. The scholars of the *Wissenschaft* movement applied modern methods of research to traditional

Jewish literature, and paved the way for the scientific investigation of Jewish history. Their achievement seems all the greater when we remember that they were not professional scholars, but rabbis, schoolmasters or businessmen. Demands for the integration of Jewish studies in the universities were met with stolid resistance. The establishment of the Jewish Theological Seminary in Breslau (Wroclaw) in 1854 at last enabled a few scholars to devote their time fully to academic research and to training a future generation of Jewish scholars, and the Breslau model was copied elsewhere. But it was hard for the seminaries to compete with the universities in attracting the best Jewish students, and it was only after the foundation of the Hebrew University in Jerusalem in 1925 that Jewish studies were fully incorporated into a university curriculum.

Wissenschaft des Judentums drew its impetus from the instability of Judaism in the early 19th century. Its leaders were motivated in part by a conscious desire to interest young Jews, who were uncertain of their allegiance, in the riches of the Jewish past and at the same time to present a more positive image of Judaism to the gentile world. They emphasized especially the achievements of medieval Jewry, notably those of the philosophers and poets of Spain. The idea of the Spanish golden age furnished an antidote to present insecurities; its influence is manifest in the Moorish revival architecture so characteristic of later 19th-century synagogues. Great names of the past, such as Philo, Maimonides and Spinoza, became potent symbols: it is no coincidence that these were Jewish thinkers who had made an acknowledged contribution to Christian tradition. Biblical history, too, attracted interest, no doubt for similar reasons. But internal Jewish tensions also influenced historical research. The conflict of Reform and Orthodoxy focused attention on the early history of rabbinism, and promoted the scientific study of the Talmud. Zunz himself wrote a notable treatise on the sermon in antiquity, showing that this controversial feature of Reform services was not a servile borrowing from the Church but the revival of an ancient practice of the Synagogue.

Local history also attracted attention, as Jews sought for their roots in the places where they were

Jacques Basnage (1653–1723): a French Protestant who wrote the first modern history of the Jews. It became the model for subsequent attempts.

Right: The heritage of the past Our knowledge of the Jewish past is increasing all the time. This map shows the major institutions specializing in research, and also places where important ancient or medieval remains survive *in situ*. In addition there are numerous smaller museums and libraries (many of them set up by private initiative or by a local Jewish community), and literally thousands of other places with historic remains, most of which still await systematic exploration. Cemeteries are particularly numerous, and they are a rich source of information about the past; it is only recently, however, that they have begun to be taken seriously by researchers, and unfortunately many of the most important ones are in countries where access by Jewish scholars is difficult, and where there is little or no surviving Jewish population to ensure their maintenance.

UNITED STATES
OF AMERICA

Los Angeles
Cincinnati
New York
Philadelphia

Ballista missiles fired by Roman forces
during the siege of Masada (72–74).

Remains of the 6th-century synagogue at Bar'am, Israel.

Detail of a capital and architrave
in the 3rd/4th-century remains
of a synagogue at Ostia, Italy.

NORTH SEA

BALTIC
SEA

Leningrad

Moscow

Manchester
Oxford
Cambridge
London
Amsterdam
Hamburg
Berlin
Warsaw
Elbe
Oder
Vistula

EASTERN EUROPE
numerous medieval cemeteries and synagogues

Rhine
Rouen
Paris
Worms
Frankfurt
Prague
Krakow
Loire
Munich
Sopron
Budapest
Dniester
Dnieper

Casale
Monferrato
Venice
Parma
Carpentras
Pesaro
Senigallia
Danube

BLACK SEA

Rhône
Gerona
Corsica
Ostia
Rome
Trani
Venosa
Stobi

Ebro
Avila
Segovia
Sardinia

ASIA MINOR
numerous ancient inscriptions

Tomar
Toledo
Palma
Balearic
Islands
Sicily
Aegina
Delos?
Sardis
Priene

Cordoba
Seville
Syracuse
Naro

Apamea

scale 1:21 500 000

0   600km

0   400mi

MEDITERRANEAN SEA
Crete
Cyprus
Dura-Europus

IRAQ/IRAN
numerous ancient and
medieval remains

Hara Sghira
(Djerba)

ISRAEL
numerous ancient synagogues
and other remains

Damascus
Bar'am
Bet Shearim
Tel Aviv
Qumran
Masada

remains from antiquity

☰ synagogue
✡ cemetery
⌐ manuscript find

from the middle ages

☰ synagogue
✡ cemetery
⌐ manuscript find

modern collection of older material

Alexandria
El Yahûdiya
Cairo
Jerusalem

Oxyrhynchus

Nile

Elephantine
RED
SEA

■ primarily Jewish museum
● museum with important Jewish section
⌐ major collection of medieval manuscripts
○ historical archive

Detail of the medieval synagogue at Cordoba, Spain.

The Beth Hatefutsoth (Museum of the Jewish Diaspora), Tel Aviv,
Israel.

INDIA

Cochin
Chenamangalam

The Cairo Genizah

Below The conservation of the fragments is a demanding technical task. Before they can be read, identified and studied each one has to be carefully flattened and treated. At Cambridge a special department of the University Library has been set up to look after the Genizah material.

Below The main credit for the recovery of the Genizah documents must go to Solomon Schechter, Reader in Rabbinics at Cambridge and subsequently President of the Jewish Theological Seminary in New York. The full tale of his journey to Cairo and of his acquisition of the bulk of the material for

The Hebrew word *genizah* refers to a pious custom of preserving documents which bear the name of God, or have been used for sacred purposes, usually with the eventual intention of burying them in the ground. It is not uncommon to see in Jewish cemeteries a grave-plot marked simply *Genizah*: it is probably filled with old prayerbooks. The astonishing haul of manuscripts and printed texts known as the Cairo Genizah was recovered, however, not from a graveyard but from a synagogue, the Ben Ezra synagogue in Fustat (Old Cairo). Several extraordinary factors combined to make this one of the most exciting historical discoveries ever made. In the first place the synagogue was an old one, dating back a thousand years or so. Secondly, it had ample room for storage in a loft, so there was no need to bury *genizah* material in the ground. Thirdly, the climate of Egypt, as is well known, is uncommonly favorable to the preservation of parchment and paper. And fourthly, Cairo had been, during the lifetime of the Genizah, one of the most important centers of Judaism, with close religious, cultural and commercial links with other parts of the Jewish world. Consequently the documents discovered there in the 1890s were not only relatively well preserved for their age, they were also of outstanding historical importance. They include Bible and Talmud, liturgy and poetry, legal and literary documents, personal and business letters, ranging in date from the 10th century and earlier right down to the end of the 19th century.

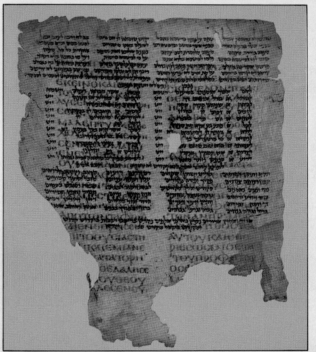

Left Most Genizah documents date from the 10th century onwards, but some fragments are older. This is a palimpsest, a manuscript whose writing has been scraped off so that the parchment can be reused. The upper writing is a Hebrew liturgical poem, but the 6th-century writing underneath, which can still be made out, is part of Aquila's Greek translation of the Bible, once very popular but now almost entirely lost.

Left There are innumerable historical documents in the Genizah, about both major events and more local or ephemeral affairs. This text is from an account purportedly by the king of the Khazars, explaining how his forebears were converted to Judaism (see p. 43).

Right The Genizah manuscripts reveal a great deal about the everyday life of a medieval Jewish community, including the education of children. The Jewish boy learned to read and write an an early age, and texts like this one show us how it was done. Each letter of the alphabet is copied out several times, with the different vowel-signs which vary its sound. The letters are copied in outline, and it may have been the child himself who colored them in, as part of the learning process.

Cambridge University is a highly colored Oriental romance in itself, full of sublime coincidences and ridiculous misapprehensions. Here he is seen at work among the crates of dusty fragments in the former Cambridge University Library. There turned out to be well over 100000 fragments in all, and

smaller but still important collections have ended up in Leningrad, London, Budapest, New York and elsewhere.

Below Among the extraordinary discoveries of the Genizah were documents written by well-known people in their own handwriting. This legal responsum was written by Moses Maimonides, who was the spiritual head of the Cairo community in the late 12th century.

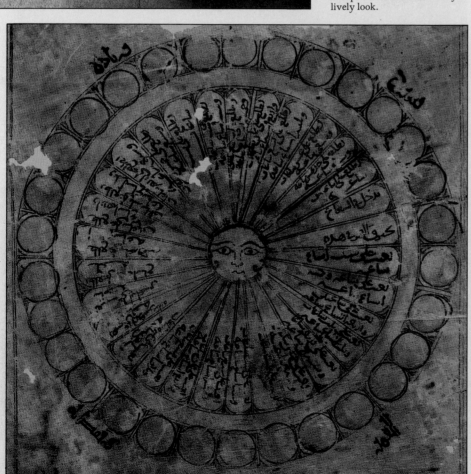

Below The Genizah manuscripts are written in a bewildering variety of languages; they include virtually every language that Jews have used, and notably Hebrew, Aramaic, Arabic, Persian and Spanish, but there are also documents of non-Jewish origin. Arabic was widely spoken and written by Jews in the middle ages, but they tended to write it in Hebrew characters. This calendar is inscribed in Arabic script. The face which occupies the center has a very lively look.

beginning to feel they belonged, and wished to demonstrate to their gentile fellow citizens that they too had an honorable past in their common land. The Jewish Historical Society of England (founded in 1893, one of the earliest learned societies of its kind) promoted research into medieval Anglo-Jewry, and similar bodies were established in other countries. Attention was also paid to the presentation and collection of historical archives. The German Jewish archive was set up in 1906 in Berlin, where the World Zionist Organization also established an archive in 1919. This was prudently transferred to Jerusalem in 1933, and the Central Zionist Archive is now an important documentary resource. An even more ambitious project was the General (now Central) Archives for the History of the Jewish People, founded at the Hebrew University in 1939. Meanwhile some important Jewish libraries and research institutes had been set up in various countries, as well as museums which presented the heritage of the Jewish past in visible form to a wider public.

The early archaeological explorations of biblical sites in the Near East attracted a good deal of interest, but Jews were not well placed to participate in them before the establishment of the Hebrew University. Some discoveries from later periods were made in the course of the 19th century—the Jewish catacombs at Rome and Venosa, the synagogue at Hammam Lif in Tunisia, the necropolis at Tell al-Yahudiyya in Egypt and the amazing manuscript hoard from the Cairo Genizah (see opposite)—but they failed at first to exert a serious influence on Jewish historiography or to capture the popular imagination. With the growth of Jewish interest in the land of Israel, however, and the spectacular discoveries which have been made there, attitudes have gradually changed. Archaeology in Israel has become almost a national sport. Jewish students from abroad have been enabled to take part in excavations. Important new finds receive immediate attention in the Jewish press both in Israel and abroad. There is a palpable excitement in the rediscovery of long-lost relics of the Jewish past, in the reforging of a physical link with the land, and in being able to identify with famous scenes of history and legend. Important discoveries have contributed to our understanding of Jewish history, such as the rabbinic necropolis of Beth Shearim, numerous remains of Roman and Byzantine synagogues, the written documents of the Judaean Desert, or fascinating tombs and buildings in Jerusalem. The excavations at the Herodian palace and Zealot fortress of Masada attracted unpaid volunteers from 28 countries. This site of suicidal resistance to foreign occupation has become a powerful symbol for Israelis and a shrine for national pilgrimage.

Whether the past can really answer the questions of the present is a moot point. More often history is invoked to buttress a religious or political prejudice. The renewal of interest in Jewish history is not just a reflection of natural curiosity: it answers to a need for reassurance in the face of bewilderment, disorientation and physical loss. Since the Nazi holocaust "survival" has become a watchword for Jews everywhere, verging at times on a blinding obsession. A preoccupation with the past may well reflect a deep-seated anxiety about the future.

THE JEWS IN THE ANCIENT WORLD

The cradle of the Jewish people lies in the Middle East, more specifically in the "Fertile Crescent" which arches from the head of the Persian Gulf up the valley of the Euphrates and south through Syria and Palestine to Egypt. This region contains all the oldest known areas of Jewish settlement, as well as providing the setting for the events which dominate the traditional accounts of Jewish origins. Geographically, most of it consists of fertile cultivated land, bordered by mountains and deserts. Historically, it was the home of several powerful empires, whose vicissitudes furnish the background for much of the biblical narrative.

The Jews in antiquity believed that their history, in common with that of all mankind, originated in Mesopotamia, but they also looked to Egypt, at the further end of the crescent, as playing an important part in their origins. Abraham, the father of the

people, was thought to have come originally from Ur, not far from the Persian Gulf, and to have lived for a while at Haran, far to the north in the land of Aram, before traveling southwestwards into Palestine and Egypt. His family tomb was pointed out, where it is still shown to visitors today, in Hebron, near Jerusalem. The other dominant figure from the remote past, Moses "the lawgiver," was born in Egypt but led the people out into the desert in preparation for their entry into the land which later bore their name.

The Hebrew Bible describes the origin of the people in terms of a coherent history, unfolding from the wanderings of the family of Abraham, through the Egyptian captivity to the exodus, from a nomadic or seminomadic life to a settled existence, and from an essentially tribal to a national organization. After a period of anarchy punctuated by the

The Fertile Crescent
The early history of the Jews was played out in this region of natural contrasts—mountain and plain, fertile land and desert. The River Euphrates waters a long plain bounded by formidable mountains and extensive deserts—a natural route for the movement of people and trade, and also for military conquest. The land of Israel is small, relying for its fertility on seasonal rainfall. But it straddles the vitally important route from Mesopotamia to Egypt—hence its role as a commercial and cultural crossroads and its destiny as a battleground. Not until the coming of the Greeks did the stage of Jewish history expand beyond the bounds of Egypt and the Fertile Crescent.

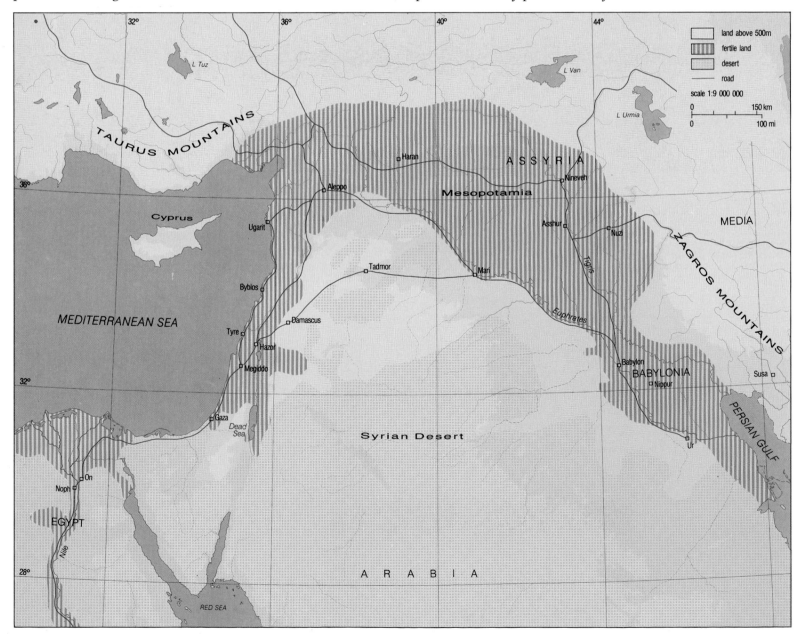

Jews in today's world are predominantly an urban population, and so it has been for many centuries. But behind the urban experience there lies a period of agricultural life which has left numerous traces on Jewish law and customs. And yet further back there is the age of the "Fathers"—desert nomads who are acknowledged as the founders of the Jewish people. The images of desert and oasis and the wandering life are intimately woven into the fabric of Jewish thought and experience to this day.
Above An oasis near Qurna in southern Iraq, traditional site of the Garden of Eden.
Right The landscape of Judaea, descending from Jerusalem towards the coast. Terrace cultivation has ancient origins on these winding slopes.

military leadership of "judges" a monarchy was established, which was soon divided into two kingdoms, Judah in the south and Israel in the north. In the absence of other narrative sources it is hard to assess the accuracy of this tradition, but archaeological evidence supports the story of the conquest of Canaan in broad outline, while casting doubt on some of the details, and suggesting that it was a lengthy process which occupied the whole of the 13th century BCE and left some areas in Canaanite hands. External evidence has not re-solved the major problems connected with the previous history of the conquerors, but there is increasing documentary information about the movements of West Semitic populations during the second millennium BCE and their social organi-zation. The early biblical narratives bear the marks of later editorial reworking of ancient traditions, some of which may well preserve authentic recollections even in their revised form. Despite intense research it is still not clear how the twelve tribes arose or precisely how and when they were welded together into a single nation. The names of the tribes are associated with particular regions of the land, and even if the tribal divisions originally reflected close blood ties, in time it was geographical rather than genealogical criteria that determined tribal identity, which in any case yielded in importance to smaller units (family and clan) as well as to the larger national identity. In the period of the monarchy tribal membership was largely symbolic: it had given way to the new realities of a centralized administration and a predominantly urban and agricultural lifestyle.

The monarchy also encouraged the development of a strong merchant class, involved in international as well as in local trade. Although concrete evidence is scanty, it is reasonable to suppose that some traders settled temporarily or permanently abroad, laying the foundations for the later mercantile diaspora. At any rate the Bible records the granting (c. 860 BCE) of a trading quarter in Damascus to King Ahab (1 Kings 20:34). The recurrent political upheavals and invasions may also have led to some movement of population, as prisoners of war or as political refugees. With the Assyrian conquest of the northern kingdom in the late 8th century the incipient diaspora takes on a more substantial reality. An inscription of Sargon mentions 27 290 deportees from Samaria in 721 BCE, and this figure must represent only a fraction of the Israelites resettled in northern Mesopotamia and further east during the Assyrian conquests, their place being taken by settlers from Babylonia and Syria. The southern kingdom of Judah lived on in the shadow of the Assyrians, and for a time at the end of the 7th century, while Assyria was defending itself in vain from the assaults of the Medes and Babylonians, King Josiah restored Judaean rule in a large part of the territory once ruled by David. But soon the Babylonians overran the kingdom and destroyed its cities, including Jerusalem with its temple (587). Large numbers of Judaeans were transported to Babylonia, while others fled to Egypt. In both these regions there may already have been settlements of Israelites. The exiles maintained their attachment to the old country, and their hope of an eventual return. They also clung to their national identity, and from this time on Judaism effectively lost its territorial basis. When Cyrus the Persian conquered Babylon (539) and permitted the Jews to return to Jerusalem and rebuild the temple, many chose to remain where they were. Neither the Babylonians nor the Persians interfered with the inner religious and social life of the Jewish communities. They lived on a level of equality with the majority of the king's subjects, and some of them achieved prominence at court. In Egypt they even had their own temple at Elephantine, although apparently no attempt was made to build a temple in Babylon. The communities preserved their distinct identity based on a common past and strengthened through family and clan loyalties. The idea of the nation was no longer linked directly to territory: God's rule extended to the whole world, even if Jerusalem was his special home.

Jewish life under Greek rule

After the Macedonians conquered Persia (331 BCE), Alexander the Great and his successors did not alter the status of their Jewish subjects, who continued to enjoy equality of treatment and limited self-government. Jews were encouraged to settle in the newly founded cities and the early years of Macedonian rule saw a massive expansion of the diaspora throughout the Greek world, particularly westward, into Asia Minor, Egypt and beyond. The Jewish communities were organized in officially recognized corporations (*politeumata*), governed by leaders and councils and having their own courts dispensing traditional Jewish law. Other minorities also had their *politeumata* in the Greek cities, and in many ways the status of the Jews was not exceptional. Their freedom to live under their own laws, however, necessarily implied certain privileges, notably exemption from worshiping pagan gods and paying divine honors to their rulers, and freedom to observe the Sabbath rest. These special privileges were an essential condition for Jewish life and therefore necessary if their rulers were to enjoy the loyalty of the Jews (which most of them did). They were a source of satisfaction to the Jews and often of resentment to their non-Jewish neighbors. Jews sometimes claimed that the much greater privilege of Greek citizenship had been conferred on them by the founders of the Greek cities. This is an exaggeration: although some individuals acquired Greek citizenship, what the Jewish communities as such possessed were privileges and immunities, which varied in detail from place to place. Greek citizenship was in any case the perquisite of a minority, and the mass of Jews, in common with the mass of non-Jews, were not members of the Greek *polis* (state or society).

The situation in the territory of Judah (called

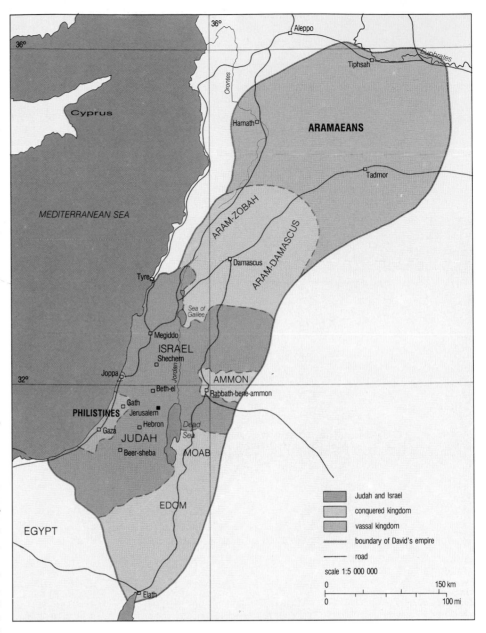

Above: The kingdom of David and Solomon
King David and his son Solomon achieved a legendary reputation for power, wealth and wisdom. As the map shows, they ruled directly or indirectly over an extensive region inhabited by a variety of populations. David established Jerusalem as his capital; it was Solomon who built the great temple which was to be the unified focus of Israelite worship and national identity. The achievements of this period (c. 1000–930 BCE) left a lasting impression on subsequent generations, traces of which are still alive today, in the Jewish liturgy, in folklore and in the political ideology of Zionism.

Judah and Israel

conquered kingdom

vassal kingdom

boundary of David's empire

road

scale 1:5 000 000

0   150 km

0   100 mi

"Judaea" by the Greeks and Romans) and its capital, Jerusalem, was different. Here the Jews constituted a majority of the population and continued to enjoy a broad measure of self-government as they had done under Persian rule. The leadership in Jerusalem was entrusted to the hereditary high priests and to a Greek-style city council. They were permitted to administer the territory under their "ancestral laws," and to apply them even to the non-Jewish inhabitants. Although Judaea formed part of the Ptolemaic, and later (from c. 200 BCE) the Seleucid, kingdom, there was little interference in the autonomy of the Jewish government until the reign of Antiochus IV (175–164 BCE). The course of

events is not entirely clear, but it appears that at the beginning of his reign Antiochus deposed the high priest, Onias, and sold the office to Onias' brother Jason, who abolished the traditional "theocracy" and constituted Jerusalem as a Greek *polis*, under the name of Antioch-at-Jerusalem. A complicated civil war broke out, in the course of which Antiochus captured Jerusalem (169), settled it with Syrian soldiers and sanctioned the introduction of pagan worship in the temple (167). Resistance, however, continued, and under the leadership of Judah Maccabee (died 160) achieved remarkable military and diplomatic successes. The eventual outcome was the establishment of Judah's family, the Hasmoneans, as the ruling dynasty in an independent Judaea. His brother Jonathan (died c. 142) was recognized as high priest and as the local governor for the king; he was succeeded by another brother, Simon, who achieved independence in the form of immunity from Syrian taxation (142). In 140 BCE a public assembly formally acclaimed Simon as national leader (ethnarch), general and high priest, with perpetual rule: in other words his position was to be hereditary. His son John Hyrkanos succeeded him (135–104), to be succeeded in turn by his sons Aristoboulos (104–103) and Alexander Yannai (103–76). Jewish rule was progressively extended, so that Alexander Yannai at his death ruled a kingdom comparable in extent to that of David. Jews were settled in the conquered territories; their populations were forcibly Judaized and some cities which resisted were destroyed. The name of Judaea was extended to the whole enlarged territory, and its rulers from Aristoboulos onwards used the royal title like other Hellenized rulers of the region. After the death of Alexander, his widow Salome Alexandra ruled as queen (76–67), and their eldest son

Family Tree of the Hasmonean Dynasty

Mattathias (c.166)

Judah Maccabee (160)

JONATHAN (c.142)
High Priest 153/2–c.142

SIMON (134)
High Priest c.142–134
Ethnarch 140–134

JOHN HYRKANOS I (104)
High Priest and Ethnarch 134–104

Rulers in CAPITALS
Date of death in brackets
All dates BCE

JUDAH ARISTOBOULOS I (103)
High Priest and King
104–103

ALEXANDER YANNAI (76)
High Priest and King
103–76

m. SALOME ALEXANDRA (67)
Queen 76–67

JUDAH ARISTOBOULOS II (49)
King 67–63

JOHN HYRKANOS II (30)
High Priest 69–40
King 67
Ethnarch 47–40

ANTIGONOS MATTATHIAS (37)
High Priest and King 40–37

Jonathan Alexander (49) m. Salome Alexandra (c.27)

daughter m.
Antipater, son of King Herod (4)

Aristoboulos (35)
High Priest 35

Miriam (29) m. HEROD (4)
King 40–4

The Jewish world in 300 BCE
The early beginnings of the wider diaspora are clearly visible in this map. Jewish settlement is still concentrated in Judaea and Babylonia, but already new offshoots are springing up along the main trade routes and in the Greek cities of the eastern Mediterranean. This distribution reflects the two main reasons for movement: commercial opportunities and a Greek policy of granting rights to settlers (for instance former soldiers who were given grants of land). At this early moment the westward expansion has hardly begun. In the course of the 3rd and 2nd centuries BCE its effects will become more marked, and so will the cultural rift between Greek-speaking and Hebrew- or Aramaic-speaking Jews.

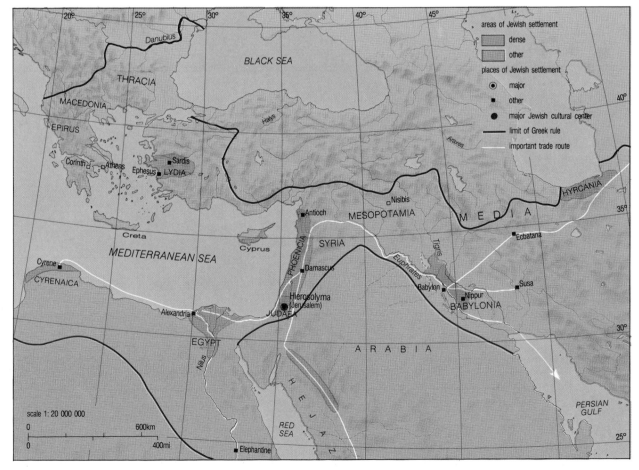

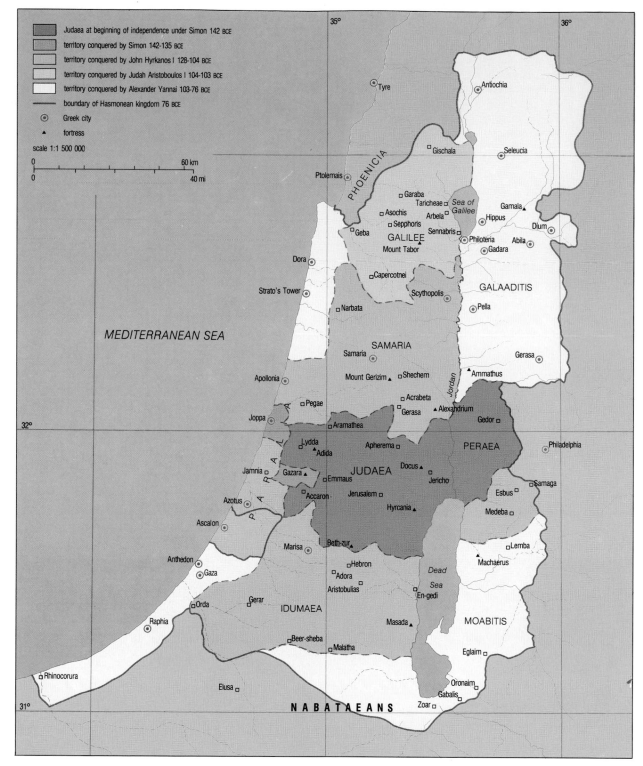

Judaea at beginning of independence under Simon 142 BCE
territory conquered by Simon 142-135 BCE
territory conquered by John Hyrkanos I 128-104 BCE
territory conquered by Judah Aristoboulos I 104-103 BCE
territory conquered by Alexander Yannai 103-76 BCE
boundary of Hasmonean kingdom 76 BCE
⊙ Greek city
▲ fortress
scale 1:1 500 000
0   60 km
0   40 mi

Left: The Hasmonean kingdom
From small beginnings the Hasmoneans eventually came to rule over a territory only a little smaller than that of David and Solomon (see p. 22). The map shows the gradual expansion of their rule. A major military achievement was the conquest of the Greek city of Samaria, after an arduous siege (c. 108–104 BCE), by Hyrkanos I, opening the way for the incorporation of Galilee into the Hasmonean state.

Hyrkanos was high priest. On the queen's death civil war broke out between Hyrkanos and his brother Aristoboulos, which was to bring to an end the period of Judaean independence. The Roman commander Pompey, who was engaged in a successful campaign in Asia Minor and Syria, intervened in the civil war, and after a three-month siege captured Jerusalem (63). The image of the Roman general and his staff entering the inner sanctuary of the temple—a place reserved exclusively for the high priest—left a lasting impression on Jewish minds. But the consequences were more far-reaching. Josephus puts it succinctly: "We lost our freedom and became subject to the Romans. We were forced to return to the Syrians the territory which we had captured from them. In addition the Romans exacted from us in a short time more than a

thousand talents, and the kingship, which was previously given to the hereditary high priests, devolved on laymen."

Judaea under Roman rule

For the next 700 years the land was, with only a few brief interruptions, ruled directly or indirectly by the Romans. On the whole they were content, like former rulers of the region, to allow the Jews to administer their own affairs, but it was they who made or ratified official appointments, and in times of stress they did not hesitate to intervene with force to maintain the Roman peace.

Under Pompey's arrangements the area of Judaea was much reduced, and it was placed under the supervision of the governor of Syria. Hyrkanos was ratified as high priest but he lost his royal title.

Below: The Jewish world in 1 CE
Jewish settlement is now far more extensive throughout the Greek world and in the Parthian empire, and is beginning to spread to the Latin-speaking west. There are probably over 8 million Jews in all (in a world population of some 170 million), more than 2 million of them in Judaea and more than a million each in Egypt, Syria, Asia Minor and Babylonia. Alexandria has a particularly large Jewish population, and is the main center of Greco-Jewish culture.

Later, Julius Caesar made him ethnarch (47 BCE), but by now the real power was in the hands of Antipater, Hyrkanos' able general. The period was marked by frequently renewed fighting, much of it led by Aristoboulos and his sons, who had not given up hope of regaining the throne. For a few years (40–37) one of the sons, Antigonos, actually reigned as king in Jerusalem by favor of the Parthians, who had overrun the region, but in the meantime Herod, Antipater's son, had been recognized as king of Judaea by the Roman senate (40 BCE), and with Roman help he reconquered the land and ruled it until his death in 4 BCE. Under Herod the high priesthood was reduced to little more than a

ceremonial function under the king's dispensation. The Jewish sanhedrin (supreme council) was deprived of political power and replaced by a new royal council. Although a Jew himself, Herod ruled over an extensive territory with a large non-Jewish population and he attempted to combine the roles of Jewish king and Hellenistic ruler. His reign was successful and prosperous, although marked by an appalling contempt for the lives of those around him (including members of his own family). His many grandiose building schemes included the rebuilding of the Jerusalem temple in a Hellenistic style, as well as several palaces and an important harbor at Caesarea. He was the last of the great Jewish kings,

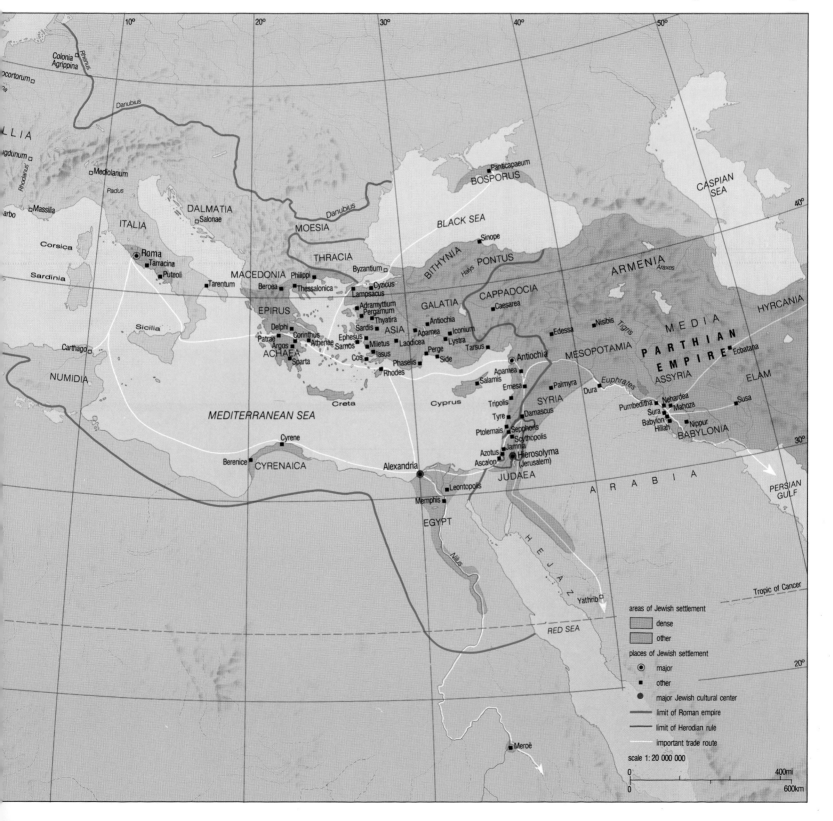

areas of Jewish settlement
☐ dense
☐ other
places of Jewish settlement
⊙ major
■ other
⦿ major Jewish cultural center
━ limit of Roman empire
━ limit of Herodian rule
━ important trade route
scale 1: 20 000 000
0   400mi
0   600km

and many aspects of his reign recall that of his legendary predecessor David. But he was always aware that his power depended on the favor of the Romans, and that his real role was to execute their policy in the region under his rule. On his death his kingdom was divided up among three of his sons, none of whom was granted the royal title. But the arrangement proved neither satisfactory nor permanent. Judaea was administered by a series of Roman governors of equestrian rank, apart from a brief interlude (41–44) when Herod's grandson Agrippa ruled it as king. One of the governors married a daughter of Agrippa, another was of Alexandrian Jewish birth, but none of them had any real connection with Judaism and most were resented by the Jewish population. Roman rule was felt to be military domination and fiscal exploitation. The high priests and their council in Jerusalem had no real power, relations between Jews and Greeks were not good and various revolutionary movements sprang up. In 66 smoldering rebellion burst into flame, with the assassination of the high priest and savage fighting between Jews and Greeks in the mixed cities. The Roman armies took nearly eight years to quell the commotion, partly owing to political uncertainties in Rome following the suicide of the emperor Nero in 68, but largely because of the determined resistance of the Jewish rebels. Jerusalem fell to the Romans in 70, and the temple was burned to the ground. The last rebel stronghold, Masada, was captured in 74.

The war marked the end of Jerusalem as the Jewish capital, and of the institutions at the heart of the old theocratic government: the temple, the high priesthood and the sanhedrin. The Romans did not, however, attempt to abolish Jewish religion and internal self-government. They allowed the establishment of a new council, consisting of sages rather than priests and autocrats. This new body dealt with internal Jewish reorganization and administration, while the province itself was detached from Syria and placed under governors of senatorial rank. In 132 a second revolt broke out, led by Simeon bar Kosiba who styled himself *nasi* (ethnarch) of Israel. This revolt lasted three and a half years, and cost the Romans heavy losses. But it was even more damaging for the Jews. Vast numbers, including prominent members of the new leadership, were killed or sold into slavery or fled abroad. Jews were banished from Jerusalem, which was refounded as a Roman city (Aelia Capitolina), and from a considerable surrounding territory. The province lost its Jewish name, and was called Syria Palaestina (a reference to the ancient Philistines and the origin of the name Palestine). Apart from some scattered settlements, Jews became a minority everywhere except for Galilee, which was flooded with refugees. For a short time the government took the quite exceptional step of trying to stamp out Judaism by banning circumcision and rabbinic education and ordination. The attempt was soon abandoned, however, and a new policy emerged. Limited Jewish self-government was restored under a hereditary ethnarch or *nasi*, who presided over the council of sages and administered the traditional law through a network of Jewish courts. The

Conflicting images of Judaea under Roman rule. *Top* A Roman image: Judaea personified as a downcast captive, her hands tied behind her back. *Above* A Zealot image: the temple of Jerusalem, long destroyed but seen here restored in all its glory. The legend reads *Shim'on* (for Simeon bar Kosiba), and above is a star, alluding to the messianic prophecy, "A star shall come forth from Jacob." Bar Kosiba's supporters called him bar Kochba, "Son of the Star."

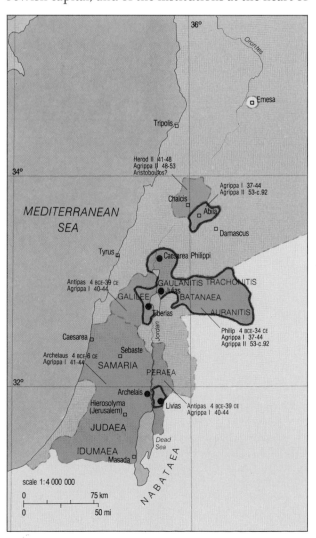

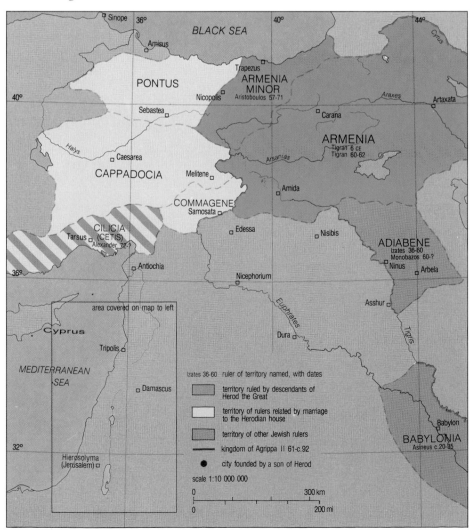

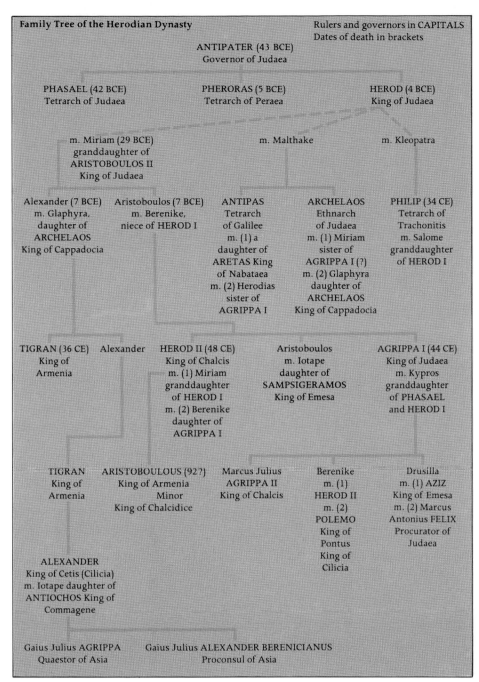

Family Tree of the Herodian Dynasty

Rulers and governors in CAPITALS
Dates of death in brackets

ANTIPATER (43 BCE)
Governor of Judaea

PHASAEL (42 BCE)
Tetrarch of Judaea

PHERORAS (5 BCE)
Tetrarch of Peraea

HEROD (4 BCE)
King of Judaea

m. Miriam (29 BCE)
granddaughter of
ARISTOBOULOS II
King of Judaea

m. Malthake

m. Kleopatra

Alexander (7 BCE)
m. Glaphyra,
daughter of
ARCHELAOS
King of Cappadocia

Aristoboulos (7 BCE)
m. Berenike,
niece of HEROD I

ANTIPAS
Tetrarch
of Galilee
m. (1) a
daughter of
ARETAS King
of Nabataea
m. (2) Herodias
sister of
AGRIPPA I

ARCHELAOS
Ethnarch
of Judaea
m. (1) Miriam
sister of
AGRIPPA I (?)
m. (2) Glaphyra
daughter of
ARCHELAOS
King of Cappadocia

PHILIP (34 CE)
Tetrarch of
Trachonitis
m. Salome
granddaughter
of HEROD I

TIGRAN (36 CE)
King of
Armenia

Alexander

HEROD II (48 CE)
King of Chalcis
m. (1) Miriam
granddaughter
of HEROD I
m. (2) Berenike
daughter of
AGRIPPA I

Aristoboulos
m. Iotape
daughter of
SAMPSIGERAMOS
King of Emesa

AGRIPPA I (44 CE)
King of Judaea
m. Kypros
granddaughter
of PHASAEL
and HEROD I

TIGRAN
King of
Armenia

ARISTOBOULOUS (92?)
King of Armenia
Minor
King of Chalcidice

Marcus Julius
AGRIPPA II
King of Chalcis

Berenike
m. (1)
HEROD II
m. (2)
POLEMO
King of
Pontus
King of
Cilicia

Drusilla
m. (1) AZIZ
King of Emesa
m. (2) Marcus
Antonius FELIX
Procurator of
Judaea

ALEXANDER
King of Cetis (Cilicia)
m. Iotape daughter of
ANTIOCHOS King of
Commagene

Gaius Julius AGRIPPA
Quaestor of Asia

Gaius Julius ALEXANDER BERENICIANUS
Proconsul of Asia

Left: Jewish rulers in the 1st century CE
Herod established a dynasty which forged marriage ties with many of the neighboring ruling houses. His descendants ruled not only in Judaea but as far afield as Armenia. Most of them did not rule as Jews, but rather as part of the complex network of Roman client-kings. Eventually they merged into the Roman senatorial aristocracy. In the Parthian empire the ruling dynasty of Adiabene were converts to Judaism, while Babylonia, with its large Jewish population, for a few years had a Jewish governor.

ethnarchs amassed considerable wealth and privilege. They held court in royal fashion (indeed they claimed to be descended from David), had their own police force and owned a fleet of ships to transport overseas the produce of their estates. A non-Jewish writer, admittedly during a period of relative anarchy in the empire (c. 235–50), describes the powers exercised by the ethnarch, with the emperor's consent, as being no different from those of a king, adding that the emperor sometimes turned a blind eye to capital sentences imposed by the ethnarch's courts.

The policy of supporting the ethnarchate, coupled with the appointment of high-ranking governors and the maintenance of a powerful army in Palestine, certainly had the desired effect of sustaining the peace. From 135 to 351 there were no Jewish revolts, and during the revolt of 351, when a short-lived attempt seems to have been made to restore the kingdom under a certain Patricius, the ethnarch appears to have remained loyal to Rome. This revolt followed (and may have been provoked by) the first offensively anti-Jewish legislation of

the Christian emperors. From this point the position of the Jews in the Roman empire progressively deteriorated, with one exceptional interlude under the pagan emperor Julian, who attempted to rebuild the temple in Jerusalem (363). The attempt was frustrated by an earthquake and by the death of the emperor shortly afterwards. It was perhaps Julian who bestowed on the ethnarch (who now bore the title patriarch) the lofty honorary status of praetorian prefect. The emperor Theodosius II canceled this honor in 415, and a law of 429 refers to the "ending of the patriarchate." Apparently Theodosius simply declined to recognize a successor to the last patriarch, and so the office died out.

Palestine was at this time divided into three separate provinces, of which only two had sizable Jewish populations. They had their own separate Jewish councils, at Tiberias and at Caesarea. The Jews in Palestine, as in the diaspora, resented the policy of Christianization and occasionally resisted it by force, but there was no serious trouble until 613, when the Jews assisted the Persian armies in their conquest of Palestine. Jerusalem fell in 614, and for a few years (to 617) Jewish rule was restored, together with sacrificial worship. In 629 the city was recaptured by the Romans, and for a second time the Jews were expelled. But shortly afterwards (634–40) the country was conquered by the Arabs, and Roman rule was finally ended.

Diaspora Jews under Roman rule

From the time of the destruction of Jerusalem in 70 there was little real distinction between the position of the Jews in Judaea and elsewhere in the Roman empire. The diaspora continued to grow and spread, partly through proselytism, although there was also some movement away from Judaism, to the state religion and to Christianity. Absolute figures are hard to arrive at, but it has been plausibly estimated that shortly before 70 there were two and a half million Jews in Judaea and well over four million in the Roman diaspora. Subsequently—especially after the revolt of 132–35—the ratio of diaspora to Palestinian Jewry increased considerably. It is likely that the Jews represented something like a tenth of the whole population of the empire, and in the places where they were most concentrated, in the cities of the eastern provinces, they may have been a quarter or more of the inhabitants. They were thus a considerable element in the population, a situation for which there are few parallels in later history, and it is obvious why the Romans took Jewish affairs seriously, quite apart from the factor of the sizable population of Jews beyond the eastern frontier (perhaps a further million or more by 70).

The general Roman policy was to recognize rights which already existed, and to preserve as far as possible the status quo. Problems which arose were dealt with on a local basis, and there was little or no attempt to formulate fundamental principles concerning all Jews, such as we find later under Christian rule. The civil status and legal rights of Jews varied from place to place and even from individual to individual within the Jewish community. In some places (and this may have been a common situation in the Greek cities of the east) the Jewish *politeuma* constituted a separate, parallel and in a sense equal structure to that of the Greek city itself. Tensions between Jews and Greeks

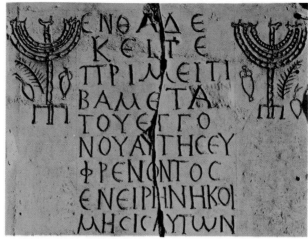

Above left The great gold lampstand (*menorah*) from the temple: it is being paraded in triumph in Rome.

Above right Many hundreds of Jewish tombstones have been found in the Roman diaspora. This one, from Rome itself, commemorates Primitiva and her grandson Euphrainon. The language is Greek, but Primitiva's name is Latin. The stylized symbols—*menorah, lulav, etrog* and oil-flask—are typical: are they a proud statement of Jewish identity, or do they convey a more specific religious message, such as the hope of redemption?

Left There are several Jewish catacombs in Rome. This one, on the Via Appia, has interesting fresco paintings.

sometimes gave rise to outbreaks of violence, as happened in Alexandria in 38 CE and in several eastern cities in 66. In such cases the Roman government intervened, with military force if necessary, to restore the peace and clarify any constitutional problems.

The success of the pragmatic Roman policy is very remarkable. The few cases where it broke down, such as the riots just mentioned, the revolts in Judaea, or the events of 115–17, when fighting between Jews and Greeks spread through Egypt, Cyrenaica and Cyprus, demonstrate how violent and bloodthirsty were the emotions kept under control by the Roman government. Despite the Jews' feeling of belonging to one nation, and known attempts to involve outside Jewish intervention in local problems or to orchestrate widespread rebellion, the incidents which did occur were mostly confined to one region or city. Even the great revolt of 66 in Judaea attracted little if any support from the Jews of the Roman diaspora. On the other hand, the Romans certainly recognized the factors binding the Jews into a single body, particularly their religion. Although they did not (as is sometimes stated) explicitly permit the Jewish religion, they tolerated it in practice and they reiterated earlier privileges or granted new ones making it possible for the Jews to continue their traditional observances. They also facilitated the sending of financial donations from the provinces to the temple in Jerusalem. When the temple was destroyed the

regular contribution was diverted to the imperial treasury in the form of a Jewish tax. Later the ethnarchs, whose authority was recognized as extending to all the Jews of the empire, were permitted to collect funds. These too passed to the imperial treasury with the cessation of the patriarchate. This fiscal policy at least indicated a recognition of the Jews as constituting a single, dispersed body within the empire. If the burdens of taxation and the odium of such specific discrimination were resented by Jews, they were compensated for by the protection of the Roman peace and the honors granted to the ethnarchs as representatives of the Jewish nation. And, apart from prohibitions on circumcising non-Jews and on settling in Jerusalem (both of which seem to have been administered rather laxly most of the time), there were no restrictions on Jewish life other than those the Jews chose to impose on themselves.

The eastern diaspora

Considerable communities remained outside the bounds of the Roman empire. They included the long-established centers in Babylonia and Mesopotamia, some of which have a continuous history extending from remote antiquity to modern times. But as some old centers (such as Babylon itself) decayed, newly founded cities and trading posts attracted Jewish settlers, and there were also some large-scale movements of population due to wars and deportations. The area of Jewish settlement was

The Jewish world in 300 CE
The frontiers of the Roman empire, shown here on the eve of its Christianization, enclose extensive areas of Jewish settlement. The expansion noticed before has continued: Jews are now found virtually everywhere in the Mediterranean basin, and are gradually extending into western Europe. Outside the Roman empire the densest settlement is still in Babylonia, but new communities are rapidly being established further afield, along the main trading routes. The details of these outlying communities are vague and their very existence is in some cases hypothetical, but it is quite possible that there were many more settlements, which have left no trace. Inside the Roman empire we rely for our information largely on inscriptions and other archaeological evidence: this too is fragmentary and accidental information, and no doubt other communities existed.

enormous, ranging from Armenia to Arabia in the south and Media and Elam (perhaps as far as Merv) in the east. At an unknown period Jews also began to spread further eastwards along the main trading routes. The most densely concentrated settlements were in Babylonia, although even here, with the exception of a few towns, the Jews constituted only one among many ethnic and religious minorities.

The Parthians, who ruled most of the region from the late 2nd century BCE to the early 3rd century CE, interfered little in the lives of their subject peoples. The Jews welcomed them and served them loyally, and seem to have prospered under their rule. For a short time, probably from 20 to 35 CE, Babylonia was actually ruled by a Jew, Asineus, with the support of the Parthian king. Conflict with Rome was a dominant feature of Parthian policy, and the Parthians made use of the Jews to further their ends. We have already seen that they briefly restored the Hasmonean monarchy in Jerusalem in 40 BCE, and it has been suggested that they had a hand in the revolts of 115–17 in Egypt and elsewhere. These events took place during a Roman invasion of Parthia, and may well be linked to Jewish participation in an anti-Roman uprising which took place at the same time in Mesopotamia, to the rear of the advancing Roman armies. In Palestine there were Jews who continued to look to Parthia for rescue from Roman domination, and a nationalistic motive for Jewish loyalty to the Parthians is not to be ruled

Below: The Jewish world in 600 CE
Christianity is by now well established in the area of the old Roman empire, but the effects of discrimination against Jews have hardly begun to be felt, and the major decline in the fortunes of European Jewry is still in the future. Settlement in western Europe has grown considerably, but the densest area of Jewish population is probably still Babylonia, which is also the foremost cultural center of the Jewish world.

Dura-Europus was an important frontier-post on the Euphrates, where Roman and Parthian empires met. The synagogue was lavishly redecorated in 245 CE with biblical scenes, only a few years before the building was partially demolished in a scheme to strengthen the city wall against an invasion. But the destruction of part of the synagogue led to the preservation of the rest.
Right Ezekiel's vision in the valley of dry bones preaches a hopeful message of national restoration.

areas of Jewish settlement

dense

other

places of Jewish settlement

● major

■ other

major Jewish cultural area

▬ limit of Christian rule

▬ important trade route

scale 1: 22 000 000

0 — 800km

0 — 500mi

CASPIAN SEA

SSANIAN EMPIRE

Ecbatana
Isfahan

Basra

PERSIAN GULF

Tropic of Cancer

Najran

HADHRAMAUT

out, although the easy conditions prevailing under Parthian rule may provide a sufficient explanation. There is evidence of eastern Jews attempting to emancipate themselves from the influence of the Jewish leadership in Palestine, and the Parthians recognized or perhaps even instituted a Jewish ethnarch (the *Resh Galutha* or "Head of the Exile") analogous to the ethnarch in Palestine. The powers and dignities of the Head of the Exile were no less, and in some respects were greater, than those of the Roman ethnarch, and the office may well have been created to provide a challenger and rival to the Roman official.

Among the many principalities which owed allegiance to the Parthian kings one, Adiabene, was ruled for a time by Jews. Queen Helene and her son Izates were converted to Judaism in the early 1st century CE. The family built impressive monuments in Jerusalem, and strongly supported the Jewish rebels in the war of 66–74, virtually the only foreign Jews to do so. Whether in backing the revolt they were consciously furthering Parthian policy is impossible to judge; the apparent total lack of response from Babylonian Jewry may suggest the contrary. The later history of the dynasty is unknown. Another ruling family, in Himyar in the Yemen, was converted briefly to Judaism, in the late

4th century and again in the early 6th century.

Under the Sassanian Persians, who superseded the Parthians c. 224 CE, conditions continued at first to be on the whole favorable to the Jews, despite periodic attempts by the rulers to impose their religion, Zoroastrianism, on the subject peoples, and despite some heavy losses in wars. The office of Head of the Exile was maintained, and indeed strengthened, and as the position of the Jews deteriorated in Christian Rome Jews from the west were attracted to the freer and more prosperous centers of the east. In the middle of the 5th century there was a period of religious persecution, in which Jews, together with Christians, suffered. Later Jewish legends about the brief establishment of an independent Jewish state by the Head of the Exile at Mahoza in the latter part of the century may be related to these persecutions, but the stories are fantastic and unreliable. About the later history of Jewish self-government we have little information, and it is possible that the exilarchate was abolished during the troubles. It may have been restored briefly during the 6th century, but the last century and a half of Sassanian rule is remembered as a dark and difficult period, and the Jews welcomed the Arab conquerors who overran the Middle East in the 630s.

The Kingdom of Herod

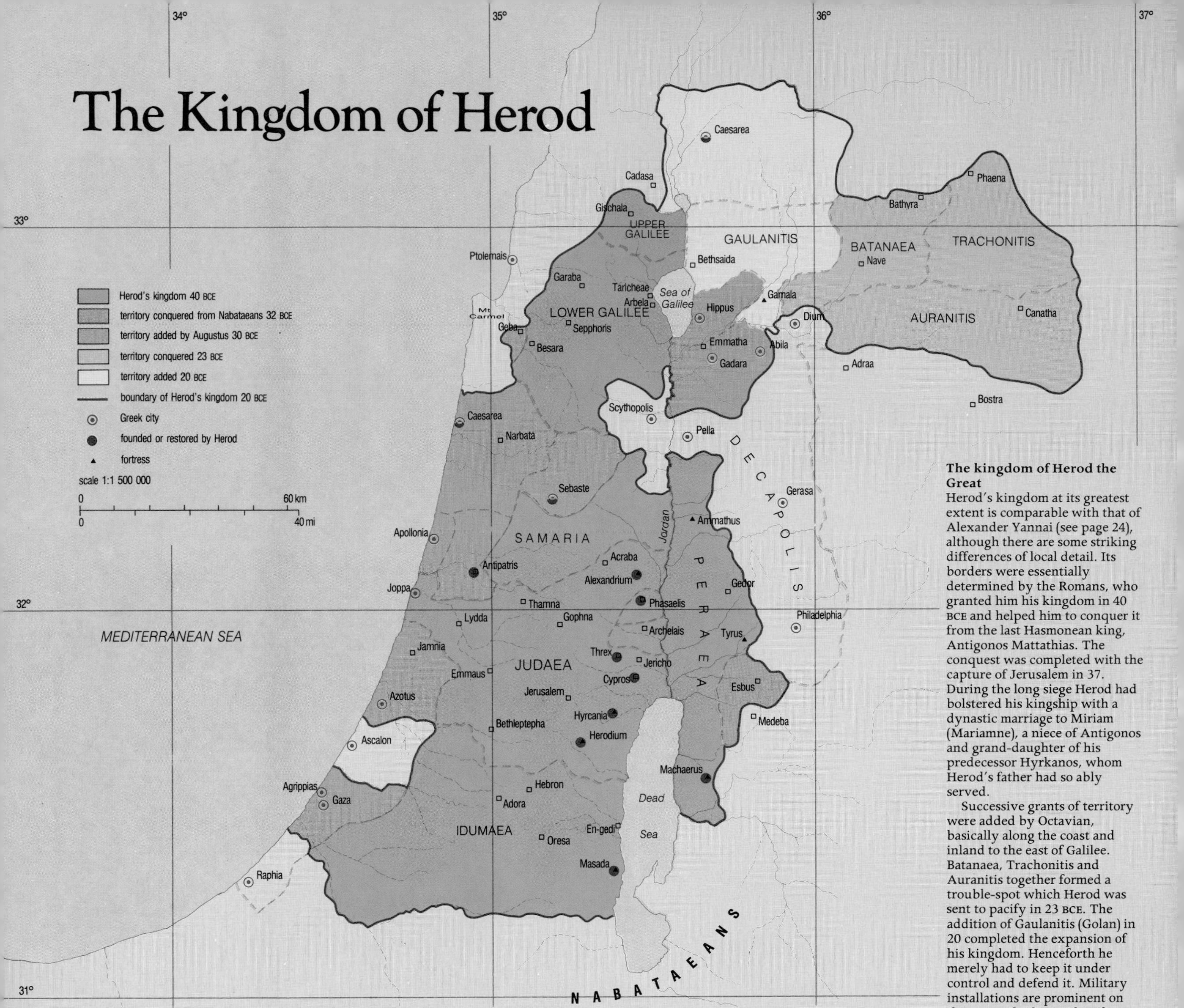
34°
35°
36°
37°
33°
32°
31°
Caesarea
Cadasa
Phaena
Bathyra
Gischala
UPPER GALILEE
GAULANITIS
BATANAEA
TRACHONITIS
Ptolemais
Bethsaida
Nave
Herod's kingdom 40 BCE
territory conquered from Nabataeans 32 BCE
territory added by Augustus 30 BCE
territory conquered 23 BCE
territory added 20 BCE
boundary of Herod's kingdom 20 BCE
Greek city
founded or restored by Herod
fortress
scale 1:1 500 000
0
60 km
0
40 mi
Garaba
Taricheae
Arbela
Sea of Galilee
Gamala
Mt Carmel
LOWER GALILEE
Hippus
Dium
Canatha
AURANITIS
Geba
Sepphoris
Besara
Emmatha
Abila
Gadara
Adraa
Scythopolis
Bostra
Caesarea
Narbata
Pella
DECAPOLIS
Sebaste
Gerasa
Jordan
Ammathus
Apollonia
SAMARIA
Acraba
Antipatris
PERAEA
Alexandrium
Gedor
Joppa
Thamna
Phasaelis
Philadelphia
Lydda
Gophna
MEDITERRANEAN SEA
Archelais
Tyrus
Jamnia
Threx
Jericho
JUDAEA
Emmaus
Cypros
Esbus
Jerusalem
Azotus
Hyrcania
Medeba
Bethleptepha
Herodium
Ascalon
Machaerus
Agrippias
Gaza
Hebron
Adora
Dead Sea
IDUMAEA
En-gedi
Oresa
Masada
Raphia
NABATAEANS

The kingdom of Herod the Great
Herod's kingdom at its greatest extent is comparable with that of Alexander Yannai (see page 24), although there are some striking differences of local detail. Its borders were essentially determined by the Romans, who granted him his kingdom in 40 BCE and helped him to conquer it from the last Hasmonean king, Antigonos Mattathias. The conquest was completed with the capture of Jerusalem in 37. During the long siege Herod had bolstered his kingship with a dynastic marriage to Miriam (Mariamne), a niece of Antigonos and grand-daughter of his predecessor Hyrkanos, whom Herod's father had so ably served.

Successive grants of territory were added by Octavian, basically along the coast and inland to the east of Galilee. Batanaea, Trachonitis and Auranitis together formed a trouble-spot which Herod was sent to pacify in 23 BCE. The addition of Gaulanitis (Golan) in 20 completed the expansion of his kingdom. Henceforth he merely had to keep it under control and defend it. Military installations are prominent on the map, whether within the cities or in isolated situations like the fortress-triangle of Masada, Herodium and Machaerus (named for the Roman commander who had helped in the original conquest of the kingdom). These stern fortresses still dominate the landscape today.

Tradition has dealt harshly with Herod, just as he himself dealt harshly with many of those around him. He has been remembered as a ruthless and hot-tempered autocrat. Even in his own day he had a reputation for cruelty, and his pro-Roman policies aroused violent opposition in some Jewish quarters. But recently a more positive image has begun to emerge. Herod was also a shrewd and able statesman, one of the most successful and powerful of the Roman client-kings of his day. Under his strong, pragmatic rule Judaea enjoyed a period of considerable stability and prosperity which compares very favorably with the decades immediately before and after his reign (40–4 BCE).

The last period of Hasmonean rule had been a time of uncertainty and internecine conflict, both in Judaea and in Rome. Herod's father Antipater had profited from the troubled situation to build up his own power, and had won recognition from Julius Caesar. After Caesar's death Herod adroitly gained the favor of Marc Antony and then, after Antony's defeat at Actium in 31 BCE, of Octavian, who was to become the first Roman emperor under the name of Augustus. Herod paid fulsome tribute to Caesar Augustus by naming in his honor two magnificent cities which he founded, the port of Caesarea and the hill-city of Sebaste. Josephus describes the splendor of the temple of Caesar built on a prominent site facing the harbor-mouth of Caesarea. Inside was a colossal statue of Caesar and another of Rome, both modeled on famous Greek originals. Here we see Herod in the typical guise of a philo-Roman Hellenistic ruler. Elsewhere, and particularly in Judaea proper, he is more respectful of Jewish religious susceptibilities and refrains from erecting human images. His greatest Jewish building, the temple at Jerusalem, was built in a Hellenistic style, but it contained no image. The fabulous beasts which adorned the base of the great golden lampstand (see page 28) recur elsewhere in the Hellenistic world surmounted by human figures. In Jerusalem they are bare. The excavations of Herod's fortress-palace at Masada have provided further illustration of the successful blend of Jewish and Hellenistic themes.

Right One of the most impressive relics of the Herodian city of Caesarea is the aqueduct which brought the city's water supply from the southern tip of Mount Carmel, over eight kilometers away to the northeast. The arches carry two separate conduits; they are built on sand and are exposed to constant sandblasting from the sea winds. Even so a large stretch survives, testifying to the sound engineering and solid construction of the aqueduct. Caesarea supplied a need for a good harbor on that smooth stretch of coast: it remained for a long time the gateway to Judaea.

Below Herod extended and embellished the city of Jerusalem, which had grown considerably to the west and north since the days of David and Solomon. The Temple Mount was still the focus. Herod refashioned the temple in Hellenistic style, and his characteristic masonry is still clearly visible in the western retaining wall of the platform. But to the west of this wall rose the Upper City, where the Hellenistic city of Antioch had been built in the early 2nd century, in and around what is now the Armenian quarter. The Hasmoneans had walled two sides of this area, and built themselves a palace in the Acra, the Hellenistic fortress. Herod completed the wall, dividing the Upper from the Lower City, and he constructed a spacious and well-fortified palace in an angle of the older wall, close by the present Jaffa Gate. He also strengthened the earlier fortress, overlooking the Temple Mount.

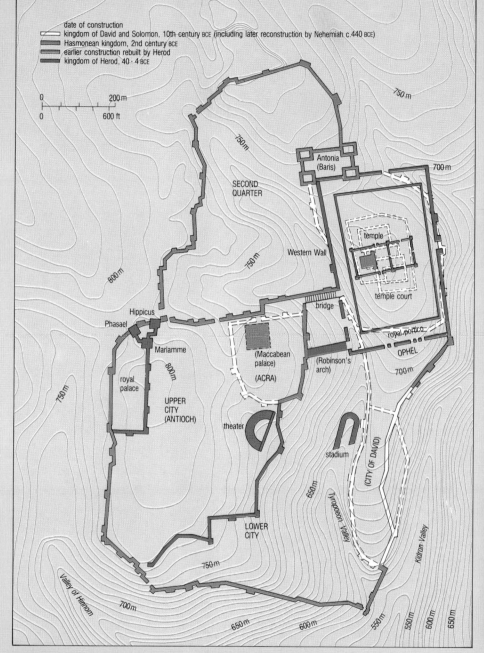

date of construction
kingdom of David and Solomon, 10th-century BCE (including later reconstruction by Nehemiah c.440 BCE)
Hasmonean kingdom, 2nd century BCE
earlier construction rebuilt by Herod
kingdom of Herod, 40 - 4 BCE

Even though most of Herod's magnificent building works have perished, enough survive to convey some idea of his achievement. *Top* The breast-shaped mound of Herodium was artificially raised to conceal the fortress-palace within. Here Herod's body was solemnly laid to rest after his death in 4 BCE. *Above* The fortress of Masada, situated atop a massive spur of rock overlooking the Dead Sea, some 64 kilometers southeast of Jerusalem. The flat-topped rock, falling away in steep cliffs on three sides, made a natural fortress, requiring only the provision of walls around the summit and huge cisterns to trap the rare but heavy rainfall. In this inhospitable aerie Herod installed a sumptuous palace, clinging to the exposed northern tip of the rock (in the foreground of the picture), descending in a series of terraces and overhanging a startlingly sheer drop. Excavations have revealed the remains of columns and richly painted walls, and, as at Herodium, the complex included a synagogue and heated baths. It was an astonishing achievement, a proud testimony to the king's power, wealth and enterprise. The site was occupied by Zealots in the revolt of 66 CE and held out for three full years after the fall of Jerusalem. A Christian monastery was later constructed on the platform.

CHRISTIANITY AND THE JEWS

The adoption of Christianity as the state religion of the Roman empire in the 4th century marked the beginning of a long period of desolation. Judaism, together with the pagan cults, fell victim to the repressive alliance of religious intolerance and political power. Christian polemic against Judaism is attested from the beginning of Christian literature; in the 4th century it displays considerable virulence and aggression, and occasionally finds practical expression in the burning of synagogues and physical attacks on Jews. Ecclesiastical legislation of the period is concerned to limit contacts between Christians and Jews and to counteract possible Jewish influence on Christians. The legislation of the Roman emperors represents an uneasy compromise (inherent in the position of the emperors as Christian rulers) between the maintenance of law and order and concessions to Christian demands. The offensive language of Christian preaching creeps into the laws very early; they

gradually become more openly discriminatory, and harsher in their penalties. The death penalty was laid down for Jews who converted their Christian wives or slaves; the Jewish clergy were subjected to the burden of the decurionate (municipal office), from which Christian clergy were exempt; marriage between a Jew and a Christian was declared to be adulterous. Early in the 5th century the situation worsened considerably. Jews were barred from the civil service and the army; the patriarchate was abolished and the jurisdiction of Jewish courts was restricted to private cases between Jews; new synagogues would be confiscated and old synagogues could only be repaired, by special permission, if they were in imminent danger of collapse.

In fact the position of the Jews was in many ways better than that of pagans and non-Orthodox Christians: the campaign against them was not a war to the death, but a policy of isolation and attrition.

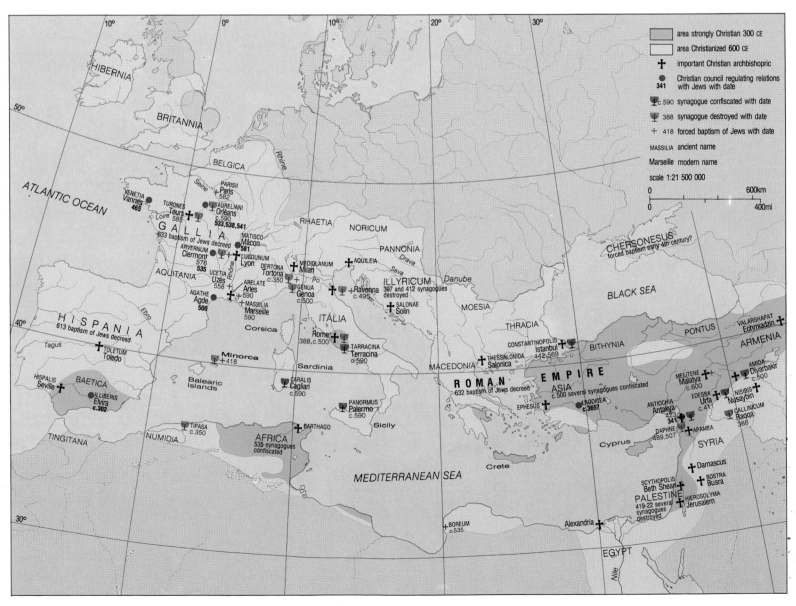

Christians had to contend with several conflicting images of the Jews: it is hardly surprising that reactions were somewhat mixed. On the one hand, Jesus, his family and his disciples were Jews. In these 12th-century scenes from the life of St Anne (*above*), from the cathedral of Paris, the grandparents of Jesus are portrayed as contemporary Jews. St Joachim wears the Jewish hat, and the priest is represented as a rabbi. The 13th-century statue from the cathedral of Strasbourg (*below*) displays a different type of image, reminiscent of the Roman image of vanquished Judaea (see p. 26). It is one of a conventional pair, showing the triumphant Church and the defeated Synagogue.

The legal and economic basis of their life was progressively undermined. Restrictions on Jewish slave-owning were particularly damaging to industry and farming, and the decurionate was a crippling burden for the wealthy. The synagogues were gradually ruined or appropriated to Christian use, and conversion to Christianity was encouraged by inducements of various sorts, and sometimes by threats or by violence.

The Jews resisted this policy where they could, but they were not in a strong position to defend themselves from Christian fanaticism which enjoyed the backing (not always whole-hearted) of the emperor. Large numbers took the easy way out and became Christians; others fled beyond the confines of the empire. Those who remained tried to adapt to the new conditions. The gradual collapse of central authority and the eventual dismemberment of the empire were factors favoring survival, since some of the local rulers, particularly those of the Arian persuasion, were less hostile. But in the early 7th century the baptism of all Jews was decreed in several kingdoms (Byzantium, France, Spain). Jewish life in Europe reached its lowest ebb at this time. In the following centuries a gradual revival is discernible, due perhaps to the useful economic role of the Jews, whose very dispersal gave them certain advantages in trade. But many centuries were to pass before they regained their numerical strength or their freedom.

Throughout the period of Christian supremacy the Jews frequently had to contend with ignorant superstition fomented by rabid anti-Jewish preaching. During the crusades there were assaults on the Jewish communities of the Rhineland, and although in some places the local rulers tried to protect the Jews there was much loss of life and property. Such attacks continued at intervals for centuries, and the total loss of life is appalling. The Jews, generally forbidden to carry arms, were unable to defend themselves, and relied entirely on the protection of

their rulers and neighbors. Too often help was not forthcoming. In several places Jews killed themselves and their families rather than fall into the hands of the Christian mobs.

Scarcely less savage, and certainly more official, were the decrees of expulsion. There were many of these in the course of the middle ages, some local, others affecting whole kingdoms. Although often incompletely implemented or revoked after a few years, they had a very disruptive effect on Jewish life, and indeed often on the economic life of the cities and countries which instigated them. The Jews were expelled from England in 1290, from France (after a long series of temporary banishments) in 1394, from Spain in 1492. In German lands a sequence of massacres in the 13th and 14th centuries gave way in the 15th to an endless round of expulsions. Populations shifted from one bishopric or principality to another and from the towns to the countryside. There was also a general movement eastwards to Hungary and Poland, or south into Italy.

In Italy the Jews actually fared better than in most other parts of Christian Europe. The political fragmentation offered, as in Germany, a refuge from persecution, and in some places they were protected from molestation, even if their status was very inferior. In the papal possessions, for example, the Jews were segregated and humiliated, but they were not butchered or evicted until the Counter-Reformation. Rome contains in fact the only major European Jewish community that can trace an uninterrupted history from ancient to modern times.

In general, Christian policy was to keep the Jews in segregation and subjection, but not to eradicate or assimilate them by force. The popes maintained this policy with considerable consistency. Although such discriminatory or coercive measures as the Jewish badge, the ghetto, book-burnings and conversionist sermons in synagogues all have their

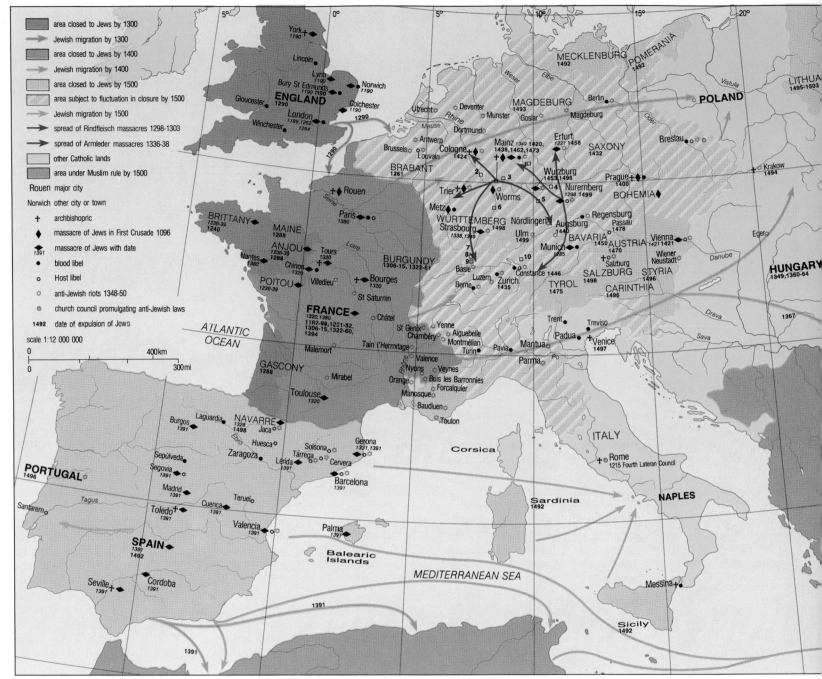

origin in papal legislation, popes strongly disapproved of forcible baptism (although victims were not permitted to return to Judaism), and condemned superstitious accusations, such as that Jews killed Christian children for ritual purposes, desecrated the Host or poisoned wells. These accusations often originated with the local clergy, and were used to stir up hatred of Jews among the people. Priests and monks encouraged violence by their preaching, and sometimes appeared at the head of marauding mobs. The preaching orders of friars were particularly zealous in rabble-rousing, and in encouraging anti-Jewish legislation and ensuring that it was implemented. The secular powers on the whole opposed such disruptive activities, and physical assaults on Jews are usually an indication of the weakness of a ruler. But not all violence was initiated by the clergy. Christian merchants and manufacturers strenuously resisted rival Jewish activities, and Jews were steadily pushed out of these spheres and into moneylending. This had previously been in the hands of the Church or

wealthy Christian laymen, but the enforcement of ecclesiastical regulations based on theological objections to taking interest made it increasingly a Jewish preserve. Jewish moneylenders were subjected to crippling taxation, which led to higher interest rates, and hence to resentment on the part of borrowers, which often led in turn to riots in which Jews were killed and records of loans burned. The slogan of Jews exploiting Christians was now added to the theological battle cries.

Intolerance and coercion naturally produced some half-hearted or insincere conversions. When baptism was imposed on a large scale, as happened in Spain in 1391 and again in 1492, and in Portugal five years later, large numbers of the converts retained a sense of Jewish identity and even kept up their old beliefs and practices in private. The war against Judaism was now carried within the Church itself. The converts and their descendants bore the stigma of their Jewish origin and were subjected to discriminatory measures and to the investigations of the Inquisition. This gruesome apparatus of re-

Above: Christian persecutions, c. 1200–1500 Relegated to an inferior position and dependent on the protection of Christian rulers, Jews were vulnerable to arbitrary decrees, religious fanaticism, economic exploitation and mob violence. Serious attacks began during the First Crusade (1096), and violence increased in the 12th century, sometimes accompanied by accusations of the ritual murder of Christian children (the "blood libel"), or of the desecration of the Host (sacramental wafer), a charge first officially recognized in 1215. The first edict of expulsion was issued in France in 1182, and by 1500 the Jews had been driven out of most of the Catholic kingdoms and principalities. Only Poland and Naples provided stable conditions in which Jewish life could flourish. Despite a similar theological odium, the Orthodox Church provides few examples of anti-Jewish violence.

pression was introduced in Spain in 1478, and extended subsequently to Portugal and to their overseas possessions. Those suspected of Judaizing were tortured to make them confess their guilt and name other guilty persons. Once condemned they were handed over to secular authorities for punishment. The impenitent were burned alive; others were garroted before burning or subjected to lesser penalties such as perpetual imprisonment or service in the galleys. The punishments were executed in "acts of faith," a form of public entertainment accompanied by elaborate and bizarre pageantry. The trials of Judaizers continued to the close of the 18th century (the Inquisition in Spain was not finally abolished until 1834). Thousands of victims were burned, and hundreds of thousands subjected to lesser penalties. Meanwhile even sincere Christians of Jewish origin were discriminated against and excluded from religious orders and offices of authority for several generations. So effective was the segregation that communities of "New Christians" survive in parts of Spain and Portugal to this day.

The Reformation movement of the 16th century offered at its outset a hope of amelioration in the lot of the Jews. Martin Luther began by professing sympathy for them, but when he found that his conciliatory stance did not win widespread conversions he turned against them with ruthless hostility. Under his influence Protestant rulers expelled the Jews or implemented the full range of medieval restrictions. The Counter-Reformation, too, renewed and reinforced the older legislation. The Jews of Rome were segregated in a ghetto by Pope

Paul IV in 1556 (it was not finally abolished until the end of temporal papal rule in 1870), and by the 1630s ghettos had been established in all those parts of Italy from which the Jews had not been bodily ejected. Similar conditions prevailed in other parts of Europe under Catholic rule, even to some extent in Poland where the favor of the monarchy and nobility protected the Jews from the worst excesses of Christian fanaticism. And side by side with official oppression Christian preachers continued to instill in the minds of their flocks an irrational hatred and resentment which poisoned human relations and ever threatened to break out into actual violence.

The complex web of Christian anti-Judaism continued to oppress European Jewry long after the humanitarian rationalism of the Enlightenment had begun to inculcate more positive attitudes. An edict of Pope Pius VI, issued in 1775, not only reiterated the medieval program of degradation but added new refinements—Jews were forbidden to ride in carriages, for example, or to erect tombstones over the graves of their dead. The ritual murder accusations continued: there was an outbreak of them as late as the 1880s, and cases have occurred even in the 20th century. So deeply had the poisonous doctrines sunk in that even anti-clerical secularists often manifested symptoms of the disease, and in Nazi Germany some influential anti-Nazi Christians equated Nazism with Judaism. It was only after the Nazi holocaust that a sincere effort was made at the official level in some churches to counteract the teaching of contempt.

Right Yet another image of the Jews—an utterly alienated one is seen in this painting of the Crucifixion by Hieronymus Bosch (c. 1450–1516). Here Jesus is no longer a Jew but the noble victim of a savage, dehumanized Jewish mob. This caricature has its origin in Christian preaching; it ominously foreshadows the stereotype of the Jew in Nazi propaganda.

ISLAM AND THE JEWS

Unlike Christianity, Islam never formulated any specific attitudes towards the Jews. Full participation in Islamic society was reserved for Muslims; Jews, in common with Christians (and Zoroastrians), had the subordinate status of protected peoples (*ahl al-dhimma* or *dhimmis*). In return for physical protection and freedom of worship they were subjected to special taxes and restrictions, including the wearing of distinctive clothing and a ban on proselytism. It has been suggested that some of these restrictions were inspired by legislation discriminating against Jews which already existed in the Roman empire. They were not always uniformly

or rigorously enforced, and the details varied in the course of time, but the status of *dhimmis*, Jews included, was always a subordinate one. It was formalized in the so-called "Pact of Umar" ascribed to Caliph Umar I (634–44) but probably codified under Umar II (717–20).

Jews were already long established in various parts of the Arabian peninsula by the time of Muhammad (570–632). In Medina (whose name is probably of Jewish origin and where Muhammad preached a new faith in God in 622 CE) they formed the majority of the population. The three main Jewish tribes there were defeated by the Muslims

Below: The Jewish world in 900
The rise of Islam has encouraged a westward movement to North Africa and Spain, while south Italy forms a bridge between the Muslim and Christian worlds and the Jewish empire of the Khazars has an important trading role. The world Jewish population is estimated between 750000 and 1500000, fairly evenly divided between Muslim and Christian rule.

Right Muhammad orders the Banu Aus to execute the Jews of the Banu Qurayza. The early expansion of Islam was won partly at the expense of the Jewish tribes. As the Quran says: "He [God] struck terror into their hearts. A part you slaughtered, and a part you took captive. And he let you inherit their lands, their homes, and their wealth." Only a handful of the Jews saved their lives by embracing Islam: the rest chose martyrdom. In this Ottoman painting, from a manuscript made for Sultan Murad III in 1594, the Jews are distinguished by their typical high red hats.

areas of Jewish settlement

| | dense |
| | other |

places of Jewish settlement

⊙ major

■ other

major Jewish cultural area

— limit of Islamic rule

— limit of Christian rule

— limit of Khazar khanate

⋯ important trade route

scale 1: 28 000 000

0 — 800km

0 — 500mi

under Muhammad: two were allowed to leave, but the third, the Qurayza, suffered a harsher fate. The men, between 600 and 900 in number, were put to death; the women and children became slaves (627). The following year the Jews of the rich oasis of Khaybar were conquered and made to pay tribute, and this victory paved the way for the establishment of Muslim supremacy in the peninsula.

The ensuing rapid Arab expansion brought large Jewish populations under Muslim rule, including the old-established communities of Babylonia, which eventually became the seat of the Abbasid caliphate. Although many Jews accepted Islam, a substantial number remained as *dhimmis*, paying the special taxes and enjoying the protection of the new faith. The institutions of Jewish internal self-government—the exilarchate, the rabbinic leadership, the Jewish law courts—continued to function. According to tradition, the exilarch was given a Persian princess as one of his wives by the Arab conqueror, a gesture suggesting a desire to conciliate an influential sector of the population.

The Arab conquests had united the vast majority of Jewry (perhaps as much as 90 percent) under a single political mantle, and the establishment of the Abbasid capital at Baghdad meant that the largest and wealthiest communities were close to the seat of power. Jewish life in Iraq was gradually transformed from an agrarian to a predominantly urban existence, and many Jews were attracted to the new capital, where in the late 12th century (long after a serious decline in the city's fortunes) Benjamin of Tudela found some 40 000 Jews with 28 synagogues and 10 academies. In Europe at this time few Jewish communities numbered more than a few hundred souls.

Meanwhile there had been a great deal of movement westwards, to the cities of Syria and North Africa, where Damascus, Aleppo, Cairo, Kairouan and Fez rose to especial prominence in the Jewish world. There was also some expansion eastwards, to Persia and beyond. Jewish merchants extended their activities from Spain and Morocco to India and China, and at many points on the trading routes communities grew up.

In recent years the detailed examination of the remarkable manuscript dump from the Cairo Genizah has begun to shed a new light on the Jewish communities of North Africa, and especially on that of Cairo itself. Cairo is now by far the best documented of all medieval Jewish communities. The communal and private life of the Jews, with their law courts and charitable foundations, their cultural and religious activities, their relations with the government and with their non-Jewish neighbors, and their far-reaching links with other parts of the world, can be reconstructed in vivid detail. The information has already served to fill out or revise the accepted picture, and there is material for much more research (see page 18).

As in Fatimid and Ayyubid Egypt, so in Umayyad Spain and in many parts of the Islamic world Jews could share in the general stability, prosperity and cultural flowering of the 10th, 11th and 12th centuries. The discriminatory legislation was often applied leniently or ignored, and outside specifically religious spheres of activity Jews could mix freely with non-Jews and participate with them in trade, in intellectual pursuits and to some extent in

the administration. Hostility certainly existed, motivated partly by religious teachings, and there were occasional outbreaks of violence, but they were sporadic and local. The massacre of the Jews of Granada in 1066 was an isolated occurrence in its severity. Equally isolated was the official persecution of Judaism under the eccentric Fatimid caliph al-Hakim at the beginning of the 11th century; in any case it was originally directed against Christianity, and it was a short-lived exception to the general rule. A more serious and long-lasting disruption was caused by the religious fanaticism of the *al-Murabitun* (Almoravids) and *al-Muwahhidun* (Almohads) who overran Morocco and southern Spain in the late 11th and 12th centuries. Many Jews fled, or, under the latter, chose Islam in preference to the sword.

In the course of the 13th century, when the world of Islam was under pressure from the Christians in the west and the Mongols in the east, the economic and social climate changed dramatically, to the disadvantage of the non-Muslim populations. The laws of *ghiyar* (differentiation) were enforced more stringently, and religious intolerance was allowed a freer rein. In Egypt distinctive dress had already been imposed by the end of Ayyubid rule (1250); under the Mamluks the subjection of the *dhimmis* was more severe and more strictly implemented. In Mongol Iraq and Iran a similar situation prevailed once the ruling dynasty accepted Islam (1295). In western North Africa the Jews were more tolerantly treated for a while, and several of the Merinid sultans employed Jewish officials. The appointment of a Jewish vizier in 1464 brought about the end of the dynasty and also the massacre of Jews in Fez and throughout the country. The downfall of a Jewish courtier had similarly led to the massacre in Granada in 1066 and to another in Iraq in 1291. In Fez, which had a long history of anti-Jewish feeling, the Jews had actually been removed to a special quarter in the wake of riots in 1438. This was the first step towards the physical segregation of the Jews in *mellahs*, which later became a feature of the Moroccan towns. Jews had previously occupied certain quarters in many towns, but this was a voluntary concentration which had roots going back to ancient times. The quarters were not exclusively Jewish, and many Jews chose to live outside them. The creation of the *mellah*, even if it was originally intended for the Jews' own protection, was felt as a humiliating ostracism, and the later *mellahs* were certainly established with this intent, like the ghettos of Christendom. The sizable communities of Morocco remained segregated and humiliated until recent times.

It is impossible, for lack of documentary evidence, to assess accurately the numbers of Jews living at various times in the different Muslim countries. Reports by Jewish travelers are infrequent, and the figures they give are open to question. Benjamin of Tudela, who traveled extensively in the east in the second half of the 12th century, gives figures for many communities, but it is not always clear whether he is referring to the total community or to heads of households only, and the manuscript tradition of figures is notoriously questionable. It is also doubtful to what extent accurate statistics were available in his day, and his account omits many places where Jews are

Below: The Jewish world in 1200
The communities of western Europe are still important, but religious persecution is making itself felt, and there is a noticeable eastward movement along the trading routes both in Europe and in Asia. A majority of the Jewish population (estimated at 1–2 million) now lives under Muslim rule. We have valuable information about this period from the travelogue of Benjamin of Tudela and the documents of the Cairo Genizah (see pages 18–19).

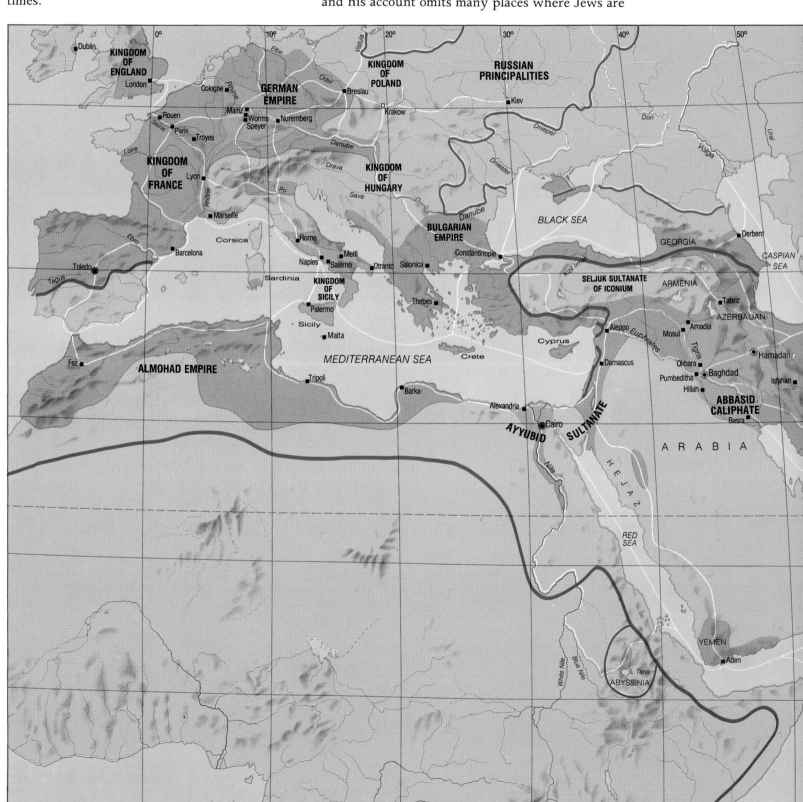

Right below "This is the gate of the Lord; the righteous shall enter through it." The Hebrew inscription on what looks otherwise like a Muslim prayer-rug is a surprise. No doubt it was made (by Jews or Muslims?) to hang in a synagogue. But the design resembles a Muslim *mihrab*, and the lamps are typical mosque lamps—or is the cup containing nine lamps meant to represent the lamps of Hanukkah? This is Turkish court work of the 18th century, and quite unique.

known to have lived. Nevertheless his report is valuable, if only because it indicates the relative distribution of Jews at the time. The largest populations he mentions are in Iraq and Iran, with extraordinary figures of 80000 for Ghazna, 50000 for Samarkand, 40000 for Baghdad and totals of 20000 or more in several other places. In Arabia he records some figures of comparable magnitude, and he mentions Jewish communities which were independent of foreign rule. On the other hand in Syria and Egypt the largest communities are respectively Aleppo with 5000 and Cairo with 7000, and in Europe, apart from Constantinople (2500), Thebes (2000) and Palermo (1500), the largest communities

he mentions total 600 or less. While some of his larger figures, in particular, have been called into question, his report illustrates the massive numerical preponderance of the Jews of the Islamic over those of the Christian world. The general picture is confirmed by the report of Petahiah of Ratisbonne a few years later, although there are some discrepancies of detail. There are no similar sources for another 300 years. Laborious attempts to deduce figures for Egypt from the charity lists of the Cairo Genizah have produced only partial and very local results, and different figures suggested for the Jewish population of Spain reveal large disparities.

It does appear that there was a general decline in population from the 13th century on, attributable to economic deterioration, war and epidemics. Persecution was only a minor factor, and there were no expulsions of Jews such as were commonplace in the Christian world at the same period. In fact, besides considerable movements of population within the Islamic world—at first from east to west and later in the opposite direction—there was a continual flow of Jews from Christian Europe to Muslim lands, which at certain moments of severe persecution became a spate. One such movement occurred at the end of the 14th century, but the most massive exodus followed the expulsion from Spain in 1492. Between 50000 and 150000 left at this time, most of them for Morocco and the Ottoman empire, which had already received a number of Jewish immigrants in the previous decades, and which from 1517 included Egypt as well as Syria and Palestine. The refugees were welcomed, and given opportunities to recreate a stable and prosperous life. The discriminatory regulations were not at first enforced, and we soon find Jews occupying prominent positions in the administration and making an important contribution to Ottoman trade and industry. Sadly, with the economic and political decline of the empire from the 17th century on, the freedom and prosperity of the Jews (as of other populations) were curtailed, but important Jewish communities survived until modern times.

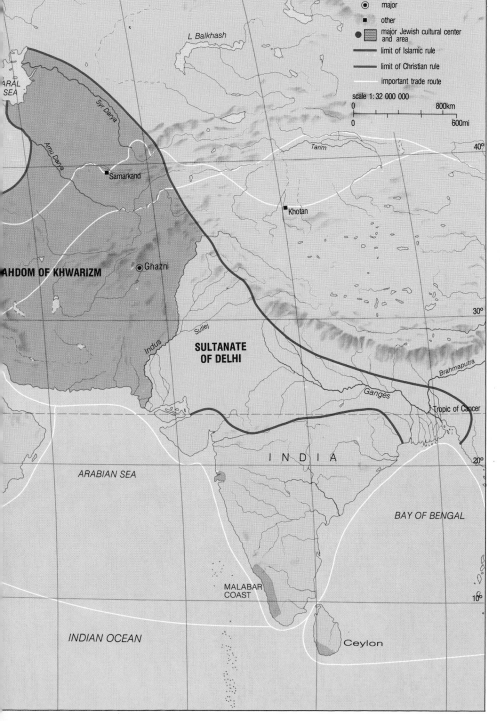

ON THE PERIPHERY

The overwhelming majority of Jews in the middle ages lived under Christian or Muslim rule, but there were exceptions. News occasionally filtered through of Jewish tribes or settlements in remote regions, enjoying freedom from Christian and Muslim domination. The reports tended to be vague and exaggerated, based often on rumors or legends. The lack of regular contact with the major centers is a significant aspect of these communities (although within the Islamic world, too, there were communities which were remarkably isolated). We know now that some of them were unaware of the very existence of other Jews. Their religion often developed along independent lines, neither influencing the main stream nor influenced by it. Their history remains obscure: we catch tantalizing glimpses of them through travelers' reports or references in the writings of their neighbors, or through the scanty remains of their own literature and monuments. A few of them survive, but are unable to provide a reliable continuous account of their own history. It is clear though that in the middle ages there were a number of such "lost tribes" (perhaps far more than we know of), and what we can reconstruct of their story furnishes an instructive contrast to the more familiar communities of the "center."

In China there were Jewish settlements in a number of towns, both on the coast and inland. One, at Kaifeng, still existed in recent times, but the rest disappeared, not through persecution but through assimilation to the tolerant surrounding culture. Confucianism was not hostile to other forms of belief, and no social or political constraints were placed on the Chinese Jews. The records of Kaifeng show Jews in the 16th century engaging in a wide range of occupations, including trade, farming, the army and the civil service. Although the Kaifeng Jews in the last century kept up some distinctive Jewish observances, they had also adopted some typically Chinese ones. They knew little Hebrew, and Chinese inscriptions in their synagogue contained quotations from the Confucian writings, and indeed identified Jewish and Confucian values. Chinese Jewry provides an example of what can happen to Judaism under conditions of extreme toleration: an effortless assimilation leading to total effacement.

In India the toleration and religious syncretism of Hinduism were combined with social segregation deriving from the caste system. Settlements on the Malabar coast and further north in Konkan were cut off for a long time from the rest of the Jewish world (and from each other); Jews from Europe joined the former in the 16th century. The barrier of caste ensured their survival, but it did not prevent them from adopting various Hindu beliefs and practices, and indeed both Jewish communities developed their own internal caste divisions.

The Mongols, who overran the eastern lands of Islam in the 13th century, were equally tolerant. "With the Mongols there is neither slave nor free

Jews came to China most probably as traders, arriving both overland, from Persia, and by sea. The earliest reference to them records a massacre of Jews in Canton in the late 9th century. The longest-lasting settlement was at Kaifeng, the capital of Honan; it was established c. 1000 and lasted into the 19th century.

Left This curious Scroll of Esther is illustrated in Chinese style.

Below A reconstruction of the synagogue at Kaifeng, based on drawings made by a Jesuit missionary in the 18th century. The synagogue was originally built in 1163, but it was rebuilt in 1653 by a Jewish mandarin, Chao Ying Ch'en. The prayerhall was approached through a series of four courtyards, leading west towards Jerusalem.

Left Falashas of Ethiopia. Little is known of their origin or history. They call themselves "Israelites," but their religion is not identical with either Abyssinian Christianity or rabbinic Judaism. They were completely cut off from the Jewish world until recent times.

Below Indian Jews (Bene Israel), c. 1830. The origin of the Jews in India is unknown, although legend ascribes their arrival to the Roman period or even earlier, and it is not impossible that King Solomon's sailors were borne to south India on the trade winds.

man, neither believer nor pagan, neither Christian nor Jew, but they regard all men as belonging to the same stock." So a contemporary Christian chronicler (Bar Hebraeus) reports, and he goes on to describe how a Jewish physician, Sa'd al-Dawla, became the all-powerful vizier of the Mongol ruler Arghun Khan (1284–91). "He treated with contempt the principal emirs and the directors of general affairs and many Jews who were on the fringes of the world gathered together to him, and they all with one mouth said, 'Verily, by means of this man the Lord has raised on high the horn of redemption, and the hope of glory for the sons of the Hebrews in their last days!'" The hope was short-lived, however. On the death of Arghun, Sa'd al-Dawla and his family and protégés were put to death, "and because of him the Jews throughout the world were hated and ill treated." The Mongols soon accepted Islam, and the short spell of toleration ended.

The extent of Jewish penetration into Africa is obscure, but reports occasionally circulated of "lost tribes" in the center of the continent. The only tribe to preserve a Jewish identity to modern times is the Falashas of Ethiopia. Their origin is unknown; they claim to have come to Africa at the time of King Solomon or even earlier, during the exodus from Egypt, but it is generally supposed that they were an African tribe converted to Judaism at a later period, perhaps by missionaries from south Arabia. At any rate they never received the Talmud, and their religion is very biblical, combined with local features such as a female equivalent of circumcision. Ethiopian chronicles from the 14th to the 17th century refer to wars waged against them by the Christian rulers of Ethiopia. At various times they were overcome and forced to accept Christianity, but they repeatedly recovered their independence until they were finally subdued in the 17th century and dispersed to various parts of the country. Those who resisted baptism remained in voluntary segregation, maintaining that contact with outsiders was a source of defilement. Their neighbors, for their part, took little interest in them and left them to pursue their distinctive faith and way of life.

Perhaps the most remarkable of the Jewish groups of the periphery were the Khazars, a Turkish people from Central Asia who settled to the north of the Caucasus, probably in the 6th century. For several centuries they remained powerful enough to command the respect of the Byzantines and Arabs. They controlled a considerable trade in furs, slaves and other commodities, and Khazar merchants were found as far afield as Kiev, Constantinople, Alexandria and Samarra. At some time in the 8th century they adopted the Jewish religion. The details of the conversion are not known for certain, but one thing is clear: it was not the conversion of a whole people, as seems to have been the case with the Falashas, but only of the ruling class, analogous perhaps with the earlier examples of Adiabene and Himyar. The Khazar kingdom contained many different ethnic and religious groups, and there is no evidence of a substantial Jewish element among the population. The Judaism of the ruling Khazars was mingled with extraneous beliefs and practices, and the principal center of Judaism in Iraq never seems to have taken a serious interest in the "Jewish empire" to the north. Petahiah of Ratisbonne traveled across Khazaria (c. 1185) without so much as mentioning its Jewish connections. Other Jewish writers mention the Jewish Khazars (we even have what purports to be an account of the conversion sent by the Khazar king to Hasdai Ibn Shaprut, a Jewish courtier of the Spanish caliph Abd al-Rahman III in the mid-10th century), but it is clear that the Khazars were not at all integrated into the Jewish world, and they must be considered something of a curiosity. Nothing is known for certain about their ultimate fate. The Khazar kingdom had ceased to exist before the coming of the Mongols in the 13th century; whether any of their descendants continued to profess Judaism is an open question.

Life for the Jews of those Christian territories which continued to tolerate their presence was hedged around with endless restrictions and humiliations. Jobst Mellern of Prague (*left*) is nicknamed *der gelb Geckl*, "the yellow fop," on account of the Jewish badge he has to wear in the form of a yellow wheel. The same badge can be seen in the etching of the attack on the Frankfurt Jewry in 1614 (*far left*). The peculiar shields displayed on the houses are another humiliating imposition. This attack illustrates the precariousness of Jewish existence under Christian rule: many Jews were killed, and the rest banished.

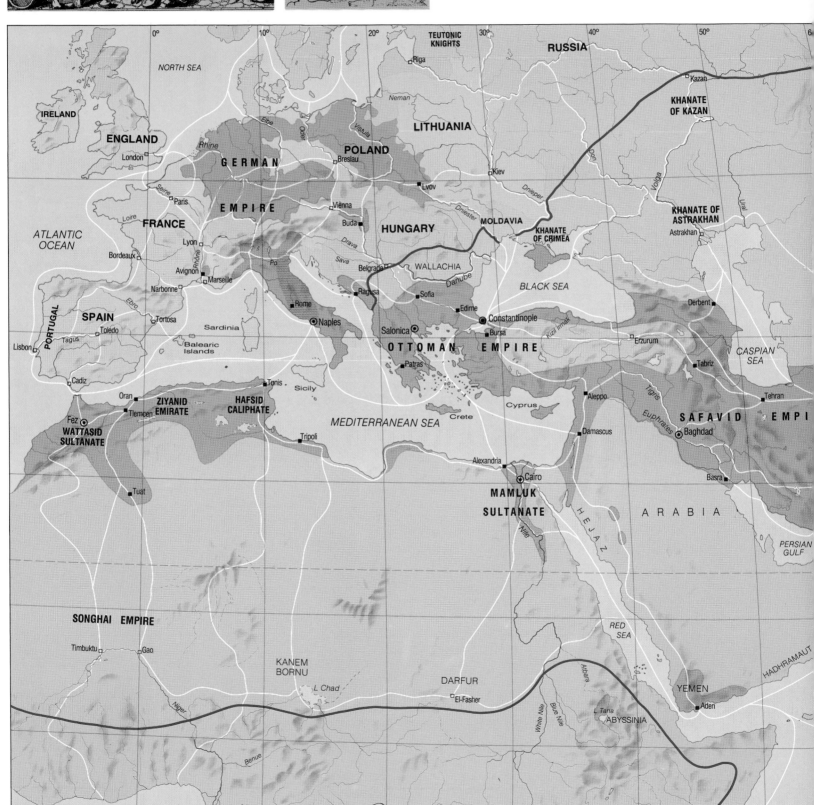

Left The expulsion from Spain in 1492 was not unexpected; it was the culmination of centuries of threats and pressures. This picture of the king of Castile's advisers urging him to expel the Jews from his kingdom dates from the early 14th century.

Far left Church militant: the Inquisition. Dominican friars lead the procession, holding aloft the banner showing justice balanced by mercy. Then come prisoners who have escaped the flames by confessing their crimes. The crucifix has its back to those who are to be burned, together with the effigies of those who died in prison.

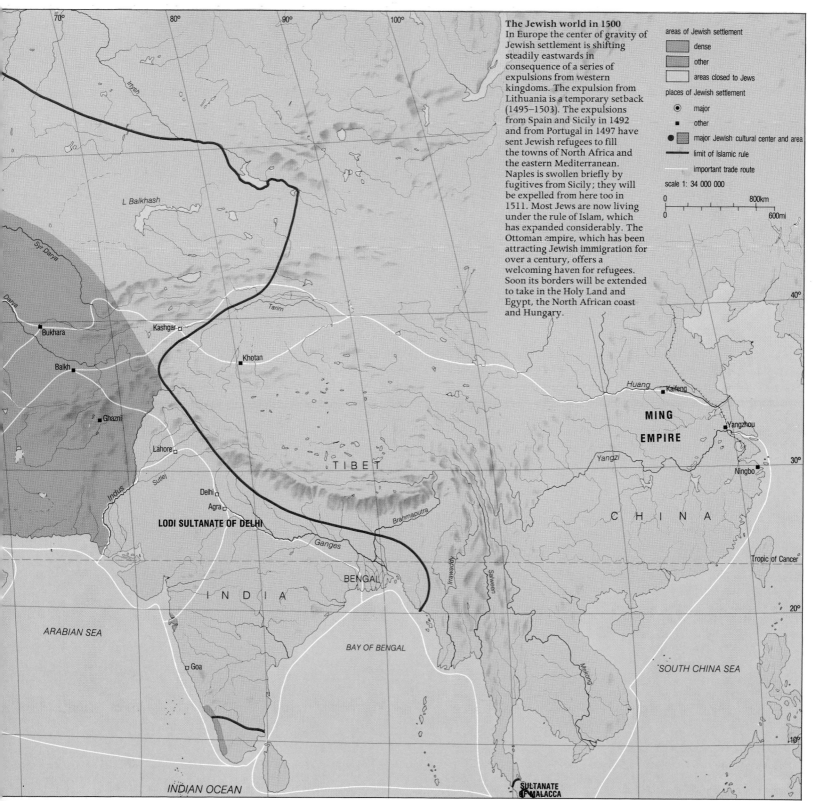

The Jewish world in 1500
In Europe the center of gravity of Jewish settlement is shifting steadily eastwards in consequence of a series of expulsions from western kingdoms. The expulsion from Lithuania is a temporary setback (1495–1503). The expulsions from Spain and Sicily in 1492 and from Portugal in 1497 have sent Jewish refugees to fill the towns of North Africa and the eastern Mediterranean. Naples is swollen briefly by fugitives from Sicily; they will be expelled from here too in 1511. Most Jews are now living under the rule of Islam, which has expanded considerably. The Ottoman empire, which has been attracting Jewish immigration for over a century, offers a welcoming haven for refugees. Soon its borders will be extended to take in the Holy Land and Egypt, the North African coast and Hungary.

areas of Jewish settlement

- dense
- other
- areas closed to Jews

places of Jewish settlement

- ⊙ major
- ▪ other
- ● major Jewish cultural center and area
- ▬ limit of Islamic rule
- ▬ important trade route

scale 1: 34 000 000

0 ——— 800km
0 ——— 600mi

THE SEPHARDI DIASPORA

The expulsion of the Jews from Spain in 1492 is remembered as one of the epoch-making events in Jewish history. Spain was the last Christian country where Jews survived in considerable numbers (perhaps 200 000 or more, not counting *conversos*) and with a certain measure of prosperity. The expulsion was decreed in the newly captured Alhambra of Granada on 30 March 1492, and by 31 July they had all either accepted baptism or gone into exile.

The largest numbers, estimated at over 100 000, took the easiest route and fled to Portugal. It was an unwise choice. Five years later, under Spanish pressure, all the Jews in Portugal were forcibly baptized, amid scenes of gruesome violence.

Italy received a number of Spanish exiles, but political conditions made it an unsatisfactory refuge. Parts of the country (including Sicily with its large and long-established Jewish population) were Spanish possessions and subject to the edict of expulsion. Other parts became Spanish not long afterwards. In the north the Counter-Reformation was soon to harden hostility.

The best hope for the refugees lay outside the Christian world. Some settled, temporarily or permanently, in Morocco and other parts of North Africa, where Jews fleeing from Christian persecution had already been settling for a century. Here their fate was not a happy one. The Muslim populace was unfriendly, and the rules of separation were harshly enforced. It was only in the Ottoman empire that the exiles were really welcomed. The Cretan rabbi Elia Capsali, whose family offered hospitality to some of the outcasts as they passed through Candia, was moved to compile a highly laudatory chronicle of the Ottomans, and he describes the Turks mocking the folly of the Spanish king who was enriching their kingdom while impoverishing his own. The Ottomans had none of the Christian (or indeed the Muslim) prejudices, and the Spaniards (known as "Sephardim" from the biblical name of Spain, *Sepharad*) were treated with particular favor, since they brought skills which were needed: medical and technical knowledge, commercial and political expertise. They settled in all the major cities and reconstructed the ruins of their shattered life and culture. Salonica soon became a mainly Jewish town, and its development into the most important commercial port of the eastern Mediterranean was largely due to Jewish enterprise. When Egypt and Palestine came under Ottoman rule in 1517 these regions too attracted Jewish immigration. Although the Sephardim, with their Spanish language and culture, dominated the Jewish communities of the empire, refugees also arrived from other countries. Some of the fugitives were able to repay their welcome by rendering extraordinary services to the Ottoman state. Joseph Nasi, duke of Naxos (c. 1515–79), and Solomon Aben-Ayish, duke of Mytilene (c. 1520–1603), both from Portugal, and the Italian

Solomon Ashkenazi (1520–1603) were among the foremost diplomats of their day and exerted a considerable influence on international affairs.

The Portuguese émigrés were Christian converts who renounced Christianity on arrival in a freer land. The general conversion of 1497 had trapped many thousands of Jews in a cloak of Christianity which they wore unwillingly and longed to discard. They watched anxiously for an opportunity to escape. Many of the most important Jewish centers of later times owe their origin to groups of Portuguese New Christians. The list includes London, Amsterdam, Hamburg and New York. By the beginning of the 17th century small settlements were to be found in every major commercial center, and they played a vital role in the development and expansion of European trade and finance. As (nominally) Christians they were in a position, through their wealth and skills, to win acceptance in the highest ranks of society, and gradually they acquired, in many places, freedom to worship as Jews. They were thus the pioneers of Jewish settlement and integration in the Western world. Their establishment laid the foundations for much larger-scale immigration of Jews from Germany and Poland. Although they were soon numerically far outnumbered, the Portuguese maintained their own distinct identity, together with their religious traditions, and many of their synagogues survive in use to this day.

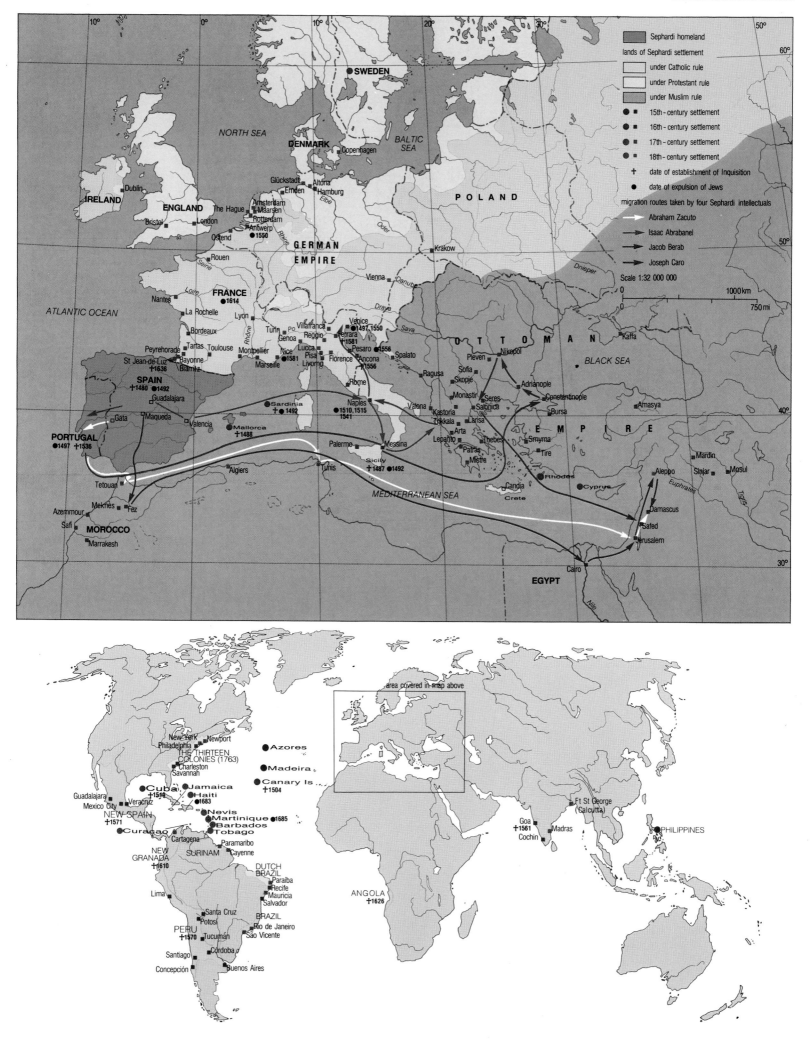

Legend:
- Sephardi homeland

lands of Sephardi settlement
- under Catholic rule
- under Protestant rule
- under Muslim rule

- 15th-century settlement
- 16th-century settlement
- 17th-century settlement
- 18th-century settlement
- † date of establishment of Inquisition
- ● date of expulsion of Jews

migration routes taken by four Sephardi intellectuals
- Abraham Zacuto
- Isaac Abrabanel
- Jacob Berab
- Joseph Caro

Scale 1:32 000 000
0   1000 km
0   750 mi

area covered in map above

The Golden Age of Amsterdam

Bernard Picart (1663–1733) was a French artist and engraver who settled in Amsterdam in 1710. In 1723 he began to issue a series of studies of the "Religious Ceremonies and Customs of all the Peoples of the World," beginning with the Jews. He was fortunate in having his Jewish material ready to hand in Amsterdam, which at the time was one of the major centers of the Jewish world. Picart visited the synagogues and attended ceremonies in Jewish homes. His drawings reveal a sympathetic interest in his subjects, a keen eye for detail and a certain sense of humor. They give us a vivid and fascinating glimpse of Dutch Jewish life at its zenith.

The law is displayed to the people
"When the lessons are over, he whose business it is to lift up the Law takes, opens, lifts it as high as he can, and thus opened and raised, turns it towards the four winds, upon which the congregation say: *Behold the Law which Moses gave to the children of Israel.*" (*Right*)

Simcha Torah or rejoicing for the law
". . . After a few prayers, all the books of the Law are brought out of the ark and carried in procession round the desk, at the head of which procession the Chanter walks . . . They read the beginning and conclusion of the Law out of two different books. The two persons appointed to read them are called Spouses of the Law." (*Left*)

The chipur or day of atonement as it is celebrated by the German Jews
"We ought to do the Jews that justice which is due to them: they observe everything that may be called the outside of repentance with extreme care, and as imitation is prevailing on such occasions the spectator himself can hardly forbear feeling a sharp remorse for his own sins at the sight . . . Some penitents pass the night and sometimes all the next day standing, without shifting place, perpetually in prayer and meditation." (*Right*)

Sounding the horn on the first day of the year
"The horn is sounded on the first day of the year, to tell the Jews that they should listen attentively and humbly to the judgment that God is about to pronounce on sinners and thank him for his favours and support during the year just ended . . . He who sounds the horn stands in the place where the Law is read. The horn is made of a ram's horn, as a reminder of the ram of Isaac. Its curved shape is explained as representing the posture of a man humbling himself." (*Right*)

The dedication of the synagogue of the Portuguese Jews at Amsterdam
"This synagogue, which is the fairest in the world, was dedicated with all imaginable solemnity the 10. of the month Menahem in the year 5435, which answers to the 2. August 1675. The most considerable men amongst the Jews there carried the Law richly adorned in procession, and distinguished the entry of their sacred books into the synagogue by devotion and extraordinary alms . . . This festival lasted eight days, and its anniversary is celebrated on the 2. of August every year." (*Below*)

THE ASHKENAZI DIASPORA

Germany was known in medieval Hebrew by the biblical name of *Ashkenaz*, and its Jews came to be called Ashkenazim. The expulsions and persecutions had not succeeded in ending Jewish life completely, but material and cultural conditions were poor. Excluded from the cities, the Jews tended to be dispersed in small towns and villages. There was a steady stream of emigration eastwards to Poland, where from the 13th century Jews had been attracted by grants of special privileges. This movement became even more pronounced during the upheavals of the Reformation.

The Ashkenazi immigrants in Poland were so numerous that (like the Sephardim in Turkey) they imposed their language and religious culture on the native Jews. They filled an important economic role as a middle class between the feudal aristocracy and the peasants, and they managed most of the internal and foreign trade. Neither class hatred nor religious intolerance could seriously undermine their security, and they shared in the prosperity and cultural richness of the Polish renaissance of the 16th and 17th centuries. With the cooperation of the rulers they developed a strong internal self-government which was unique in the Jewish diaspora, and the "Council of the Four Lands" (Great Poland, Little Poland, Podolia and Volhynia; there was a separate council in Lithuania) exercised wide-ranging quasi-parliamentary powers.

This golden age of Polish Jewry was brought to an abrupt and violent end during the Cossack rebellion of 1648. Among the aims of its leader,

Among the earliest physical relics of Polish Jewry are 12th-century coins with Hebrew inscriptions, like this one which reads *berakhah* ("blessing").

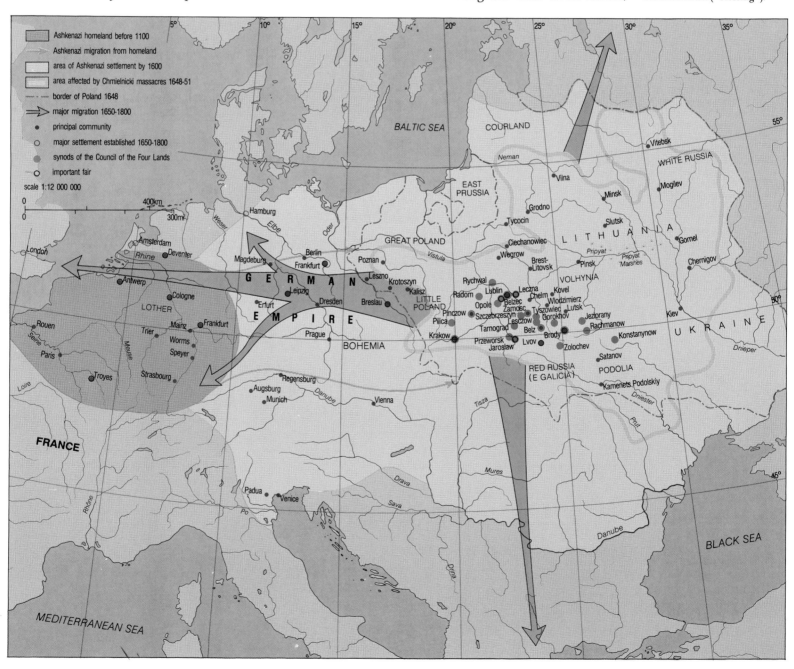

Ashkenazi homeland before 1100

Ashkenazi migration from homeland

area of Ashkenazi settlement by 1600

area affected by Chmielnicki massacres 1648-51

border of Poland 1648

major migration 1650-1800

• principal community

○ major settlement established 1650-1800

synods of the Council of the Four Lands

○ important fair

scale 1:12 000 000

Jewish settlement of Poland, mainly from the west, increased after the economic chaos of the Mongol invasions of the 13th century, and was encouraged by persecutions in Germany. *Left* Jews being expelled from a German city, c. 1428.

Overleaf The ceiling of the synagogue at Chodorów, near Lvóv, the first wooden synagogue, built in 1651 during a period of expansion. The ceiling features signs of the zodiac, pious texts, animals and ornamental plant motifs.

dispersal in the countryside began to be reversed. The trend to urbanization became very marked in the centuries that followed. The war also provided opportunities for enrichment to small traders connected with the army, and the supplying of armies became, until the late 18th century, a characteristic Jewish occupation all over Europe and even in North America. The numerous German courts with their extravagant habits also offered opportunities to financiers and dealers in luxury goods. Some of the "court Jews" (*Hofjuden*) in the late 17th century and the early 18th were amazingly wealthy and powerful. Such men were exceptional, but by their established position in German society they paved the way for a greater degree of social acceptance of Jews as such (perhaps reinforcing in the process certain anti-Jewish prejudices). They gathered around them larger circles of Jews who became progressively assimilated to the prevailing culture. But meanwhile the German communities were being swollen by immigration, and the sumptuous lifestyle of the court Jews contrasted starkly with the poverty and overcrowding of the *Judengassen*.

The Ashkenazi diaspora spread gradually westwards. By the end of the 18th century there were some 20 000 Jews in Alsace (against the German trend they were scattered over a large number of small centers), perhaps only slightly fewer in England (again surprisingly dispersed, although the majority were in London) and, remarkably, rather more in the single city of Amsterdam, whose Jewish community had for a century been the largest in western Europe and was by now probably the largest of any city in the world. Very few of the Ashkenazim belonged to the upper crust of wealthy financiers, jewelers and importers; most eked out a tenuous existence as small traders or semiskilled workers. Despite a gradual process of acculturation the Ashkenazim in some places continued to speak Yiddish well into the 19th century. The common language helped in the integration of new waves of immigrants as well as facilitating contacts with other Ashkenazi communities. It also tended, together with other cultural differences, to distinguish Ashkenazim from Sephardim. Whereas in Mediterranean lands the Ashkenazi minorities were generally assimilated within the Sephardi communities, in the northern European centers, such as Amsterdam and London, where the Ashkenazim formed the large majority, there was little fusion of the two groups. Intermarriage was frowned on (particularly by the Sephardim, with their sense of superior culture and, perhaps, a deeply engrained feeling of racial purity deriving from the hard years in the Christian Iberian peninsula), and separate synagogues and communal organizations were maintained. In time some of the barriers were broken down, and the differences only rarely occasioned real animosity, but the descendants of the two groups still feel a sentimental attachment to their distinctive pasts.

Left: The Ashkenazi diaspora, c. 1600–1800
The story of Ashkenazi migrations in Europe involves a two-way movement: first eastwards to Bohemia and eventually to Poland-Lithuania, and then, after the nightmare of the Chmielnicki massacres (1648–51), back to the west. But the center of gravity remained in the east, where the settlers had put down deep roots and developed a rich and distinctive culture. They also evolved an autonomous administrative structure, the Council of the Four Lands (with a separate council for Lithuania), which governed Jewish life over a wide area. Ashkenazim differed from Sephardim in their cultural outlook and way of life, in their spoken language (Yiddish) and their pronunciation of Hebrew, and in their liturgical traditions. Direct competition between the two groups was rare, since for the most part they were geographically separate; where they did coincide they generally maintained their distinct identities.

Bogdan Chmielnicki, was the eradication of Judaism in the Ukraine. Huge numbers of Jews were killed, baptized or forced to flee. According to Jewish chroniclers, over 100 000 were put to death and 300 communities were destroyed. The massacres left a deep wound on the Polish Jewish mind, and the image of the rampaging Cossacks still haunts some Ashkenazi Jews to this day: it has entered Jewish mythology in the same category as the crusades and the Spanish expulsion. The Chmielnicki massacres were only a foretaste of violence which was to beset the Polish Jews periodically, culminating in the Nazi holocaust. Their immediate result was to inaugurate a gradual movement back towards the west, at first to Germany and ultimately to those new centers that had been pioneered by the Portuguese.

Poland was not emptied of Jews—in fact its Jewish population continued to grow dramatically, so that by the early 19th century it contained over half the Jews in the world—but the Ashkenazi diaspora became a permanent and dominant feature of the map of world Jewry.

Conditions in Germany had in the meantime become more stable. Although Jews were still banned from many places, some smaller states had begun to readmit them. During the Thirty Years' War (1618–48) Jews had been allowed into several of the large cities, and the previous tendency to

INTO THE MODERN WORLD

The middle period of Jewish history is characterized by the enforced segregation of Jews from non-Jews. At its most extreme and concrete this segregation is symbolized by the physical barrier of the ghetto walls. But even when there was no physical barrier there was an invisible wall separating what were in effect two different worlds. Jews were divided from non-Jews not only by their religion but by their political and legal status, by the social and economic structures of their communities, by their intellectual culture and by the very rhythm of their everyday lives.

The leadership of the Jewish community was in the hands of the rabbinate, the self-perpetuating learned class who were the curators of the traditional religious culture. The rabbis enjoyed considerable independence, even from each other. As judges and religious authorities they wielded real power, generally with the consent and support of non-Jewish rulers who allowed the Jews a great measure of judicial autonomy and self-government. There were rebellions against rabbinic authority, but they were infrequent and rarely institutionalized: even the Karaite movement, the most concerted and successful challenge to rabbinism, developed its own style of rabbinate. The rabbis were able to wield the potent sanction of the *herem*, a kind of excommunication, whose victim was excluded from the religious, social and economic life of the community. Since there was no scope for Jewish existence outside the structure of the community, this was a very effective weapon. The mere threat of *herem* was generally sufficient to ensure conformity.

The segregation, although brought into being and maintained by the non-Jewish powers, was generally accepted by the Jews themselves. The system had the great advantage of permitting them to live under their own laws, which were considered to be divinely revealed. A potential source of serious conflict was thus avoided. Drawing on precedents from earlier times and on texts from the sacred scriptures, the Jewish leadership developed the notion of Israel as a holy people, separated from "the nations" to the service of the one God. So long as they were not physically maltreated the Jews could see the separation in a positive light as a legitimate expression of their special function in the world.

Naturally the negative side of the system was plainly visible to anyone who had eyes to see it. Even if, exceptionally, under tolerant rulers individual Jews rose to positions of power and prominence the Jews as a group were (as we would now say) second-class citizens, and worse when there were other classes of people above them in the hierarchy of rightlessness. The opportunities for abuse were unbounded—witness all the expulsions and massacres which, while far from being the everyday lot of medieval Jewry, are cataloged in such gruesome detail by the 19th-century historians. But such incidents were easily accommodated by the victims themselves in a world view which cast them in the role of erring children doomed to punishment for ancestral sins by a just and loving father whose blows were often inscrutable but never undeserved. The medieval poets protest against the sufferings of the people, and cry out against the cruelty of the nations, but they rarely question the justice of divine dispensation. They look forward to eventual relief in the form of a cosmic act of reconciliation when the gentile yoke will be broken and the dispersed will be gathered in to their land.

The Christians, for their part, also theologized the status quo: the Jews were being preserved in subjection as a testimony to their sinfulness in rejecting Christ and so as to bear witness by accepting him at his second coming. Even the massacres and expulsions could be justified by the doctrine of the sinfulness of the whole Jewish people.

Changing attitudes to the Jews

It is impossible to pinpoint a single moment at which these attitudes began to be seriously questioned. In mid-17th-century Amsterdam, at the same time as Baruch Spinoza was laying the foundations of a universalist philosophy which strictly limited the validity of the divine legislation, there was a marked upsurge of millenarian enthusiasm among Jews and Christians alike, and even a Jew as steeped in the western humanist tradition as Manasseh Ben Israel was laying stress on the messianic hope of Israel. He exploited messianic arguments in his successful campaign for the readmission of the Jews to England, one outcome of which was John Locke's pioneering *Letter Concerning Toleration* of 1689. A hundred years later the integration of the Jews in European society was being widely canvassed among enlightened thinkers. In 1781 C.W. Dohm produced his influential treatise *On the Civil Improvement of the Jews*; a year later Moses Mendelssohn, in his introduction to Manasseh Ben Israel's *Vindication of the Jews*, linked the improvement of the status of the Jews to human progress in general, and in the following year, 1783, he published his seminal *Jerusalem* in which he argued for the separation of Church and State. In 1785 a competition was launched at Metz for an essay on ways of making the Jews of France more useful and happy, and it elicited several distinguished responses. Of course the question of the Jews was only one of many issues that preoccupied the thinkers of the Enlightenment, but the prominence it received at this time betrays a growing awareness that the segregation and subordination of the Jews constituted a sickness in European society. Not that the diagnosis was always the same, or the prescribed cure. For some it was a wrong to be challenged in the name of human rights: the Jews should be granted basic civil equality, or at least toleration and religious freedom. Others had more ambitious pro-

These German Jews, congregating outside their synagogue after the Sabbath service, seem to be caught between two worlds. The women and children are in modern dress. The men have preserved their traditional costume for synagogue, but their beards are neatly trimmed and there is nothing outlandish about their appearance. The date is c. 1800, and there are momentous changes in the air. The next generation will see the establishment of the movements for "Jewish culture" and religious reforms, and also a massive defection from Judaism. Is it the early hints of such

developments that these Jews are discussing so gravely?

jects: full integration, with an end to the dominance of superstitious religion, or else ultimately conversion to Christianity. Such programs implied a measure of coercion, and the Jewish response was naturally guarded. But few of the reformers were concerned with what the Jews themselves wanted. It was presumed that they would be grateful for the benefits conferred upon them.

By the beginning of the 19th century reforms had actually been implemented in a number of countries. They varied greatly in their scope and in their aims. The variations illustrate the different perceptions of the problem, as well as the different local conditions.

In revolutionary America the position of the Jews

as immigrants and refugees from religious oppression hardly distinguished them from their neighbors. The liberal political ideas of the Enlightenment were well established and the Jews were able to demand and obtain not "toleration" but full equality, in keeping with the guiding principles of the Revolution. The constitution of 1787 explicitly forbade religious tests for public office (although some states retained them until much later), and the Bill of Rights of 1791 guaranteed total freedom of religion. The American Revolution thus inaugurated the new era of political emancipation for the Jews. Only a few thousand were directly affected at the outset, but the ultimate implications were enormous, thanks to a massive immigration of Jews and the gradual rise of America to a dominating position on the stage of world history. And from the start the central implementation of such a radical reform had an impact on developments in other countries.

In France, too, it was the Revolution that put an end to the medieval segregation of the Jews, as to so many other abuses of human rights. Emancipation was debated on several occasions in the early meetings of the National Assembly, but resistance was strong. A vote at the end of 1789 was lost by 408 votes to 403. But the passion for freedom was too strong for the problem to be shrugged off, particularly since the Jews themselves appealed to the Assembly for recognition of their civic equality. After the arrest of the king the balance of power in the Assembly changed sufficiently for a decree of enfranchisement to be passed, on 27 September 1791. The subsequent modification of some of its provisions and the ambiguities about the position of the Jews in France which have survived until recent times have led some commentators to play down the significance of the decree, or even to represent it as a retrograde move for the Jews. The fact remains that it was, for its time and place, a remarkably radical statement, and its impact all over Europe was considerable. Emancipation for the Jews became a feature of the revolutionary program, and wherever French influence or power extended it was debated or abruptly implemented. In Holland equal rights, including freedom of religion, were proclaimed with the setting up of the Batavian Republic in 1795, and the first National Assembly passed a Jewish enfranchisement bill the following year. Two Jewish deputies from Amsterdam were elected to the second Assembly in 1797, and from then on Dutch Jews lived on terms of complete equality with their neighbors until the Nazi occupation. In Italy the ghetto walls were pulled down by the armies of the republic, Jewish badges were torn off their wearers' clothes, and "liberty trees" were planted outside synagogues. Even in western Germany the ghettos were abolished, and the Jews were temporarily granted citizenship in the Prussian constitutional reforms of 1812.

In England the revolution had occurred much earlier, in the mid-17th century; it had given the Jews the right to assemble freely for the practice of their religion. By the late 18th century the wealthiest Jews were well integrated in the higher ranks of society, but apart from the minority who were born in the country they were not citizens (some immigrants had acquired the more limited rights of denizens), and even those who were citizens were subject to some civic disabilities, which they shared to varying degrees with other non-Anglicans. The campaign for emancipation therefore centered on two distinct questions: citizenship for immigrants (which was largely a Jewish problem) and the removal of religious tests for admission to public office and to certain other activities (which was a more general issue). The campaign was waged in an orderly and pragmatic fashion, by appeal to public opinion and established democratic processes. The question of naturalization was settled in 1826, and most of the religious tests were abolished in the course of the following half-century.

Quite different was the case of the Hapsburg empire. Here the Jews not only had no share in the

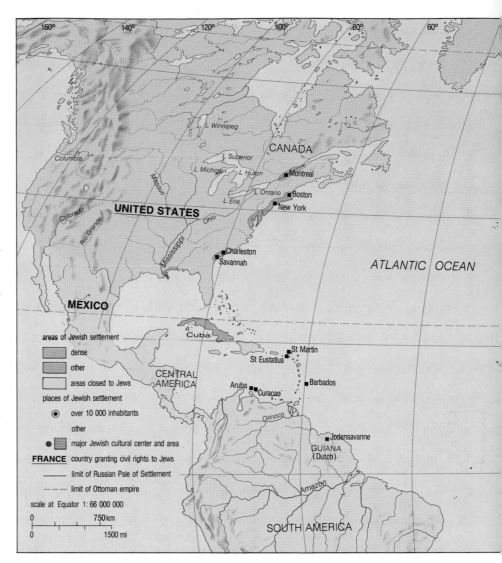

The French Revolution was a watershed for the Jews in Europe. The principle was established that Jews, too, could be citizens equal before the law. But the practical implications of such a radical principle took a long time to work out, and it was not easy to persuade the Jews themselves to give up the privileges of separatism. Napoleon, in a characteristically dramatic gesture, convened a Grand Sanhedrin in 1807 to ratify the renunciation of these privileges. On this bronze medal (*left*) he is seen imperiously presenting the tablets of the new laws to a submissive and grateful Moses. *Above* Amsterdam Jews enthusiastically welcome their king, Louis Bonaparte. (The Portuguese synagogue is on the left, the Ashkenazic on the right.) In reality the community was deeply divided, and emancipation, which threatened the traditional autonomy of the *kehilla*, was strongly resisted by the conservative establishment.

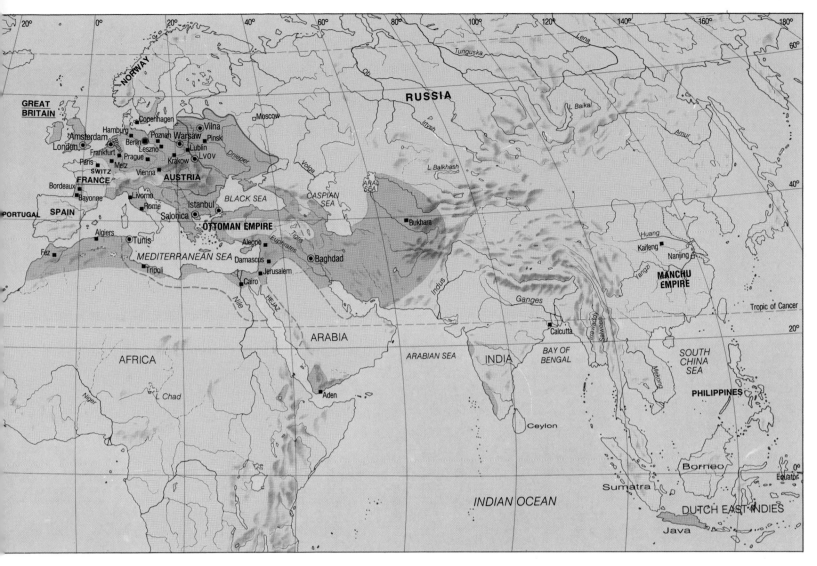

body politic, they were socially ostracized and subjected to the full range of medieval Christian regulations, including the wearing of the yellow badge. They were excluded from agriculture and from most trades and crafts, and from schools and universities, and were liable to a multitude of special taxes. Between 1781 and 1789 the emperor Joseph II issued a series of Letters Patent directed to the various provinces, abolishing many of the disabilities and at the same time imposing new obligations. The Jews were to adopt German names, and were encouraged to use the German language. Primary schooling was made compulsory, either in Jewish or in Christian schools, and secondary schools and universities were opened to Jews. Eventually Joseph made them, for the first time, liable for military service, and the military oath was modified so as to omit any specific Christian references.

Emancipation and relief
These various reforms only affected a minority of the Jews in the world, and in Europe many of them were reversed during the period of reaction which followed the battle of Waterloo (1815). But the progress could not be entirely obliterated, and even under the most reactionary regimes the memory of emancipation endured. The Jews became increasingly impatient of the burdens of discrimination, and many took an active part in the revolutions of 1848, which led to the brief adoption of liberal

constitutions in many countries. Jewish emancipation had become so much a part of the liberal program that in the course of the 1860s it was gradually established in most countries of western and central Europe. By 1871, when the German Imperial Constitution incorporated the principle of freedom of religion for all, only Switzerland, Norway, Spain and Portugal still held out. Eastern Europe was another matter, but even in Russia, where half the Jews in the world were living under conditions of extreme disadvantage in a country hardly touched by the economic, technical, educational and social progress which had transformed the face of western Europe, the reforms of Alexander II had brought some relief and held a promise of better things to come.

The complexity of the responses to the pressure for Jewish integration extended to the Jews themselves. For many, emancipation came as a shock that was too sudden to be absorbed. The image of the Jews stumbling dazed and blinded from the darkness of the ghetto into the light of liberty appropriately describes the experience of many in 19th-century Europe. Some quickly adapted themselves to the new conditions, and in several countries Jews were soon to be found in the army, the government, the liberal professions and a wide variety of occupations. But integration tended to imply a loss of Jewish identity, which the Jewish leadership at least was unprepared to accept. An assembly of Jewish notables convened by Napoleon in 1806

firmly asserted the brotherhood of Jews and Frenchmen, but on one point, the permissibility of marriage between a Jew and a Christian, a cautious response was offered: Jewish law does not forbid such marriages, and the Jewish partner is still considered a Jew, but the rabbis oppose mixed marriages because they cannot themselves officiate at them. Intermarriage became quite common in the course of the 19th century: it has remained a focuspoint of anxieties about Jewish survival and the limits of integration.

A common response to the uncertainties of the new age was conversion to Christianity. At first the converts came from the fringes of Jewish society, but soon the movement involved large numbers. In some German cities in the early 19th century perhaps as much as half the Jewish population accepted Christianity. Baptism did not lead to immediate assimilation. The converts did not sever their links with the Jewish community—in fact they mixed freely with unbaptized Jews who had abandoned the beliefs and practices of Judaism. On the other hand they were not accepted unreservedly into Christian society, which became increasingly sensitive to the problems raised by the wave of conversions. Some Christians, like the influential Protestant theologian Schleiermacher, warned against the age-old danger of "Judaization" of the Church. The converts were not allowed to forget their Jewish origins; many of them continued to be regarded, and even to regard themselves, as Jews.

Those who remained within the Jewish fold had some difficulty, as Jews and citizens, in defining their identity. A formula which was widely embraced, particularly in western countries where the structure of Christian society provided a model for the existence of religious minorities within the state, spoke of Frenchmen (or Englishmen, or Germans) "of the Mosaic persuasion," suggesting that Jewish identity could be reduced to a purely religious label. In America a conference of rabbis at Pittsburgh in 1885 proclaimed: "We consider ourselves no longer a nation but a religious community."

In a sense, though, the preoccupation with religious labels was already an anachronism. The age of the religious community as a major political

unit was over, and it was becoming merely an incidental element in the nation state. This was the nub of the "Jewish problem" in the modern world. Those Jews who opted for the status of a religious community were seeking the same kind of compromise that Christian religious denominations were making with the modern state. There is little fundamental difference between the arrangements that Napoleon made with the Jews and with the Catholic and Protestant Churches in France. The religious bodies were to receive official recognition and certain limited privileges in return for the surrender of their corporate political powers and the acceptance of state interference in their affairs. This type of model was adopted sooner or later in most European countries. The main alternatives were the total separation of Church and State, as in the United States, or a partial separation as in Britain. In each case the results, as far as the Jews were concerned, were similar. The Jewish community effectively ceased to exist as an autonomous political entity, and the rabbinic courts lost most of their jurisdiction. The new community was in effect a private corporation, and affiliation became for the individual a matter of personal choice. If he chose not to affiliate, he need not suffer any undue hardship. The religious leadership, for its part, had to exert itself to win and maintain the adherence of the individual. But for those who opted out, there was no alternative formal structure in which to express a Jewish identity.

In eastern Europe, however, different tendencies emerged. The Jews were surrounded by peoples engaged in a struggle for national selfdetermination, and even religions tended to take on a national identity. Emancipation and integration came about more slowly, and were preceded by secularism. The Jewish enlightenment movement, while combating the dominance of traditional Jewish religion, encouraged the development of a specifically Jewish secular culture. If the Jews were to play a corporate part in the modern state (it was increasingly argued) it should be as a national, not as a religious, minority. The idea was slow to find concrete expression, but eventually it was to have a very significant effect on the course of Jewish history, both in eastern Europe and worldwide.

Citizenship implied both privileges and responsibilities. The admission of Lionel de Rothschild to the British parliament in 1858 without being obliged to take the Christian oath (*above left*) was seen as a crucial step in the struggle for Jewish emancipation, even though British Jews in practice suffered from very few disabilities by this time. But the right of those who could not subscribe to the principles of the established Church to take degrees at the ancient universities of Oxford and Cambridge was not won until 1871. Such reforms, of course, did not only benefit Jews: they are part of the evolution of the modern state, with its tolerance of dissent. A major obligation of citizenship was military service, which became an important step in the integration of Jews in the wider society. Even in Russia, where the Jews did not yet enjoy citizen rights, they became subject to universal conscription under a law of 1874, and thousands served as soldiers in the Russo-Turkish war three years later (*above*).

THE LAST HUNDRED YEARS

The reemergence of the Jewish people into the arena of history has been painful and often tragic. The past hundred years have seen the completion of the process of emancipation which began in the preceding century, but have also seen it severely tested and for a time brutally reversed. They have witnessed the emergence of two new forces, antisemitism and Jewish nationalism, both of which have divided Jew against gentile and Jew against Jew, and which have given rise in swift succession to two new epoch-making events: the Nazi holocaust and the establishment of the state of Israel. The map of the Jewish world has been changed beyond recognition by destructions and migrations, and the optimistic mood of the 1860s and 1870s has been converted into one of uncertainty and self-questioning.

The decade of the 1880s opened ominously for the Jews of Europe. On 13 March 1881 the reforming czar Alexander II was assassinated. Six weeks later a wave of pogroms erupted, which lasted well into the following year. In more than 200 places Jews were attacked by savage mobs who killed, raped and plundered with impunity and apparently with official encouragement. In May 1882 a program of discriminatory legislation (the May Laws) reversed the recent reforms and imposed intolerable restrictions on Jewish life. In the same year in Germany an international antisemitic congress was convened, and an antisemitic party won seats in parliament, while in Hungary there was a revival of the medieval blood libel.

It is a sad reflection on human nature that the era which granted freedom to the downtrodden Jews also gave birth to a new kind of hostility. Whereas the old Christian anti-Judaism justified itself by theological arguments, the new "anti-Semitism" (a sinisterly pseudo-scientific term first coined in 1879) appealed to a supposed biological inferiority and represented the Jews as an alien and corrupting virus in European society. Antisemitism fed on the older anti-Jewish prejudices, which the churches, which had borne and nurtured them, did nothing to combat, but it derived a strong impetus from the rapid course of change in European society (of which Jewish emancipation was one ingredient) which posed a threat, real or imagined, to many deeply entrenched interests. By focusing their anti-liberal political program on the "Jewish peril" the antisemites may seem to have been propounding a simplistic and implausible diagnosis of the ills of society. It is a measure of the deep roots of anti-Jewish sentiment that the doctrine spread with dramatic success from Germany through France, Austria and even Russia.

In Germany the antisemitic Christian Socialist Party was founded by the Protestant pastor Adolf Stöcker, who presided at the 1882 international antisemitic congress in Dresden. Similar parties were formed in several countries, inciting primitive hatred and pressing for the repeal of the Jewish franchise. A spate of anti-Jewish literature was published, cloaking prejudice in the guise of reasoned argument, and soon anti-Jewish riots began to break out.

In Russia the pogroms of 1881 were followed by repeated spasms of officially sponsored terror, and the May Laws were harshly enforced. The beginnings of an integration of Jews into Russian life, resulting from the liberalizing legislation of the 1860s, were abruptly stifled by this combination of

"It's his fault!" A cartoon by Abel Pann (1915). All the troubles of Europe are blamed on the Jew, the universal scapegoat.

Legend

areas of Jewish settlement
- dense
- other

places of Jewish settlement
- ⊙ over 100 000 inhabitants
- ▣ over 20 000
- ▪ significant
- ○ other
- · small and isolated

major Jewish cultural area

AUSTRALIA country granting civil rights to Jews

—— limit of Russian Pale of Settlement

scale at Equator 1: 80 000 000

0   1600km
0   1200mi

below
Jewish population by country
- over 1 million Jewish inhabitants
- over 100 000 Jewish inhabitants

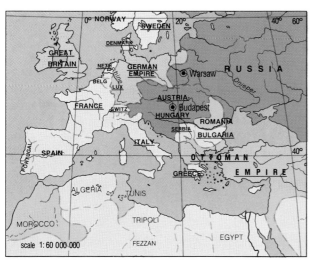

scale 1:60 000 000

physical violence with legal aggression. It was also in Russia that a new twist was given to the antisemitic arguments by the publication in 1903 of a spurious document purporting to contain a Jewish plan for world domination: the *Protocols of the Elders of Zion*. It was translated into many languages and published in virtually every European country, as well as in North and South America. The *Protocols* still feature in antisemitic propaganda today, even though they were long ago demonstrated to be a malicious forgery. Henceforth the Jews were portrayed not only as an alien presence but as a subversive underground political movement. Their wealth and influence were grotesquely exaggerated as part of the myth, and they were blamed for events as diverse as the Boer War and the Bolshevik Revolution.

The Jewish world in 1880
On the eve of the great migration there are about 7·7 million Jews in the world, of whom 90 percent live in Europe, and most of these in the eastern half of the continent. There are more Jews in Warsaw alone than in the whole of Britain or France. Thus although the emancipation movement is now well advanced, it still only affects a minority of Jews, and most still suffer from rightlessness and hostile discrimination. Outside Europe the same is true: the main concentrations are in the Muslim world, and the communities of the Americas, South Africa and Australasia are small and scattered. New York is a notable exception: it numbers 80000 and is growing fast.

One outcome of all these developments was a dramatic increase in the rate of emigration, especially from Russia. The 19th century was a period of migration for the Jews, as indeed it was for Europe as a whole. Huge numbers of people were on the move, both within the continent and to the new territories being opened up beyond the seas, in the Americas, southern Africa and the antipodes. The main cause of the movements was economic. A rapid growth in population led to increasing hardship, and industrialization attracted large numbers of the people to the cities, which had difficulty in absorbing the influx. The Jewish population explosion was particularly traumatic. Between 1800 and 1900 the total world population approximately doubled, but the Jewish population underwent a fourfold increase, from some 2·5 to 10·6 million. What is

even more remarkable is that the bulk of the increase took place in eastern Europe, especially in the Russian Pale of Settlement whose Jewish population rose from 1·6 million in 1820 to four million in 1880 and some 5·6 million by 1910—and this despite continuous emigration. The region constituted a sort of reservoir, constantly replenishing the Jewish communities of central and western Europe, which were being depleted through emigration overseas, assimilation and demographic decline attributable to the effects of rapid urbanization. After the beginning of the pogroms, what had been a noticeable trickle became a veritable flood. Between 1881 and 1914 some 2·75 million Jews left eastern Europe—more than a third of the Jews of the region, and more than a quarter of all the Jews in the world. Population movement on this scale was

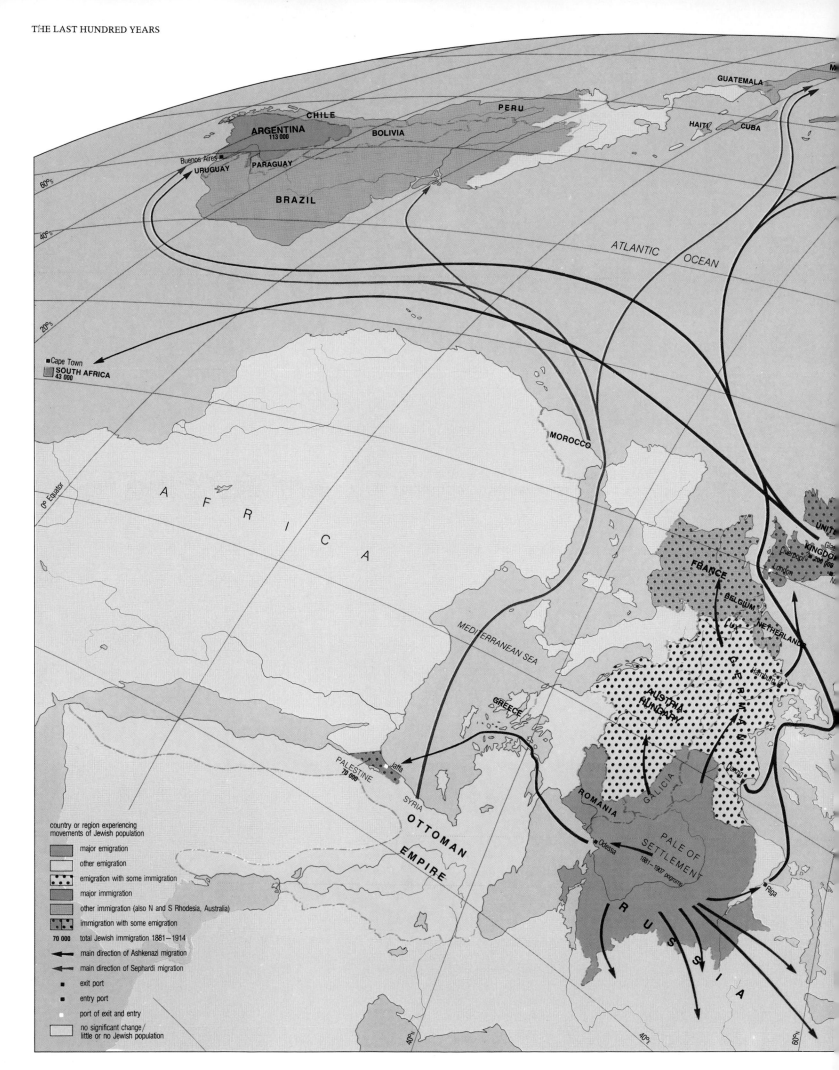

GUATEMALA

CHILE
PERU
ARGENTINA
113 000
BOLIVIA
HAITI
CUBA
BUENOS Aires
URUGUAY
PARAGUAY
BRAZIL

ATLANTIC   OCEAN

60°S
40°S
20°S

Cape Town
SOUTH AFRICA
43 000

0° Equator

MOROCCO

A F R I C A

UNITED
KINGDOM
Glas
Liverpool 200 000
London

FRANCE
BELGIUM
Lux
NETHERLANDS
Hamburg
GERMANY
AUSTRIA
HUNGARY
Cracow
GALICIA

MEDITERRANEAN SEA

GREECE

ROMANIA
Odessa
PALE OF
SETTLEMENT
1881–1907 pogroms

PALESTINE
70 000
Jaffa
SYRIA
OTTOMAN

R U S S I A

EMPIRE

Riga

country or region experiencing
movements of Jewish population

major emigration

other emigration

emigration with some immigration

major immigration

other immigration (also N and S Rhodesia, Australia)

immigration with some emigration

70 000   total Jewish immigration 1881–1914

◄—   main direction of Ashkenazi migration

◄—   main direction of Sephardi migration

■   exit port

■   entry port

□   port of exit and entry

no significant change/
little or no Jewish population

40°N
40°E
60°E

Left: The Great Migration, 1881–1914
In many parts of rural Europe a population explosion caused poverty and social tensions on an unprecedented scale, and millions of people left their homes in search of better opportunities, either in the growing cities or in other continents. This explosion was most dramatic in eastern Europe, where adverse political conditions gave the Jews an added reason to leave. Over 2 million Jews emigrated from Europe in this period (compared to some 200000 in the previous 40 years); 85 percent of them settled in the United States, where they constituted one of the largest immigrant groups. A further 760000 Jews left Europe between 1915 and 1931.

Right The Statue of Liberty, inscribed with famous lines by the Jewish poet Emma Lazarus, symbolizes the hope of a new life for these European immigrants. The religious traditions they brought with them from Europe (*right below*) are about to be challenged and transformed in the New World.

virtually unprecedented in Jewish history; it had a very marked effect on the overall picture of the Jewish world.

In western Europe the modest and relatively well-integrated Jewish communities were inundated with immigrants, whose poverty was a heavy burden on communal resources and whose different culture gave rise to internal conflicts. In Britain by 1914 the newcomers outnumbered the native Jews by five to one; they were concentrated in the larger cities, where they were overcrowded and exploited. In the United States, the land of seemingly unbounded opportunity and freedom which attracted the vast majority of the migrants, the earlier central European settlers had followed the expansion of the country to the west and south, where they had easily found a livelihood as traders and craftsmen. The eastern European influx of the 1880s coincided with the growth of large industry, and concentrations of immigrants grew up in New York, the main port of entry, and in other big cities, many of the newcomers being employed in clothing factories. And so here too a Jewish urban proletariat developed, with all the attendant problems of poverty and unrest. The immigrants were assisted by the longer-established settlers, and they helped each other. They also subsidized further immigration from Europe, which was facilitated by improved means of transportation; the immigration fueled itself. By 1900 the Jewish population of the United States had reached one million, and a further 1·3 million arrived by 1914. New York itself by now had a million Jewish inhabitants, making it by far the largest "Jewish city" in the world. Meanwhile other countries were being put on the Jewish map for the first time, or enhancing their position on it. This was partly due to the work of the Jewish Colonization Association (ICA), established in 1891 by the financier Baron Maurice de Hirsch. Hirsch spent a huge fortune on the relief of Jewish misery.

His original plan was to educate Russian Jews and train them in agriculture and handicrafts, but when his overtures were rebuffed by the Russian government he decided that emigration was the only solution. The ICA sought not only to tackle the most urgent problems of poverty and persecution by means of properly organized emigration, but to offer a long-term improvement in Jewish life by establishing self-sufficient colonies on virgin territory in free countries. Argentina was especially selected for agricultural colonization, but help was also lavished on projects in Canada, Brazil, Palestine and elsewhere.

Palestine was of course a special case. The opportunities here, whether economic or political, were not obvious. Such Jewish immigration as there was (and it was little, even compared with the modest influx into Canada or Argentina) was motivated by determined idealism, which was often frustrated by the unpromising conditions in the country. But with the help of outside benefactors and relief organizations the lot of the immigrants slowly improved, and a number of agricultural colonies were established (there were 43 by 1914).

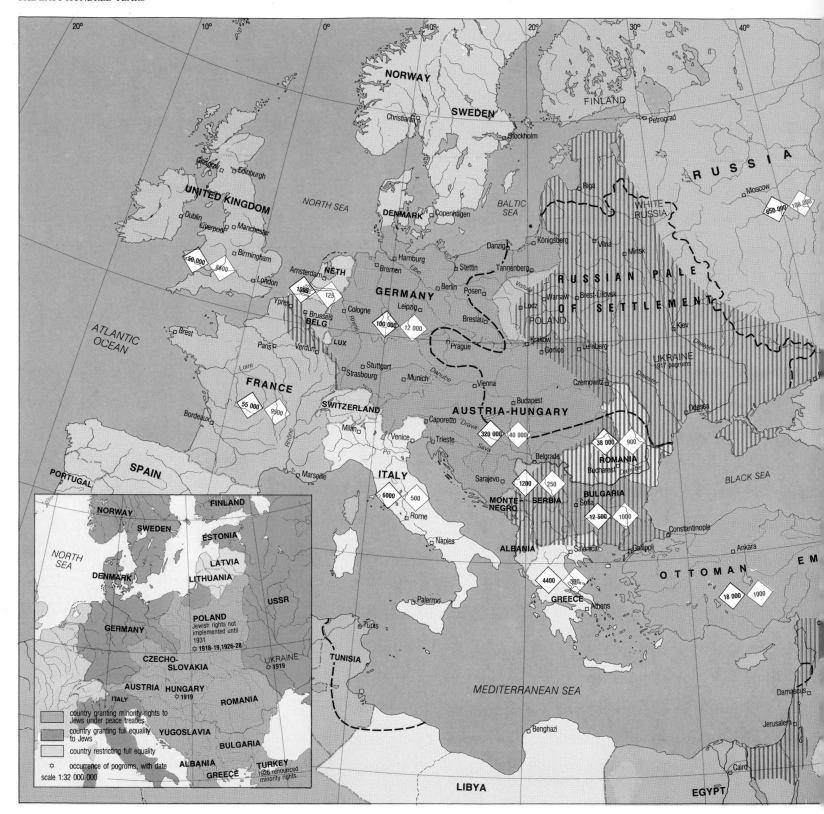

Nationalism or socialism?

Whereas in other countries the problem was the integration of the Jews as a group within a predominantly non-Jewish society, in Palestine the aim of the Zionists was to build a Jewish society which would eventually become autonomous. Zionism can be seen as radical rejection of assimilation, or as itself a form of assimilation to the model of European nationalism: the difference is a matter of emphasis. The movement arose in response to the denial of Jewish integration implicit in the concerted antisemitism of the 1880s and 1890s. Although it absorbed and developed earlier nationalist ideas, it was antisemitism which gave it its rationale and its

popular appeal. Leo Pinsker published his *Auto-Emancipation* in reaction to the 1881 pogroms; Theodor Herzl wrote his *Jewish State* (1896) after experiencing French antisemitism at the time of the Dreyfus trial. Their ideas won little support among western Jews; it was in pogrom-stricken Russia that they first caught the popular imagination, and they were subsequently spread among the masses of Russian émigrés in western countries. Their appeal was particularly strong among Russian socialists, who saw in the Jewish state an opportunity to establish an egalitarian society free from religious dominance, economic exploitation and the curse of antisemitism. The first Zionist Congress, held at

World War I
The war was fought in some of the densest areas of Jewish population, and caused severe suffering to civilians, in addition to large numbers killed or wounded as soldiers on both sides. The Jews of Russia were at last emancipated after the revolution of 1917, and the postwar peace treaties incorporated guarantes of minority rights for the Jews of central and eastern Europe (see inset). Nevertheless discrimination and outbreaks of anti-Jewish violence continued in several countries.

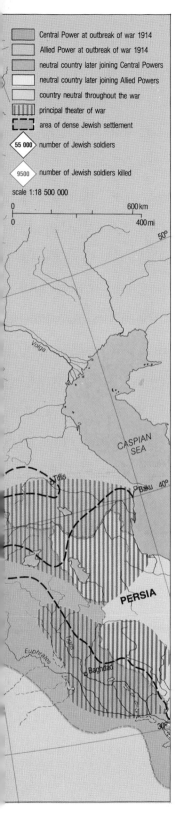

Central Power at outbreak of war 1914
Allied Power at outbreak of war 1914
neutral country later joining Central Powers
neutral country later joining Allied Powers
country neutral throughout the war
principal theater of war
area of dense Jewish settlement
55 000 number of Jewish soldiers
9500 number of Jewish soldiers killed

scale 1:18 500 000

0   600 km
0   400 mi

The case of Captain Alfred Dreyfus (*below*) in 1899 brought powerful currents of anti-Jewish prejudice to the surface, and illustrated how far the Jews were from winning acceptance even in a country such as France, which prided itself on its humanitarian principles. The scandal boosted the appeal of Zionism, which became more than a dream when the British captured Jerusalem from the Turks in 1917 (*bottom*). Another challenge to the liberal conscience in the West was the Kishinev pogrom of 1903, in Russia, in which 47 Jews were brutally massacred. "Cursed be he who cries 'Revenge!' Vengeance for the blood of a child the Devil himself has not yet devised," wrote the Hebrew poet Bialik. Children orphaned in the pogrom were cared for in the United States by HIAS, the Hebrew Immigrant Aid Society (*left*). Meanwhile ORT (Organization for Rehabilitation through Training) set up factories like this one (*below left*) in Argentina.

Basle in 1897, chose a flag and a national anthem and established an international organization to pursue the aim of setting up a Jewish homeland in Palestine. The Zionist leaders were not united in their objective or on the means to achieve it, but they all agreed that emancipation within the countries of Europe, whatever opportunities it might offer to the individual Jew, was incapable of solving the problems of the Jews as a nation.

Not all Jewish socialists were attracted to Zionism. Jews had a long history of involvement in socialism, going back to the early days of Moses Hess (1812–75) and Ferdinand Lassalle (1825–64). In general, they looked to social revolution to end the Jewish problem which they described as a product of bourgeois society and capitalist economy. After the early pogroms the various radical movements in Russia attracted Jewish adherents, who often drifted restlessly from one world-reforming ideology to another. At first the language barrier impeded the spread of socialism among the mass of Yiddish-speaking Jewish workers, but in 1897 a specifically Jewish socialist movement was established in Vilna. The Bund (officially entitled the "General League of Jewish Workers in Lithuania, Poland and Russia") adopted from the start the aim of defending the interests of Jewish workers and

areas of Jewish settlement
- dense
- other

places of Jewish settlement
- ⊙ over 1 million inhabitants
- ▣ over 100 000
- ■ over 50 000
- ○ other
- • small and isolated
- ▤ major Jewish cultural area

scale at Equator 1: 80 000 000

0   1600km

0   1200mi

combating anti-Jewish discrimination, "because Jewish workers suffer not only as workers but also as Jews." The movement received strong support, and the specifically Jewish content of its policies became progressively more important. In 1901 the Bund adopted Jewish nationalism as a policy, and four years later it accepted the idea of cultural autonomy for Russian Jewry, calling for the recognition of Yiddish as a legal language. A three-sided ideological conflict ensued between Bundists, Zionists and socialists of a more universalist persuasion. The socialists dismissed the Zionists as "bourgeois nationalists," and Lenin (who was deeply sensitive to the sufferings of Russian Jewry) called the Bundists "Zionists who are afraid of being seasick." Both the Jewish movements, while bitterly hostile to each other, were suspicious of residual anti-semitism even within the socialist ranks. Meanwhile both socialism and nationalism were opposed

in the Jewish world on a broad front ranging from religious traditionalists who still hankered after the relative autonomy of an earlier age to religious modernists (in the west) who maintained a confident faith in enlightenment and progress. These two groups carried on a fierce polemic against each other. The divisions were reminiscent of the sectarian conflicts that characterized the end of the Second Temple period.

World War I and Jewish history

World War I was disastrous for Europe as a whole, but for the Jews it brought unprecedented losses. Not only did large numbers die as soldiers on both sides (the total number of Jewish servicemen killed has been estimated at 140 000, the majority of them Russians), but for the first time the theaters of war included areas of dense Jewish population in eastern Europe. Apart from civilians killed in fighting,

The Jewish world in 1930
The Jewish world is now at its zenith, in terms of extent, overall numbers and conditions of life generally. There are over 15 million Jews in the world. Half of them still live in eastern and central Europe, where they form 6 percent of the total population. In Poland the 3 million Jews are nearly 10 percent of the population, and they are still the majority in some places. But emigration has brought about some momentous changes. The USA has now achieved its position as the country with the largest Jewish community in the world, with well over 4 million members (3·6 percent of all Americans), while in British-ruled Palestine the small but growing Jewish population of 160 000 is nearly 18 percent of the total. Many communities figure for the first time on this

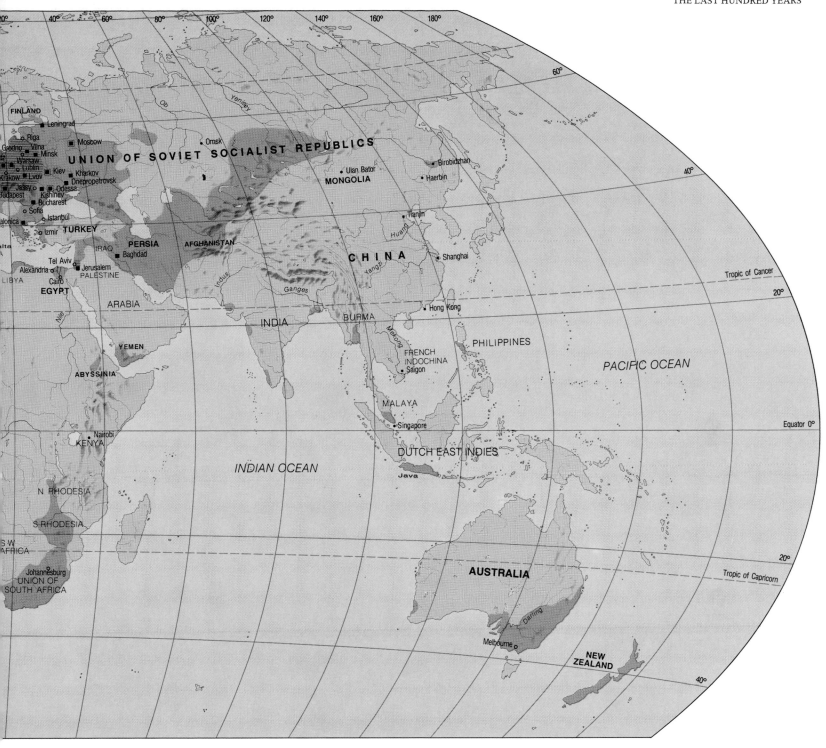

map. Few countries impose serious restrictions on Jewish life; in many places Jews are now well integrated at all levels of society. Despite economic uncertainties there is a widespread sense of progress and satisfaction. But this is the lull before the storm: already the clouds are gathering for the most nightmarish ordeal in Jewish history.

many fled the war zones as refugees and succumbed to starvation and epidemics. In the aftermath of war pogroms broke out in Hungary, Poland and the Ukraine which left tens of thousands of Jews dead or homeless. The war also brought emigration to a halt. The exodus was resumed after 1918, but emigration was now discouraged, and the countries of immigration gradually imposed restrictions on entry.

Three major developments took place during the war which were to have a significant effect on Jewish history: the Russian Revolution, the British conquest of Palestine and the emergence of America as a world power.

The revolution of March 1917 in Russia swept away at a stroke all the restrictive and oppressive anti-Jewish legislation, and was enthusiastically welcomed by Jews of all persuasions. Even the Bolshevik seizure of power eight months later was

not at first perceived as a danger, since the Bolshevik leaders had affirmed their sympathy for the Jews as prominent victims of czarist oppression, and some of them were Jews themselves. But the Bolsheviks failed to eradicate anti-Jewish prejudice in Russia, and they added to it their own ideologically motivated persecution of Jewish religion and of the "counter-revolutionary" Bundist and Zionist movements. Individual Jews, however, benefited from the new opportunities, and many rose to prominent positions in the Communist Party and the government.

The British military advance into Palestine coincided with the British government's official recognition of Zionist aspirations in the Balfour Declaration of 2 November 1917. The aim of a Jewish national home was subsequently incorporated in the League of Nations Mandate for Palestine, and for the first time it seemed to be a realistic objective.

The Zionist movement now began to win greater support from Jews in the west, but anti-Zionism also increased, and Jewish communities were passionately divided. The ending of Turkish rule also strengthened Arab nationalism in the Middle East, and a three-cornered struggle evolved, the British clumsily holding the balance between the rival national movements whose conflict became increasingly violent.

The American intervention in the European war was accompanied (in fact preceded) by an assumption of responsibility by American Jews for their brethren in Europe. Concern for the predicament of east European Jewry had led to relief work and even political intervention for some years previously, and in 1906 the American Jewish Committee had been set up (on the model of western European organizations such as the Anglo-Jewish Association and the Alliance Israélite Universelle), with the aim of defending Jewish rights in any part of the world and alleviating the consequences of persecution. In 1914 the AJC brought a multiplicity of separate groups together to coordinate fund raising and relief work through the American Jewish Joint Distribution Committee (JDC). On the political front, the American Zionists took over the organizing role of the World Zionist Executive, which was paralyzed in Berlin, and an American Jewish Congress was established to secure the rights of European Jews after the end of the war. American Jewish leaders played a prominent role in the Committee of Jewish Delegations at the Versailles peace conference, which was instrumental in obtaining guarantees for the rights of minorities in the new eastern European states. Reality unfortunately lagged behind the ideal, and only a few of the new states granted their Jewish minorities full equality before the law, but the international guarantees were an important safeguard, and helped to ensure that abuses of civil rights were publicly aired and, where possible, redressed.

The gathering of the clouds

Antisemitism continued to be a problem in Europe throughout the 1920s, particularly in Romania, Poland and Hungary, where official government policy was unfavorable to the Jews. In Weimar Germany Jews for the first time enjoyed full political and civil equality, and the government generally took a firm stand in punishing antisemitic outrages, but right-wing parties were active in spreading scurrilous propaganda. Even in America there was a wave of xenophobia which found expression in anti-Jewish polemic, discrimination and, most significantly, immigration quotas. The economic crises of the late 1920s exacerbated prejudice, while causing a severe cutback in the funds available for charitable relief work.

Meanwhile a demographic decline of Jewish communities was giving serious cause for concern. The population explosion of the 19th century had been sharply reversed. Already before World War I a German sociologist had warned that a declining birthrate and the tendency to intermarriage would lead in time to the disappearance of German Jewry, which was only being maintained by immigration. After the war these trends became even more pronounced. The Jewish birthrate everywhere in Europe was markedly lower than that in the

population at large, and in some large centers deaths actually outnumbered births. In many places a third or more, sometimes over a half, of marriages involving Jews were with non-Jewish partners, and the children of such unions were generally raised as non-Jews. Large numbers of Jews were leaving the community, either by converting to Christianity or by declaring themselves as "non-religious." Even a modest natural increase in the Afro-Asian communities, due to improved health care, could not offset the losses. In 1930 the world Jewish population was estimated at 15 million, indicating a slight decline against estimates for previous years. Eastern and central Europe still accounted for half the total, but the clouds were already gathering for the catastrophe that would eradicate the long-established dominance of this region on the map of world Jewry.

Few people at the time, however, foresaw the scale of the disaster that was in store, for Europe as a whole and for its Jews. Life continued much as normal for a while even after the National Socialists, with their record of antisemitic rabble-rousing and violence, came to power in Germany at the beginning of 1933. The Jewish response was fragmented and in some circles pathetically optimistic. The Nazi policies of isolating, disfranchising and eventually expelling the Jews were implemented gradually, and were accompanied by hypocritical propaganda which masked or distorted their effect. In retrospect it seems extraordinary that there was neither more determined protest nor a stronger sense of urgency in Jewish reactions. A petition to the League of Nations actually secured the revocation of the racial laws in Upper Silesia, but such resistance was rare. The Nazi leaders themselves were surprised at how easily their anti-Jewish policies were implemented.

"Black milk of daybreak we drink it at nightfall we drink it at noon in the morning we drink it at night" (Paul Celan). The darkest hour of European Jewry is fast approaching, and an indicator is the renewed pace of emigration. Between 1932 and 1939 over half a million Jews left Europe. And for the first time a significant proportion—46 percent—went to Palestine (*above*). If the causes of the emigrations 50 years earlier had been primarily economic, now they were primarily political. Antisemitism, which had never died, was raising its head again all over Europe, and especially in Germany (*far left*). "Death comes as a master from Germany." By stages the Jews were deprived of their citizenship, their livelihood, their human dignity. On the night of 9–10 November 1938 hundreds of synagogues were destroyed (*left*) and thousands of Jewish homes and shops were raided. In the following days huge numbers of Jews were taken to concentration camps. Many more fled the country. But places of refuge were few. At the Évian Conference of July 1938 representatives of 32 countries discussed the problem of Jewish refugees: all expressed sympathy, but there were pitifully few offers of help.

The non-Jewish population, after years of indoctrination, accepted them with little protest, and anti-Nazi demonstrations abroad were ineffectual. The Jews were slow to reconcile themselves to the need to emigrate, even after the Nuremberg Laws of September 1935 deprived them of their citizenship. Emigration did speed up considerably, however, in 1938, after the annexation of Austria in March and of the Sudetenland in October, and after the pogroms of 9 November (*Kristallnacht*) when in one night hundreds of synagogues were burned down and nearly a hundred Jews were killed in the streets. Between 1933 and 1938 about 150 000 of Germany's half-million Jews left; a similar number fled in the single year preceding the invasion of Poland in September 1939. So a majority of German Jews managed to escape the "Final Solution."

It was a different story in most of the other countries which came under Nazi occupation. For many of the Jews escape was impossible in wartime conditions, and too often those who could leave had nowhere to go. The British strictly limited immigration to Palestine, and closed the doors of the colonies to refugees, and few other countries were willing to accept large numbers. Ships loaded with fugitives were turned away from port after port. In any case the Nazis had settled on a policy of extermination, not expulsion. They pursued it with ruthless efficiency and single-minded zeal.

Destruction and resurgence

In all about six million Jews were murdered by the Nazis and their collaborators between 1941 and 1945. The numbers hardly bear contemplation. The knowledge that a similar number of non-Jewish civilians were killed during the same period in a cataclysm of unprecedented intensity and brutality does not mitigate the sense of desolation and horror at the fate of the Jews. It is not only a question of numbers. They were deliberately dehumanized, made into outcasts from society and scapegoats for all the ills of the world. No conceivable military or political objective could be served by their death. It was pure irrational hatred, the most bestial of human instincts, that hounded and destroyed them. They were powerless, friendless, hopeless, often disowned and betrayed by their own neighbors. Even those who survived were broken, and dis-

The Nazi holocaust
It is impossible to do justice to the enormity of the Nazi nightmare, but the figures on this map tell their own story. In all some 6 million Jews were herded up and killed, and over a million more made homeless, all in conditions of indescribable brutality and horror and over and above the ravages of a terrible war. Although the Jews were by no means the only people to be victimized by the Nazis, they were hounded with a ruthless and single-minded passion that came to dominate the whole Nazi enterprise, so that it is no exaggeration to speak of a "war against the Jews."

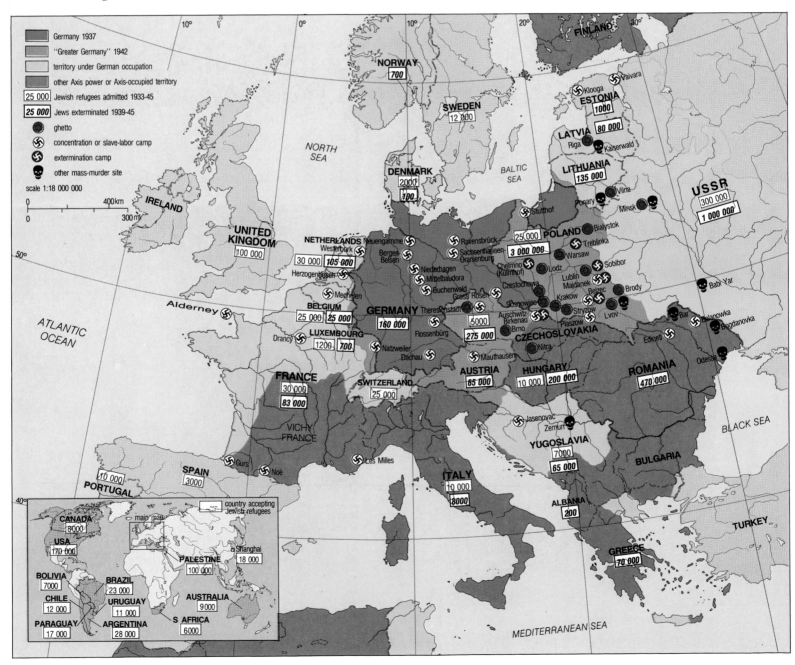

To reduce the holocaust to statistics is another way of dehumanizing the victims. Each one was a face, a unique human being.

*How beautiful is my love
with her everyday clothes
and a comb in her hair.
Nobody knew she was so beautiful.*

*Maidens of Auschwitz,
Dachau maidens,
Have you not seen my love?*

*We saw her on a distant journey,
she no longer had her clothes
or a comb in her hair.*

*How beautiful is my love,
pampered by her mother,
and her brother's kisses.
Nobody knew she was so beautiful.*

*Maidens of Mauthausen,
Maidens of Belsen,
Have you not seen my love?*

*We saw her on the frozen square
with a number on her white hand
with a yellow star on her heart.*

Iakovos Kampanellis, *Song of Songs*

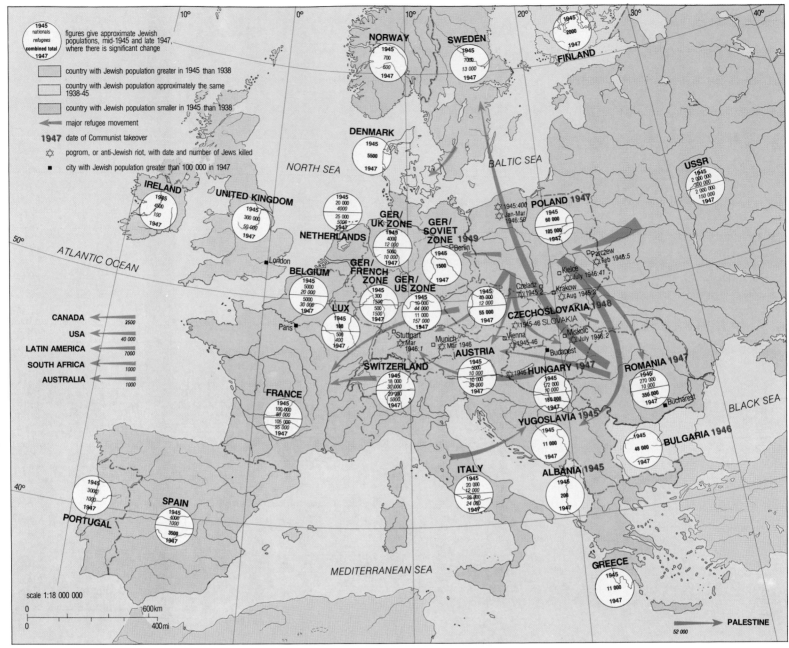

oriented by the loss of their families, their homes, the whole familiar landscape of their lives. Beyond the personal tragedies, the loss for the whole Jewish people was incalculable. More than a third of world Jewry had been murdered. Europe, especially central and eastern Europe, had become a Jewish wilderness. The very foundations of Jewish life among the nations had been swept away in the countries which had occupied the center of the stage of Jewish history for generations.

For those Jews who remained among the ruins there was to be no immediate return to normal life. The shattered remnants had to be pieced together slowly and painfully, in conditions of political and economic chaos. The survivors succumbed to sickness and despair in the camps, or migrated from country to country in search of a permanent home. The restoration of former Jewish property was fraught with obstacles, and in several countries there were renewed anti-Jewish riots and pogroms, notably in Poland where amid widespread political violence hundreds of Jews were murdered. The introduction of Communist regimes in countries liberated by the Russians subjected the survivors to

further economic upheavals and provoked fresh emigrations.

The evolution of America to the dominant position in world Jewish affairs, which had begun during the migrations of the 1880s and first became manifest during World War I, was now complete. The five million Jews of the USA now represented almost half of world Jewry, and it was the only major center of Jewish population to be largely untouched by the ordeal of the war. European Jewish organizations had transferred their headquarters there, or at least opened branch offices, and in 1943 an American Jewish Conference had been set up to plan the immediate rescue of European Jewry and to deal with postwar problems. After the war America's Jews contributed unprecedented sums for relief and rehabilitation, and American Zionists played the leading role in promoting the cause of the Jewish national home. In fact the objective was now explicitly defined as the establishment of Palestine as a "Jewish commonwealth." This controversial decision had been taken, under the influence of David Ben-Gurion, at an extraordinary conference held at the Biltmore

The Jews in Europe, 1945–47
In the aftermath of the holocaust one of the most pressing problems to be resolved was the fate of the survivors, many of them living precariously as stateless refugees or in temporary camps. Some tried to regain their former homes, but restitution of property was resisted by those who had acquired it, and in many places antisemitism was rife, flaring up occasionally in renewed violence. Others sought to settle down in the countries where they found themselves, or looked for a new home overseas. But few countries were willing to accept refugees in large numbers, and resettlement was a slow and painful process. By the end of 1947 there were still over 200000 Jewish displaced persons in Europe. Britain adamantly resisted pressure for free immigration to Palestine, and it was not until Israeli independence in 1948 that this way out was secured.

The plight of the Jewish survivors in Europe was highlighted by the incident of the *Exodus 1947*. When this ship, overloaded with some 4500 refugees, arrived at Haifa, the passengers were sent back to France under guard. After they refused to land in France they were forcibly put ashore in the British Zone of Germany. It could only appear as an act of the most heartless indifference, and the British were branded as fascists by Zionist propaganda. The UN Special Committee on Palestine was collecting evidence at the time. When the Committee recommended the partition of Palestine between Jews and Arabs, the British response was to announce an early withdrawal.

Hotel in New York in 1942. It represented a dramatic departure from traditional Zionist policy, which had been to concentrate on the practical task of building the "National Home," and to avoid formulating the ultimate political aims of the movement. That the crucial decision was taken in New York and not in London or Jerusalem was seen, rightly, as a clear indication that the USA had become the natural center for Zionist political activities.

One result of the ordeal of the "war against the Jews" was that the Zionist organizations received new and massive support from Jews who had previously been lukewarm about the idea of a National Home. On a different front, a World Jewish Congress had been established, under the impact of Nazi aggression and against opposition from leading Zionists. The first and only international organization representing Jews of all religious and political affiliations, the WJC has played an important dual role, in strengthening the solidarity of Jews everywhere and promoting their rights and interests and at the same time in providing a united voice for world Jewry at the United Nations and other international assemblies.

It was the plight of the survivors of the European holocaust which demanded and received most urgent attention in the postwar years. Although many were gradually resettled within Europe or in the few overseas countries that were willing to take them, there remained considerable numbers for whom emigration to Palestine was seen as the only hope. The British government, however, was resolutely opposed to an increase in Jewish immigration. During the war, when conditions in any case impeded immigration, the restrictions had been justified by appealing to a need to prevent the Arabs joining the Axis. After the war the position was

entirely changed, but it became clear that the new Labour government in London would maintain its predecessor's policy of cultivating Arab friendship and thwarting the aims of the Zionists. Efforts were redoubled to bring European refugees into the country illegally, and the different Zionist military factions coordinated sabotage activities against British installations. A crisis came when the British government declined to implement the unanimous recommendation of a joint Anglo-American Committee of Inquiry in 1946 that 100 000 Jewish refugees should be transferred immediately from Europe to Palestine. Even the Jewish Agency, which had previously been opposed to terrorist activity and had attempted to work through cooperation with Britain, was now brought into confrontation with the British authorities. The desperate plight of the refugees won sympathy for the Zionist cause not only in world Jewry but among non-Jewish observers as well. In August 1947 a United Nations Special Committee on Palestine recommended that the Mandate should be terminated and replaced by an independent Palestine. The majority of the committee recommended partition of the country into a Jewish state and an Arab state, and this recommendation was endorsed by the UN General Assembly on 29 November. The Arab states opposed partition and the British refused to implement it. It was therefore left to the initiative of the Jews in Palestine to establish their own independent state. This they did. On the afternoon of 14 May 1948, the date announced by the British for their withdrawal, the National Council met in Tel Aviv and issued a Declaration of Independence.

Israel and the Jews in the modern world

Tragically and perhaps inevitably the vision of the Zionist founders was achieved not in a spirit of

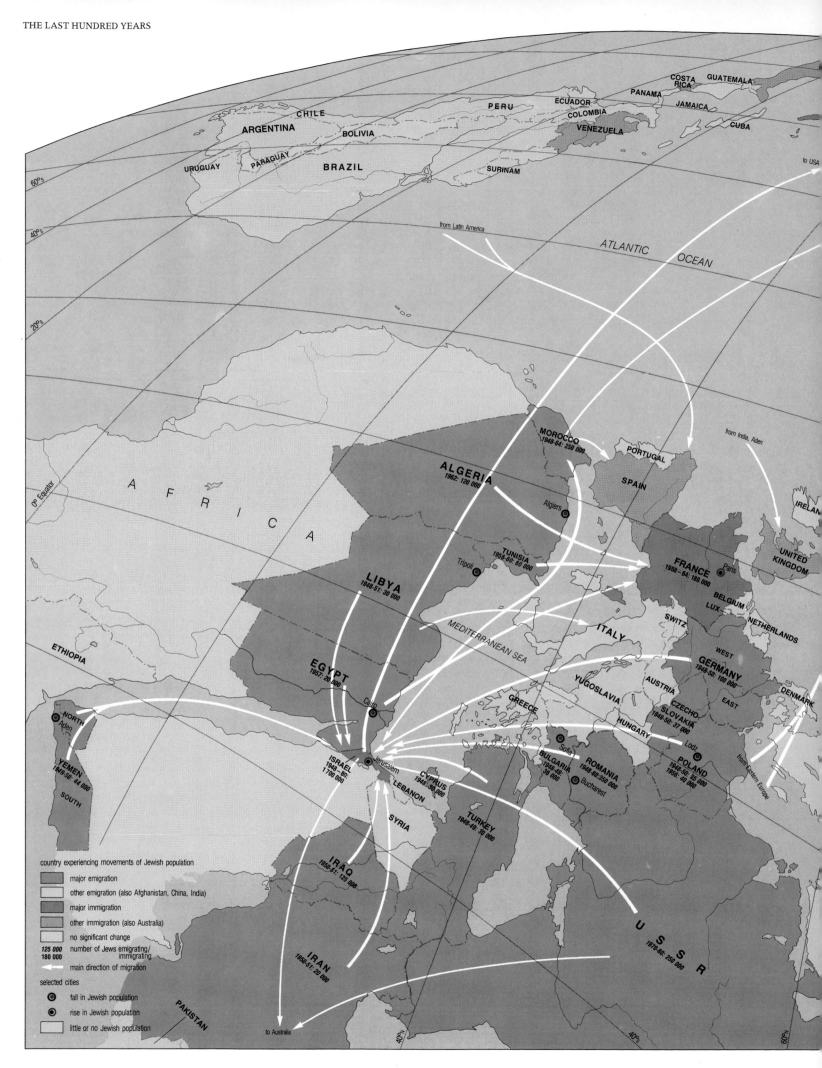

country experiencing movements of Jewish population

major emigration

other emigration (also Afghanistan, China, India)

major immigration

other immigration (also Australia)

no significant change

125 000 number of Jews emigrating/
180 000 immigrating

→ main direction of migration

selected cities

◉ fall in Jewish population

◉ rise in Jewish population

little or no Jewish population

MOROCCO
1948-64: 250 000

ALGERIA
1962: 120 000

TUNISIA
1956-60: 80 000

LIBYA
1948-51: 30 000

EGYPT
1957: 20 000

FRANCE
1958-64: 180 000

WEST GERMANY
1948-50: 100 000

CZECHO-SLOVAKIA
1948-50: 37 000

BULGARIA
1948-49: 38 000

ROMANIA
1948-80: 350 000

POLAND
1948-50: 25 000
1956: 40 000

HUNGARY

YEMEN
1948-50: 44 000

ISRAEL
1948-80: 1 700 000

CYPRUS
1948-51: ?

TURKEY
1948-49: 30 000

IRAQ
1950-51: 125 000

IRAN
1950-51: 20 000

U S S R
1970-80: 250 000

from Latin America

from India, Aden

from Eastern Europe

to USA

to Australia

Jewish migrations, 1948–80
The population movements of this period are comparable in scale to those of the decades before World War I (see pages 62–63), but there are notable differences in the direction of migration. America has continued to exercise an attraction, but the main center of immigration has been Israel (although in some years emigration has exceeded immigration here). The overall effect of the migrations has been to complete the elimination of the old centers of dense population in eastern Europe and the Muslim world, while boosting the new centers in Israel and the New World and assisting a renewal of Jewish life in western Europe.

Below left David Ben-Gurion, as first prime minister of the new state of Israel, inaugurates the first Knesset in Jerusalem on 13 December 1949. After the first Zionist Congress in 1897 Herzl had written in his diary: "At Basle I founded the Jewish state . . . Perhaps in five years' time, certainly in fifty, everyone will realize it."

Below right Soviet Jewish emigrants arrive in Israel, 1971.

harmony and reconciliation but in a mood of strife, despair and grim determination. It was achieved too late to save the six million, and the bitter frustrations of the war years had led to a sense of isolation, to rancorous conflicts within the Zionist movement and to physical violence directed against Arab, British and even Jewish targets. The struggle for Israeli independence, which entailed a hard-fought war against the superior invading forces of six Arab states, helped to unite the Jewish factions and perhaps to push the traumatic memory of the holocaust to some extent into the background of the collective Jewish psyche. Success brought its own reward. The voice of Jewish anti-Zionism was almost silenced, and Israel received the whole-hearted backing of the majority of Jews everywhere. The immigration restrictions were abolished and European refugees began to stream into the country, to be followed by refugees from Arab countries whose position there had been made insecure by the Middle East conflict. The state was recognized by most countries, and in May 1949 was admitted to the United Nations. But the Arab states implacably refused to recognize Israel's right to exist, and the legacy of the war of independence was a siege existence which put a continuous strain on her international relations and posed the recurrent threat of renewed invasion.

Meanwhile the Jews of the Soviet Union fell victim to a frenzied campaign against "cosmopolitanism" and Zionism, in which thousands were deported to slave-labor camps or summarily murdered. Lifelong Communists and Soviet citizens were subjected to fabricated accusations of disloyalty, and many leading Jewish figures were liquidated in what have come to be known as the "Black Years" (1948–53). On a more positive plane, in West Germany (where a few Jews had resettled since the war) a conscious effort of atonement and conciliation was being made. In a momentous speech to the parliament in Bonn in 1951, Chancellor Adenauer spoke of the obligation to make moral and material amends for the "unspeakable crimes perpetrated in the name of the 'German people'," and announced the government's willingness to "bring about a solution of the material reparation problem, in order to facilitate the way to a spiritual purging of unheard-of suffering." The following year an agreement was concluded with Israel and with a Jewish representative body in which Germany undertook to pay out considerable sums for the relief and rehabilitation of survivors and for cultural and educational projects. The "spiritual" dimension was not neglected: the churches expressed a new spirit of fellowship and groups of young Germans traveled to Israel to work side by side with Jews in a gesture of contrition and reconciliation.

Israel's involvement in the Anglo-French Suez campaign of 1956 inaugurated a period of strengthened relations with the Western powers and with

Peace! President Sadat of Egypt applauds as Prime Minister Begin of Israel and President Carter of America embrace. The peace agreement between Israel and Egypt of 1979 was a triumph of personal diplomacy by these three men. Sadat and Begin were rewarded with a joint Nobel Peace Prize. Sadat was assassinated by Muslim extremists in 1981. Begin resigned in broken health in 1983.

emerging Third World states, but increased tension with her Arab neighbors. In 1967 Egypt, with Soviet backing, provoked a confrontation which sparked off the Six Day War. Israel secured a dramatic victory, which left her in control of Old Jerusalem and occupied territories several times her own size. The victory brought relief and jubilation in the country and among Jews abroad, but lost much of the international sympathy which had formerly accrued to Israel as the underdog. It also gave rise to a renewed spate of anti-Zionist propaganda in the Soviet Union and her satellites, as well as among left-wing intellectuals in the West, with strong overtones of old-style antisemitism. If Israel was the embodiment of Jewish peoplehood, political rhetoric against Israel could exploit anti-Jewish prejudice, and the "Zionist peril" could in turn be invoked in anti-Jewish hate-mongering. In Poland a scurrilous propaganda campaign drove Jews out of all official positions and eventually out of the country. In the Soviet Union one effect of the anti-Zionist campaign was to crystallize Jewish self-awareness among people who had grown up as Soviet citizens but who now felt they were aliens in their own country. In 1970 a group of Jews from Leningrad tried to hijack a plane to take them to Israel. They were arrested and severely sentenced, but the demand for the right to emigrate spread all over the Soviet Union, and, under the biblical slogan "Let my people go," was taken up by Jews in the West. Amazingly the demand was met with an increase in exit permits, which encouraged further applications on a massive scale. Life was not made easy for the applicants—they were stigmatized as traitors and parasites—but considerable numbers succeeded in leaving before a policy of renewed repression began to emerge in the early 1980s.

In 1973 Israel fought off another Arab invasion, which shattered the mood of post-1967 self-confidence. Anti-Israel agitation was intensified. In 1974 the head of the Palestine Liberation Organization was invited to address the UN General Assembly, and the following year the Assembly adopted by 72 votes to 35 (with 32 abstentions) a resolution equating Zionism with racism. This public endorsement of anti-Zionist rhetoric only contributed to bolstering the instinctive Jewish support for Israel at a time when even some Zionists were beginning to voice some sympathy for the plight of the Palestinian Arabs. Since then both tendencies have become more marked, and have come increasingly into conflict. After Israel's first real change of government in 1977, when the Labor alignment gave way to a right-wing coalition, overseas supporters of Labor Zionism felt free, as they had not done in the past, to criticize the government's policies while asserting their continued loyalty to Israel. A spate of violent attacks on Jewish targets by neo-fascist and Arab terrorists in Europe and elsewhere brought home to Western Jews the fact (long familiar to Jews in the Arab and Soviet bloc states) that their personal destinies were intimately bound up with Israel. The invasion of Lebanon in 1982, which began as an anti-terrorist action and culminated in the conquest of Beirut, provoked deeply divided reactions in the Jewish world and the first widespread and open condemnation of Israel's policies from Jews who were self-declared Zionists. This diaspora response was the corollary to the jubilant identification with Israel which followed the Six Day War 15 years earlier, and perhaps marked the beginning of a return to a more balanced and realistic appreciation of the relationship between Israel and world Jewry.

PART TWO
THE CULTURAL BACKGROUND

JEWISH IDENTITY

One does not have to eavesdrop for very long on the Jewish world today—on its publications, sermons, public speeches or serious conversations—before one discovers an intense preoccupation with two major themes: identity and survival. The preoccupation with survival is easily attributed to the shock of the holocaust, but it has older roots, in the drift away from Judaism and in the demographic decline which began in the 19th century. The preoccupation with Jewish identity also derives from the upheavals of this earlier period. It reflects in fact the drastic changes in the status of the Jews brought about by the process of emancipation and by the dislocating effect of the migrations.

The preoccupation with identity takes many forms. It finds expression in discussions about support for Israel, about Jewish day schools or intermarriage, in the anguish of teenagers torn between the attitudes of their parents and their friends, or in articles about the "Jewishness" of Kafka, Freud or Schoenberg. It is ever present in the work of Jewish clergymen, youth leaders and committee members. It is visible in the formation of Jewish sporting clubs, student societies or political groups, as well as in the many-faceted activities of the synagogues. And it is a matter of urgent public debate in Israel, where "Who is a Jew?" is the code name of a political issue which has several times threatened to bring down the government.

Left The eternal question mark. This picture postcard from the turn of the century encapsulates the uncertainties of Jewish existence. What are the Jews? What should they be in the modern world? Are they a nation or a religion? Can they survive with their identity unimpaired? If they opt for assimilation will they be accepted? Where, if anywhere, can they live in peace and security? And does being a people necessarily entail having a territory of one's own? These are questions which have still not been clearly answered.

Below A medieval view. It was at Sinai that the Jews were welded into a people: peoplehood and religion are inseparable. From a prayerbook for Shavuot made in southern Germany c. 1320. Moses is kneeling to receive the tablets of the covenant. Behind him is Aaron in the priestly miter. The male Israelites wear the characteristic medieval Jews' hat; the women have animal heads, no doubt so as to avoid distracting the male worshiper from his devotions.

Medieval cohesion

It was not always so. Medieval Jews did not search for a "Jewish identity": their identity was an unquestioned fact which had been constant for countless generations. The lack of questioning was a function of a very real lack of choice. If you were born a Jew you were naturally a member of a closely knit and clearly defined community. The only way out of it besides death was to join another community, which meant not only changing your religion but severing your links with your family and friends. The bounds of the community were clearly drawn, sometimes by the physical barrier of the ghetto wall but always by a separation from the non-Jewish environment which embraced not only religion but law, language, education and culture, even eating habits and the calendar. Jews could not intermarry with non-Jews, nor could they attend the same schools. The segregation was specific and public, openly recognized and officially sanctioned. All this was to change with the emancipation, and it is hardly surprising that the shock was profound and disorienting.

The proponents and opponents of emancipation, whether Jews or non-Jews, were fascinated by the question of what sort of community the Jews constituted. Was it religious, national, economic, cultural, racial—or what? The echoes of the debate are still heard today. But as far as the medieval community is concerned the question is largely an academic one. All the ingredients were present and it was segregation which fundamentally defined Jewish existence. It is conventional to see the Jews as a religious community, because religion is what most obviously distinguished them from Christians or from Muslims. But medieval Hebrew hardly has a word for "religion," and medieval Jews tended to see the essential difference as one of "nation" or "people" (in the biblical sense) rather than belief. They used the names of biblical nations, Edom and Ishmael, to refer to Christians and Muslims, while referring to themselves by the national title "Israel." Religious community and nation were coextensive, but religion could be seen as one of a number of incidental features which distinguished the nations from each other.

The economic and cultural differences which so preoccupied the 19th-century reformers were clearly incidental consequences of medieval segregation. In antiquity the Jews had no distinctive economic role. They were perfectly capable of sharing, and contributing to, the wider culture. Even in the middle ages there are examples of such participation, particularly in the Arab world. The question of race is a little more complicated. Preoccupations about intermarriage with outsiders go back to remote antiquity, but ancient Jewry accepted, and sometimes even sought, proselytes. A talmudic definition, which is still influential today, lays down that a Jew is either the child of a Jewish mother or a proselyte duly admitted through the ceremonies of immersion in water and (in the case of males) circumcision. Since both Christian and Muslim law laid down the death penalty for apostasy, such proselytes were rare in the middle ages and the Jewish community became, perforce, primarily a community of blood. In due course inbreeding did produce some genetic differences between Jews and non-Jews, but they were very localized: there were not, and never have been, genetic characteristics common to all Jews.

If the community was perceived as a national entity by its members, its institutions must appear to us as religious rather than secular. Such power as was delegated by non-Jewish rulers was vested in the rabbis, who as custodians of the learned tradition were religious authorities: the Torah was revealed by God and expressed his will. Although the combination of political, judicial and religious functions in the rabbis has a precedent in Jewish antiquity, it also reflects the practice in the Christian and Muslim communities, where essentially religious figures exercised political powers and dispensed religious law. The Jews never acknowledged a single spiritual head, comparable to the pope or the caliph. The cohesion and uniformity of the scattered Jewish communities was due to the voluntary adherence of the rabbis to the discipline of the divinely sanctioned Torah, as well as to the network of contacts they maintained among themselves.

This cohesion was not absolute. Communal unity was occasionally disrupted by conflicts of a personal or ideological character. A number of sectarian movements sprang up in the east, probably under the influence of a similar tendency in Islam, and one of them, Karaism, presented a real and enduring challenge to rabbinic authority. The movement spread from Iraq to the whole of the Middle East and eventually to eastern Europe too. The Karaites maintained their own communities, often side by side with the Rabbinite ones. They certainly considered themselves, and were considered by others, to be Jews, but they were always something of a special case. After 1795 the Karaites in Russia were exempted from the disabilities to which Jews were subject, and the Nazis, who eventually waged a war of extermination against them in the Crimea, were uncertain at first whether to classify them as Jews.

The Karaites are an extreme case, but there are other examples of separate Jewish communities existing side by side in the same place. In Fatimid Egypt and Palestine (10th–12th centuries CE) there were "Palestinian" and "Babylonian" synagogues, following different religious rites and recognizing different legal authorities. After the influx of western Jews into the Ottoman empire in the late 15th and early 16th centuries the newcomers established their own synagogues and some towns had a number of different communities, distinguished by the name of their country or province of origin, each preserving its own language and ritual. In northwest Europe and America too, separate Sephardi and Ashkenazi congregations coexisted, and subsequent waves of immigration increased the diversity. So even before the emancipation movement there were precedents for the fragmentation of Jewish identity—the loyalty to subgroups—which has become so marked in modern times.

The challenge of emancipation

The problem with emancipation was that it undermined the basis of a long-established and relatively stable system without offering anything concrete to take its place. A new concept of the state had rendered the separate "national" identity of the

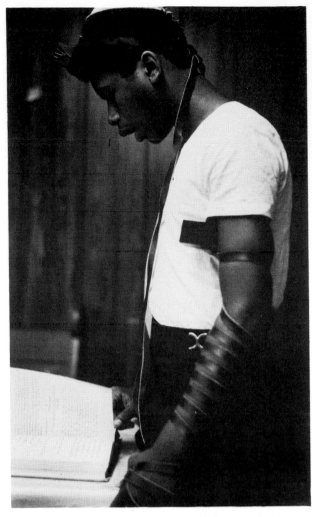

Jew obsolete. The idea was forcefully enunciated by one of the speakers in the debate on Jewish enfranchisement in the French National Assembly in 1789: "To the Jews as a nation everything must be refused; as individuals, everything must be granted to them. They must be citizens. It has been suggested that they do not wish to be citizens. Let them say so and be banished. There cannot be a nation within a nation." In fact the separate existence of the Jews was officially recognized, in France and in other European countries, in religious communities, in which the rabbis, shorn of most of their powers and brought under state control, continued to exercise a function of spiritual leadership. The new role of the rabbis was modeled on that of the Christian clergy. But the granting of citizenship and the abolition of enforced segregation introduced a crucial element of choice for the individual. Henceforth each Jew had to decide for

himself to what extent he wanted to retain his Jewish identity and in what way he wanted to express it. If a group of Jews chose to turn their backs on the new opportunities and, as it were, rebuild the fallen ghetto walls they were free to do so, within the constraints imposed by citizenship. But the vast majority had no desire to cut themselves off from the new perspectives which were opening up to them.

Many opted for baptism as a way out of an uncomfortable dilemma. It may seem strange that the Church attracted more Jewish converts in an age of freedom than it had ever succeeded in winning over during its era of supremacy. It should be remembered that conversion in the new age was easier precisely because the ground rules had been changed. The convert was no longer compelled to sever his links with the Jewish community, and indeed Christianity was no longer seen as the

Who is a Jew? The old man at prayer (*left*) conforms to a widespread image. He is wearing the *tallit* and *tefillin*, distinctive Jewish articles and both symbols of commitment to the God of Israel. But there are others who also claim the name of Israel. The New York *yeshivah* student (*far left*) is committed to the same God; he presents a less familiar face of Judaism. The Samaritans (*center left*) consider themselves to be the true Israel, and regard Jews as deviants. The Falashas of Ethiopia (*center right*) refer to themselves as the "House of Israel": they have had a hard struggle to win even nominal acceptance by Jews. No less disputed is the status of the Karaites (*above*). There are other groups too whose claims are challenged: small groups like the Bene Israel of India or the various Judaizing sects in Latin America, or larger groups like the Reform Jews, and particularly their proselytes. Christians also call themselves the true Israel, but this is interpreted in a spiritual sense.

antithesis of Judaism. The rise of a secular, even anti-religious, culture placed Christianity and Judaism on the same side of one important fence. (The phrase "Judeo-Christian tradition," in common use today, would have seemed bizarre in the middle ages, when there was no alternative tradition on hand.) There is no doubt that for many converts baptism was a formal act, a measure of convenience or an escape from irksome burdens. Benjamin Disraeli's father had his children baptized following a rift with his synagogue when he refused to pay his dues. Karl Marx's father accepted conversion rather than lose his job. These two celebrated 19th-century "New non-Jews" exemplify the flimsiness of baptism as a way out of the dilemmas of Jewish existence: both Disraeli and Marx were seen by their contemporaries (and continue to be described today) as Jews, and both, in their very different ways, testify in their writings to their obsession with Jewish identity.

Christianity was only one way out of the dilemma. The rationalist universalism of the Enlightenment looked to an age when there would be neither Jew nor Greek. There were Jews who shared this vision, which seemed to accord with the universalism of the biblical prophets. As early as 1762 Isaac de Pinto in France asked Voltaire to recognize him as a European man, and in the 19th century Jewish intellectuals participated eagerly in every movement which sought to eradicate particularism and to establish universal human values. Many Jews, however, simply drifted out of the Jewish community. Their education and social ties made traditional Jewish life meaningless to them. Loyalty to the state replaced loyalty to the Jewish community. Captain Dreyfus, a man pathetically unsuited to become a symbol of the Jewish victim of gentile intolerance, was reluctant to press for the vindication of his innocence because it would cast a slur on the honor of the army and of French justice.

The fate of Dreyfus is a tragic illustration of the inability of the liberals to deliver the goods they advertised. They could call on the Jews to emerge from the shell of the ghetto, but they could not command the gentile world to accept them as equals. On the contrary, Jewish assimilation fueled the savage reaction. Racial antisemitism, with its deep roots in medieval prejudice and its plausible cloak of scientific reason, undermined the effort for integration by categorizing the Jews as an alien breed. Even Jews who opted for assimilation were taunted with their origins. If they changed their names, their former Jewish names were added in brackets as a pointed reminder. They were mocked for their fickleness, or accused of sinisterly infiltrating and subverting gentile society.

It is hardly surprising that Jews, already troubled perhaps by guilt for having abandoned or questioned their Jewish heritage, felt confused and frustrated when confronted with signs of rejection from the very society which was urging them to assimilate. The well-known phenomenon of the alienated Jewish intellectual—alienated both from Judaism and from gentile society—highlights the common predicament of European Jews in the age of antisemitism. So do the ideological conflicts which divided the Jewish communities and of which the focus was the question of how to respond as Jews to the dual challenges of emancipation and gentile

distrust. Liberal and Orthodox Jews, German nationalists and Jewish nationalists, all claimed to have *the* answer to the problems of being Jewish in the modern world. In the 1920s, while the Jewish Communists in the Soviet Union were waging war on the Jewish religion as well as on Zionism and Bundism, the main Jewish organization in Germany, significantly entitled the Central Union of German Citizens of Jewish Faith, was opposing both the assimilationism of the Association of National German Jews and the growing Zionist movement. Even in America the American Jewish Committee, founded in 1906 by the wealthy elite of American Jewish society to protect the interests of the Jewish community as a whole, was being challenged by the multifarious and vocal Zionist and socialist groups, which claimed to represent the Jewish proletariat. The religious establishment, too, was deeply divided, even though the Synagogue Council of America was set up in 1926 to coordinate certain activities.

The Nazi holocaust heightened the anguish of the Jewish condition, by forcibly demonstrating the failure of assimilation even in countries which had pioneered it. Totally assimilated Jews, even second-generation Christians, were classified as "non-Aryans" and deprived of their citizenship together with religious Jews and Zionists. Loyalty to the state, social integration with its various forms of camouflage, even the ultimate step of baptism, had proved to be no escape in the moment of trial. Many of the survivors of this war of extermination understandably came to see Jewish survival as an end in itself: not just the survival of the individual but the survival of the people as a whole. Hence the momentous postwar upsurge of enthusiasm for Zionism in America and other Western countries, typically manifested not in a personal desire to emigrate to Palestine but in a commitment to the idea of a state where the survivors of the holocaust could reconstruct a Jewish national existence. The establishment of Israel in 1948 provided a powerful stimulus for the sense of national Jewish identity among Jews all over the world. It also offered an entirely new model for Jewish identity within the context of the modern state. At the same time it raised new problems about Jewish identity, both for the individual and for the state as a whole.

In Israel the process of assimilation—the social integration of minorities, acculturation to the dominant ethos and lifestyle, the weakening of religious ties and the strengthening of loyalties to the state—takes places within a Jewish society. This means that the main factors which give rise to tensions in the area of Jewish assimilation in other countries—erosion of the Jewish community, non-Jewish influence on Jewish life, the fear of antisemitism—are not present. The state makes no provision for intermarriage between Jews and non-Jews, and Jewish parents can rest assured that their children will have a Jewish upbringing. At the same time Jews can identify fully with the state and participate in all aspects of its life without restriction. The result is that Jews in Israel (particularly if they are not religious) tend to identify themselves as Israelis rather than Jews. It has been remarked that non-religious Israeli emigrants rarely join the Jewish community in their new country, perhaps partly because of a difficulty in accepting the centrality of

Who is a Jew?

Problems in formulating Jewish identity inevitably entail doubts in individual cases. Does Jewish identity depend on parentage, or religion, or both, or on something quite different? Can one stop being a Jew? And if so, how? The pictures on these pages are of people whose Jewish status is not entirely obvious or straightforward.

Abraham

The biblical patriarch Abraham is often described as the founder of Judaism. But was he a Jew? A later Jewish tradition insists that he observed the commandments of the Torah, even though they had not been revealed in his day.

The figure of Moses too looms large in all three monotheistic faiths. Jewish tradition looks to him as the greatest of all the prophets, the mediator of God's revelation to the Jewish people, the ideal type of leader, intercessor and teacher.

Moses

Jesus of Nazareth

Jesus of Nazareth, who considered himself a Jew throughout his life, is also remembered as a prophet by Muslims, while for Christians he is a superhuman figure with a spiritual message for all mankind. Jesus the man has left little if any trace in Jewish tradition, but as the figurehead of triumphant Christianity he has too often appeared in the guise of persecutor of the people into which he was born.

Inquisition Spain was deeply sensitive to the Jewish origin of "New Christians." Nevertheless there is no clear evidence that Columbus was of Jewish extraction, as many people have believed.

Baruch Spinoza, the greatest philosopher the Jewish people has ever produced, was a member of the Sephardi community of Amsterdam until he was charged with holding heretical views and excommunicated. Refusing to be baptized, he remained outside any community until the day he died.

In the early 19th century many German Jews were baptized, although they did not always make sincere Christians. Some, like Karl Marx, were baptized in childhood. Marx was six when he was baptized; in later years he wrote a pamphlet on the Jewish Question which betrays an excess of anti-Jewish sentiment.

As the 19th century wore on, there were increasing numbers of Jews who moved out of the Jewish community without feeling any need to become Christians. Some drifted restlessly from one ideology to another; many were preoccupied by their rift with Judaism. In the writings of people as different as Sigmund Freud, Marcel Proust and Franz Kafka we can detect a certain anxiety about Jewish identity and its meaning in the modern world. On the other hand one would be hard put to it to discover a trace of their Jewish origins in the paintings of Pissarro or in the music of Mahler.

For some Jewish intellectuals the universalistic appeal of socialism offered a way out of the repressive cycle of Jewish rejection and withdrawal. Among the closest collaborators of Lenin were several Communists of Jewish origin: they included Leo Kamenev, Yakov Sverdlov (for whom the city of Sverdlovsk was named), and of course Leon Trotsky. The Russian Jewish artists who came to maturity around the time of the Revolution faced a difficult choice, as did Jewish intellectuals all over Europe, between Jewish particularism and a more universal stance. The writer Ilya Ehrenburg is typical of the assimilated intellectuals who were not permitted to forget their Jewish background. Boris Pasternak adopted a more enigmatic pose; having abandoned Judaism and Christianity in turn, he is said to have described himself in later years as "an atheist who has lost his faith." The filmmaker Sergei Eisenstein is remembered as a Jew: in fact like so many he was the product of a mixed marriage, and since his mother was not Jewish he would not be accepted by the rabbinate; for others, any measure of Jewish blood is a qualification.

In more recent years there has been no shortage of people, who, while not denying their Jewish background, have expressed no interest in a specifically Jewish identity, whether religious or national. Dr Bruno Kreisky, the Social Democratic Chancellor of Austria from 1970 to 1983, is an example. Another is the noted American statesman and political theorist Dr Henry Kissinger. To stand aloof from one's known background is this way demands in a public figure a good measure of clearheaded determination; it is a path which is less difficult for private individuals, who have followed it in large numbers.

Christopher Columbus (1451–1506)

Can one be a Jew and a Christian? A British bishop, Dr Hugh Montefiore, has claimed that he is both. In recent years there has also been a certain amount of conversion to Judaism, much of it for matrimonial reasons. Marilyn Monroe, who became Jewish to marry the playwright Arthur Miller, is one of a number of showbusiness personalities who have taken this step.

Baruch Spinoza (1632–77)

Franz Kafka (1883–1924)

Karl Marx (1818–83)

Sigmund Freud (1856–1939)

Camille Pissarro (1831–1903)

Gustav Mahler (1860–1911)

Leon Trotsky (1879–1940)   Ilya Ehrenburg (1891–1967)

Henry Kissinger (1923–)

Hugh Montefiore (1920–)

Marilyn Monroe (1926–62) and Arthur Miller (1915–)

the synagogue in diaspora Jewish identity. Meanwhile religious Jews in Israel display many symptoms of a minority complex, even to the extent of forming political parties to safeguard their rights and privileges. They also maintain their own educational, social and charitable institutions. At its most extreme this phenomenon is visible in the small ghettoized community which does not recognize the Jewish state and has expressed a preference for non-Jewish rule. Thus Israel manifests both a tendency to extreme assimilation and a resistance to assimilation, just like diaspora Jewry. What makes it special is that the state itself maintains and fosters a sense of Jewish identity and gives official recognition to Jewish identity in its institutions.

Israeli citizens are allocated a national status and a religious status, which are entered in their official papers (in the case of the Jewish majority the two are effectively coterminous). Registration as a Jew has important consequences for the individual, in terms of privileges and restrictions (for example, a person registered as Jewish may only marry with the consent of the rabbinic courts). The regulations are the result of a long process of conflict and compromise between secularist and religious Zionists, and they continue to give rise to acrimonious debate which centers on the official definition of Jewish identity. In 1958 the Mizrachi (religious Zionist) members withdrew from the government coalition in reaction to a cabinet decision that anyone who wished to be registered as a Jew should be so registered provided the applicant had not been received into another religion. In the political storm which ensued the prime minister, David Ben-Gurion, addressed a letter to prominent Jews in Israel and abroad soliciting their opinions, particularly on the problem of the registration of children of a Jewish father and non-Jewish mother. The 43 replies mainly upheld the talmudic definition, but the problem is still far from being resolved. A succession of difficult legal cases highlighted the anomalies, and there is mounting pressure from secularists for the separation of religion from the state and from the religious parties for a narrower definition which would exclude Reform and Conservative proselytes.

In another major center of Jewish population, the Soviet Union, Jewish identity is also officially recognized but gives rise to different problems. For historical rather than ideological reasons the Jews are regarded as a nationality, and their Jewish nationality is entered on their papers. In other respects Jewish identification labors under severe handicaps. There are no Jewish communal or social organizations, at local or state levels, and Jewish schools are forbidden. Religious congregations are permitted, but suffer from a lack of rabbis and of facilities for rabbinic training, and from a ban on religious education for children and other disadvantages. Zionism is illegal, antisemitism is common. In recent years there have been complaints of discrimination against Jews in higher education and bars on advancement in academic careers, and Jews have been virtually eliminated from the upper echelons of the Party, the civil service and the army. In these circumstances it is not surprising that assimilation is rife. Mixed marriages are very common, and the children normally adopt the

Russian or the dominant local nationality. But a sense of Jewish identity remains strong. In a secret survey carried out in 1976, 87 percent of respondents said they would go to Jewish cafés or restaurants if they existed. Since 1970 many Jews have risked harassment by attending private Hebrew classes and seminars on Jewish subjects or by gathering together on Jewish festivals. This great upsurge of interest, which is linked to the movement for emigration and to some extent to political dissent, is not primarily religious but social and cultural. National Jewish sentiment is surprisingly muted, considering the official definition and the stress on Zionism in anti-Jewish propaganda, and in recent years most Jews who have succeeded in emigrating have chosen not to go to Israel, despite intense Zionist pressure.

In most other countries the state takes no official cognizance of the identity of its Jewish citizens, even if in a few cases the religious institutions are to some extent incorporated in the state system. In America religion is strictly separated from the state. Judaism is widely recognized as one of the major religions and is entirely respectable. Indeed, there is some social pressure on Jews, as on Americans generally, to affiliate to a religious community. At the same time the existence of numerous ethnic minorities may encourage a different perception of Jewish identity, in which religion takes second place to social and cultural considerations. The synagogue, which in Israel and the Soviet Union exists to provide religious services, serves as a community center and offers a wide range of activities including some of a purely social nature. In other countries the situation is similar, even if local conditions encourage a slightly different perception of the place of the Jews in the wider society. As a minority group Jews tend to be sensitive about their status and experience certain tensions, either at group or individual level. Jewish representative organizations keep a watchful eye on legislation and political developments which may threaten the interests of the Jewish community and they often take an initiative in cultivating relations with other religious or ethnic groups. Israel provides an important focus for Jewish identity, expressed through Zionist organizations and, increasingly, in the activities of synagogues and representative organizations. Most Jews, however, identify themselves primarily with the country in which they live and resent any imputation of dual loyalties.

Contemporary dilemmas

For all the multiplicity of responses to the challenge of emancipation, the basic problem remains the same everywhere: how to define and express one's identity as a Jew without falling into conflicts and contradictions. The old definitions have become obsolete, but none of the proposed solutions has so far proved satisfactory. Emancipation was essentially a political issue, and it provoked political responses. Of these the most enduring was Zionism, but most Jews have no desire to express their Jewish identity in political terms. In fact no attempt to define Jewish identity in ideological terms has won general favor: even religion, which was such a cohesive force in medieval Jewish society, has proved to be neither a necessary nor a sufficient foundation for Jewish identity in the modern age.

Zionism and Judaism are seen as options available to people who consider themselves as Jews. Both claim to offer a way of leading a purposeful and fulfilling Jewish life, but neither maintains that only its own adherents are Jews. Large numbers of Jews belong to synagogues or Zionist organizations, but for only a minority of these is Judaism or Zionism central to their lives, and many people with a strong sense of Jewish identity have no formal attachment to any Jewish institution.

Of course the Jews are not alone in facing this problem of identity. Greeks, Basques, Armenians, Welshmen and many others are familiar with the problems of minority existence, of militant nationalism, of intermarriage, of maintaining a distinctive religious and cultural heritage. In countries as different as Canada, Argentina and the Soviet Union, the Jews are only one among a variety of minority communities attempting to preserve their culture and identity in conditions of civil equality. Each of these communities knows tensions at the personal and collective levels, and pressures on the younger generation to conform to traditional values. For it is always the youth who feel the dilemmas most acutely, having to contend with their parents' anxieties as well as the ambiguities of their own situation.

Prominent among the expressed preoccupations of Jewish parents and communal leaders is "assimilation." For most Jews some measure of assimilation is inevitable and indeed positively desirable: the problem is where to draw the line. In contemporary Jewish rhetoric, however, "assimilation" is always a pejorative term. It signifies defection from an ideal Jewish life, and is equated with estrangement from the community, perhaps even conversion to another religion. In practice it is often used as a euphemism for intermarriage, which has come to be seen as the main threat to the survival of the Jews as a group. This is the area where the challenge of changing times is most noticeable, and where the response of the Jewish leadership has been most inadequate. Intermarriage has been steadily increasing for generations: it is an inevitable consequence of emancipation and social integration. It is resulting in ever-growing numbers of people with some Jewish ancestry, but whose Jewish identity is uncertain and whose attachment to the organized Jewish community is problematical. If one adds to these the children of Jewish parents who have been given little or no Jewish upbringing, it is clear that the doubts and questions about Jewish identity beset far more people than just the committed Jews whose situation in the modern world compels them to reexamine the character and strength of their Jewish commitment and the place of Judaism in their lives.

It is difficult to foresee where the present uncertainties are leading. Jewish history provides several striking examples of periods of crisis and change. The encounter with the Greek world was one such period: many of the contemporary preoccupations are vividly evoked in the literature of that distant age. It was a time of upheaval and painful adjustment, but it led to a great enrichment of Jewish culture and to extraordinary opportunities for Jews to influence the culture of the wider world. The same could be said of the encounter with Islam, and of the later encounter with the European Renais-

For young American Jews, religion constitutes a natural expression of Jewish identity (*above*). In Russia (*right*) the synagogue is a vital focus for an identification which may be predominantly "national" rather than religious.

sance. Each of these encounters gave rise to anxious debates about the legitimate scope for the assimilation of external influences, which are echoed in our own time. The debates were often acrimonious, and one result in each case was a deliberate narrowing of horizons, a withdrawal into Jewish tradition, albeit a tradition transformed and enriched by the encounter. But those encounters also produced Philo, Maimonides and Spinoza (to name only the outstanding representatives of each phase), brilliant and original thinkers who made enduring contributions to wider culture. Their modern counterparts are Marx, Freud, Einstein and a host of creative talents. Clearly the larger benefits of cultural interchange are not to be underestimated.

The historical lessons are complicated, however, by the greater freedom deriving from political emancipation. This freedom is an undoubted gain for the individual Jew, but it has raised widespread fears for the future survival of the Jews as a group, and for their religion and culture. If it were a question of a straightforward choice between survival under oppressive conditions or freedom leading to dissolution there would be an intolerable conflict of interests between the individual and the group. But the alternatives are not that simple. It is true that some Jewish communities have largely or entirely disappeared through assimilation. But others have been eliminated by massacre or forcible conversion. Subordination in itself is no guarantee of survival. Jews, like other minorities, require and demand personal security, freedom of religious and cultural expression, and also freedom from coercion, from pressure to abandon their distinctive heritage in the interests of conformity. It is this pressure which has done the greatest damage to the continuity of Jewish identity and culture under conditions of apparent liberty. Where minorities are tolerated and allowed to be themselves they can survive whether in free or restrictive political conditions: this is one clear lesson from the experience of Jewish history.

One other lesson of history may help in predicting future trends: problems of identity are more acute in small than in large communities. For all the anonymity of large cities, where the main centers of Jewish population are located, it is the smaller and more isolated groups that are most exposed to the pressures of assimilation. Our survey of the Jewish world today will demonstrate the tendency for smaller communities (whether at the national or local level) to become smaller, while larger ones maintain their strength or even grow through immigration. The Jews are increasingly becoming concentrated in fewer and fewer localities. This concentration does not in any way solve the problems of assimilation, but it does to some extent mitigate its most threatening effects.

The rebirth of Israel as a major Jewish center has important implications for the self-perception of Jews everywhere. Even if the political ramifications have given rise to unwelcome tensions for Jews in some countries, all Jews can look to Israel in the way that overseas Greeks, say, look to Greece or Irish Americans to Ireland. A national homeland is a powerful asset to a scattered people, and it offers rich opportunities for cultural growth and collective self-confidence.

The Lifetime of a Jew

The important moments which punctuate the Jew's passage through life are marked by appropriate ceremonies, which underline the fact that the individual is not alone but belongs to a larger community, reaching out both vertically, in time, and horizontally, in space.

Birth is closely followed for boys by circumcision (*brit milah*), traditionally carried out on the eighth day. The operation is performed by a specialist called a *mohel*, and to hold the baby is considered an honor. This is also the moment when the boy receives his name.

The child becomes of age in Jewish law at puberty, and is then liable to observe all the commandments. This occurs, for a boy, at the latest on the day after his 13th birthday, and from now on he can play a full part in the ritual of the synagogue. Consequently at the heart of the family celebrations is an attendance at synagogue when he will exercise his right for the first time, generally by reading from the Torah and Prophets. The corresponding age for girls is 12, and the more modernist synagogues have devised ceremonies to mark the occasion. They have also tended to introduce a "confirmation" ceremony for boys and girls at the age of 16.

Marriage has its origin in ancient property law, and the ceremony still involves the giving of a ring by the bridegroom to his bride, together with a document (*ketubbah*) recording his undertaking to respect and maintain her, and itemizing the agreed financial settlement. Divorce has no special ceremony: it too is effected by means of a document (called a *get*), releasing the wife so that she is free to remarry.

There are many other occasions marked by special religious ritual: recovering from a serious illness, for instance, or completing a dangerous journey, or moving into a new home. These are moments which deserve a ceremony of thanksgiving, and appropriate forms have been evolved. Conversion to Judaism, too, is accompanied by distinctive rituals, including immersion in water (*tevilah*) and, for males, circumcision.

Burial is carried out simply. The presence of a rabbi is not required (nor is it for the other ceremonies mentioned here), and there are no flowers. The body is wrapped in a shroud, and nowadays it is usually encased in a plain coffin. Mourning is observed intensely for the first week, less intensely for the first month, and more lightly still for the remainder of the first year. After that the mourner returns to normal life, save for an annual act of commemoration.

"You shall circumcise the flesh of your foreskin, and it shall be the sign of the covenant between us." The requirement of circumcision goes right back to the Torah, to Abraham who circumcised his son Isaac a week after his birth: Jewish babies are still circumcised at this age (*below*). It is a social occasion: family and friends share the parents' joy. Special implements are used, and in the past they were often beautifully made (*below right*), since circumcision is not only a surgical operation but a major religious observance.

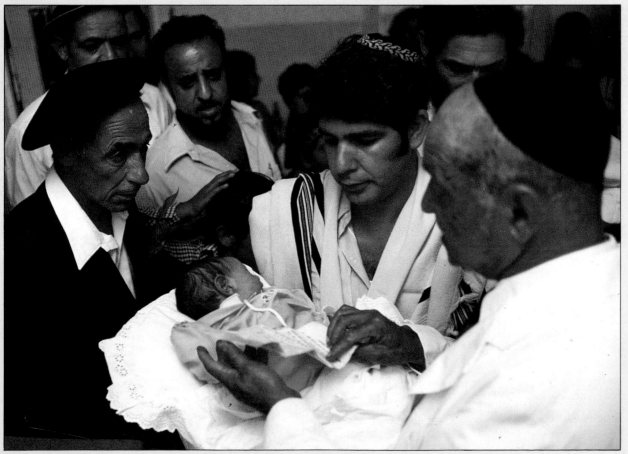

Right "At thirteen, the commandments." The *bar mitzvah* (the term properly applies to the person rather than the ceremony) is initiated into the adult community by putting on the *tallit* and being called up to read the Torah and the *haftarah* in synagogue, usually during a Sabbath service. Here he is seen reading from the Torah scroll: notice the hand-shaped pointer (*yad*) used by the rabbi, to avoid touching the parchment scroll.

Left "The voice of joy and rejoicing, the voice of bridegroom and bride." Marriages are usually performed nowadays in synagogue, although some traditionalists protest that this is due to Christian influence, and insist that the ceremony should take place at home, or preferably in the open air. What is indispensable is the *huppah*, a canopy which covers the bridal pair. Blessings are intoned over wine, the *ketubbah* is read out, and the bridegroom places a ring on the bride's right forefinger. In former times betrothal rings were often very elaborate (*below*).

Below "The Lord gives and the Lord takes away; blessed be the name of the Lord." Death is accepted with resignation, and the community has an important role of comforting and supporting the mourner. Precise rules govern the preparation of the corpse for burial, and it used to be considered a privilege to belong to the *Hevra Kadisha*, the "Holy Society" which undertook this task. The Society would meet for an annual banquet on the seventh of Adar (the traditional date of the death of Moses), when they would drink from glasses decorated with appropriate motifs (*right*).

The Jewish Year

The Calendar

The Jewish calendar regulates the rhythm of life of observant Jews everywhere. It is a lunar calendar: the months match the lunar cycle, and the festivals always fall at the same phase of the moon. The months are alternately of 29 and 30 days' duration; the first day of each month (and the 30th day if there is one) is observed as a minor feast-day. To keep the lunar year of 354 days in step with the solar year of 365 days an additional month is inserted seven times every 19 years. This adjustment ensures that the festivals fall in the same season each year, unlike the Muslim festivals which can occur at any date in the solar calendar, but there is still a certain fluctuation in the civil date of the Jewish festivals from year to year.

The smaller units of the calendar are the day, which begins and ends at nightfall, and the week, culminating in the Sabbath, a holy day of rest which falls every Saturday. The Sabbath dominates the observant Jew's week as an ever-present reminder of his religion. The Sabbath rest looks back to the creation of the world—since according to the Bible God rested from his task on the seventh day—and it also looks forward to the final redemption, often being described as a "foretaste of eternity." It is a time for repose and recreation, a retreat from worldly cares, and a chance for the family to come together in shared activities.

The year also has its regular rhythm, rising to a peak of activity during the two festive seasons in the autumn and the spring. The major festivals have biblical origins, associated with the thrice-yearly pilgrimage to Jerusalem at harvesttime. The harvest theme has long since ceased to dominate the observance of these festivals (although it has been revived to some extent in modern Israel), but the biblical influence is still very strongly felt. *Sukkot* (Tabernacles) takes its name from the harvest huts, bedecked with fruit and greenery, which call to mind the tents in which the Israelites dwelt during their wanderings in the wilderness after the exodus from Egypt. In antiquity *Sukkot* was the high point of the year, and the ancient rabbis refer to it simply as "the Festival"; nowadays it has been somewhat thrust into the shade by the New Year festivities and the solemn Day of Atonement which immediately precede it. The exodus itself is celebrated annually at *Pesah* (Passover), and seven weeks later *Shavuot* (Weeks or Pentecost) commemorates the giving of the Torah at Mount Sinai. But each of the festivals also has its spiritual message: the transience of human life in the case of *Sukkot*; liberation from oppression for *Pesah*; divine revelation for *Shavuot*. And each also comes with the flavor of its own time of the year—the ripeness of autumn, which in the Middle East is a time of fresh rain and new life, the promise of spring and the fullness of summer. The New Year period has a special tone of introspection and penitence, in which the joy of renewal is mingled with reverent self-searching.

Many other observances have grown up over the

Tishri	Heshvan	Kislev	Tevet	Shevat	Adar
1 ROSH HASHANAH (New Year)	1	1	1	1	1
2	2	2	2	2	2
3 Fast	3	3	3	3	3
4	4	4	4	4	4
5	5	5	5	5	5
6	6	6	6	6	6
7	7	7	7	7	7
8	8	8	8	8	8
9	9	9	9	9	9
10 YOM KIPPUR (Day of Atonement)	10	10	10 Fast	10	10
11	11	11	11	11	11
12	12	12	12	12	12
13	13	13	13	13	13 Fast of Esther
14	14	14	14	14	14 PURIM
15 SUKKOT (Tabernacles)	15	15	15	15 New Year for Trees	15
16	16	16	16	16	16
17	17	17	17	17	17
18	18	18	18	18	18
19	19	19	19	19	19
20	20	20	20	20	20
21	21	21	21	21	21
22 SHEMINI ATSERET	22	22	22	22	22
23 SIMHAT TORAH*	23	23	23	23	23
24	24	24	24	24	24
25	25	25 HANUKKAH	25	25	25
26	26	26	26	26	26
27	27	27	27	27	27
28	28	28	28	28	28
29	29	29	29	29	29
30		30		30	

ואשמח בשמחת תורה

Nisan	Iyyar	Sivan	Tammuz	Av	Elul
	1	1	1	1	1
	2	2	2	2	2
	3	3	3	3	3
	4	4	4	4	4
	5 Israeli Independence Day	5	5	5	5
	6	6 SHAVUOT (Pentecost)	6	6	6
	7	7 *	7	7	7
	8	8	8	8	8
	9	9	9	9 Fast	9
	10	10	10	10	10
	11	11	11	11	11
	12	12	12	12	12
	13	13	13	13	13
of the tborn	14	14	14	14	14
AH sover)	15	15	15	15	15
	16	16	16	16	16
	17	17	17 Fast	17	17
	18 Lag Ba'omer	18	18	18	18
	19	19	19	19	19
	20	20	20	20	20
AH Day	21	21	21	21	21
* 22	22	22	22	22	22
	23	23	23	23	23
	24	24	24	24	24
	25	25	25	25	25
	26	26	26	26	26
caust embrance Day 27	27	27	27	27	27
	28	28	28	28	28
	29	29	29	29	29
	30		30		

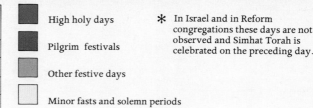

High holy days
Pilgrim festivals
Other festive days
Minor fasts and solemn periods

* In Israel and in Reform congregations these days are not observed and Simhat Torah is celebrated on the preceding day.

centuries, and the calendar is dotted with fast-days and minor festivities. Two celebrations in particular have won a firm place in the affection of all Jews: *Hanukkah* in midwinter is an eight-day festival of light, commemorating the rededication of the temple by the Hasmoneans, while *Purim*, the celebration of relief from Persian persecution as recounted in the biblical book of Esther, is observed with fancy-dress parties and riotous fun. In recent years an attempt has been made to establish two new dates in the calendar: the declaration of Israeli independence on the fifth of Iyyar and a day of remembrance for the victims of the Nazi holocaust a week earlier. Both of these dates are especially observed in Israel. The same is true of other, older-established, observances, such as the 15th of Shevat, a day of tree-planting, or the 18th of Iyyar (*Lag Ba-Omer*), a day for bonfires and picnics. For most of the Jewish world there are two times of the year which stand out above all others: the Days of Awe (New Year and the Day of Atonement), when the synagogues are packed with worshipers, and Passover, when families are reunited to celebrate the feast of liberation.

One other detail of the calendar needs a word of explanation. In the diaspora the custom has arisen of observing an additional day for each of the pilgrim festivals (including both the first and the last day of *Sukkot* and *Pesah*). This custom, which has its origins in antiquity, has been abandoned by Reform and some Conservative Jews, who, like Israelis, follow the observance laid down in the Bible.

The years are numbered from the traditional date of the creation of the world, in 3761 BCE. Thus the year beginning in the autumn of 1984 is AM (*Anno Mundi*) 5745.

Each festival of the year has its own particular flavor. *Far left Simhat Torah* marks the end of the solemn period of New Year celebrations, which for the very pious has lasted the best part of two months; it also marks the end of the annual cycle of Torah readings. The theme of the festival is joy, which may easily verge on the riotous, as in this woodcut from Russia of c. 1920. Note the participation of children in the synagogue dancing: traditionally they wave special flags, of which this is actually an example. *Left* Although no less joyful, *Pesah* is more restrained. It is inaugurated at home, in an evening meal which is part banquet, part religious service and part history lesson. Here too the participation of children is encouraged. The service book is called *Haggadah* ("Narration"), and this illustration itself comes from a Haggadah produced in 14th-century Spain. *Right* The zodiac and four seasons, from a 6th-century Byzantine floor mosaic in a Galilean synagogue (Beth Alpha). The function of such mosaics is an intriguing enigma.

The Festivals

Below left "Blow the *shofar* on the new moon!" New Year at the Western Wall in Jerusalem: the *shofar* utters a call to repentance. *Bottom right* "Take the fuit of citrus trees, palm fronds, leafy boughs and willows from the brook, and rejoice before the Lord your God." *Sukkot* at the Western Wall.

Below "We kindle these lights to commemorate the wonders, the heroic acts, the victories and the marvelous and consoling deeds which you performed for our fathers in those days at this season." On the last night of *Hanukkah* all eight lights are lit.

Days of Awe

In English they are often called the high holy days, in Hebrew the Awesome Days (*Yamim Nora'im*): ten solemn days which begin with *Rosh Hashanah* (New Year) and culminate in *Kippur* (Atonement). This is the time of judgment: the book lies open, and each individual's destiny will be inscribed according to the balance of his or her deeds. "On *Rosh Hashanah* it is written, and on the fast-day of *Kippur* it is sealed: how many will pass away and how many will be created; who will live and who will die; who at his allotted end and who prematurely . . ." The words of the liturgy are awe-inspiring, yet they also carry a reassuring message of comfort and forgiveness.

Hanukkah

In the dark of midwinter, eight days of light and festivity. *Hanukkah* commemorates the victory of the Hasmoneans over the armies of Antiochus IV (164 BCE). "Afterwards your children entered the sanctuary of your house, cleared your temple and lit lamps in your holy courts. Then they instituted eight days of *Hanukkah* to thank and praise your great name." *Hanukkah* means "dedication," but to generations of children it has meant candles and presents. The *menorah*, the seven-branched lampstand which stood in the temple, has been skillfully transformed into the *hanukiyyah* of nine branches: one light for each day of the festival and a ninth (the *shamash*) to light the others.

Sukkot

Close after *Kippur* comes *Sukkot*, which takes its name from the festive huts (*sukkot*) roofed with greenery and decorated with fruit and flowers. It is a pious custom to begin building the *sukkah* on returning from the *Kippur* service. Where the climate permits, families eat and sleep in the *sukkah* for the duration of the festival. The other special observance of *Sukkot* is the "four species": a palm frond, sprigs of myrtle and sprays of willow, all bound up together to form the *lulav*, and accompanied by the *etrog*, a citrus fruit of delicate scent if of unexceptional taste. The four species are carried in procession, and shaken and waved in six directions, to the accompaniment of the chanting of *hosannas* (prayers for deliverance); they make a stirring spectacle. *Sukkot* lasts for seven or eight days, and it is immediately followed by *Simhat Torah*, when similar but more exuberant processions occur, this time parading the Torah scrolls.

Top left "For the Jews there was light and joy, gladness and honor." Bukharan Jews celebrating *Purim*. As they read the scroll of Esther do they recall their own Persian origins? *Center left* "For seven days no leaven may be found in your homes." Burning the *hametz* in Jerusalem.

Bottom left "On that day you shall tell your son, 'This commemorates what the Lord did for me when I came out of Egypt.'" A Passover *seder* in America. Note the ritual foods on the plate which is being held up.

Purim

Nearly halfway through the year comes *Purim*, which commemorates the failure of the plot by the wicked Haman to annihilate the Jews of the Persian empire (5th century BCE). Like *Hanukkah*, it is not a full festival, but a normal working day distinguished by specific observances and a mood of joy. The Book of Esther, which tells the story of the original *Purim*, is read aloud from handwritten scrolls, and drinking is unrestrained.

Preparation for Passover

Only a month separates *Purim* from Passover, and for those concerned with the practical tasks of preparation it passes all too quickly. The Torah insists that homes shall be free from leaven, and this is commonly seized as a suitable pretext for some more general springcleaning. There is a visible bustle in any Jewish community before the advent of Passover, as homes are cleaned out, furnishings and clothes are laundered or replaced and the kitchen undergoes a complete transformation. It is not uncommon in traditional circles for whole new sets of crockery and kitchen utensils to be bought, and stores of provisions are laid in for the week's feasting and entertaining. Unleavened bread (*matzah*) must be baked or, more usually, bought, and there is a wealth of traditional recipes which make a virtue of the restricted diet by the lavish use of ground almonds, cinnamon and other such tasty ingredients. The day before Passover Eve the preparations are essentially complete, and the remaining *hametz* (leaven) is ceremoniously destroyed.

Passover

The week-long festival begins in the evening with one of the most popular of all Jewish ceremonies: the *seder* meal. The family is united, and Jews who are away from home or living on their own are offered hospitality. All formal Jewish meals begin with blessings, for wine and bread and for the day itself, but the *seder* ritual is especially elaborate: the recitation of the biblical story of the exodus from Egypt is interwoven with meditations on the themes of liberty and rescue and with songs of praise to God. Children play a leading role: it is the youngest present who traditionally begins the proceedings by asking the leading question "Why is this night different from all other nights?", and what follows—the narration of the exodus—is the reply to this inquiry. There are "teaching aids" in the form of symbolic foods: a roast lamb's bone and egg for the paschal sacrifice, *matzah*, as a reminder of the haste with which the Israelites were forced to leave Egypt, and horseradish or other bitter herbs as a reminder of their sufferings. The ritual of the *seder* preserves features of the Greco-Roman banquet; it also looks forward to the messianic banquet of the coming age. The evening concludes with some popular songs, which help to hold the children's interest to the very end.

JEWISH LIFE

The often-echoed aphorism that Judaism is "not so much a religion, more a way of life" is perhaps intended more as a reflection on Jewish religion than on Jewish life. It is true that Jewish identity is very often a social commitment in which religion is only one ingredient among many, and equally true that Jewish religious literature has always placed a firm emphasis on real life rather than abstract thought or faith. But Jewish life, as lived and as opposed to the ideal blueprint of sermons and manuals, is a curiously intangible thing, varying widely from place to place, from time to time, and even among groups or individuals within the same community. This variety is very marked today, probably more so than at any previous time, but it would be unduly romantic to imagine that it is a purely modern phenomenon. What has changed is that the social cohesion and uniformity of the medieval community have broken down in the new conditions of an open society, and this breakdown has given rise to multifarious attempts to preserve and express Jewish identity without the constraints of enforced segregation and a powerful internal leadership. As often happens, an essentially political change has brought about a transformation of economic and social life which has in turn demanded a reappraisal of the theoretical basis of traditional institutions and habits.

The disintegration of the medieval community has been a gradual process over the past two or three hundred years; it is not yet complete. There are still places where medieval conditions of life persist, though they are few and small and ever decreasing. The vast majority of Jews today live in countries where the formal basis of such an existence has been removed, and where Jewish life is a matter of individual or collective choice. In these new conditions it has been possible to recreate an existence which approximates to the traditional life-style, and this option has been taken up by a small minority, but since it represents a voluntary choice it is fundamentally different from the older model on which it is based, and it is to be judged as one aspect of modern diversity rather than as an authentic survival. Traditional forms of life do continue to exercise a powerful influence on Jews today, particularly on those for whom emancipation has been a recent experience, but in the course of two or three generations this influence becomes attenuated, surviving often in the form of a sentimental instinct. Meanwhile new forms of social life have been developed, consciously or unconsciously, and old institutions have been abandoned or reinterpreted, old values have been rejected or revised and new institutions and values have taken their place. The process is neither regular nor anywhere complete. For many (those whose medieval communities were shattered in the 1940s or later) it has hardly begun. It is a kaleidoscopic picture whose final outcome, if there can be such a thing, is impossible to predict.

The medieval community

In medieval Jewish communities Jewish identity was officially recognized, proselytism and intermarriage were forbidden and Jews were often compelled to wear distinctive clothing and inhabit separate quarters: social segregation resulted in cultural separation. Although some influence was inevitable, Jews were cut off from the culture of the majority and developed their own life-style in relative isolation. In many places they even spoke a different language from their neighbors. There was often a noticeable difference in cultural levels between Jews and non-Jews (particularly in those places where illiteracy was widespread among non-Jews). Religion of course was a clearly divisive factor, as much a cause as a product of separation, although very often there was some mutual religious influence, both at the intellectual level and at the popular.

The medieval community was highly organized and maintained salaried functionaries to administer its various activities and institutions, including religious and educational establishments, taxation and public charities. It was a highly cohesive society, welded together by a defensive bond of common interest as well as by an ideological sense of common purpose. There was a strong sense of social responsibility—the more prosperous members assisted the less fortunate through charitable foundations and individual beneficence. Although each community was autonomous, there was also inter-communal cooperation. Rabbis sought each other's advice and assistance (very occasionally they came together in regional synods), law courts exchanged information about cases transcending local jurisdiction and charities cared for unfortunate travelers and ransomed captives.

The constraints imposed upon the Jews led to considerable economic and occupational specialization. Restrictions on slave owning had very nearly pushed them out of agriculture and industry, and they were soon debarred from owning land. A prohibition on joining guilds excluded them from a wide range of crafts, and they were generally disqualified, explicitly or implicitly, from participating in the army, the government and the "liberal professions" (with the exception of medicine). In medieval Europe they were increasingly driven into moneylending and into a small range of commercial activities. This specialization emphasized the separation of Jews and non-Jews and also contributed to their unpopularity with the populace at large, particularly with commercial rivals and debtors. They tended to be concentrated in specific quarters of cities. In eastern Europe, where cities were few, they were dispersed in small towns and villages, but even here economic and social constraints made them a class apart.

The basic unit of Jewish life was the family; perhaps this was the real strength of the system. Families were large and strong and loyal. In a society

Aspects of everyday Jewish life in the middle ages.
Above From a Haggadah painted at Hamburg in 1740 by Joseph Leipnik, one of the outstanding Jewish painters of the period. Although purporting to illustrate the text, about Jewish laborers in ancient Egypt, the picture shows contemporary Jews against the background of a German city.
Right From an early 14th-century Spanish manuscript. The caldron is used to purify pots and pans.

in which the community tended to be valued above the individual and which never glorified celibacy and monasticism, it was the family which provided stability and continuity and formed the immediate social, economic and religious setting for the life of the individual Jew. Religion began at home and moments of the religious year were celebrated within the family, just as the crucial moments in the life of the individual and the family were marked by religious observances. Religion also supplied the strict code of sexual conduct whose aim was the preservation and sanctification of the family. Childlessness and bereavement were family misfortunes, which the family attempted to repair or mitigate. Marriages were arranged, often within the wider family or between families already linked by marriage bonds. Such a bond joined all the members of both families in a special relationship. The fame of a relative or ancestor was a source of pride to all the family, while a disgrace in the family brought shame on all its members. The old were respected and cared for, the young were cherished as representing the continuity of the family into the future. Education and instruction in a trade were, at least in theory, family responsibilities.

The system favored men above women. Power and authority were male monopolies, and while sons were educated from an early age daughters were hardly educated at all. They were excluded from the active religious life of the synagogue: if they attended they were hidden in a gallery or behind a screen. Rules of modesty and ritual purity were applied strictly to women, rather than to men, whereas religious observances were mostly a male preserve. Women had a legal status similar to that of slaves or minors (except that it was permanent). They could not give evidence in a law court. They were barred from public life, and from most gainful occupations. (The often-quoted exceptions only prove the general rule.) It was only within the home that women enjoyed a certain freedom and respect, and even here there was a clear separation of functions, the more honorable part being reserved to males.

The medieval community was a closed society. Few entered it except by birth or left it except by death, and the destiny of the individual was largely governed by factors beyond his or her control. Individualism and dissent were not encouraged, and members were expected to subordinate their personal desires to the welfare of the group. In many ways Jewish life reflected the ethos of the non-Jewish world, which was directly responsible for many of its features.

Modern Jewish life

The homogeneity of medieval Jewish life in Europe began to disintegrate slowly in the 17th and 18th centuries when wealthy merchants and bankers mixed with gentile society and began to adapt their way of life to that of their non-Jewish acquaintances. But popular religious movements such as Sabbataeanism and Hasidism represented a more insidious and certainly more widespread challenge to traditional values. The European Enlightenment, which called into question the accepted relationship between State and Church and eventually led to the political emancipation of the Jews, also had a profound effect on Jewish life-styles as social

integration gradually became more acceptable both to non-Jews and to Jews themselves.

Since for most of the 19th century the mass of Jewish population was concentrated in the countries which provided least scope for radical change, the transformation in Jewish life was slow. By the 1880s, however, when massive westward migration from Russia and the Near East began, there was a very marked contrast between Jewish life in eastern and western countries. Newcomers arriving from traditional eastern communities were scandalized by the sight of assimilated western Jews, indistinguishable from gentiles in their dress, speech and habits, and apparently moving with total freedom and assurance among non-Jews. By 1880 native-born Jews in western Europe and North America were almost entirely non-Orthodox in their religion and had relaxed or abandoned such observances as Sabbath rest, dietary restrictions, daily prayers and ritual baths. In the east, by contrast, observance was strong among religious Jews and religious reforms were virtually unknown. Even Hasidism, which had begun in an upsurge of reforming zeal, had conformed to the patterns of traditional religion. With large-scale immigration older patterns of Jewish life were temporarily restored in western countries, and in due course the process of acculturation was repeated, with the addition of still more varieties of compromise and reaction. Successive waves of migration, notably from central Europe during the Nazi era and from Arab lands since 1948, have added further complexities to the picture.

With the removal of restrictions on residence in the various countries Jews have tended to conform to prevailing patterns of settlement. There is a certain tendency for unofficial Jewish quarters to

CONGREGATION BETH SIMCHAT TORAH
NEW YORK'S GAY SYNOGOGUE

Aspects of Jewish life today.
Left Jews participating in a Gay Pride parade in New York.
Center left A wholesale poultry butcher in London.
Below left An informal wedding in Los Angeles.
Right Bargaining for fish in New York's Lower East Side.
Below Togetherness at a Sabbath retreat for members of a New York *havurah*.

continue, and as people have moved to the suburbs of big cities new areas of relatively dense Jewish population have sprung up with their own shops and religious facilities. In most countries one or more large cities account for the majority of the Jewish population, even if smaller communities and even isolated families are dispersed over a wide area. In Israel the pattern is exceptional: with mass immigration Jews have been settled all over the country in towns and villages, many of them new, most of them exclusively Jewish.

The economic specialization of the ghetto has given way to great diversity. Although in some places, by force of tradition or local circumstances, Jews remain prominent in banking, commerce and manufacture, they are found today in every kind of occupation. Surveys in Britain, North America and elsewhere have produced clear evidence of upward economic mobility, away from manual occupations towards "white collar" work and the professions. This tendency is more prominent with successive native-born generations. No longer forbidden to bear arms, Jews serve in armies both as conscripts and as professional soldiers. There has also been a return to agriculture, at first in experimental colonies in 19th-century Russia, later in South America and Palestine. A large part of the Israeli Jewish population is involved in agriculture, either

in collective or cooperative settlements or in more traditional farming communities. The legal profession, academic life, medicine and scientific research have all proved attractive to Jews, and they are represented in a wide spectrum of political parties in different countries, although few have reached the highest offices of state (Israel, of course, proving again to be the exception). All these remarks, naturally, apply to countries where integration is well established. There are still some countries, notably in the Arab world, where opportunities for Jews are severely restricted, and some from which Jews are totally excluded.

Specifically Jewish culture, which was such a strong feature of medieval Jewry, has become very much attenuated through integration, although there have been isolated attempts to keep Yiddish language and literature alive. Culture is the area where change has been most complete. In most countries there is no appreciable difference in general culture between young Jews and non-Jews—this is particularly true where they attend the same schools and absorb the same values and outlooks. Jews also make their contribution to the cultural life of the countries in which they live, and in general they do so without any specific Jewish emphasis, even if some writers and artists concentrate on Jewish themes.

In the sphere of religious life acculturation has taken many forms, and it is hard to make meaningful generalizations. Synagogue membership, for example, varies greatly from country to country, and so does the role of the synagogue in the life of the individual Jew. In the United States a large proportion of all Jews belong to a synagogue, but relatively few attend services frequently or regularly. Many members, in fact, attend rarely or never. Synagogue membership should not therefore be seen in itself as a religious gesture; it is as likely to answer to a social need. In Israel, at the other extreme, the role of the synagogue is exclusively religious, although many religious Jews do not formally belong to a synagogue. Attendance also varies greatly, from Russia, where few functioning synagogues remain, and Argentina, where there are many synagogues but few Jews go to them, to Israel, where 5 percent of respondents to a survey in 1969 said they attend every day and a further 13 percent every Sabbath. In that survey 27 percent said they never attend a synagogue; the corresponding figure in the United States ranges from 10 percent or so in small communities to as much as 30 percent in large cities. Most of the main national communities show a similar pattern for religious observance in general as for synagogue attendance: a small minority maintains a high level of observance and a similar minority observes little or nothing but the majority keep up some religious observance, even if they do not regard themselves as being particularly "religious." The most popular ceremonies are circumcision, *bar mitzvah* and the Passover meal (*seder*), and the only times when synagogues are regularly crowded are the high holy days (New Year and Day of Atonement). Many Jews mark the Sabbath in some way (often by lighting candles at the Friday evening meal) and observe some dietary restrictions, but very few observe the Sabbath and dietary regulations in their full traditional rigor. The level of observance is naturally higher in more traditional communities, but studies have revealed surprisingly similar ranges of practice between nominally Orthodox, Reform and secular Jews. The details of this complex picture are to be explained only in part by specifically Jewish considerations; Jewish attitudes usually conform to local conditions and are the result of assimilation to prevailing modes of behavior.

The traditional strength of the Jewish family has been steeply eroded in recent years, largely owing to the process of assimilation which smooths away whatever is most distinctively Jewish. In general there is now no observable difference between Jewish and non-Jewish families beyond a sentimental hankering after the old ways and a pressure on young people to better themselves, to marry and specifically to marry Jews. In most countries the state has taken over the educational and charitable roles previously filled by the family and the community and a cultural gap between immigrants and the first native-born generation has tended to undermine the traditional continuity of culture. Geographical and social mobility have also weakened family bonds. Intermarriage between Jews and non-Jews is widespread wherever social integration is advanced. In many western countries a third or more of Jews marry non-Jews; in some places the figure is much higher. The Jewish leadership, whether religious or secular, has taken little cognizance of this tendency—beyond deploring it—although some rabbis, particularly at the more liberal end of the religious spectrum, encourage and facilitate the conversion of the non-Jewish partner. The children of mixed marriages are often, although by no means always, lost to the Jewish community. The weakening of the family structure and the increased independence of young people have not been matched by an adaptation of the synagogue institutions to cater for the needs of single Jews, but some effort has been put into chaplaincy work among students, and the Zionist youth movements have provided an attractive alternative to the religious community. In North America, however, there has been a steady growth of less conventional religious fellowships, reflecting the distinctive ethos of American youth. A few gay synagogues have also been established, indicating a sense of alienation among some homosexual Jews from what is perceived as the excessively family-based character of the typical Jewish congregation. A similar feeling of despair at the male dominance of Orthodox and traditional synagogue life has led to the formation of some women's groups, but in most congregations women try to improve their status by working within the established framework. In any case the non-Orthodox denominations have already done a great deal to remedy the inequality and segregation of women in traditional Judaism. In the Reform movement the sexes enjoy a theoretical equality, and in Conservative synagogues too the disabilities suffered by women are gradually being removed. A similar situation prevails in Britain, where in the Liberal and Reform movements prejudice against women is gradually being eroded, but here, unlike North America, the non-Orthodox groups are small and there are still very few women serving as rabbis or holding communal office. In other countries the position of women in Judaism continues to be very subordinate, and even the secular organizations tend to be dominated by men.

In the years ahead, if present trends continue, the tendency to social integration and acculturation will become more marked among recent immigrants in the west and in countries where Jews have only recently or not yet acquired full civic equality. No one country's experience can be taken as a model for another, since experience has shown that local conditions tend to determine the course of developments in the Jewish community. In countries where religion in general is declining, for example, Jewish religion is unlikely to survive unimpaired. But American Jewry is likely to have an increasing influence in the Jewish world simply because of its size and vitality and because of the important place of the USA in the world; certain features of American Jewish life may well be reproduced elsewhere. Israel, too, is likely to wield an influence, particularly in bolstering the Jewish identity of the younger generation, but so far Israel has not produced any notable new developments which are applicable in the diaspora, and conditions in Israel are so unusual that it is hard to envisage the Israeli experience being of direct relevance to Jewish communities abroad. Indeed it is more likely that some problematical features of Jewish life in Israel will be resolved along lines already familiar in the larger diaspora communities.

JEWISH RELIGION

Day of Atonement, by Jacob Kramer. On the Day of Atonement the Jew stands naked and defenseless before God. All his wrongdoings testify against him, and his sole recourse is to throw himself, with prayers and sincere repentance, on the mercy of God. On this day alone Jews kneel and prostrate themselves in synagogue, and the liturgy recalls the atonement ritual in the ancient temple, when the high priest, on this one most sacred day of the year, would enter the Holy of Holies, the most sacred spot on earth, and pronounce the most sacred name of God. So sacred was this name that the secret of its pronunciation was lost after the fall of the temple. Something of the awesome character of this day has survived right up to the present.

Judaism is a member of the monotheistic family of religions, of which the largest representatives are Christianity and Islam. All three religions share certain common features beyond the worship of one God. In the first place they all look back to a common origin, rooted in the Middle East and dominated by God's self-revelation to Abraham and Moses, even though these founders are overshadowed for Christians by Jesus and for Muslims by Muhammad. Theologically, God is conceived in similar terms in all three traditions: he is the creator and ruler of the world, loving mankind and intervening directly in human affairs; he is infinite and absolute, all-knowing and all-powerful, incorporeal and unchanging. All three religions have a strongly rooted opposition to selfish materialism, idolatry and polytheism. All three represent a blend of Semitic and Greek elements, and of speculative and practical teachings ranging from the metaphysical to the legal and political. All three believe in the power of words and of knowledge and have rich scholarly traditions. They also all have similar traditions of worship involving readings, prayers and songs, with some sects worshiping through ecstatic trances and bodily movements. And all three have notable mystical traditions, which have influenced the main streams while standing somewhat outside them.

On the other hand, despite a great deal of mutual influence down the ages, all three religions have their distinctive traits. Judaism stands in between Christianity and Islam, and shares some features with both. Like Islam, Judaism has traditionally been more concerned with this-worldly preoccupations, with social justice and morality, than with metaphysics and abstract speculation. Creeds and dogmas have been less important than rules and precepts. Judaism and Islam lack, of course, the specifically Christian doctrines such as the incarnation, and are more suspicious of anything suggesting polytheism or idolatry. At the same time they are both rather less "monopolistic" than Christianity and tolerate diverse responses to God, so long as certain basic principles are respected. Judaism and Christianity share their sacred scriptures (although the Christian Bible is somewhat longer than the Jewish one), and this common heritage brings these two religions close at many

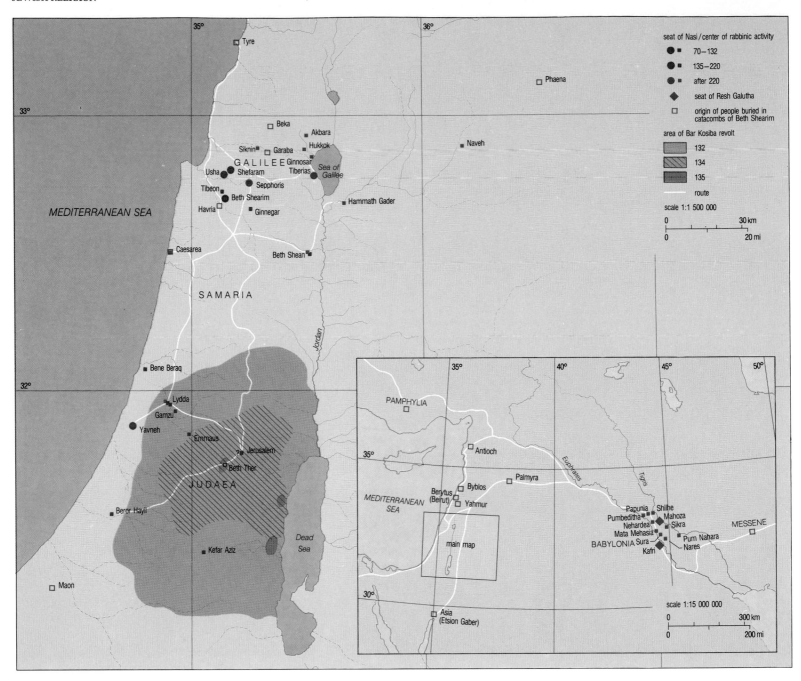

Above: The origins of
Rabbinism
The earliest activities of the
rabbis are associated with the
center at Yavneh, established
during the first Roman war
(66–74 CE). The collapse of the
bar Kosiba revolt (135 CE) drove
the rabbis north into Galilee,
where they consolidated their
influence over the Jewish
population. The excavations at
the necropolis of Beth Shearim
have illustrated how widespread
were the ramifications of this
influence. Meanwhile rabbinic
schools had been established in
the strong Jewish settlements of
Babylonia, and it was here that
Rabbinism continued to flourish
after the eclipse of the Palestinian
center under Christian rule. The
Babylonian Talmud, a
compilation of the discussions
and decisions of both western
and eastern centers over a period
of several centuries, remained
the authoritative guidebook of
Jewish life and thought until the
threshold of modern times.

points in vocabulary and symbolism. They have
also both been dominated, at least in recent centuries, by their western traditions, and the interac-
tion of Judaism and Christianity in Europe has led to
many similarities in forms of worship, religious
philosophy, biblical scholarship and general ethos.

Among the features of Judaism not shared with
the other religions are the retention of Hebrew as a
language of biblical reading and worship, a distinctive religious calendar and a variety of practices and
observances. Prominent among these are infant
circumcision and dietary restrictions. Whereas
Muslims are enjoined to refrain from pork and wine,
the Jewish restrictions extend to a wide range of
animals and also to the way foods are prepared. The
calendar represents a complicated compromise between the lunar and the solar years. The Sabbath is
observed on Saturday, by abstention from work
and by pleasurable pursuits, and there are various
festivals, each with its own characteristic observances. All these customs and regulations are
grounded in the Bible, but many details have been
elaborated over the centuries. They are discussed in

the Talmud and in rabbinic *responsa* and codified in
various handbooks and compendia. Although
similar discussions and codes are certainly found in
the Christian and Muslim traditions, Judaism is
probably unique in the attention paid to these
minutiae of religious observance.

The historical varieties of Judaism

The most long-lived and influential of the different
varieties of Judaism was what may be called (for
want of a better term) Rabbinism. Its two distinctive
characteristics are the institution of the rabbi,
conceived of as a blend of scholar, judge and
religious leader, and adherence to the scholarly
tradition grounded in the Talmud, a corpus of
esoteric literature produced in Palestine and
Babylonia in the formative period of the movement
(corresponding roughly to the first five Christian
centuries). The origins of Rabbinism are obscure: its
roots are diverse, and include priestly, scribal and
pietistic elements, but it represented a new departure in ancient Israel and became extraordinarily
influential over a wide area after the destruction of

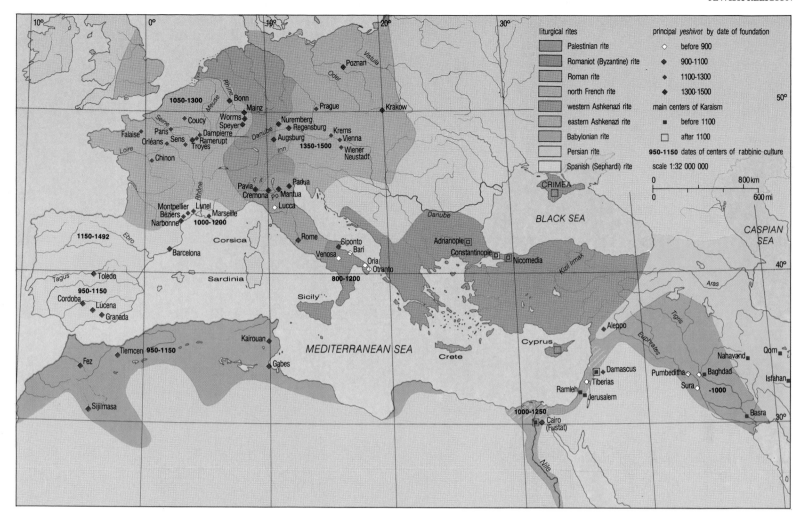

Above: The spread of Rabbinism, c. 650–1500
Rabbinic Judaism spread westwards from Palestine to Italy and eventually to northern Europe, and from Babylonia to North Africa and Spain. The lines of influence can be discerned in the different liturgical rites, some of which have continued in use to the present day. Rabbinic culture was disseminated through the *yeshivot* (talmudic schools); the leading *yeshivot* attracted students from far afield. The main challenge to Rabbinism came from Karaism, a movement which began in Persia and Iraq and soon established strong bases in the eastern Mediterranean and even for a time in Spain.

Map legend:

liturgical rites
- Palestinian rite
- Romaniot (Byzantine) rite
- Roman rite
- north French rite
- western Ashkenazi rite
- eastern Ashkenazi rite
- Babylonian rite
- Persian rite
- Spanish (Sephardi) rite

principal *yeshivot* by date of foundation
- ◇ before 900
- ◆ 900-1100
- ◆ 1100-1300
- ◆ 1300-1500

main centers of Karaism
- ■ before 1100
- ▫ after 1100

950-1150 dates of centers of rabbinic culture

scale 1:32 000 000

the second temple (70 CE), partly through the acquisition of political privileges by the rabbis and partly through their missionary activities among the Jewish communities. So strong was its influence that even rival or alternative trends such as Karaism and Kabbalism could not free themselves fully from it.

Karaism, which first arose in 8th-century Iraq and Persia in opposition to talmudic Rabbinism, maintained the institutions of the rabbi and the synagogue and in fact remained very similar to Rabbinism, the only external differences being in the calendar and in some religious laws and customs. Kabbalism, a form of gnosticism mingled with asceticism and sometimes with magic, remained institutionally within Rabbinism. One of its most prominent luminaries in the 16th century, Joseph Caro, was also the author of two of the most authoritative compendia of rabbinic law. Later movements, such as Hasidism and Reform, even while rejecting many of its beliefs and practices, have always clung to the main institutions of Rabbinism, although the nature of these institutions may have been transformed.

Rabbinism was based on tradition and consensus. Rabbis enjoyed local autonomy and theoretical equality, although outstanding scholars or saints acquired a certain additional authority. The Talmud was revered as the repository of all wisdom, and it was mastery of talmudic learning that was the essential distinction of the rabbi. More attention was paid to practical wisdom than to speculative science, although there have been some distinguished rabbinite philosophers. Disputes were

settled by reference to the Talmud, or by arguments based on talmudic reasoning. The Bible, especially the first five books (the Torah), was revered as holy truth and was prominent in public worship and preaching, but it was interpreted by the rabbis in the light of talmudic canons of exegesis. It was the Talmud rather than the Bible that came to be studied in the rabbinic academies.

Over a long history the rabbis gave mainstream Judaism its direction and definition as much by what they rejected as by what they accepted. Early in the movement came the rift with Christianity. The details are undocumented: it seems likely that the impulse to separation came from the Christian side rather than the Jewish. At any rate the Talmud hardly mentions Christianity, and there is little or no Jewish polemical literature against Christianity to compare to the large body of anti-Jewish writing in the Church. More evident in the early period is the campaign against dualism and gnosticism (a similar campaign is attested in early Christianity). In the 10th century there is a polemic against Karaism. In the 13th century there is some argument about the admissibility of Aristotelian philosophy, but this was an internal rabbinic dispute arising out of the work of the outstanding 12th-century Aristotelian rabbi Moses Maimonides. Kabbalism, on the other hand, was never condemned outright, although every effort was made to confine it to a small circle and to prevent it from reaching the public at large. That this was a prudent policy is shown by the wide popularity of the two movements led by Shabbetai Zvi (1626–76) and the Baal Shem Tov (1700–60). The first was apocalyptic in character, the second (Hasidism) pietistic, but both were steeped in Kabbala and both were, in their different ways, diametrically opposed to Rabbinism. Shabbetai Zvi proclaimed himself the messiah and declared the rule of the Torah to be at an end. The Hasidim condemned what they saw as the arid scholasticism of the rabbinic schools and academies and viewed talmudic study as a barrier between man and God. They sought a union with God through fasting, dancing and ecstatic prayer, the joys of nature and human fellowship. The rabbis waged a fierce campaign against the Hasidim, especially in Lithuania where the civil power was invoked against them and where in 1772 a rabbinic synod formally banned them. Despite these attacks, Hasidim won many adherents among the poor, ignorant and downtrodden masses in Poland. But so great was the power of Rabbinism that in time Hasidism became assimilated to it. The Hasidic *zaddik* became less like a village saint and more like a rabbinic sage; Hasidim and Misnagdim (opponents) became reconciled, and Hasidic scholars started writing commentaries on rabbinic law codes.

New ideas and their effects on Rabbinism
It was a development outside Judaism that ended the dominance of Rabbinism in Europe: the Enlightenment, with its anticlericalism and rationalism, and its pressure for Jewish emancipation and secular education. Rabbinism was essentially a medieval phenomenon and relied for its strength on medieval institutions. The power of the rabbis was underpinned by their control of the Jewish communities, by the segregation of those communities and by the support of the government. Faced with dissent they could rely on the civil powers and on the ban (*herem*), as the Lithuanian rabbis did against the Hasidim. In the 18th century bans were hurled around with wild abandon in western Europe, and had less and less effect. A Jew under ban no longer became an outcast from society (the case of Spinoza had in the 17th century long ago shown that), and the traditional independence of the rabbinate for once worked against the system. New ideas entered the Jewish community, often through the rabbis, who could use their position of authority to promote them. Napoleon found a number of enlightened rabbis to join his Sanhedrin, and Reform Judaism spread through the German rabbinate. In 19th-century eastern Europe, however, the main attack on Rabbinism came from secularist "enlighteners" (*maskilim*), like J.L. Gordon (1830–92), a Hebrew

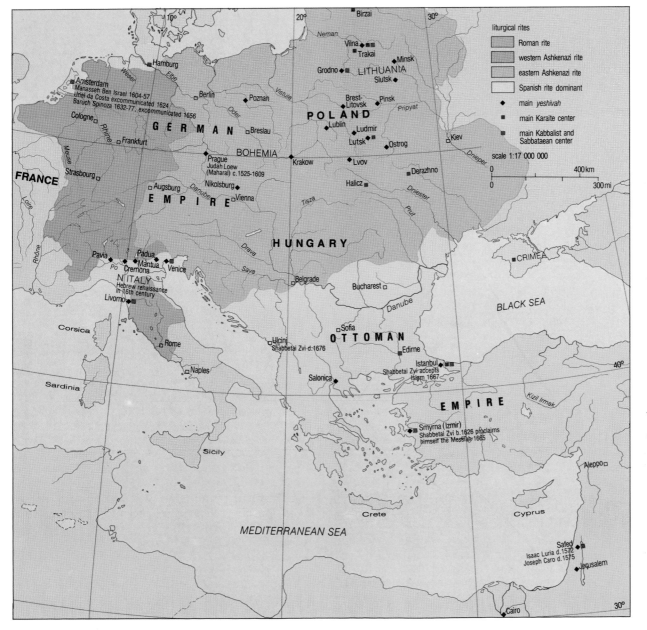

Left: Religious upheavals in the 16th and 17th centuries
The dramatic developments of this period were due largely to political factors. The expulsion from Spain in 1492 led to the implantation of Sephardi Judaism all over the eastern Mediterranean region and the eclipse of the various native traditions, while the consolidation of Ashkenazi Judaism in north Italy, Bohemia, Poland and Lithuania is visible in the establishment of important *yeshivot* in these places. Meanwhile the dominant centers of Karaism shifted north to the Crimea and Lithuania. Changing patterns of contacts between the various groups favored the emergence of new ideas; so did the encounter with Christian scholarship in Renaissance Italy, and in the Sephardi centers of northern Europe, where many New Christians reverted to Judaism. Political upheavals also led to a resurgence of mysticism, notably in the Kabbalistic center at Safed, and messianic fervor, which reached its height in the movement led by Shabbetai Zvi.

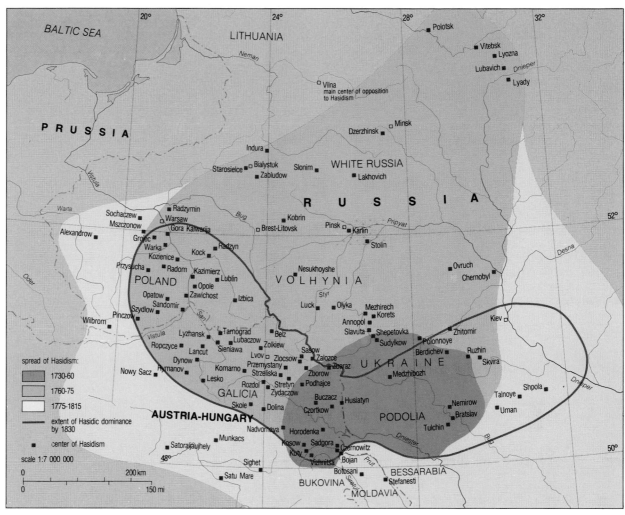

Right: The rise of Hasidism
Hasidism, a movement combining elements of *kabbalah*, messianism and popular piety, arose at a time of political upheaval and profound religious questioning. The founder, Israel ben Eliezer, the Baal Shem Tov (fl. 1730–60), taught mainly at Medzhibozh, but his influence spread further afield, and the generation after his death witnessed an impressive expansion, reaching far to the north and even establishing a foothold in Vilna, the main center of opposition led by the famous Talmudist Elijah ben Solomon. By 1830 the period of thrusting expansion was over; Hasidism was by now established as the dominant mode of Judaism over a wide area, stretching from Warsaw to Kiev, and had a considerable following throughout most of central Europe.

Shabbetai Zvi, the messiah from Smyrna, attracted an enormous following all over Europe. Eventually, confronted with the choice between Islam and death, he preferred life. Many of his adherents followed him into Islam, where they formed the sect of the Dönmeh.

poet who wrote a number of trenchant stories exposing the arrogance and corruption of the rabbis and the injustices caused by rabbinic law.

The new ideas showed themselves at first in liturgical rather than in theological or legal reforms. In the early 19th century the issues which provoked debate included prayer in the vernacular, the introduction of sermons and music, the shortening of the service and the decorum of worshipers. It was only later that a theoretical basis for reform was sought with the help of theologians and historians. Theological discourse had become alien to the rabbis since the decline of Aristotelian philosophy in the 14th century. Now it was revived, and the debate centered on the nature of revelation and on the authority of tradition. It was not dissimilar to contemporary debates in western Christianity, and it resulted in a diversity of points of view. Very few in the west maintained the traditionalist viewpoint that all change was to be deplored, and that even

emancipation was of questionable worth if it led to the disintegration of traditional Jewish observance. The old ways were unappealing to a generation who were, or wished to be, modern Europeans.

The new ways found expression in a wide spectrum of formulations, from the extreme theological conservatism of Samson Raphael Hirsch (1808–88) to the extreme liberalism of Samuel Holdheim (1806–60) and Abraham Geiger (1810–74). Characteristically these three German rabbis had all enjoyed both a talmudic and a secular university education, and Hirsch devoted much of his anti-traditionalist polemics to justifying the combination of the two traditions.

Holdheim formulated the influential view that changing times demand changes in the law, even if the law is agreed to be of divine origin. He went further, however, than most of his colleagues could follow him when he transferred the Sabbath services in his Berlin temple to Sunday, abolished several festivals and officiated at marriages between Jews and gentiles. Holdheim relied on the distinction between the religious and the national elements in Judaism: the latter (echoing Spinoza) he declared to be obsolete since the loss of the temple in Jerusalem. In practice he was willing to abandon many purely religious observances: what were important were the beliefs and ethics of Judaism.

Geiger's religious philosophy was similar in many ways. He stressed the belief in progress: the Bible and Talmud represent an early, primitive stage in a revelation which is still continuing. Many traditional ceremonies (such as circumcision) are distressing to modern sensibility or incompatible with

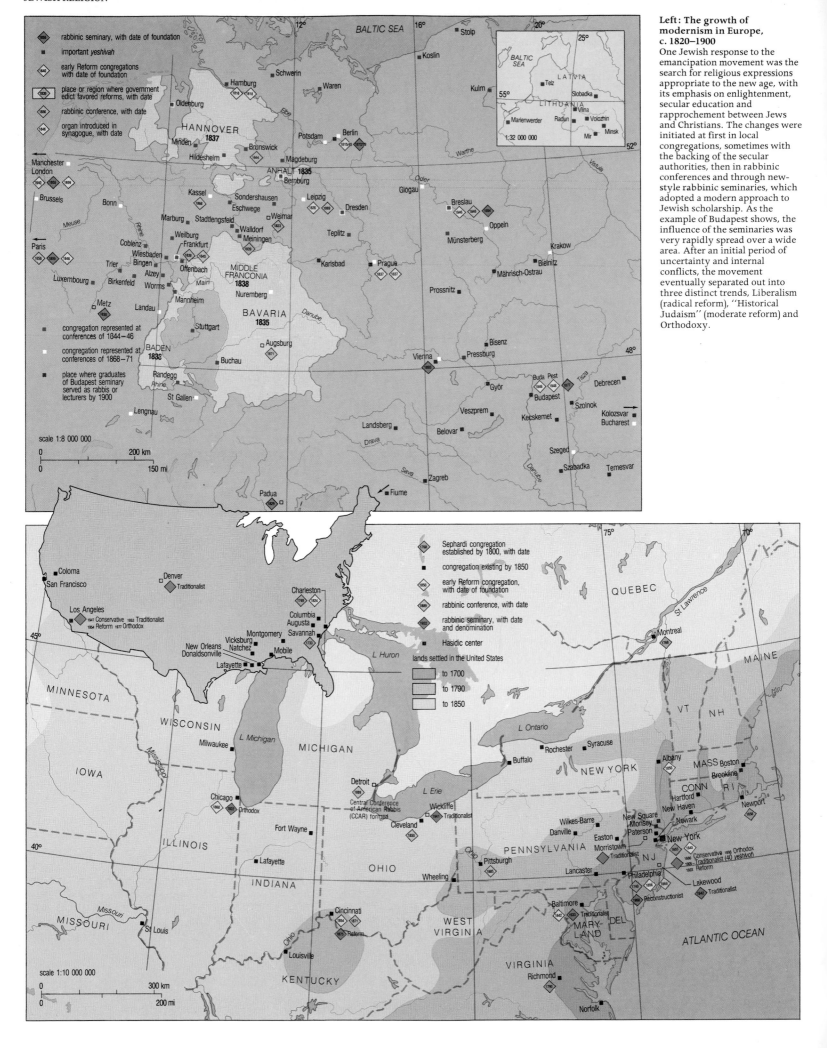

Left: The growth of modernism in Europe, c. 1820–1900
One Jewish response to the emancipation movement was the search for religious expressions appropriate to the new age, with its emphasis on enlightenment, secular education and rapprochement between Jews and Christians. The changes were initiated at first in local congregations, sometimes with the backing of the secular authorities, then in rabbinic conferences and through new-style rabbinic seminaries, which adopted a modern approach to Jewish scholarship. As the example of Budapest shows, the influence of the seminaries was very rapidly spread over a wide area. After an initial period of uncertainty and internal conflicts, the movement eventually separated out into three distinct trends, Liberalism (radical reform), "Historical Judaism" (moderate reform) and Orthodoxy.

Right Sacred nostalgia: praying at the Western Wall in Jerusalem.

Left: Judaism in America
The reforms initiated in Europe found fertile ground for growth in America, where the restraints which hampered innovation in Europe were absent. By 1880 Reform was the dominant mode. The subsequent immigration introduced traditionalist forms of religion, and also led to the emergence of Conservative Judaism, a distinctively American compromise with roots in the "Historical Judaism" school in Europe. Reconstructionism is another uniquely American development. Religious Jewish culture now flourishes in America as nowhere else in the world, with no one trend exercising a dominant force, but with a great deal of fruitful cooperation and cross-fertilization.

modern life. In any case, the law of God is essentially ethical, not ritual. Moreover, historical study shows that the rituals themselves have changed and developed and there is evidence of this change in the Bible and Talmud themselves. Geiger became increasingly aware of the need to "dethrone the Talmud." He supported the critical study of the Bible and wished to extend the critical methods to the talmudic literature.

Hirsch's approach was completely different: he would not allow any attempt to displace the Talmud from its traditional role. He frowned on biblical criticism and he deplored the overuse of the slogan "progress." It was the Jews, not Judaism, who were in need of reform, he argued. He hoped through education to breed a better understanding of Judaism, which would make radical reforms unnecessary.

The disagreements between Hirsch and Geiger (who had been friends and fellow students at Bonn University in 1829) and between their respective followers found expression in polemics as bitter as those between modernists and traditionalists. From the literature it is clear that underlying the debate about observance and ceremonies is a genuine theological difference and, for once, an issue of belief. For Hirsch the belief in the inspiration, integrity and authority of the Bible, the Talmud and the whole corpus of rabbinic law becomes an article of faith. To budge from it even by an inch is to open the door to unrestrained reform. Maybe that is why he was particularly firm in his opposition to Zechariah Frankel (1801–75), a very conservative modernist who was himself an avowed enemy of what he called "negative reform leading to complete dissolution" and who can be seen as a founder of what is now called Conservative Judaism. But articles of faith are alien to the spirit of authentic Judaism—so at least the Reformers argued. They named the new-style traditionalism "Orthodoxy," to highlight its dogmatic character. The name stuck.

Jewish religious groupings in the 20th century
The controversies between modernist theologies in 19th-century central Europe became institutionalized in formal factions which still exist. The differences make themselves felt in liturgy, education and to some extent in theology and ritual observance, but they are hard to define precisely and there is considerable overlap at the edges. The factions are not distinct sects. Even if there is some reciprocal polemic, the members of one group would be accepted into another without any formality (with the proviso that because of differences in procedure some non-Orthodox proselytes would not be automatically accepted by Orthodox authorities). There are some local, national or international associations of congregations and of rabbis, but many congregations are independent and even those that are affiliated to one or more of the associations enjoy a large measure of autonomy.

In the United States there are three main groupings: Reform, Conservative and Orthodox. The Union of American Hebrew Congregations was founded in 1873 as a centrist body, but because of the dominance of Reform elements it soon became the national organization of Reform congregations. It now has some 700 member congregations, representing about a million souls. The Central Conference of American Rabbis (founded in 1889) is the assembly of Reform rabbis, and the rabbinical seminary of the movement is the Hebrew Union College–Jewish Institute of Religion, with four campuses, in Cincinnati (1875), New York (1922), Los Angeles (1954) and Jerusalem (1963). The corresponding institutions of the Conservative movement are the United Synagogue of America, founded with fewer than 30 congregations in 1913, now representing more than 850 congregations with well over a million members; the Rabbinical Assembly (1919); and the Jewish Theological Seminary in New York (1886), Los Angeles (1947) and Jerusalem (1962). The main Orthodox organizations are the Union of Orthodox Jewish Congregations (1898), numbering about 700 congregations with some 750 000 members, the Rabbinical Council of America (1923), and the two major rabbinical colleges, Yeshivah University in New York (1896) and the Hebrew Theological College in Chicago (1922). The six congregational and rabbinic bodies cooperate through the Synagogue Council of America. The reasons for a congregation or an individual choosing one movement rather than another are often fairly arbitrary. Traditional class-differences between the various groups are becoming less marked as are differences of ritual and practice; some synagogues opt for a blend of Orthodox, Conservative and Reform ritual in their services. A fourth, much smaller and newer movement is Reconstructionism, which rejects supernaturalist theology and sees Judaism as a civilization grounded in the life of the Jewish people, while traditionalism is also very much alive and maintains a number of *yeshivot*.

Whereas in North America the three main groupings are roughly equal in size and structure, elsewhere the situation is entirely different. The modernist movements are a western phenomenon which have hardly touched the large communities of eastern Europe and the Muslim countries, where the experience has rather been one of polarization between traditionalism and secularism. Even in countries like Britain and France, where modernism is long established, successive waves of immigration have maintained the numerical dominance of traditional Judaism, even if the intelligentsia and the communal leadership tend to belong to the modernist streams. Radical modernism, under various names (Liberal, Reform, Progressive), holds its own as a minority trend in western Europe as well as in South Africa, Australia and other places of western immigration, and it has recently been introduced, against strong opposition, in Israel. In all these places it has to endure uncompromising hostility from the traditionalist rabbinate. Modernist Orthodoxy, which occupies the middle ground, has been put into an uncomfortable position by this rift and has tended increasingly to side with the traditionalist camp. In fact modernism is currently in considerable disarray behind the facade of labels and organizations, and demands for reforms among Orthodox Jews are balanced by a hankering for tradition on the more radical wing.

Problems facing Jewish religion today

Judaism today faces many challenges, of which the strongest is the loss of faith due to the experience of the holocaust and to the alienation from traditional life caused by the recent migrations. These features, coupled with a growing secularism in society at large, have led many Jews to question the meaning and value of religion. Even among religious Jews there are doubts about the traditional conception of God and about the relevance of the old codes of practice. The last definitive formulation of the *halakhah*, the program for the ideal Jewish life, took place in the 16th century, in the wake of the expulsion from Spain. Many Jews feel that it needs to be revised in the light of the new age, while others feel that the whole concept of a life guided by minute regulations understood as divinely revealed is an anachronism. Uncertainty leads to extreme and irrational reactions. Fundamentalism, which never entirely died, has undergone a revival in recent years, and in Israel has become linked in some circles to extreme nationalism, as has also happened in neighboring Muslim countries. On the other hand the severe rationalism of 19th-century theology has given way to an existentialist approach, of which the pioneers were Martin Buber and Franz Rosenzweig. In this new theology the four main elements

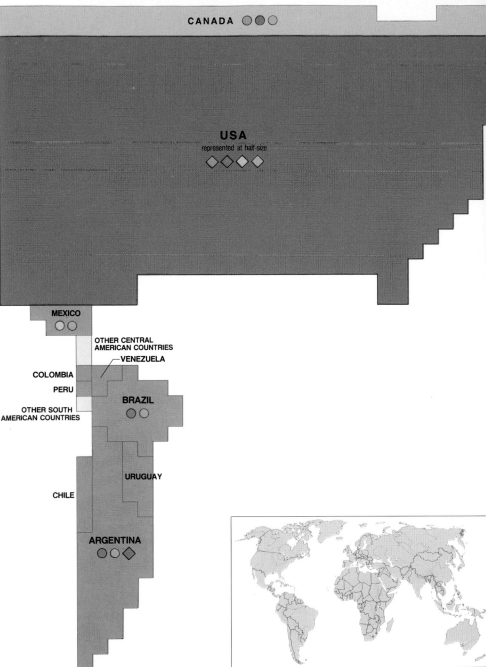

of classical Judaism—rationalism, scholasticism, mysticism and messianism—are fused together in a more balanced blend, and some persuasive solutions have been advanced to counter old problems.

Judaism today presents a fragmented appearance when compared to the homogeneity of talmudic Rabbinism. There may be a parallel with a still earlier period, that of the late second temple with its various competing sects. Many of the questions of that period have been revived, such as the relative merits of piety and scholarship, the legitimate scope for innovation, the relationship between religion and politics, and accommodation to external influences (including the use of the vernacular in worship). There are significant differences, however. The Jewish people is more widely dispersed, and lacks a single focus—a "direction"—for religious sentiment, such as was formerly provided by the temple in Jerusalem. Hopes that Jerusalem might once again become a "source of Torah" have not so far been fulfilled. America has come to exercise a considerable influence, at least in intellectual leadership, but is

Jewish religion today
This map is a cartogram, a geometric presentation which enables us to relate the distribution of the various religious trends to the size of the Jewish population in each country. It must be stressed that these trends are not distinct sects, and that the labels mean different things in different countries. "Traditionalism" here includes both the unselfconscious survival of old forms, and also their deliberate preservation in the "new ghetto," while "Conservatism" ranges from liberal Orthodoxy to conservative Reform. Despite this lack of refinement the overall picture is clear. Various forms of traditional religion still dominate a large part of the Jewish world, from the old (and much depleted) heartlands of eastern Europe and the old Ottoman empire to the largely immigrant communities of France, Spain and Latin America. Modernist Orthodoxy commands an important following in

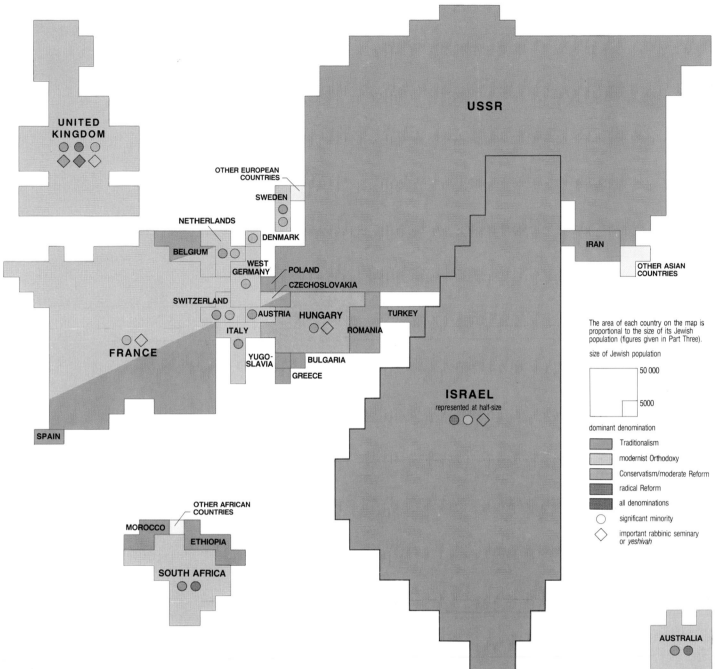

UNITED KINGDOM

OTHER EUROPEAN COUNTRIES

SWEDEN

NETHERLANDS

DENMARK

BELGIUM

WEST GERMANY

POLAND

CZECHOSLOVAKIA

SWITZERLAND

AUSTRIA

HUNGARY

TURKEY

ITALY

ROMANIA

FRANCE

YUGO-SLAVIA

BULGARIA

GREECE

SPAIN

USSR

IRAN

OTHER ASIAN COUNTRIES

ISRAEL

represented at half-size

The area of each country on the map is proportional to the size of its Jewish population (figures given in Part Three).

size of Jewish population

50 000

5000

dominant denomination

Traditionalism

modernist Orthodoxy

Conservatism/moderate Reform

radical Reform

all denominations

◯ significant minority

◇ important rabbinic seminary or *yeshivah*

OTHER AFRICAN COUNTRIES

MOROCCO

ETHIOPIA

SOUTH AFRICA

AUSTRALIA

western Europe and the former British empire, while Reform Jews constitute a substantial minority in English-speaking countries. By far the most important centers, in terms both of religious life and of *yeshivot* and seminaries, are the USA and Israel.

incapable of constituting a real religious focus. Meanwhile Jews in different countries are acquiring their own characteristic attitudes and customs. While the development of "national churches," along Christian lines, is unlikely, national differences are already as marked as they are, say, within the Roman Catholic Church, without the benefit of a central religious authority to ensure unity. That function is filled at present by a strong sense of ethnic identity, but mere sentiment is a frail and unpredictable force and further fragmentation cannot be ruled out.

Uncertainty also prevails over the whole question of the place of religion in Jewish society. It has now become clear for the first time that Jewish national feeling can be strong enough to endure without, or even in conflict with, religious faith. It is possible to envisage (at least in theory) the Jewish people abandoning religion altogether and continuing to exist as a nation. This scenario, however implausible, raises many disturbing questions, not least for the religious leadership. All the main religious organizations are attempting, tacitly or openly, to

woo Jews back to religion, although so far the dynamic campaigns of the Lubavitch Hasidim in America or the efforts of the *yeshivot* in Jerusalem to bring "penitents" back into the fold are isolated phenomena. Even rarer are campaigns to win gentile converts to Judaism, despite mounting realization that the Jewish population is on the decline. However the conversion of non-Jewish marriage partners is increasingly encouraged, particularly on the more radical wing of Judaism. Meanwhile a process of secularization is discernible within the religious institutions, as synagogues become social and cultural centers and rabbis are expected to act as social workers and organizational managers. In a sense Judaism has less to fear than Christianity from such secularization: the Jewish institutions were never as "spiritualized" as the corresponding Christian ones in the first place, and the very nature of Judaism is less exclusively "religious" than that of Christianity. But to the extent that Judaism has now become integrated in modern society and culture, it would be a mistake to suppose it to be immune to general trends.

The Synagogue

Architectural Variety

Variety is the keynote of synagogue architecture, with local influences more prominent than any distinctive tradition. There are no rules about the size or shape of synagogue buildings, although the orientation towards Jerusalem sometimes imposes constraints. Social factors often have their say: the need for discretion, moderation, even physical defense, or by contrast a wish to make an assertive public statement. Modern western synagogues are usually in the current architectural idiom, distinguished perhaps (not necessarily) by an orientalizing flavor in the design or by a Hebrew inscription. They can be very grandiose. Earlier synagogues were usually more discreet, sometimes tucked away in a courtyard or alley, but in largely or entirely Jewish areas there was scope for more ambitious designs. The synagogue building may serve as a community center, with meeting and study rooms attached, and sometimes baths, kitchens, a library, or even (nowadays) sports facilities.

Below The wooden synagogues of Poland are a rare example of a distinctive style of vernacular synagogue architecture. Several hundred of them were built in the 17th and 18th centuries, but they were very vulnerable to accidental or deliberate destruction, and scarcely any now remain. They often had a series of roofs, with a curious upward curve to the eaves, and richly painted interiors. They reflect the ready availability of timber and a strong native tradition of craftsmanship.

Left Medieval synagogues in Europe were usually modest in size and appearance, making use of current Romanesque or Gothic styles. The Old-New Synagogue (*Altneuschul*) in Prague, built in the late 13th or early 14th century, is uncharacteristically imposing, perhaps because it was built in the heart of a Jewish quarter. Its striking brick gables were added in the 15th century.

Below Helmut Goldschmidt's synagogue at Bonn (1959), replacing earlier synagogues destroyed in the *Kristallnacht* attacks in 1938, is one of a number he has built in postwar Germany. Its calm simplicity contrasts with the self-conscious pomp of an earlier age, and its small size is a silent reminder of the tragic destruction of German Jewry.

Right Dutch and Oriental influences mingle in the Paradesi synagogue of the ''White Jews'' in Cochin, south India. Dating originally from 1568, it was enlarged in 1761, when the clock tower was added.

Above The emergence of grand synagogue buildings in the cities of Europe and North America coincided with a period of somewhat aimless eclecticism in western architecture. In the second half of the 19th century there was a distinct preference for Moorish styles, conjuring up memories of the Jewish Golden Age in Spain, as against the (supposedly Christian) Gothic. One of the most dramatic Moorish revival synagogues is the new synagogue of Florence (1874–82); echoes of the Alhambra adorn a building whose plan is inspired by St Sofia in Constantinople.

Left Since World War II it is in the USA that most synagogue building has taken place. Modern trends in architecture have been harnessed to the needs of wealthy and imaginative congregations to produce some exciting new buildings, many of them in attractive situations away from urban centers. This spectacular synagogue was built in 1959 for the Beth Shalom congregation at Elkins Park, near Philadelphia, by the eminent non-Jewish architect Frank Lloyd Wright.

Above left Synagogue building in modern Israel tends to be nondescript. An exception is this eyecatching design for the Hebrew University Synagogue at the Givat Ram campus in west Jerusalem by Heinz Rau.

Interior Arrangement

The activity which dominates the synagogue service, and which determines the interior arrangement of the prayer hall, is the reading of the Torah. The scrolls are kept in the ark, situated in the wall facing Jerusalem, and they are read from a flat-topped desk. In traditional synagogues the reader faces the ark, and the desk is placed in the middle of the hall or at the far end, creating a "bipolar" focus; this raises problems for the orientation of the seating and the location of the preacher and of the precentor who leads the congregation in prayer. In many modern synagogues the desk is placed immediately in front of the ark, so that the reader, prayer leader and preacher all operate from the same area and all face the congregation. Apart from the ark and reading desk there are no essential furnishings, but the grander synagogues tend to be lavishly adorned with architectural features, carvings and other decorations, often incorporating Hebrew inscriptions and symbolic motifs.

Below The ark dominates the synagogue interior. It is approached by steps, and is usually elaborately wrought, with carvings and Hebrew texts. Its Hebrew name (*aron ha-kodesh* or *heikhal*), together with those of its lamp (*ner tamid*) and curtain (*parokhet*), conveys reminiscences of the ancient sanctuary, and the ark is treated with the solemnity and reverence due to the Torah which it houses.

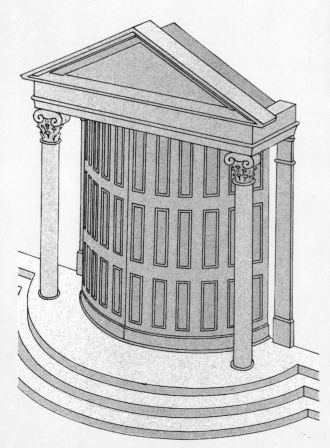

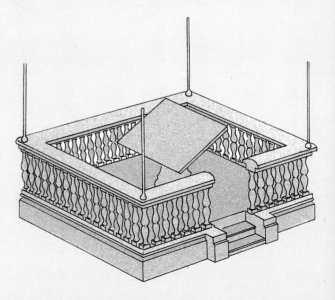

Right The reading desk stands in a raised enclosure, called by Sephardim *tebah* ("chest," an old Hebrew name of the ark), by Ashkenazim *almemar* or *bimah* (from Arabic and Greek words meaning "platform"). In some synagogues the prayers are read from the desk, but its main function is to accommodate the scrolls of the Torah, which are large and unwieldy when opened for reading. In the traditional synagogue sermons were rarely given, and were delivered from the *almemar* or from before the ark. The Reformers placed greater emphasis on the sermon, and many synagogues now have a pulpit near the ark, often incorporated in a single architectural unit including the reading desk. This arrangement, which is found in many western Orthodox, as well as Reform, synagogues, doubtless reflects Christian practice.

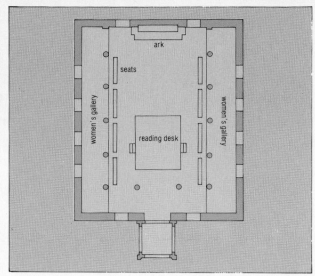

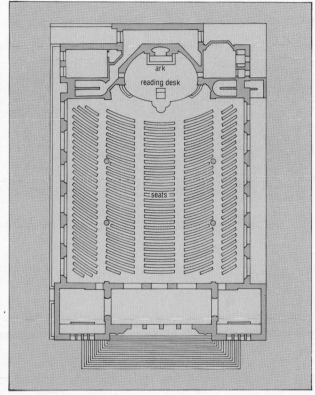

Right It is not known when women were first segregated from men in the synagogue, but some medieval synagogues have separate accommodation for women, either in a hall of their own (*Frauenschul*) or in a gallery. Sometimes they were hidden behind a grille or curtain, and a ''learned woman'' might lead them in prayer in the vernacular. The separation of the sexes has been continued in Orthodox synagogues, but in the other modern movements the sexes have been reunited.

Above left A traditional synagogue (Nefusot Yehuda in Gibraltar). The reader standing at the desk faces the ark, which is flanked in this case by seats for the communal officials. The desk is conventionally covered with a cloth, and many older synagogues preserve the candles and oil lamps which sometimes have a ceremonial as well as a practical function. The ark is here opened to show the scrolls with their mantles and silver ornaments; normally it is kept closed.

Above These two plans demonstrate the effect of moving the reading desk to the vicinity of the ark. In the traditional synagogue (*top*) much of the central space is taken up by the *tebah*, and the seating is mainly along the sides facing inwards. The columns support the women's gallery. In the large Reform temple (*above*) all the action takes place at the front, and the rest of the hall is freed for seating. The effect is theatrical, and the congregation is more clearly separated from the officiants.

Folk Religion

Right Purim masquerades remain one of the most popular manifestations of folk Judaism. They are an expression of sheer fun, with no overtly religious purpose, yet they are inseparably associated with the festival, and the characters of the *Purim* story are favorite models.

Side by Side with "official" Judaism, which lays down statutory obligations derived from the Torah and the rabbinic codes, there exists a rich variety of religious observances based on popular custom. Many of these customs are local traditions, but some are very widely observed, and they tend to exercise a powerful appeal. For many Jews they are the living soul of the religion, while the official regulations and theological doctrines are merely dry bones.

Purim provides a striking example of a widespread and popular custom. *Purim* is officially observed by reading the scroll of Esther and making donations to charity. But for countless Jews all over the world, and especially for children, *Purim* stands for dressing up in fancy dress. The custom has become inseparable from the festival.

There are other customs which, although evidently popular or folkloric in origin, have become absorbed into the official handbooks of Judaism. Such is *tashlikh*, when at New Year sins are cast away onto water, or *kapparot* at *Kippur* when an expiatory chicken is waved aloft. These ceremonies are not widely observed today. But some well-established customs—such as *bar mitzvah* celebrations or the festival of *Simhat Torah*—owe their origin ultimately to popular demand.

An example of locally strong observance is the reverence of saints and shrines. There is no real basis in official Judaism for crediting holy men and women, whether living or dead, with superhuman powers. But in some communities the reverence of saints and their shrines plays a dominant part in religious life. This tendency seems to be particularly associated with Kabbalism. It is strongest in North Africa and the Middle East, and also among the Hasidim. The reputed tomb of Rabbi Shim'on bar Yohai, revered by Kabbalists as the author of the anonymous mystical work the *Zohar*, is a place of prayer and pilgrimage, especially on *Lag Ba-Omer*, the supposed anniversary of his death or *hillula*, when his soul was spiritually wedded to the divine. There are other tombs in Galilee where lamps are lit and prayers are said, and there are holy caves as well. But the country where these folk observances are strongest is Morocco, where they are also shared by Muslims: an investigator in the 1940s found 13 Muslim saints revered by Jews and no fewer than 50 Jewish saints revered by Muslims.

Veneration of shrines is a remarkable instance of Jewish folk religion: very strong in some countries, totally unknown in many others, it plays no part in official Jewish teaching. *Right* Galilee is particularly rich in shrines of holy men. Hasidim gather once a year to pray at a tomb in Tiberias. *Far right* The tomb of King David, on Mount Zion in Jerusalem, receives a steady stream of devout visitors. *Above right* Morocco is another country remarkable for the number of its shrines. These Jews of Asni in the Atlas Mountains were photographed in 1955 during a pilgrimage to the tomb of a saint.

Above Kapparot on the eve of the Day of Atonement: a chicken is taken and swung around the head. This may be a relic of the expiatory sacrifices of antiquity; it may also have less reputable antecedents.

Left Galilee is the scene of the annual pilgrimage to the tomb of Rabbi Shim'on bar Yohai at Meiron: there is ecstatic dancing around bonfires, and children have their hair cut for the first time.

No Graven Images

Below The restrained decoration of the Torah shrine in the synagogue at Dura (c. 245 CE) contrasts with the exuberance of the rest of the decoration. The symbolic images, like the worshiper, look towards Jerusalem. The figures in the scene of the offering of Isaac are seen from behind, and above is the earliest known representation of the hand of God.

"Thou shalt not make unto thee any graven image, or any likeness ..." The biblical prohibition has been observed in different ways but in general the problem has been approached cautiously: no statues, and strong inhibitions about human figures (particularly in a religious context), with a latent tendency to iconoclasm. Above all, no pictures of God and no veneration of images. The wall paintings of the synagogue at Dura are unlikely to have been unique in antiquity (few ancient synagogue walls survive), but in medieval and modern synagogues artistic representation is restrained or, more commonly, avoided. Illustration in Bibles and prayerbooks is now also rare (except for the Passover Haggadah), although many fine illuminated manuscripts survive from the middle ages and the Renaissance. But even where figurative art has been tolerated in a religious context, signs of inhibition are often apparent. They take no consistent form, but include the avoidance of human figures or of human faces. The presence of God in a biblical scene may be indicated by a hand descending from the sky—a persistent motif from ancient times on.

Above ''The Giving of the Torah'': Moses stands on top of Mount Sinai and receives the two stone tablets from God, whose hand is shown protruding from the cloud. The theme is a favorite one in manuscript illumination. In this German Haggadah of c. 1300 all the human figures have birds' heads.

Left The Coming Age represented as a banquet: the closing illustration from the three-volume Ambrosian Bible (Germany, 1236–38). The avoidance of human faces is a typical feature of 13th-century German Jewish art; there are Muslim and Christian parallels, but the influence of ascetic German Hasidism may also play a part.

Right One of a series of stained-glass windows designed by David Hillman (1895–1974) for the Central Synagogue in London. The theme is *Hanukkah,* represented by appropriate Hebrew texts as well as images. The avoidance of human faces (the figure at the top is completely shrouded in the *tallit*) revives the medieval practice.

Ritual and Art

Below Most Jewish homes contain a *kiddush* wine-cup, used for the "sanctification" of Sabbaths and festivals. It is generally of silver, though this English example (dated 1803) is of coconut with a rosewood stem.

Below Sabbath lamps often consist of a pair of candlesticks, but a favorite older style was the *Judenstern*, a hanging oil lamp with six or more spouts. This handsome example, with its crown, ball, seven-wick lamp and drip-pan, was made by the London Sephardi silversmith Abraham d'Oliveira in 1734.

In the past great care was lavished on the manufacture of the various material objects associated with the religious rituals of home and synagogue. They were generally made in the finest materials, by the best available craftsmen, and with an eye to both traditional style and artistic creativity. Even in this age of mass production, distinguished and original specimens are still being made, although the ready supply of cheap replicas has had a debasing effect.

The objects display great variety of styles, reflecting the taste of their very different countries and periods of origin. They were often, but not always, made by Jews, and certain symbolic themes became very common. Lions and crowns are frequently woven into the design, especially in the case of synagogue art, which is closely associated with the scrolls of the Torah and the ark in which they repose. There is also a natural tendency to incorporate biblical images or texts. A curiously popular feature is the *colonna santa*, the spirally fluted bronze column in St Peter's, Rome, which was said to have come from the temple in Jerusalem; other reminiscences of the temple and its own ritual implements are also found.

In the home, where the ritual objects range from fixtures such as the *mezuzah* to equipment for special occasions such as the *kiddush* cup or lamps for Sabbath and for Hanukkah, both art and symbolism tend to be subtly different. All however reveal a desire to devote to God's service whatever is most beautiful and precious.

Below The Torah scroll was decorated with a silver breastplate or shield which received correspondingly lavish embellishment. This example is more ornate than most, but it conforms essentially to a stereotyped pattern which became common in central Europe. Note the *colonna santa* and the lions and crowns, all thoroughly characteristic of synagogue art. This piece was made in Berlin c.1820.

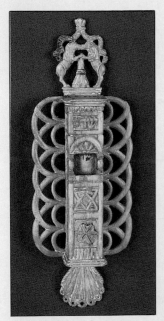

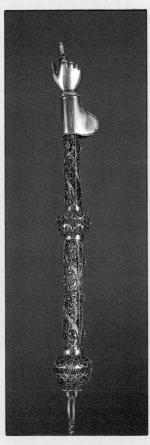

Above The *mezuzah*, a tiny parchment scroll inscribed with biblical texts and enclosed in a case, is the visible outward sign of a Jewish home. This bone case is 15th-century Italian work.
Right The Torah scroll is too sacred to touch and so a silver pointer (*yad*), usually in the shape of a hand, is used by the reader.

Left This gilt Hanukkah lamp was made in Germany c.1770. Note the shrine with the *colonna santa* on either side, and the Hanukkah scene below.

Above The scroll of the Torah is covered in the west with an embroidered mantle (in eastern countries it is set in a wooden case). Ashkenazic mantles are often elaborately decorated; this 18th-century English specimen has a more simple elegance. The silver finials are 17th-century Venetian.

Left Finials take many forms, but they regularly feature tinkling bells which were derived from the priests' vestments in the temple.

LANGUAGE AND LITERATURE

Pride of place among the languages of the Jews must be ascribed to Hebrew, the language with the longest continuous history of Jewish use. Hebrew is a Semitic language, closely related to Aramaic and Arabic. Its origins are lost in antiquity: according to a fanciful myth it was the language in which God created the world. At any rate it is the original language of most of the Bible and therefore has the status of a classical language among Jews. For centuries traditional Jewish education has been based on the Bible, and children began their schooling by learning the *aleph beth* (the Hebrew alphabet). At the same time Hebrew has also been the dominant language of Jewish worship and as such was familiar to learned and unlearned alike, even when it was no longer a spoken language. It has thus never really been a "dead" language and has in fact been in continuous use, with a continuously changing development, from ancient times to the present day. It is the language of many of the old rabbinic writings, of sacred and secular poems, of medieval law codes and commentaries, and it has often served as a means of communication between Jews in different countries. In modern times it has been revived as the main spoken language of Israel. Although non-Jews (notably Christian scholars with an interest in the Bible) have studied Hebrew, it must be regarded as in a unique sense a Jewish language. Among Jews it has often been known as "the holy tongue."

Another language which holds a special position is Aramaic, which was once in use over a vast area stretching from Egypt to India. There are passages in Aramaic in the Bible, and Jewish Aramaic manuscripts survive from as early as the 5th century BCE. Aramaic was the language of a large number of Jews in antiquity, particularly in Israel and Babylonia, and their literature includes the Talmud as well as the Targums (translations of the Bible). Because of this background Aramaic continued in use even when it was no longer spoken. The classical text of the Kabbalah, the *Zohar*, was written in Aramaic in 13th-century Spain, and even today Aramaic is used for legal documents and in well-known prayers and hymns. Very few Jews now speak it, but it has survived in Kurdistan with an extensive oral and written literature.

Hebrew and Aramaic are the only languages which enjoy such a long unbroken history of Jewish use, which have been used by Jews in all parts of the world regardless of their origins and religious denomination and which have been regarded as "official" languages for religious purposes. In ancient times they had a powerful rival in Greek, which was introduced into the land of Israel after the conquests of Alexander the Great in the 4th century BCE and gradually became the lingua franca of the whole eastern Mediterranean region as well as further afield. The detailed history of the use of Greek by Jews in Israel is a matter of intense scholarly controversy, but there is abundant evidence from inscriptions and literary sources of Jews speaking, reading, writing and even praying in Greek during the Roman and Byzantine periods, even though Hebrew and Aramaic continued in use (indeed some Jews used all three languages). In other Mediterranean countries Greek enjoyed unchallenged supremacy. The surviving Greek Jewish literature includes translations of the Bible and the voluminous writings of the historian Josephus and of the philosopher Philo. These two writers offer an interesting contrast. Josephus was born in Jerusalem and ended his days in Rome: he wrote originally in Aramaic and only later turned to Greek. Philo lived in Alexandria and there is no evidence that he knew any language other than Greek. Both authors wrote with both Jewish and non-Jewish readerships in mind. In other circumstances Greek might have remained as important a language for Jews as it has been for Christians. Its failure is due to several factors, among them the success of Christianity in Greek-speaking lands, the rabbinic insistence on Hebrew and Aramaic and, later, the popularity of Arabic. Greek did continue in use among Jews throughout the middle ages and down to modern times, but in a very limited geographical area and without producing any noteworthy literature.

The linguistic map of Jewry in ancient times, then, is relatively simple: the Jews, in common with other people, spoke, thought and wrote in a few languages which were not peculiarly theirs and which were the official languages of large empires (Latin was used by Jews in the west, although here too Greek persisted for some time). In addition, Hebrew continued to be used for religious and literary purposes. In time, owing to various historical processes, this simple picture became enormously complicated. In the west, for example, various Romance languages and dialects emerged from Latin. The Jewish population participated in this development while retaining Hebrew for those purposes for which Christians used Latin. A Jewish poem in Italian dating from the 12th century is one of the earliest Italian poems extant, and several distinct Jewish dialects of Italian came into being, some of which can still be heard today. Judeo-Provençal (Shuadit), now extinct, has a history which can be documented from the 12th century to the beginning of the present century. French, Catalan and other Romance languages were used by Jews in the middle ages as well. The most widespread and persistent of the "Judeo-Romance" languages is Judeo-Spanish (Judezmo or Ladino). In the middle ages Jews in the Iberian peninsula spoke various languages and contributed to local literature, not least as translators. The Jews expelled from Spain in 1492 carried their languages to the lands of their migration; in some places they have continued to speak and write them to the present day.

This brief glance at some of the Romance lan-

Above A scribe correcting a Torah scroll. Parchment, pen and ink are all hand-made, and the writing of every letter is governed by a minutely precise tradition. If a single word is illegible or wrongly written the whole scroll is invalidated for ritual use.

Left Bilingualism has been a common Jewish experience; it has not been unusual for Jews to use even three or more languages in some circumstances. This hymn in an 18th-century hymn book from Corfu is written in three languages, all written in Hebrew letters: successive lines are in Hebrew, Greek and Italian. The sense carries on from language to language, and pairs of lines in different languages rhyme. Whoever wrote this hymn felt at home in all three languages, and, more significant, so presumably was the congregation which sang it.

guages reveals the convoluted history of Jewish language without touching on some of the major complicating factors. Scholars have difficulty in deciding whether some of the early vernacular writings are in the form of the language current at the time among non-Jews or whether they represent a distinctive Jewish dialect. There is also the problem of multilingualism. Not only do we have writings in Castilian, Catalan, Arabic and Hebrew, all produced by Jews in Spain, we even have some poems written in a mixture of languages. (Multilingualism is in fact a marked feature of medieval Spain by no means limited to Jews.) In France Rashi (1040–1105) wrote commentaries on the Bible and Talmud in Hebrew, but frequently gives French translations of words and phrases. "Glosses" of this sort in different languages are found in various medieval Hebrew texts. The spoken and written language of Jews, even if it approximates to that of their neighbors, often reveals the influence of Hebrew, either in vocabulary (since Jews needed words for objects and concepts unfamiliar to non-Jews, or wished to avoid expressions which were too heavily loaded with Christian connotations) or

in syntax and morphology (either unconsciously or from a deliberate desire to preserve Hebrew patterns of thought and expression). Some of the Judeo-Spanish translations of the Bible and prayers are so heavily influenced by Hebrew that they read very strangely to anyone who knows Spanish but not Hebrew. Again, the Spanish of the Jews who emigrated to the Ottoman empire or Morocco absorbed influences from other languages, such as Arabic, Greek and Turkish. In Holland and other countries where Jewish communities remained in close contact with the Iberian peninsula, spoken and written Spanish and Portuguese remained closer to the forms of the languages current in the peninsula.

This complex pattern of development can be paralleled in many other parts of the world. In northern Europe Yiddish, a Germanic language with some Hebrew, Slavonic and other elements, spread eastwards from Germany in the later middle ages and became *the* language of a huge Jewish population, extending at various times from Holland and the Rhineland to Latvia and western Russia with more recent offshoots in North and South America

These maps illustrate two basic facts. The first is that the Jews have never, since remote antiquity, spoken a single common language. The second is that on the whole they have spoken the same language as their neighbors. Like all sweeping generalizations, these statements demand some

qualification. First, in the areas of rabbinic ascendancy Hebrew has always been available as a language of communication between Jews of different origins. Secondly, Jews have sometimes had their own dialects of the languages in question. Thirdly, migrations have often resulted in Jews speaking a

distinctive language, and while this has generally been a temporary phenomenon there are some striking exceptions, notably the persistence of Judeo-German (Yiddish) in Slavic lands and Judeo-Spanish (Ladino) in the Ottoman empire.

Below: Jewish languages in antiquity
The picture is relatively simple. Most Jews speak Greek or Aramaic. There is a real culture gap between the two groups, with Palestine forming a bridge between them.

Bottom: Jewish languages in the middle ages
Here the picture becomes more complex and fragmented. Greek and Aramaic both yield to other languages, and are gradually reduced to a small area. The most widely spoken languages are Arabic, Yiddish and (eventually) Ladino. "Canaanite" was a Slavic

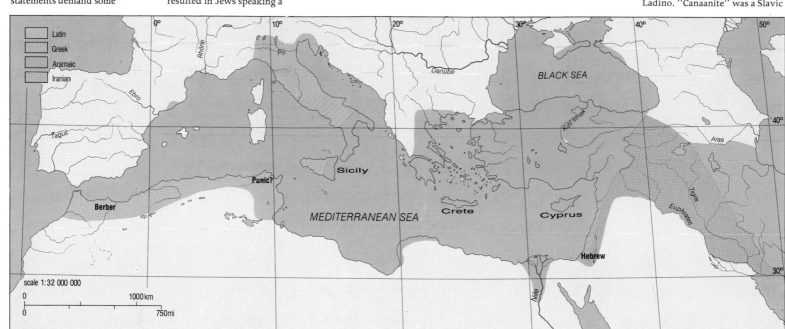

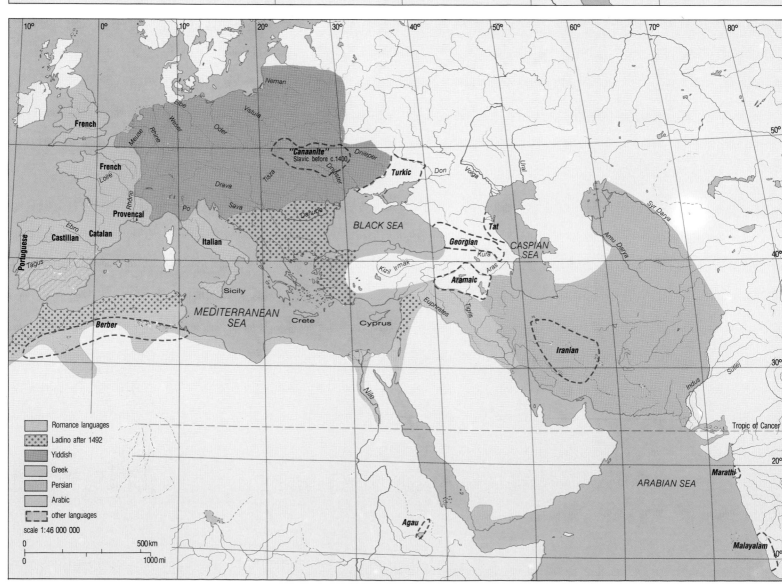

language which was superseded by Yiddish in the 14th and 15th centuries.

Jewish languages today
Apart from some local survivals, and exceptions due to migration, Jews speak the national language virtually everywhere. English is the language of half of world

Jewry. In Israel Hebrew is mainly spoken by Jews, while non-Jews generally speak Arabic. But many Jews also speak Arabic, and a wide variety of other languages is in use among immigrants.

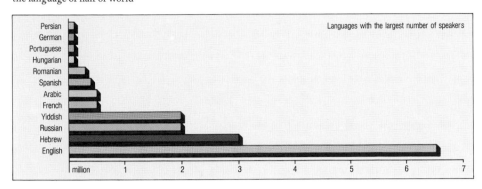

Languages with the largest number of speakers

Lillian Hellman (1905–), American

Saul Bellow (1915–), American

Primo Levi (1919–), Italian

major languages spoken by Jews today

- English
- Hebrew
- Russian
- French
- Arabic
- Spanish
- Romanian
- Hungarian
- Portuguese
- German
- Persian
- other countries where Jews mainly speak the national language

Arabic minority language

scale 1:34 000 000

0 ___ 1000km
0 ___ 750mi

Alberto Moravia (1907–), Italian

and indeed throughout the world. The spread of Arabic, from the 7th century on, profoundly affected many communities which had formerly spoken Aramaic or Greek. Arabic quickly began to establish itself as the spoken—and to a large extent the written—language of Jews in the lands under Arab rule, from Spain and Morocco in the west to Babylonia (Iraq) in the east. This vast territory included most of the oldest and most prosperous and important Jewish communities of the world, and throughout the middle ages Arabic remained one of the major Jewish languages, counting among its productions the main works of Jewish philosophy, such as Maimonides' *Guide of the Perplexed*. Various forms of Arabic are still spoken by many Jews today, and indeed it is widely taught in Jewish schools in Israel.

Further east, Persian was very widely used in the middle ages. The earliest surviving texts in modern Persian were written in Hebrew characters by Jews, beginning with an inscription in a remote corner of Afghanistan and a letter found in Sinkiang, both probably dating from the 8th century. There is an extensive Jewish literature in Persian, which has

only recently begun to be studied seriously in the west, and various forms of Persian and related Iranian languages are still spoken by thousands of Jews in Iran, Central Asia and the Caucasus.

In the past 200 years the process of linguistic assimilation has once again made itself strongly felt. At the end of the 18th century most Ashkenazi Jews spoke Yiddish, and many spoke no other language. But the use of the vernacular was already growing in the better-integrated sectors of society. By the end of the 19th century Yiddish was giving way to local languages everywhere in Europe, and in western Europe it was spoken only by immigrants, although in Russia 97 percent of Jews named it as their mother tongue in the census of 1897. Among Sephardim in western Europe the tendency to assimilation was even more marked, although Spanish held its ground in the areas which were (or had been) under Ottoman rule (it was spoken by 90 percent of Bulgarian Jews in 1925, 84 percent of Turkish Jews in 1927). Gradually, with improved social integration and the growth of secular education, Jews everywhere came to speak the language of the local majority, or of a socially dominant

Below: The spread of Yiddish
The story of Yiddish is closely tied to the story of Ashkenazi Jewry (see page 50). The German Jews who migrated eastwards retained their language and developed it in relative isolation, until it became a distinct Germanic language, enriched by Slavic and other influences, with dialects of its own and with a uniquely Jewish resonance. Subsequent movements spread the language far beyond its historic homeland, and by 1939 it was estimated that there were over 10 million Yiddish speakers dispersed over the entire globe. The holocaust and rapid linguistic assimilation have drastically reduced that figure, but Yiddish continues to be cherished by its devotees, and has recently begun to undergo a modest revival. The award of the Nobel Prize for literature to Isaac Bashevis Singer in 1978 (*inset*) drew attention to a continuing Yiddish literature which reposes on a long and significant tradition.

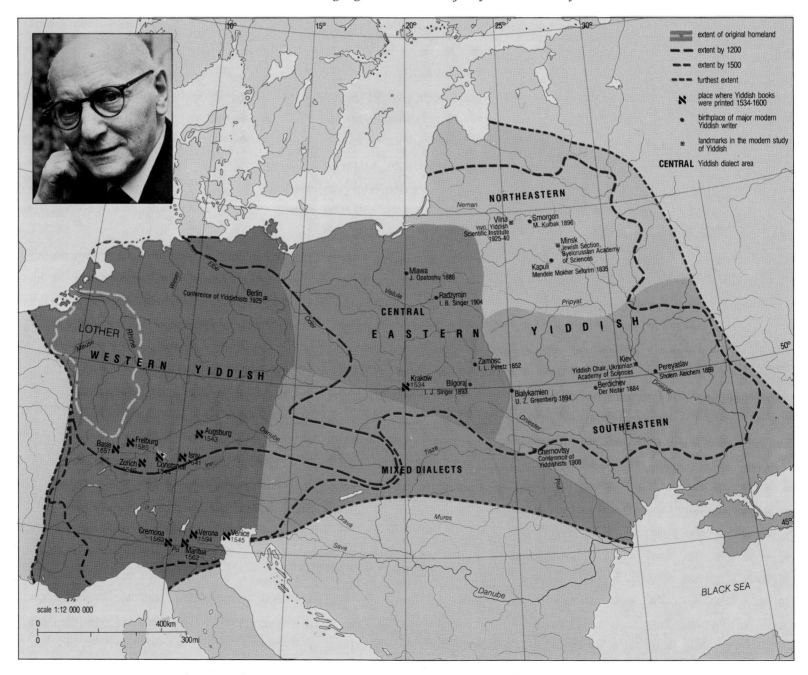

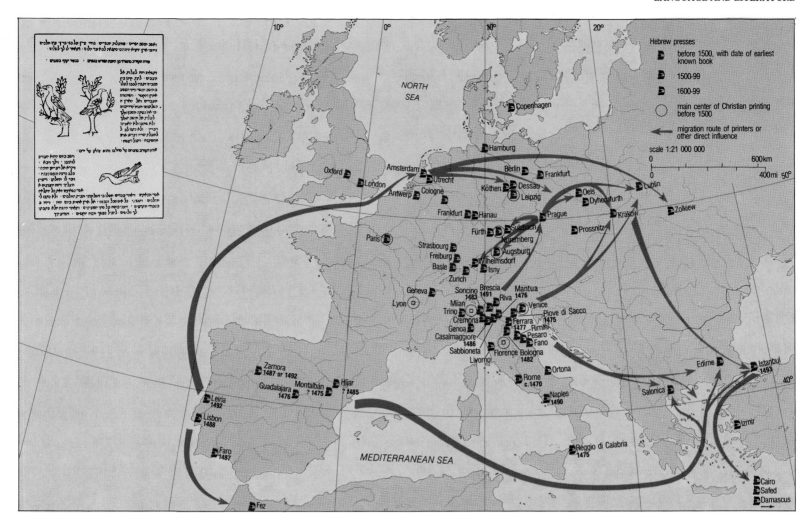

Hebrew presses
🅑 before 1500, with date of earliest known book
🅑 1500-99
🅑 1600-99
◯ main center of Christian printing before 1500
➤ migration route of printers or other direct influence

scale 1:21 000 000

0 ——— 600km
0 ——— 400mi

The spread of Hebrew printing

Jews were quick to seize on the possibilities offered by the invention of printing with movable metallic type (c. 1445). By 1500 nearly 200 different Hebrew books had been printed. Many of the early Hebrew printers were Christians. One of these, Daniel Bomberg, printed some 200 Hebrew books at Venice in the first half of the 16th century; among them were the first printed editions of the Bible with rabbinic commentaries and of the two Talmuds. Printing had a profound effect not only on the dissemination of Jewish culture but also on the character of Jewish scholarship and on the standardization of liturgical rites.

Inset Printing tended to run in families, and some of the printers were amazingly peripatetic. Gershom (Jerome) Soncino was a member of one of the most famous printing families, and was among the most prolific printers of his day, in Hebrew, Latin, Greek, Italian and perhaps also Yiddish. He printed books in some ten different towns in Italy from 1489 to 1527, before moving to Salonica and eventually to Constantinople. This book, a collection of moral aphorisms and animal fables by Isaac ibn Sahala, was probably printed by him at Brescia in 1491. It was the first Jewish book to be printed with illustrations.

minority, with their previous language sometimes lingering on for a while as a second language. German spread steadily in Germany and Austria-Hungary from the early 19th century, and by 1900 there were more than a million German-speaking Jews. English also became a significant Jewish language, with over a million speakers in 1900. It is now the first language of half the Jews in the world. Meanwhile the use of French was spread in North Africa and the Middle East through the schools of the Alliance Israélite Universelle.

The process of linguistic assimilation affected the written word as well as the spoken. Jewish writers have adopted the language and literary forms of prevailing cultures, writing in English, French, German, Italian, Spanish, Russian and a wide range of other languages. In many places they have made an acknowledged contribution to the national literature. Sometimes they exploit Jewish themes in their works, but frequently their writing has no distinctively Jewish characteristics whatever.

The one notable exception to this tendency to assimilation has been the strengthening of Hebrew. As we have seen, Hebrew was widely used as a written and liturgical language throughout the middle ages, and this activity has continued. Even with the adoption of the vernacular for worship in a number of western rites Hebrew has nowhere been permanently unseated as a liturgical language, and for most Jews it remains the primary language of worship. In the 19th century, under the influence of the European Enlightenment, a strong movement grew up to extend the use of Hebrew to the strictly secular domain (though there was already a long

tradition of Hebrew secular poetry, notably in Italy). The object was to give the Jews access to European civilization in the framework of a linguistic culture of their own, but not through Yiddish, which was regarded as a debased German jargon. The Romantic movement fostered the growth of a copious Hebrew prose and verse literature, including translations from other languages. The authors of this literature all spoke other languages, and many of them wrote in other languages as well.

In the latter part of the 19th century groups of enthusiasts, mainly in Russia, began to revive Hebrew as a spoken language, in an attempt to combat assimilation and to assert Jewish national identity. After all, a nation must have a language of its own. The language was fostered at first in small cultural circles; eventually it was introduced as the language of instruction in Jewish schools, in Palestine, Poland and elsewhere. Since the revival of spoken Hebrew was a Zionist undertaking, it is not surprising that its greatest success should have been achieved in Israel, where it is now the main official language of the state, supported by a language academy, a full apparatus of educational institutions and in particular by the remarkable *ulpan* system of instruction by which immigrants are quickly given a working knowledge of the language. It has been successfully adapted to modern needs and already there is a large and rich Israeli Hebrew literature. Meanwhile the revival of Hebrew as a spoken language in Israel has stimulated Jews all over the world to learn and use it. It is one of the great linguistic success stories of modern times.

121

Hebrew

Hebrew seems to be a truly eternal language. Just at the point where it ceased to be a spoken language, in the Roman period, it came into its own as a learned and liturgical language. In this guise it was spread to every part of the world, and continued effortlessly in use for centuries. Then just when it seemed that it was doomed, through the force of linguistic assimilation, the Hebrew Enlightenment revived it to a wide range of uses, from lyric verse to scientific articles. Finally the wheel turned full circle, with the resurrection of Hebrew as a spoken language, and its adoption as one of the official languages of Israel.

There has never been a time when Hebrew was not developing and changing. And yet an Israeli schoolchild can read and understand much of the Bible without any special training. The modern Hebrew speaker, consciously or unconsciously, is constantly using words and phrases which can be found in the earliest recorded strata of the language, some 3000 years ago. But the most up-to-date objects and ideas can be named and discussed in Hebrew, and the rich and varied modern literature draws both on more recent influences from Europe and on native Hebrew traditions of writing reaching back across the centuries.

Sacred or secular tongue? Link with the past or with present-day Israel? Language of spiritual or national yearnings? Hebrew is many different things to Jews today. In Israel it can be taken for granted, as the language of speech and broadcasting, education, comic-strips and military service. In Soviet Russia it is a precious heritage for which men and women risk their freedom.

Below Ornamental writing on a *Wimpel*, or binder for a Torah scroll, dated (5)596 (1836). It was a German custom to make the linen cloth used at a circumcision into a binder, and to embroider or (as in this case) paint it with the name of the child, his date of birth, and the pious message: "May God let him grow up for Torah, for marriage and for good deeds."

Right The Hebrew alphabet consists of 22 characters, representing consonants only. The vowels can be added in the form of dots and dashes, but generally they are omitted. The alphabet has taken many different forms, of which only the main ones are shown here. The letters can be used as numerals, being combined to make the appropriate sum.

Name	Numerical value	Pronunciation	Ancient Hebrew	Final form	Primary form
Aleph	1	–			א
Bet	2	b,v			ב
Gimel	3	g			ג
Daled	4	d			ד
He	5	h			ה
Vav	6	v			ו
Zayin	7	z			ז
Het	8	h (kh)			ח
Tet	9	t			ט
Yod	10	y			י
Kaph	20	k,kh		ך	כ
Lamed	30	l			ל
Mem	40	m		ם	מ
Nun	50	n		ן	נ
Samekh	60	s			ס
Ayin	70	–			ע
Pe	80	p,f		ף	פ
Tsade	90	ts		ץ	צ
Koph	100	k			ק
Resh	200	r			ר
Shin	300	sh,s			ש
Tav	400	t (t,s)			ת

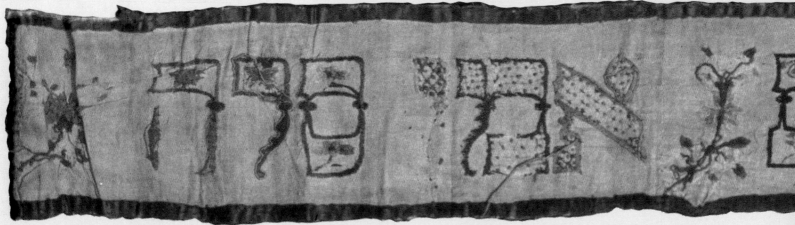

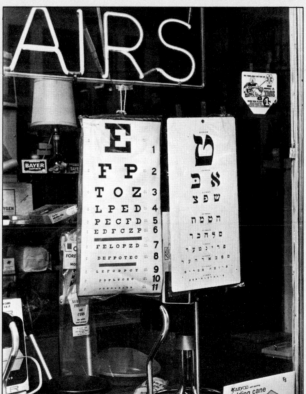

Left To teach one's children Torah is a basic religious duty (although often the task is farmed out by the parent to the *melammed* or teacher). Literacy has therefore generally been high among Jews, and since Hebrew was the basis of education the Hebrew alphabet was also used for writing other languages.

Below Graceful Hebrew lettering on the foundation inscription of a synagogue in Cordoba, dated 1315. Notice how well the rather square-shaped characters are suited to monumental use, and also how easily the letters can be squeezed or stretched to fit the space available.

Center The "Moabite Stone," an important historical inscription by Mesha, king of Moab (*c.* 850). The language is very close to Hebrew, and the writing too is similar to that used for early Hebrew texts. It is the ancestor of Greek and Latin writing, and was still being used at the time of bar Kosiba's revolt.

Left The more familiar square letters began to oust the older alphabet long before the latter disappeared, and they have remained in use down to the present day, as this eyesight testing chart displayed in a shop-window in New York shows. It is probably intended for use with Yiddish-speakers, who have the same alphabet.

The Bible

The Bible has remained the foundation of Jewish life, thought and worship from ancient times right down to the present day. It is read and preached upon in the synagogue and studied in the school; to quote from it at need is the refinement of the cultivated Jew, and no Hebrew writing can entirely escape its influence. It is essentially a written and a holy text, and it has been copied with such pious care down the generations that the manuscript tradition—especially of the Torah, which is the holiest and most authoritative portion of scripture—displays amazingly little variation when compared even with much more recent texts such as the Christian Gospels. The earliest surviving biblical texts date back over 2000 years, and the process of copying the text by hand continues to this day, since the Torah is still read in synagogue from manuscript scrolls. The art of illuminating biblical manuscripts may go back to antiquity, although no ancient examples survive. But we have some wonderful specimens from the middle ages, and biblical themes continue to inspire today's artists.

Below Here too the word is paramount. There is no representational illustration, only a decorative design which holds the eye and adorns the page, and the design itself is largely made up of Hebrew text, written in minute characters. Such "carpet pages," with their exploitation of writing for artistic effect, their use of gold paint and their rigorous avoidance of human figures, are typical of early Bible illumination in Muslim lands.

Below Muslim influence and the impact of the Torah's prohibition on images combine to make figurative art rare in manuscripts of the Bible. It is much commoner in less sacred texts, such as the Passover Haggadah which has a rich tradition of illustration going back at least to the 14th century. Shown here is a modern example from a celebrated Haggadah by Ben Shahn (1898–1969). It illustrates the Ten Plagues.

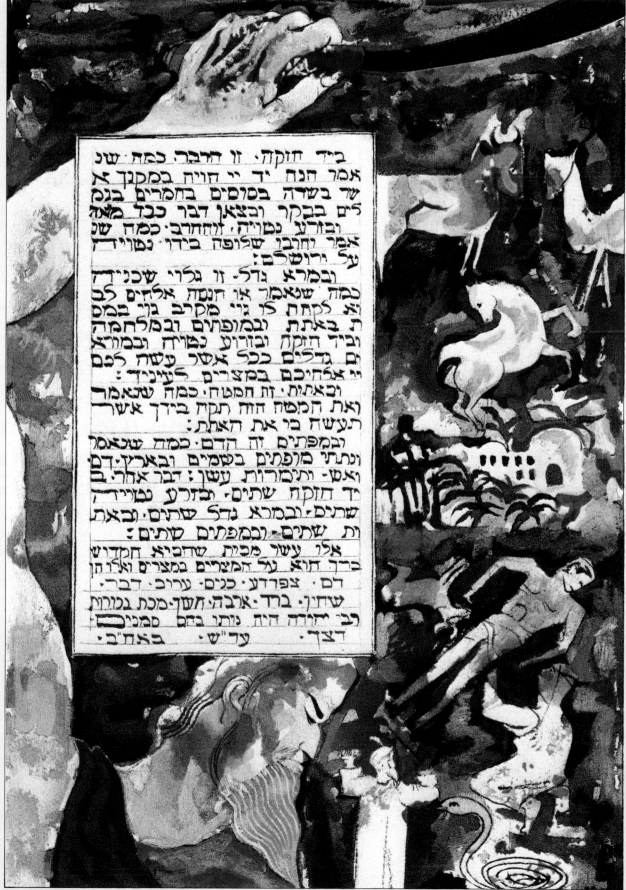

THE IMPACT OF THE HOLOCAUST

Like Hiroshima, Auschwitz stands as a boundary stone in history, marking an end and a beginning, a gruesome monument to the mistakes of the past and perhaps a signpost to a better future.

We are still too close to the events of the holocaust to judge them dispassionately. Many of the participants are still alive. Many of the victims (a million and a half of them were babies and small children) would be in their prime now had they been spared. Too many people nurse grievances, guilt feelings and nightmares. But already it is clear that the holocaust will never be relegated to a safe position in the story of the dead past, even to a simple entry in the awesome catalog of Jewish sufferings and of European wars. There had never been anything like it before in the history of Europe or of the Jewish people.

The very term "holocaust," as applied to the systematic destruction of European Jewry by the Nazis, indicates a recognition that this was something new, deserving a new name. The term first came into general use at the end of the 1950s. Before that writers used vaguer and less distinctive terms, such as "catastrophe" or "disaster." But these proved inadequate to encapsulate the enormity and novelty of what had taken place. The word "holocaust," with its implications of massive destruction and the theological resonance of its technical meaning (a sacrifice wholly consumed by fire) found favor partly because it had not been preempted by any earlier historical event.

What was new about the holocaust is hard to define exactly. It was not only the magnitude of the catastrophe, although destruction on this scale was unprecedented in the history of the Jews, and perhaps of any other people. Nor was it only the ruthless efficiency of the operation—the harnessing of modern technology to the ideology of destruction, although this certainly contributed to the shock. The Jews of Europe had known earlier trials and calamities—riots and massacres, discrimination and expulsion—but they had never had to face an orchestrated policy of extermination such as the Nazis pursued in what they themselves termed *die Endlösung der Judenfrage in Europa* ("the Final Solution of the Jewish question in Europe"). The portentous "finality" of this program, even if in the end it was frustrated, could not but send a profound shudder through a people accustomed to call itself "the eternal nation," which prided itself on its powers of survival and even felt that its destiny was assured by the Almighty himself. Hence the theological questionings which ensued from the disaster, over and above the individual experience of disillusionment and loss of faith. But even for nonreligious Jews the "Final Solution" raised questions unknown in the middle ages, and here perhaps is the heart of the problem.

Just as emancipation had created a new basis for Jewish existence, the Nazi degradation of the Jews represented a new kind of attack. Medieval Jews were a people apart: they did not expect to be treated the same way as other people. The victims of the Nazi race laws were for the most part citizens of modern European states. Many of them had fought for their countries in the Great War, and some of them had made distinguished contributions to public life. They had been brought up with expectations and beliefs which made it hard to accept this rejection, emanating from a nation which was considered to be at the forefront of European civilization. Of course the Jews were not the only victims of the Nazi crusade, but they were singled out for special treatment: they were made the objects of an elaborate demonology and were eliminated with such single-minded ruthlessness that the whole Nazi effort could appear as a "war against the Jews." For the Jews themselves Nazism was not only an attack on the European culture they had come to share, it was a denial of all the progress which was the very foundation of modern Jewish life.

All this was more true in the west of Europe than in the east, where the physical losses were heaviest and where the Jews were far less well integrated into the fabric of society. The memories of the pogroms were more recent and vivid here too, and the new catastrophe could be more easily assimilated into the traditional Jewish view of the world. But precisely because the destruction was so total in eastern Europe, and because traditional Jewish faith was so strong, the impact of the holocaust transcended the character of the earlier pogroms and called into question the whole basis of Jewish existence.

All these factors have made it difficult for Jews to accept the holocaust as a simple fact of history. The generation which survived has had to wrestle with this awesome experience. In the midst of the physical struggle for recovery and reconstruction, Jews have been obliged not only to come to terms with the terrible loss but to rethink the inherited norms so as to make sense of the catastrophe. On one level this has meant studying the actual events: uncovering their origins, tracking their progress, investigating what really took place in a thousand different localities, and trying to discover who was to blame, what could have been avoided, who perished and when and where and why. "Holocaust studies" have become a distinct and fertile branch of history, with its own research institutes and libraries and an enormous mass of literature. (By 1968 "Holocaust" had become a heading in the Library of Congress Catalog because of the huge volume of material that had appeared in print.) It was not only a matter of studying the disaster itself; earlier history too came to be reconsidered in the light of what ensued, particularly the history of Christian–Jewish relations, antisemitism and the whole emancipation movement.

On a different but interlocking level the theologians have had to investigate the implications of

Pope John Paul II's historic pilgrimage to the site of the extermination camp at Auschwitz (Oswiecim) was a moving reminder of the sufferings of the Nazi era. The name of Auschwitz has become a symbol of the horror and destruction of that era, which posed a gruesome challenge to European civilization and to the possibility of normal Jewish coexistence with gentiles. If there is a positive message to emerge from the ashes of Auschwitz, surely it is to be sought in the effort of reconciliation which has brought Christians and Jews together in an attempt to eradicate the misunderstandings of the past and to prevent such a catastrophe occurring again in the future.

realization of what had happened. There were no easy answers to any of these questions and in the meantime practical decisions had to be taken.

Decisions were taken. Reparations were negotiated and accepted, albeit with repugnance. Some of the money was used for documentation projects and for memorials to the victims. Educational courses were devised, so were practical schemes for reconciliation between Jews and gentiles. But the fundamental questions remain, and continue to torment the Jewish conscience.

Some historians have declared their opposition to what they call the "mythology" of the holocaust. It was a historical event, albeit an exceptionally traumatic one, they argue, and it needs to be described and analyzed like any other historical event. This argument is a protest against a tendency among theologians to indulge in generalized abstractions which often appear remote from the real suffering of millions of individual people. At the other extreme, theologians have taken exception to the tendency among academic historians to lose sight of the central problems in a forest of footnotes and statistics. Both criticisms are justified. The task of understanding and coming to terms with the holocaust needs the combined efforts of both historians and theologians. An occurrence of this magnitude invites easy generalization. The detailed facts are hard to reassemble (much of the evidence has been deliberately destroyed) and the effort is daunting as well as harrowing. But any generalization must be grounded in historical knowledge if it is not to be meaningless or simply false. And the attempts of revisionist historians to whitewash the Nazi record (even to the point of denying that the holocaust ever took place) demand painstaking rebuttal. But the historian cannot overlook the "mythical" element in the history itself. The Nazi ideology was sustained by a myth, and the apocalyptic character of the *Endlösung* has clear theological overtones. The actual response of the victims, too, was often conditioned by religious presuppositions. Historians may complain of the traditional Jewish inclination to judge all of history in theological terms, but they must recognize that the story of the holocaust contains ideological ingredients that require *historical* investigation. The approach of the theologians, however, is rooted not in the scientific need to discover what happened but in the psychological need of the survivor to make sense of what he has been through. They must address themselves to the shocked disillusionment, the aimlessness and loss of faith of a bereaved generation. Precisely because Jews have always seen history as the arena of God's activity they need an answer to the question: "Where was God at Auschwitz?"

Affirmative responses to the holocaust

This question ineluctably leads to many other questions, about where the ultimate responsibility for what happened lies, and about the positive lessons which can be drawn from the disaster. One simple answer is that persecution is a problem for the persecutors, not for their victims. The implication is that it is gentiles, and particularly Christians, who are confronted by the phenomenon of Auschwitz: it is they who have to face up to the destructive effects of their own beliefs. In fact Christian theologians have made a serious effort to

the holocaust for the traditional Jewish understanding of God and Israel and relations between the two, of suffering and faith and of the nature of mankind in general. These are not merely abstract, academic questions. The survivors were in urgent need of guidance and of reassurance. Many had lost their faith in God or in man; they were unhinged by anguish and despair. There were doubts about the proper response to such a devastating calamity: should one dumbly accept it, or rebel against the divine decree? Should one assign blame and demand revenge or restitution, or rather try to exercise forgiveness? These were not only questions for religious leaders, but for educators, psychologists and politicians. The trial of the Nazi Adolf Eichmann in Jerusalem in 1961 raised them in a dramatic form and provoked a painful public debate, as had the issue of German reparation money a decade earlier. There was the problem of what to teach children, whether to protect them from the trauma or to prepare them for the later

Memorials to the victims of the holocaust have been set up in many countries, and they take widely differing forms. Among the most poignant is the Pinkas synagogue in the old Jewish quarter of Prague (*top*). The building itself dates back to the 16th century and beyond, testifying to the former vitality of this now almost defunct Jewish community. The walls have been inscribed with the names of the Jews of Bohemia and Moravia who perished under the Nazis, together with their dates of birth and death or deportation. Other memorials have been erected far from the scene of the disaster, in lands where the survivors have forged a new life. The monument in the West Park Cemetery in Johannesburg (*above*) was designed by the sculptor Herman Wald (1906–70), who was born in Hungary but settled in South Africa during the Nazi period. The grounds of Yad Vashem, the official Israeli martyrs' memorial, are set with sculptures evoking the agony of the victims and the heroism of those who resisted. This is *The Silent Cry* by Leah Michelson (*right*).

The memorial at the concentration camp of Dachau (*left center*), some 16 kilometers from Munich, is one of several which have been put up on the sites of the camps themselves. And throughout the countries of Europe in which Jews were massacred or deported to their death the Jewish cemeteries display monuments to those who were killed. This memorial in the cemetery at Oslo (*left*) bears the names of the 620 Jews of the Norwegian capital who perished, including 18 members of a single family. A group of statues in the memorial park of Yad Vashem (*right*) bears eloquent silent testimony to the tragedy of victims and survivors alike. Those who suffered in the holocaust from the Swedish town of Malmö will also never be forgotten (*far right*).

Left Holocaust commemoration: individual memories, collective memories. To remember, to be reminded, is a solemn duty and a deepfelt need. At this memorial ceremony in the principal synagogue of Paris on the thirtieth anniversary of the liberation of Auschwitz the participant in the foreground is wearing camp prisoner's uniform. As the years pass, memories have to be renewed and refocused, and the unspeakable events have to be explained to a new generation.

come to grips with the implications of Auschwitz for Christian theology, especially for the traditional Christian anti-Judaism on whose foundations modern antisemitism was erected. But this approach says nothing to those Jews who have a desperate need to understand how God could have allowed such a terrible catastrophe to fall on the Jewish people. Auschwitz is not merely a problem for the persecutors, it is a problem for everybody who believes in a loving and faithful God, and it is a problem for everybody who believes in human perfectibility and progress. Few Jews would go all the way with the radical theologian Richard Rubenstein when he argues that the only honest response to the death camps is to conclude that God is dead, but most would agree with him that the problem of God and the death camps is the central problem for Jewish theology in the 20th century.

The theologians who wrestle with the problem of God and Auschwitz are aware of treading in the footsteps of the prophets, who wrestled with the problem of the destruction of the first temple and the Babylonian exile, and of the rabbis, who wrestled with the problem of the second destruction and the banishment from Jerusalem. It was their reflections which molded the traditional Jewish response to suffering, that it is a just punishment for sin. This belief, attached to the doctrine of God's abiding love for his people, distilled a message of hope from the repeated experience of disaster and helped the Jews to weather subsequent catastrophes. Some contemporary theologians have reiterated their faith in this timeworn formula, but, however modulated, it fails to carry conviction in the face of the mass murder of a million and a half children. Hence the extreme response of Rubenstein, who condemned it as an affront to the memory of the victims and an impossibly contradictory view of God: how could a loving God have willed the slaughter of a third of his chosen people?

At the other extreme is the profound faith of Ignaz Maybaum, which leads him to assert just that: God willed the destruction and Hitler was his agent, just as he willed the first destruction through Nebuchadnezzar and the second destruction through Titus. The six million were not, however, being punished for their sins: they were innocent victims of an act of destruction which was brought upon a guilty world. The holocaust, like the two earlier destructions, was an epoch-making event which brings one era to an end and inaugurates a new one. This is progress, and a visible sign that God does act in history.

Between these two extremes there is a whole gamut of theological reflections on this incomprehensible event. The purpose of the explanations, however, is not only to make sense of the past but to draw out guidance for the present. For the existentialist Rubenstein the discovery that history is meaningless puts the burden on man to inject meaning into his life. Whatever else the holocaust did, it reasserted the unity of the Jewish people. "If all we have is one another, then assuredly we need one another more than ever." He can therefore find a value for traditional Jewish observance, even if it is not the value that the tradition itself attributes to it. For Maybaum the holocaust imposes an urgent obligation on man to respect God's purpose for the world. For another influential theologian, Emil Fackenheim, the holocaust reveals a new commandment to the Jewish people—to survive: "Jews are forbidden to hand Hitler posthumous victories." Survival, even as an end in itself, is a divine imperative.

All contemporary Jewish theology links the catastrophe of the holocaust with the rebirth of Israel. (Here the theologians are happy to join hands with the historians.) Israel serves as a metaphor for consolation, hope, renewal—or simply (in Fackenheim's terms) survival. Without the sequel of Israel the story of the holocaust would seem different and far more somber. With the existence of Israel there appears to be more room for faith. Even a theologian like Maybaum, who is deeply critical of Jewish involvement in the politics of statehood (on which he blames the tragedies of human history), is prepared to see in the return to Zion the voice of God the redeemer leading his people home.

Within Israel the commemoration of the holocaust has entered the official ideology of the state. As early as 1951 Israel's parliament proclaimed an annual Holocaust Remembrance Day. Two years later it established an official "Martyrs' and Heroes' Remembrance Authority" (Yad Vashem), and conferred posthumous citizenship on the six million. The Authority is entrusted with the task of collecting and publishing all the evidence of the holocaust and of the Jewish resistance to Nazism, as well as establishing memorials and promoting the observance of Holocaust Remembrance Day in Israel and throughout the Jewish people. Its imposing memorial in Jerusalem has become a national shrine, comparable to the tomb of the unknown soldier in some other countries. Attached to it is a research institute devoted to the Herculean task of documentation. The whole complex is intended to perpetuate the memory of the victims, but also to foster an awareness of the lessons of the holocaust.

What the lessons are precisely is not always clear. Israeli schoolchildren are taught the history of the holocaust in all its horrifying detail, but often they do not make any direct connection between the victims of the disaster and themselves: they seem to inhabit two different worlds. The deliberate emphasis on the resistance groups is intended perhaps partly to bridge the gap between the helplessness of the victims, which seems totally incredible to the young Israeli, and the self-defense he takes for granted. There is a real danger of despising the victims for their passivity—a sentiment clearly visible at the time of the Eichmann trial. There is deep sensitivity in Israel to the issue of the holocaust, but it gives rise to conflicting and disturbing emotions. The national dimension provides a definite focus for reflection, but it may also lead to a certain devaluation, since the meaning of the holocaust is inevitably subordinated to the idea of Israel. It furnishes emotive catchphrases for political rhetoric, and has often been invoked in support of extremist political policies. Voices have been raised in protest against such abuses, but it was perhaps inevitable that once the holocaust was made into a national symbol it would be exploited for political ends.

On a more positive note, one consequence of the calamity has been the emergence of a serious effort for reconciliation between Christians and Jews. Soon after the end of the war an emergency conference of Christians and Jews was convened at Seelisberg in Switzerland to study the phenomenon of antisemitism and suggest possible ways of combating it through educational and religious activity. This early initiative has been followed by many others. The first assembly of the World Council of Churches, held in Amsterdam in 1948, called on its members to "denounce antisemitism as irreconcilable with the practice of the Christian faith and a sin against God and man." In 1964 the Second Vatican Council issued a Declaration on the Jewish People which (while pointedly omitting any direct reference to the holocaust) contains the significant statement that "The Church, mindful of the patrimony she shares with the Jews and moved by the spiritual love of the Gospel and not by political reasons, decries hatred, persecutions, displays of antisemitism, directed against Jews at any time and by anyone." These public proclamations, together with pioneering work by Christian theologians, have inaugurated a new age in Christian–Jewish relations. Christians have begun to dissociate themselves from the hurtful teachings and actions of the past, and Jews have begun to acknowledge the sincerity of this painful effort and to accept the hand held out in friendship. There is a realistic awareness, however, that centuries of prejudice cannot be eradicated overnight. Many Jews were shocked and disappointed that Pope John Paul II, during his historic visit to Auschwitz, did not mention the Jews by name, and the refusal of the Holy See to recognize Israel gives cause for resentment. But the barriers have at least begun to be broken down, and in many countries, especially in North America and western Europe, there is a positive sense of cooperation between churches and synagogues. It is only sad that it took a calamity on the scale of Auschwitz to bring about this reconciliation.

ZIONISM

Zionism has several interwoven and sometimes conflicting strands. Theodor Herzl was a western intellectual, seen here (*below*, seated at the back) in his natural habitat, a Vienna café. The date is the early summer of 1897. A few weeks later the first Zionist Congress will meet amid pomp and ceremony in Basle: a kind of international Jewish parliament, it will adopt a specific political program.

If the mind of Zionism was in the west, its heart and its muscles were in the east. The mass of Russian Zionists espoused the idea of resettling their lost homeland with a passionate fervor, blended for many with a socialist faith in the dignity of labor and the brotherhood of the toiling masses. Here is the young Ben-Gurion (*center right*), with his family and fellow members of the *Poalei Zion* ("Zionist Workers") party, in Plonsk shortly before his departure for Palestine in 1906.

A third strand was militant nationalism. Vladimir Jabotinsky, seen in Acre gaol in 1920 (*below right*), had founded the Jewish Legion which fought in the British army in World War I. In 1935 he was to form the New Zionist Organization (later to become the *Herut* Party), and also the National Military Organization (the *Irgun*), which would undertake terrorist action against British rule in Palestine.

The Viennese writer Theodor Herzl (1860–1904) painted a vivid and idealized picture of a future Jewish commonwealth in his last novel *Altneuland*. The name *Altneuland* ("Oldnewland," of which *Tel Aviv* is a very approximate Hebrew translation) encapsulates the vision of an ancient people returning to its ancient land, renewing it and being renewed in turn.

"Zionism" is a nebulous and emotive term which has meant many different things to different people, but at heart it represents a radical approach to the old questions of Jewish identity and the place of the Jews among the nations. For the Zionist the Jews are neither a religious community nor a loose association of ethnic minorities in different countries, but a single people with its own homeland: no longer a unique and indefinable exception to the general rule, but a normal people on an equal footing with the other peoples of the world. Zionism is one of the extreme attempts to discover a simple formula to resolve the complexities of the "Jewish problem." In practice simplicity has proved beyond the grasp even of the Zionists. After 100 years of Zionism there is still no clear and broadly accepted definition of Zionist aims, and in Zionist rhetoric the old slogan "normalization" has begun to yield once again to the language of "uniqueness."

In part the ambiguities are due to the fact that Zionism did not originate in a single place, among a single group or in the vision of a single individual. It arose over a period of time in different places in response to a complex of problems and under the influence of various other ideologies. Herzl himself was an assimilated western Jew. He was born in Budapest, lived in the Vienna of Sigmund Freud, Otto Weininger and Karl Kraus, and came to his personal crisis in Paris at the time of the Dreyfus scandal. His experience of western antisemitism led him to the realization that assimilation, for the Jews, was a chimera, and so to the formulation of a political program for the creation of the "Jewish State." This was the title of his pamphlet of 1896 which triggered off the political Zionist movement. Herzl's program was summarily dismissed by the leading Jewish philanthropists, Baron de Hirsch and the Rothschilds, but it was received with enthusiasm among groups of eastern European Jews, who were already groping their way towards a national solution of the Jewish problem. In the eastern Europe of the 1890s conditions were entirely different from those in the west. The Jews formed a large and cohesive population, unassimilated and unemancipated, victims of poverty and pogroms, desperately eager to seize on any formula which offered a way out of their intolerable circumstances. Nationalism, antisemitism, religious intolerance and political autocracy all flourished in cruder, stronger and more open forms than in the west, and radical underground movements for social and political reform were rampant.

It is hardly surprising in these circumstances that some Jews were turning to a nationalism of their

own or, in a region where emigration was taking on massive proportions, were beginning to think of Palestine as a possible home. Two witnesses of the Odessa pogrom of 1881, both destined to occupy honored places in the Zionist pantheon, anticipated Herzl's call for salvation through national self-determination. Moses Lilienblum (1843–1910), a former convert from traditional Judaism to Russian positivism, demanded massive Jewish colonization of Palestine. Leo Pinsker (1821–91), a respectable physician, did not at first think of Palestine as a solution but argued forcefully for an end to the "alien" status of the Jews and for normalization through territorial independence. His pamphlet *Auto-Emancipation* was issued anonymously in Berlin in 1882, and Herzl later confessed that if he had known it he would never have written *The Jewish State*. That same year the BILU movement was formed and founded the settlement of Rishon leZiyyon, the first step in the serious Jewish colonization of Palestine.

The roots of Zionism

The idea of a Jewish return to the land of Israel was not a new one. Napoleon Bonaparte, in 1799, had issued a call to the Jews of Africa and Asia to reestablish the ancient Jerusalem under his banner, and Lord Shaftesbury had put forward a "Scheme for the Colonization of Palestine" in 1840. Writers like Disraeli, George Eliot and Alexandre Dumas *fils* had publicized the romantic notion of a return to the Holy Land. Even among the Jews there were a few who had translated the currents of European nationalism into Jewish terms. Such were the German Communist Moses Hess (1812–75) and the rabbis Judah Alkalai of Sarajevo (1798–1878) and Zvi Hirsch Kalischer of Posen (1795–1874). These were suggestive precursors of Zionism, and so were the intellectuals of the Hebrew Enlightenment, who had labored tirelessly for the creation of an autonomous Jewish culture. The Hebrew essayist Ahad Ha'am (pseudonym of Asher Ginzberg, 1856–1927) is remembered as the founder of "cultural Zionism," a movement which views the resettlement of Palestine as part of a comprehensive revitalization of Jewish culture and national spirit on a worldwide scale.

Romantic nationalism, however, is only one strand in the complex web of early Zionism. Equally strong was the influence of the various radical movements which flourished in Russia at the turn of the century, especially socialism. Leaders and supporters of Zionism had links with many different streams of the radical movement, and they found different ways of expressing the heady blend of revolutionary fervor and Jewish renewal. One of the most influential, if least readable, is Ber Borochov (1881–1917), who propounded an elaborate fusion of Marxist and Zionist ideas, and was a leading ideologist of the *Poalei Zion* ("Zionist Workers") party, created in 1906 out of a mosaic of "proletarian" Russian-Jewish movements. The Poalei Zion transplanted their ideas to Palestine where, in the same year, they formulated their combination of Jewish nationalism and world socialism in the "Ramle Platform." (Among those present was David Ben-Gurion, later to become the first prime minister of Israel.) This step, together with the emergence among the pioneers of the

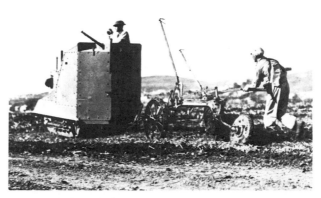

Left A fourth strand in Zionism was religious Zionism, which voiced the centuries-old longing for redemption and return in political language. The religious Zionists were for a long time a small minority both of Zionists and of religious Jews. Despite a good deal of compromise and conciliation there are still today some Jews who are unable to stomach Zionism, as this wall slogan in Jerusalem makes plain. For the Guardians of the City and others whose motives for inhabiting Jerusalem are purely spiritual, the Jewish state is at best an irritant, at worst a blasphemy.

The *halutz*, or farming pioneer, was the model of the Zionist settler of the early generations. The *halutzim* reclaimed the land for agriculture and settlement with their own hands, often in the face of attacks by the Arab population. The armored tractor (*left*) symbolizes one aspect of the Zionist enterprise of the 1930s.

Another aspect was immigration. Under the British the cry was "Free immigration!" Later, after the British departure, it became a reality, and the absorption of tens of thousands of immigrants, many of them destitute, by a fledgling state was an enormous practical problem. The newcomers were housed in primitive, overcrowded camps (*above*) until their plight could be alleviated.

The reception and absorption of immigrants was largely in the hands of the Jewish Agency, a wing of the Zionist Organization which is now one of the largest and most powerful elements within the Jewish state. It channels hundreds of millions of dollars annually into the settlement of immigrants, education and other activities. Dr Herzl and Dr Weizmann (*left*) look down gravely on the 1983 Annual Assembly of the Agency.

Above Rabbi Zvi Hirsch Kalischer (1795–1874) may deserve the title of the first Zionist. He wrote pamphlets calling for a return to the soil in Israel, and he actually persuaded Sir Moses Montefiore, the British financier, to buy an orange grove there in 1841—the first to be owned by a Jew.

Top "Hebrew Shepherd": this picture postcard offers an idyllic view of the life of a *halutz*. The reality was less relaxed, but it is certainly true that many *halutzim* were students and intellectuals who occupied their leisure time in reading or in heated discussions of literary or ideological issues. "Hebrew" was the preferred adjective of the pioneers, avoiding any religious overtones.

Hapoel Hatzair ("Young Worker") party, introduced party politics into the New Yishuv (as the Zionist settlers came to be called, to distinguish them from the pre-existing Jewish inhabitants of Palestine, the Old Yishuv). The Hapoel Hatzair were less preoccupied with socialist theorizing and more with the practical tasks of agricultural pioneering. Their spiritual mentor was A.D. Gordon (1856–1922), an original thinker who had a passionate belief in manual labor as the only road to spiritual redemption. The two movements, despite ideological conflict, came to share fundamental aims. The idealism and hard work of the pioneers laid the foundations for many of the institutions, as well as the dominant ethos, of the state.

But the Zionist movement drew its real strength not from the theories of the ideologists, not even from the self-sacrificing labors of the pioneers, but from the very real and widespread menace of antisemitism. In retrospect it is remarkable to what extent the movement accepted the presuppositions and even some of the language of the antisemites. If Zionism represented a reaction against antisemitism it was also in a sense a concession of its major premise, that the Jews represented an alien and unassimilable element in gentile society. The solution of mass emigration which the Zionists propounded was one which was not uncongenial to the antisemites themselves.

Prominent among the enemies of Zionism were the assimilationists of all hues: Jews who wished to

be nothing but full citizens of the countries in which they lived, liberals and socialists who wanted to demolish the historic barriers which had caused so much hatred and exploitation in the past. Liberal Jews renounced any hint of Jewish particularism. The Bolsheviks waged war on Zionism and eradicated it by force. (And yet those Zionists who preached "normalization" were, in their way, advocating assimilation; only it was an assimilation which would preserve a Jewish national entity.) Other opposition sprang from different motives. The Bund saw it as a duty of Jews to remain in their native lands and work towards improving society as a whole. The bulk of Jewish traditionalists viewed Zionism as a dangerous secularist heresy, substituting this-worldly for otherworldly redemption and in effect trying to force God's hand. And there were those to whom the Zionist enterprise posed a real threat—the Old Yishuv and the Arabs of Palestine.

The naivety of the early Zionists in the matter of the Arabs seems astonishing in hindsight. Some of them seem to have been genuinely unaware of the existence of Arabs in Palestine, and they were very slow to show any real appreciation of the rising tide of Arab nationalism. Herzl was certainly aware of the existence of the Arabs, but he thought they would be grateful for the benefits of economic progress. Others romantically saw them as long-lost Semitic brothers, who would eagerly join hands with the new Jewish settlers. (A few Arabs actually seem to have shared this rosy vision.) The reality of the clash between Zionist and Arab interests was not fully absorbed by some of the settlers until long after it had begun to claim lives on both sides. The growing conflict of the 1920s and 1930s ensured that the Jewish state would eventually be born in blood and fire, not in Semitic fellowship or the brotherhood of the toiling masses. It has given rise to a situation where even some Israeli Zionists have spoken of the Palestinian Arabs as the "new Jews," and have talked of "Arab Zionism."

Meanwhile the apotheosis of European anti-semitism in the Nazi holocaust has totally transformed the world in which Zionism had grown up. Nazism, with its absolute denial of Jewish assimilation, seemed to provide irrefutable evidence of the truth of the Zionist claims. Many Jews turned to Zionism in the 1930s and 1940s, even in places which had previously resolutely resisted it. Tragically the Jewish homeland came too late to save the majority of the victims, and Zionists were condemned to the role of impotent spectators of the destruction of their brethren, prophets of doom whose warnings have been vindicated. The holocaust created a mood favorable to the realization of Zionist demands, and the land received a massive influx of refugees and broken survivors. The wounds of that time have been slow to heal. The triumph of Zionism was born out of humiliating failure. The land of the pioneers was peopled with fugitives. The conflict with the Arabs brought in a further influx of refugees, who had shared neither the Zionist struggle nor the traumatic experience of the holocaust, and whose culture and expectations were at odds with those of the Russian founders. The vision of those founders survived in the new state, as did the institutions they had created, but the Labor Zionists' dream dissolved in the harsh reality of protracted war, economic chaos and social strife, which in 1977 led to their defeat in the polling booths. If there is a class struggle in Israel today, it is one in which the founders and their heirs are seen as the ruling class; despite the nobility of their aims and their self-denying endeavors they have fallen victim to their own rhetoric of colonialism and exploitation.

Zionism and world Jewry

It is otherwise with world Jewry. The Zionists failed in their aim of liquidating the diaspora, but the diaspora came to realize, in 1942 or in 1948, how much it needed the Zionists. The holocaust brought the Jewish people to its knees; Israel allowed it once again to hold its head up high. Anti-Zionism was all but silenced and Jews everywhere took pride in the achievements of Israel and supported the state with their voices, from their pockets and, in moments of grave crisis, with their blood. People who had lost or shrugged off their Jewish identity rediscovered it through Israel. Hebrew replaced Yiddish as the Jewish second language. Progressive Judaism gave Zionism its stamp of approval, even transferring its world headquarters to Jerusalem. Orthodoxy, too, shared in the enthusiasm, although with deeper theological reservations. Jews abroad endorsed every action and every declaration of the government in Jerusalem more vociferously than even the Israeli public did: dissent was equated with treachery.

This blind enthusiasm, born from the holocaust,

was sustained by the continuing Arab–Israeli conflict. It reached fever pitch at the time of the 1967 war. It really seemed then that "Zionist" might be an obsolete term: the dream had been achieved and Israel was the throbbing heart of an undivided Jewish people. But immediately the cracks began to appear. The Soviet Union's renewed anti-Zionist campaign was echoed by Jewish adherents of the New Left. The plight of the Arab refugees began to exercise not only a few alienated Jewish intellectuals but committed Jews including some religious leaders. Doubts were expressed about the effects of Zionism on diaspora communities, which were being drained of funds and vital manpower. There was dissension over the right of Soviet Jewish émigrés to settle in the diaspora, and mounting criticism of the policy of planting Jewish settlements in the occupied territories. The change of government in 1977 introduced a new element: Labor Zionists, the staunchest American supporters of Israel, argued now that criticism of Israeli policy was legitimate and did not imply disloyalty to the state as such. Religious conflicts in Israel brought traditionalist Jews onto the streets of London and New York carrying banners equating Zionism with Nazism. The Israeli invasion of Lebanon in 1982 precipitated a real crisis. Jewish communal leaders, even sincere Zionists, were perplexed. Called on to support Israeli action, they prevaricated or even expressed their condemnation. Rabbis preached belatedly about the corrupting effects of power and the need for a just settlement of the Palestinian Arab problem. The new mood gave rise to uncertainty and anxiety. Critics of Israel were accused of siding with the enemies of the Jewish people. Anti-Zionism was equated with antisemitism. Some Jews pointed to the high level of dissent within Israel, and asked why diaspora Jews should be expected to display a unity lacking in Israel itself.

The appearance of the first Jewish pimps and burglars in Palestine was hailed as a healthy sign of "normalization," and the dissolution of blind jingoistic enthusiasm for Israel should perhaps be judged in the same light. Zionism provided a valuable rallying cry for Jews disheartened and disoriented by the holocaust. It still offers a focus for Jewish identification for people who feel, for one reason or another, estranged from the society in which they live. But increasingly it is Israel which is the issue, not Zionism. Jews everywhere feel a common bond with Israel, they feel that their destiny is somehow bound up with that of the Jewish state. They have sympathy with Israel's problems and follow her progress with anxious interest. They pray devoutly for her peace and welfare. But they no longer look to Israel to end the problems of the diaspora, and they increasingly resent the Zionist idea that Israel has a right to speak for world Jewry and to intrude in the affairs of diaspora communities, particularly when the diaspora is denied the reciprocal right of proffering advice and criticism to Israel. The ideal relationship between Israel and the Jewish diaspora has yet to be satisfactorily defined, but in the meantime a healthy and fruitful symbiosis is developing, in which Israel is able to give a great deal to the diaspora, and not merely, as in the past, to take. Ahad Ha'am's vision of Israel revitalizing the culture and national spirit of world Jewry is thus becoming a powerful reality.

PART THREE
THE JEWISH WORLD TODAY

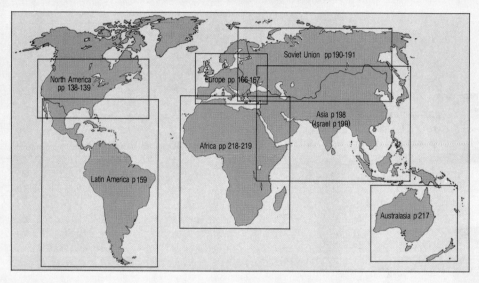

North America
pp 138-139

Europe pp 166-167

Soviet Union pp190-191

Asia p 198
(Israel p 199)

Africa pp 218-219

Latin America p 159

Australasia p 217

THE SHAPE OF THE JEWISH WORLD

Any attempt to estimate the number of Jews in the world or in any particular country must inevitably be based to a large extent on conjecture. Few countries specifically identify Jews in their national censuses and, even if they do, Jewish identity is such a subjective matter that the results are always open to question. Most published statistics are based on information gathered by the local Jewish communities, and here the problem of subjectivity is even more acute. What should the investigators be looking for? People who consider themselves to be Jews? Those conforming to the "talmudic definition" of Jewish status? Members of synagogues? There is a wide range of disagreement about these basic questions of definition, quite apart from the immense practical difficulty of collecting information. Consequently all overall figures should be taken with a grain of salt, as useful approximations but little more.

On any reckoning, however, the broad outlines are clear enough. Most Jews in the world are concentrated in a few countries. Three—the USA, Israel and the Soviet Union—account between them for over 80 percent of the total, and the nine largest communities (those estimated at over 100 000 members each) constitute probably as much as 95 percent of world Jewry.

Another way of looking at the figures is in terms of the ratio of Jews to the total population. Here, on a national basis, Israel is totally exceptional, with Jews constituting nearly 85 percent of the population (excluding the administered territories). Only five other countries (USA, Gibraltar, Uruguay, Canada and France) have 10 or more Jews per 1000 inhabitants. In all other countries the Jews are numerically insignificant.

According to the most acceptable estimates, there are about 13 million Jews in the world today. Half of them live in the Americas, and about a quarter each in Europe and in Asia (mainly in Israel). Well over half the Jews live in English-speaking countries. Migration, after the massive upheavals of the past century, now seems relatively stable. Recent years have seen some emigration from countries where political conditions are not propitious (such as Afghanistan, Iran and Zimbabwe) and continuous movement into and out of Israel. The only really momentous net emigration has been from the Soviet Union. About 250 000 Jews left in the 1970s. This movement has now been virtually halted, but it is known that considerable numbers of Jews have applied for exit permits, or would apply in more favorable circumstances.

The Jewish population is predominantly urban. Virtually everywhere Jews are more concentrated in the largest urban centers than is the general population. In many countries more than half of them live in the capital or largest city, and perhaps a quarter or less of world Jewry live in small towns and rural areas. Urbanization is by no means a uniquely Jewish phenomenon, but its effects are especially marked among the Jews, especially since the holocaust obliterated most of the agricultural settlements of Jews in eastern Europe.

The Jewish population is increasing more slowly than the general population, both worldwide and in individual countries. This is due to a number of reasons, of which the most significant seems to be a relatively low birthrate. This factor, coupled with emigration and defection from the community, has produced in many countries a situation where the Jews are an aging population which cannot hope to maintain its numbers, still less keep pace with the rising general population. On the other hand, the larger centers (with the exception of the Soviet Union) tend to attract younger Jewish immigrants. The trend towards the concentration of Jews in a few countries is therefore likely to continue, while the world Jewish population increases only very slowly, and may even soon come to a standstill.

World Jewish Population, 1800–1980
Any assessment of Jewish population can only be approximate, but this diagram brings out the main developments in the modern period, and in particular the terrible damage done by the Nazi holocaust. Before 1940 eastern Europe consistently accounted for more than half of the world Jewish population, despite continuous emigration reaching massive proportions at times. Since the holocaust, America has become by far the largest center, with Israel claiming a rapidly growing share of the total.

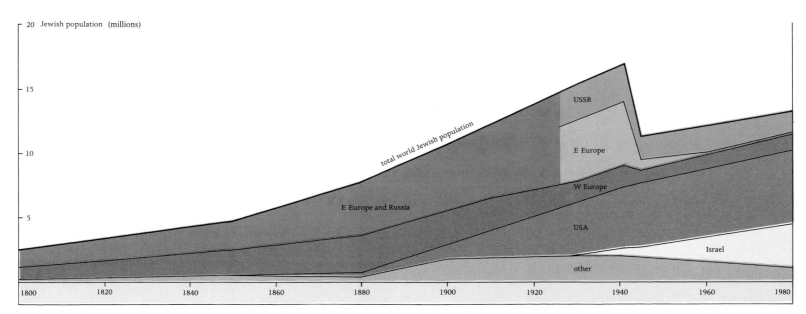

The shape of the Jewish world
These two world maps show two ways of looking at the distribution of Jews in the world today. As the top map indicates, more than 80 percent of all Jews live in only three countries, while a single city, New York, accounts for some 15 percent of the total. The bottom map makes

it plain what a tiny element of the population of each country the Jews are, with the outstanding exception of Israel. Over much of the world's surface, and especially in the "Third World," most of the population can never have seen a Jew (discounting the occasional tourist). This phenomenon is

heightened by the noteworthy concentration within each country of the Jewish population in one or two large cities.

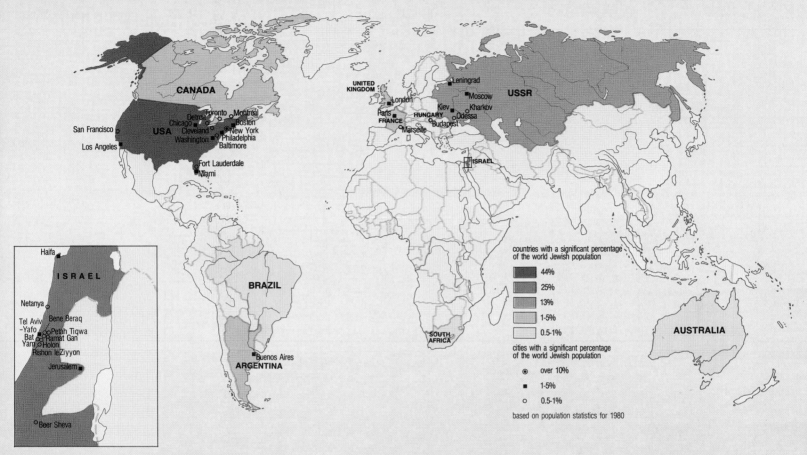

countries with a significant percentage of the world Jewish population
- 44%
- 25%
- 13%
- 1-5%
- 0.5-1%

cities with a significant percentage of the world Jewish population
- ◉ over 10%
- ■ 1-5%
- ○ 0.5-1%

based on population statistics for 1980

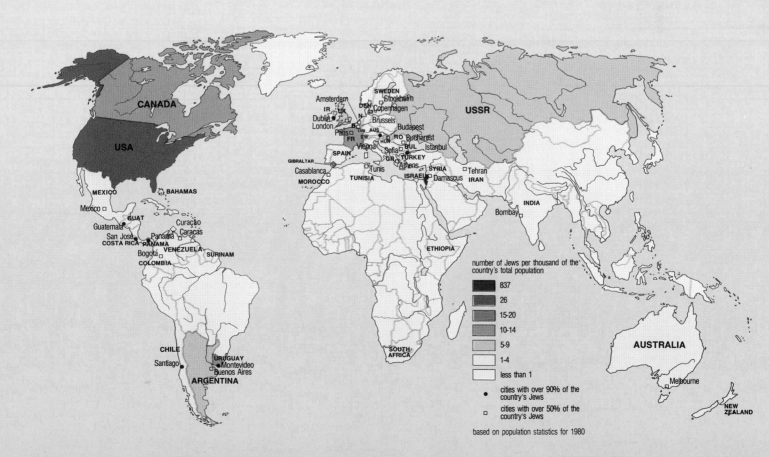

number of Jews per thousand of the country's total population
- 837
- 26
- 15-20
- 10-14
- 5-9
- 1-4
- less than 1
- ● cities with over 90% of the country's Jews
- □ cities with over 50% of the country's Jews

based on population statistics for 1980

NORTH AMERICA

Jewish settlements

- major community:
  estimated over 100 000
- important community:
  estimated over 10 000
- sizable community:
  estimated over 1000
- smaller community:
  estimated under 1000
- small community
  with some communal organization

scale 1:12 000 000

0 — 400 km
0 — 250 mi

ATLANTIC OCEAN

GULF OF MEXICO

QUEBEC
ONTARIO
NEWFOUNDLAND
James Bay
Gulf of St Lawrence
PRINCE EDWARD I
NEW BRUNSWICK
NOVA SCOTIA
MAINE
NEW YORK
VT
NH
DELAWARE
MD
PRINCE GEORGES COUNTY
W VA
VIRGINIA
KENTUCKY
TENNESSEE
NORTH CAROLINA
SOUTH CAROLINA
GEORGIA
ALABAMA
MISSISSIPPI
FLORIDA
OHIO
INDIANA
ILLINOIS
MICHIGAN
WISCONSIN
CANADA

L Superior
L Michigan
L Huron
L Ontario
L Erie

St Johns
Halifax
Sydney
Glace Bay
Moncton
Fredericton
St John
Yarmouth
Bangor
Calais
Waterville
Augusta
Lewiston/Auburn
Portland
Dover
Portsmouth
Concord
Keene
Laconia
Claremont
Rutland
Glens Falls
Saratoga Springs
Gloversville
Manchester
Bennington
Amsterdam
Herkimer
Utica
Rome
Syracuse
Auburn
Newark
Geneva
Rochester
Batavia
Buffalo
Niagara Falls
St Catharines
Hamilton
Brantford
Kitchener
Guelph
London
Sarnia
Oshawa
Toronto
Peterborough
Belleville
Kingston
Cornwall
Ottawa
Montreal
Sherbrooke
Quebec
St Lawrence
Burlington
St Johnsbury
North Bay
Sudbury
Sault Ste Marie
Timmins
Kirkland Lake
Iron Mountain
Fort William/Port Arthur
Quad Cities
Wausau
Green Bay
Appleton
Oshkosh
Fond du Lac
Sheboygan
Manitowoc
Madison
Milwaukee
Racine
Kenosha
Waukegan
Beloit
Rockford
Sterling
Dixon
Elgin
Aurora
Joliet
Kankakee
Chicago
CALUMET REGION
Champaign-Urbana
Bloomington
Lafayette
Muncie
Anderson
Marion
Decatur
Indianapolis
Terre Haute
Bloomington
St Louis
Evansville
Louisville
Lexington
Huntington
Paducah
Kennett
Nashville
Oak Ridge
Johnson City
Knoxville
Asheville
Hendersonville
Chattanooga
Dalton
Gadsden
Anniston
Birmingham
Tuscaloosa
Selma
Montgomery
Meridian
Hattiesburg
Jackson
Biloxi/Gulfport
Mobile
Pensacola
New Orleans
Baton Rouge
Clarksdale
Greenwood
Memphis
Florence
Huntsville
Columbus
Macon
Augusta
Athens
Columbia
Orangeburg
Sumter
Columbus
Fitzgerald/Cordele
Albany
Valdosta
Dothan
Tallahassee
Gainesville
Jacksonville
St Augustine
Daytona Beach
Orlando
BREVARD COUNTY
Tampa
St Petersburg
Lakeland
Fort Pierce
Sarasota
Port Charlotte
Fort Myers
Lehigh Acres
PALM BEACH COUNTY
Boca Raton/Delray
Fort Lauderdale
Hollywood
Miami
Key West
Winston-Salem
High Point
Greensboro
Chapel Hill/Durham
Raleigh
Goldsboro
Fayetteville
Wilmington
Gastonia
Charlotte
Spartanburg
Greenville
Florence
Savannah
Brunswick
Charleston
Atlanta
Martinsville
Danville
Roanoke
Lynchburg
Petersburg
Hopewell
Richmond
Williamsburg
Newport News
Norfolk
Portsmouth
Charlottesville
Harrisonburg
Staunton
Winchester
Cumberland
Hagerstown
Frederick
Chambersburg
Altoona
State College
Washington DC
Annapolis
Salisbury
Wildwood
Alexandria
Fredericksburg
Bluefield/Princeton
Charleston
Parkersburg
Clarksburg
Morgantown
Wheeling
Uniontown
McKeesport
Pittsburgh
New Kensington
Johnstown
Aliquippa
Steubenville
Canton
Wooster
Zanesville
Columbus
Cincinnati
Hamilton
Middletown
Springfield
Dayton
Lima
Marion
Mansfield
Akron
Sandusky
Elyria
Lorain
Cleveland
Warren
Youngstown
New Castle
Sharon
Jamestown
Erie
Detroit
Windsor
Mt Clemens
Chatham
Ann Arbor
Jackson
Battle Creek
Kalamazoo
Benton Hr
Michigan City
South Bend
Fort Wayne
Lafayette
Flint
Saginaw
Bay City
Grand Rapids
Muskegon
Mt Pleasant
Lansing
Toledo

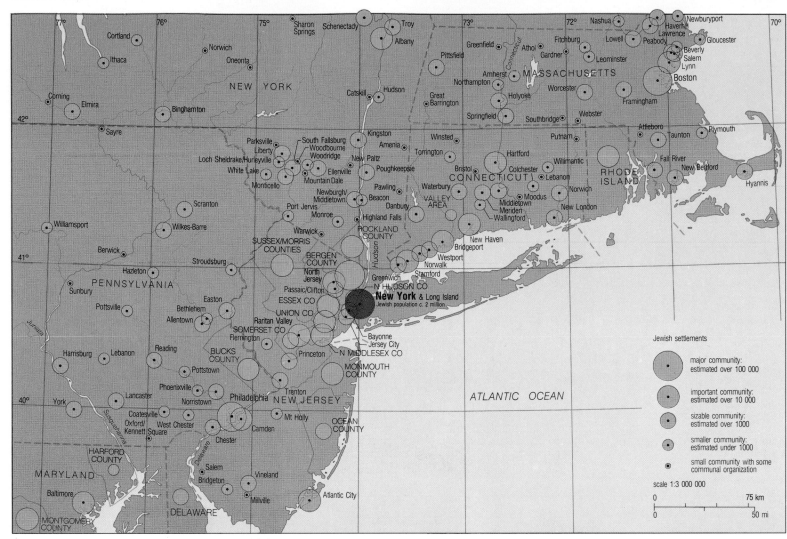

Jewish settlements

○ major community:
estimated over 100 000

○ important community:
estimated over 10 000

○ sizable community:
estimated over 1000

○ smaller community:
estimated under 1000

◉ small community with some
communal organization

scale 1:3 000 000

0   75 km

0   50 mi

**Above: The northeastern
United States**

Leonard Bernstein (1918–), US conductor and composer

Wherever Jews have been
allowed to feel at home there has
been no shortage of Jewish
individuals who have made
outstanding contributions to the
public life and culture of their
country, not as Jews but simply
as members of the wider society
to which they belong. On this
and subsequent pages in Part
Three of the Atlas we see the
faces of some of these
individuals—a random selection,
by no means representative or
complete, but simply a hint of
the wealth and variety of such
contributions.

George Gershwin (1898–1937), US composer

The Marx Brothers, US comic actors

	1930		1980	
	Approx. Jewish pop.	*Jews per thousand*	*Approx. Jewish pop.*	*Jews per thousand*
Canada	156 000	15	308 000	13
USA	4 228 000	36	5 750 000	26
Alabama	13 000	5	9000	2
Alaska	700	12	1000	2
Arizona	1500	3	45 000	17
Arkansas	9000	5	3500	1
California	123 000	28	754 000	32
Colorado	20 000	19	32 000	11
Connecticut	92 000	56	102 000	33
Delaware	5500	22	9500	16
District of Columbia	16 000	30	40 000	63
Florida	13 000	10	467 000	48
Georgia	23 000	8	36 000	7
Hawaii	80	1	5500	6
Idaho	1000	2	500	1
Illinois	346 000	47	266 000	23
Indiana	27 000	9	23 000	4
Iowa	16 000	7	8000	3
Kansas	8000	6	11 000	5
Kentucky	20 000	8	12 000	3
Louisiana	16 000	9	16 000	4
Maine	8500	11	7000	6
Maryland	71 000	44	186 000	44
Massachusetts	226 000	53	241 000	42
Michigan	89 000	20	90 000	10
Minnesota	43 000	16	35 000	9
Mississippi	6500	4	3000	1
Missouri	81 000	23	72 000	15
Montana	1500	2	650	1
Nebraska	14 000	10	8000	5
Nevada	250	3	15 000	18
New Hampshire	3000	6	4500	5
New Jersey	225 000	60	437 000	59
New Mexico	1000	3	7000	6
New York	1 904 000	167	2 139 000	122
North Carolina	8500	3	15 000	2
North Dakota	2500	4	1000	2
Ohio	174 000	26	144 000	13
Oklahoma	8000	3	6500	2
Oregon	13 000	15	11 000	4
Pennsylvania	405 000	42	414 000	35
Rhode Island	25 000	36	22 000	23
South Carolina	7000	4	8500	3
South Dakota	1500	2	600	1
Tennessee	23 000	9	17 000	4
Texas	47 000	9	73 000	5
Utah	3000	6	2300	2
Vermont	2000	6	2500	5
Virginia	26 000	10	59 000	11
Washington	15 000	9	22 000	5
West Virginia	7500	4	7500	4
Wisconsin	36 000	12	30 000	6
Wyoming	1300	6	300	1

G. Herzberg, Can. physicist

Leonard Cohen (1934–), Can. poet, songwriter, singer

N. Mailer (1923–), US novelist

Bob Dylan (1941–), US singer

Albert Einstein (1879–1955), US physicist

S. Davis, Jr (1925–), US singer

Henry Morgenthau, Sr (1856–1946), US diplomat

S. Goldwyn (1882–1974),
US producer

Woody Allen (1935–),
US director

Aaron Copland (1900–),
US composer

B. Baruch (1870–1965),
US financier

L. Brandeis (1856–1941),
US jurist

New York: The Immigrant Experience

Where would the Jews or Judaism be today without the two million immigrants, refugees from poverty and pogroms, who poured through the port of New York between 1880 and 1915? The question is a rhetorical one, but on any showing the situation would be very different without them, and probably it would be very bleak. A people without a land still needs to have a base, a kind of headquarters which can offer guidance and support without itself being threatened. There had always been a base of this sort, and for centuries it had been in Europe. But in the 1880s conditions in Europe were becoming less propitious, and we now know that at the end of that trail lay utter destruction. America offered liberty and economic opportunity—neither of which should be taken for granted—together with a powerful intellectual and spiritual stimulus and a possibility of influencing political events worldwide. It was a potent and attractive combination, and the consequence of the mass immigration was (it is no exaggeration to say) the salvation of the Jewish people and the Jewish religion.

The street plan (*right*) is taken from a guidebook published in 1891, in the heyday of the eastern European immigration. The area in which the immigrants first established themselves is at the southern tip of Manhattan Island.

The immigrant arriving from Russia (*below*), after a long, disorienting and nightmarish journey by train and steamship, still has to face the ordeal of the immigration authorities: batteries of questions, medical examinations, language difficulties and total confusion. This will take place on Ellis Island. Then, all being well, to the East Side and, with luck, a job of sorts, a shared room, perhaps an encounter with a long-lost friend or relative from the old country. At one time the Lower East Side was solidly Jewish, and with a population of a million and a half. Now the Jews have mostly been replaced with other immigrants.

✡ cemetery

■ hospital or home

○ educational or charitable institution

⚑ synagogue

◪ Lower East Side: principal reception area for Jews from eastern Europe, 1870–1920

◪ direction of Jewish migration

Below A pushcart peddler on the Lower East Side. The dream of rising from rags to riches came true for only a very few immigrants; the vast majority endured poverty and hardship. Many of them worked in the sweatshops of the garment industry. Conditions of work were often appalling, but the workers hesitated to press for improvements until in 1909 the shirtwaist (blouse) workers called a general strike; from then on labor began to be better organized and better working conditions were gradually achieved. Samuel Gompers, the union leader (*left*), was himself a Jewish immigrant.

Center The Lafayette St offices of HIAS, the guardian angel of the immigrants and one of the first American organizations to be set up by the Russian Jewish immigrants themselves.

Above A Talmud school in Hester Street. Education, traditionally important to Jews, suffered in the struggle for survival.

Gradually standards were improved, community schools were opened, and secular subjects were introduced into the curriculum.

Right Hester Street, in the heart of the Jewish Lower East Side, in 1899. At this time this was the most densely populated area in New York.

United States of America

When the Jewish leaders in Roman Palestine complained in the 3rd century that the Jews of Sassanian Babylonia had neglected their duty of settling in the land of Israel, the Babylonians replied that God had exiled them there on purpose, so that they could "eat dates and study Torah." American Jewry has now inherited the Babylonian mantle from eastern Europe, that powerhouse of Jewish scholarship and creativity. But the eastern European Jews never possessed the prosperity and self-assuredness that are the hallmark of American Jewry.

The case of America is a powerful counterbalance to the vortex of assimilation and alienation which has long perplexed the Jews of Europe. Free and equal almost from the start, the Jews of America have sustained a strong sense of Jewish identity and cohesiveness, while being an authentic and integral part of the country they can truly call theirs. America has made them, and they have made America. There is scarcely an aspect of American life to which Jews have not made a contribution; by the same token, there is scarcely an aspect of Jewish life in America that has not received a characteristically American stamp.

"The majority of our people are composed of minority groups—religious minorities or racial minorities. This diversity of its composition is the strength and richness of America. It is not a melting pot as much as an orchestra." This rosy judgment by a leading Jewish politician, speaking at a civil rights rally in 1954, holds the key to the success of the American Jewish experience. A minority in America is free to be itself, without being suspected of separatism or subversion. In this respect America is virtually unique among the countries of the world. It is hardly surprising that it has long been the most favored country for Jewish immigration.

Numerically, the Jews of America constitute by far the largest Jewish community in the world. The dominant position of America on the world stage endows them with a special role in world Jewish affairs.

There are no reliable figures for the Jewish population of the USA. Estimates of the total population in 1980 ranged between 5·5 and six million. The detailed figures rely heavily on guess-work and are open to substantial revision, but it would seem that more than a third of the total (about two million) live in the New York City Metropolitan Area, and a further half-million in the Los Angeles Metropolitan Area. In all, well over half the Jewish population is located in the northeastern states, which contain little more than 20 percent of the total American population, but the Jewish population of this region shows signs of falling, while in the south and west it is rising.

Jews constitute some 2·6 percent of the total population of the USA, but in several states the percentage is much higher—around 6 percent in New Jersey and the District of Columbia and more than 12 percent in New York State. In New York City the percentage is reckoned at 16, and as much as 20 in Manhattan.

America continues to be a country of Jewish immigration: in recent years the majority have come from Israel, the Soviet Union and Iran. But most American Jews are now native born. Immigration helps to balance a low birthrate, which is close to or even below replacement level. Meanwhile a marked trend towards intermarriage is compensated for by a tendency for non-Jewish marriage partners to be converted to Judaism, and for the children of many mixed unions to be raised as Jews.

The first permanent synagogue building in America was erected in New York in 1730, but the origins of Jewish settlement there go back to the "Jewish Mayflower," a boat called the *Saint Charles* which in 1654 disembarked 23 Jews, fugitives from the Portuguese reconquest of Brazil, in the port of New Amsterdam. By the time of the Revolution there were between 1500 and 3000 Jews in the whole country, mostly of Sephardi stock, well integrated and enjoying a modest prosperity. They already possessed civil rights, and the divorce of Church and State in the revolutionary constitutions removed the test acts debarring non-Christians from holding public office. In the course of the 19th century several Jews entered Congress, the judiciary and the diplomatic service.

Between 1840 and 1880 the Jewish population increased considerably, from an estimated 15000 to more than 250000. The newcomers were known as "Germans," though they hailed from various parts of central Europe. They benefited from the rapidly expanding economy, and from humble beginnings many large fortunes were made. It was a time of geographical expansion too, and whereas earlier settlements had been concentrated on the east coast, Jewish communities now appeared in Chicago and Cincinnati, Saint Louis and San Francisco.

The period of really momentous Jewish immigration began in the 1880s. By 1900 the Jewish population had quadrupled to about one million; by 1910 it was estimated at over two million, by 1914 at almost three million, and in the mid-1920s at four million. The new immigrants came mainly from eastern Europe. They were typically very poor, and they arrived at a time when the old opportunities for trade and small manufacture in the developing territories were giving way to a demand for industrial labor in the fast-growing cities. They tended to congregate in New York and a few other cities such as Philadelphia, Chicago and Boston, and they found employment predominantly in the clothing and tobacco industries, and to some extent in building and retail trades. Despite low wages and frequent unemployment and disease they gradually improved their status by hard work and self-help: they moved out of the crowded ghettos into more salubrious districts, they eagerly took advantage of educational opportunities, and they soon graduated into white-collar occupations and the professions. Of all the immigrant groups, they were the most dramatically successful.

A rising tide of American xenophobia and racialism after World War I produced antisemitic agitation, immigration quotas and a *numerus clausus* in more prestigious universities. The effects were nothing like as severe as they were in Europe at the same time, and the only really damaging consequence was to prevent the immigration of large numbers of desperate refugees from European anti-

semitism. Meanwhile the "Germans" in their turn had established themselves; they were to be found in Congress, state legislatures and city councils, and under the presidency of F.D. Roosevelt (1933–45) several occupied influential positions in the federal government. At the same time the Russian immigrants and their children continued to adapt themselves to the prevailing culture and to improve their economic and social status.

Jews are now well integrated into American society, but they also maintain very high levels of Jewish awareness and community life. They see no contradiction in this, since other minority groups display the same mixture of attitudes. It is favored by the separation of Church and State, combined with total freedom of religion. In 1980 concern began to be expressed about an increasing encroachment of religious issues on American politics, and particularly the assertiveness of the "Christian New Right." At the same time there was a startling outbreak of antisemitic incidents, on a scale unprecedented in decades (about 500 attacks on individuals and property were reported). While it would be disproportionate to attach too much significance to these manifestations of marginal extremism (a Gallup poll in 1981 reported 40 percent of respondents as having a "highly favorable" opinion of Jews, and only 2 percent being "highly unfavorable"), they do indicate a continuing and perhaps mounting problem of intolerance. Relations between State and Church continue to be a sensitive issue, involving such questions as public funding for parochial schools and religious worship and instruction in public schools. In 1983 the New York State Court of Appeal ruled by a narrow majority that Jewish religious marriage contracts can be enforced by state courts, although one of the dissenting judges expressed concern that this would mark an unconstitutional intrusion into Jewish religious questions, an attitude which indicates the depth of sensitivity on this general issue.

Previous page Sukkot in a New York Hasidic synagogue. Hasidism is a good example of the sturdy survival of an immigrant group over several generations.

The early Jewish settlers in America were few in number and were concentrated, like the population generally, on the Atlantic coast. Massive immigration, largely from central Europe, in the period 1820–80 coincided with a rapid westward expansion in America and with the beginnings of industrialization. Jews now spread across the continent, most often as small traders or artisans. There is a grain of truth in this humorous sketch of a "kosher prairie wagon" (*above left*): there were Jewish pioneers, Jewish cowboys, even a few Jewish Indians! Otto Mears (1841–1931; *above*) had been a cowhand and a soldier before settling down to become a prominent railroad builder in Colorado. In the pioneering days few Jews settled on the land; after the start of the great migration from eastern Europe, however, some Jewish farming colonies were set up, like this one in New Jersey (*left*).

Right Most Jews favored the patriot side in the American Revolution. Haym Salomon, a Polish immigrant, was a successful fundraiser for the revolutionary government. On this monument in Chicago he is commemorated together with Robert Morris, founder of the Bank of North America.

Below The bilingual (English and Yiddish) nameplate of the United Jewish Council of the East Side is a nostalgic reminder of the immigration from eastern Europe.

Bottom American servicemen celebrating Yom Kippur during the Vietnam War.

Bottom right Antisemitism has never been as virulent or officially sanctioned in the USA as it has been in Europe and in some Latin American countries. These troopers of the American Nazi Party are guarding their headquarters after an attack by the Jewish Defense League. The date is 1972.

ROBERT MORRIS · GEORGE WASHINGTON · HAYM SALOMON

★ ★ ★

THE GOVERNMENT OF THE UNITED STATES
WHICH GIVES TO BIGOTRY NO SANCTION · TO PERSECUTION
NO ASSISTANCE · REQUIRES ONLY THAT THEY WHO LIVE UNDER
ITS PROTECTION SHOULD DEMEAN THEMSELVES AS GOOD CITIZENS
IN GIVING IT ON ALL OCCASIONS THEIR EFFECTUAL SUPPORT
PRESIDENT GEORGE WASHINGTON 1790

★ ★ ★

Communal organizations

Diversity, arising ultimately from the different backgrounds of immigrant groups, has characterized American Jewry. Among other results, it has always hampered the emergence of unified communal institutions, at both local and national levels. In 1859 a Board of Delegates of American Israelites was set up on the model of the British Board of Deputies. It lasted for 20 years before being absorbed into the Union of American Hebrew Congregations, which in turn signally failed to accomplish its aim of speaking for united American Jewry. A representative body of New York Jews, the New York Kehilla, was established in 1909 after a shocking announcement by the city police commissioner that half the criminals in New York were Jews. It brought together more than 200 different organizations and achieved a good deal in a short time, but died after 13 years' existence.

Of the representative bodies which have succeeded in attracting wide-ranging support the most effective over a long period has been the American Jewish Committee, set up in 1906, at a time of growing antisemitism, by the American Jewish (typically "German") elite, men like the banker Jacob Schiff, Oscar Straus (a founder of Macy's department store and subsequently ambassador to Turkey), the lawyer Louis Marshall and the scholar Cyrus Adler. They were men with established positions in American society and a deepfelt concern for Jewish welfare both at home and abroad. Their concern was not only social and political but also cultural and spiritual. They had already been

responsible for the establishment in 1888 of the Jewish Publication Society of America and in 1892 of the American Jewish Historical Society, and for the revival in 1902 of the Jewish Theological Seminary of America; they had repeatedly interceded with Theodore Roosevelt (president 1901–09) on the subject of Jewish persecution in eastern Europe and had devoted mighty efforts to fundraising on behalf of the victims of the pogroms. The AJC was conceived as an elitist rather than a democratic organization; it favored moderation and the discreet approach. In its distinguished history of involvement in campaigns against discrimination and prejudice it has frequently met with opposition from other groups, particularly those of an outspoken socialist or Zionist complexion.

More vocal and partisan has been the American Jewish Congress, a "grass roots" organization with a decidedly Zionist orientation. But the Zionists have their own organizations, headed by the Zionist Organization of America (founded 1897) and the women's Zionist organization, Hadassa (founded 1912). There is a plethora of other representative bodies, voicing different interests and emphases and pursuing both overlapping and to some extent conflicting aims.

The one organization that has cultivated a mass membership in the USA and engaged in a truly international range of activities is the B'nai B'rith. It began life in 1843 as a fraternal order of Masonic type, but is now a broadly based organization, particularly devoted to combating antisemitism, to youth work and to student counseling.

For variety and vitality American Judaism is unrivaled. Establishment Judaism exists under three distinct labels—Orthodox, Conservative, Reform—each with its own theology, ethos and organizational structure. But all three share basic features of institutional religion, with an inherent instinct for the large and showy. There are many minority strains, however, all different and each catering to different needs, whether it be the need of an immigrant group to conserve its own traditions or the need of a new native-born generation to challenge the traditions inherited from the past. One example of the latter trend is Reconstructionism, a combination of traditional Jewish life-style with a radical theology in which everything is to be questioned. Another is the mushrooming of *havurot*, small groups seeking authentic religious experience in the intimate spontaneity of close personal interrelations. Spontaneity is also visible in the devotions of these Black Jews (*above*) who have blended with their Judaism ingredients from other sources to produce a heady mixture. Their Yom Kippur service displays a rapturous enthusiasm, reminiscent of early Hasidism, which contrasts strikingly with the remote and somewhat theatrical flavor of the Reform temple opposite.

Below The Touro synagogue in Newport, R.I., now designated a national historic site, is a relic of the Sephardi Judaism of the colonial settlers. It was dedicated in 1763 by Isaac Touro, an immigrant from the West Indies. It was a branch of the oldest congregation in North America, Shearith Israel of New York.

Center Yeshivah University was the first general academic institution to be established under Jewish auspices. Originally founded in 1886 as a *yeshivah* on the eastern European model, it now offers a full range of studies from rabbinic training to medicine.

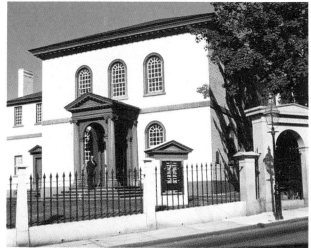

The multiplicity of organizations works well in practice. It reflects certain real differences (although there is an inevitable tendency for institutions to outlive their usefulness), and on crucial issues there is a willingness to pool resources and efforts. Cooperation is visible in the United Jewish Appeal (founded 1939), which channels considerable funds raised in a massive annual campaign into a wide range of deserving causes. Its foremost beneficiary is Israel, which has received enormous sums destined particularly for the absorption of immigrants, but help is given to humanitarian projects in a large number of countries. Two other important organizations which continue the American Jewish tradition of rendering practical assistance to the less fortunate are the Hebrew Immigrant Aid Society (HIAS, founded 1880) and the American Jewish Joint Distribution Committee (JDC, founded 1914). HIAS is a worldwide migration agency which does invaluable practical work in the resettlement and rehabilitation of refugees. Its efforts are not restricted to Jews. In 1981 it spent some 12 million dollars (including US government grants) helping nearly 13000 refugees: more than half were Soviet Jews, but 4000 were non-Jewish refugees, mainly

Immigrant Judaism. These recent newcomers from Soviet Central Asia (*below* and *right*) have established their own community, where their distinctive customs are preserved. Who knows how long such separate communities may last? If past experience is any guide, they may be very durable,

even in the "melting pot" of America.

Center "You don't have to be Jewish . . ." Nowhere else in the world, perhaps, but in New York could such an advertising campaign be mounted.

from Indo-China. The JDC works largely to relieve Jewish hardship overseas—in Israel, North Africa, eastern Europe and elsewhere—but it also offers help to non-Jews: in 1982, for example, it organized emergency supplies for victims of the fighting in Lebanon.

Judaism in the USA

American Judaism is as dynamic, as varied and as unique as American Jewry. It has developed along paths of its own in response to the demands of the American Jewish experience, that is the experience of successive waves of immigrants of very different backgrounds acclimatizing themselves to a free and open society.

The few congregations of the colonial period were Sephardic and traditionalist, looking to London for religious guidance. The "German" immigrations of the 19th century brought Ashkenazi leaders from Europe, schooled in European Jewish modernism, whether Orthodox, like Isaac Leeser of Philadelphia, who was instrumental in founding the first American rabbinic seminary, Maimonides College, or Reform, like Isaac Mayer Wise, founder of the more enduring Hebrew Union College in Cincinnati. The mass of Jewish immigrants were untroubled by doctrinal issues; of adventurous yet compromising temper, they readily introduced the religious reforms which were being fought for so controversially in Germany and which conveniently suited their new living conditions. By 1880 there were over 200 congregations and all but a handful were Reform.

The enormous immigration which followed was mainly from traditionalist Russia. Even though many of the immigrants were avowed secularists

You don't have to be Jewish

to love Levy's
real Jewish Rye

with a rooted aversion to all religion, most were accustomed to the old-style religious institutions of the ghetto. Unable to identify with the American flavor of even the existing Orthodox synagogues they founded their own at a prodigious rate. (Between 1880 and 1890 the number of synagogues in America doubled to over 500.) As the easterners established themselves and moved out of the new ghettos they joined American synagogues, but they also accommodated their own traditional religion to American life in a new style of Orthodoxy, not far removed in practice from the more conservative wing of the older American Judaism. Meanwhile immigrants from the old Ottoman lands introduced a Sephardi traditionalism which was far distant from the ethos of the established American Sephardi synagogues, and they founded synagogues of their own in their new settlements.

The later refugees from Nazi Europe introduced further diversity. They included adherents of the

New York: there are few cities in the world nowadays that can offer the spectacle of a street market selling the "four species" for Sukkot (*far right*). This is a graphic testimony to the vitality of Jewish life in the "New Babylon." The Lubavitch Hasidim have their world headquarters in New York. They are particularly committed to education (*right*) and maintain a worldwide network of schools.

Below A pause for prayer: a religious supervisor in a winery producing millions of gallons of kosher wine which will be certified as fit for Passover use.

Right The head of one of New York's Hasidic dynasties, the Bobover Rebbe, embraces his granddaughter at a wedding.

Below By way of contrast, the first woman rabbi, ordained at the (Reform) Hebrew Union College. This is a development which was anticipated long ago by the Hasidim, but the pioneering first steps were not followed up. With the decision by the Conservative rabbinic seminary to ordain women more than half the pulpits in America are now open, at least in principle, to rabbis of either sex.

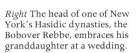

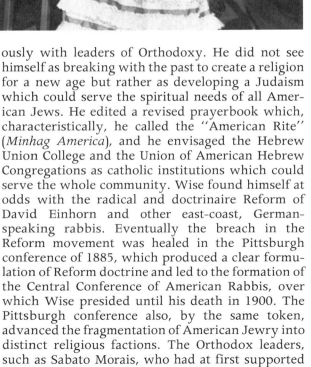

Above These Hasidic children live in Williamsburg. It is the main center of Hasidic life in America, if not in the world.

Right The new ghetto, now voluntary in character, provides for the needs of its own residents and for those of Jews who have moved away into pastures new. This row of shops could have come straight out of the old European ghetto, but notice that the signs are now in English, even if it is an English which is only comprehensible to the initiate.

more evolved forms of European Liberalism, as well as communities of Hasidim with a highly developed folk tradition strongly resistant to external cultural influences. Only the latest waves of immigration, from the Soviet Union and Israel, have had nothing to offer to American Judaism, since they stem from highly assimilated societies in which religion has ceased to be a living force.

The divisions within American Judaism defy neat classification, even if its highly organized institutions (congregational unions, rabbinic assemblies and seminaries) convey a superficial impression of clear dividing lines. It is conventional to distinguish three main trends—Reform, Conservative and Orthodox—but each trend has its own subdivisions and there is a great deal of overlap between them all in religious observance and ideology. They have all accepted influences from each other, as well as from outside (from Zionism, for example, or from developments in Christian theology and worship).

Isaac Wise, the main founder of American Reform, was an experimental and pragmatic reformer who opposed extreme change and worked harmoni-ously with leaders of Orthodoxy. He did not see himself as breaking with the past to create a religion for a new age but rather as developing a Judaism which could serve the spiritual needs of all American Jews. He edited a revised prayerbook which, characteristically, he called the "American Rite" (*Minhag America*), and he envisaged the Hebrew Union College and the Union of American Hebrew Congregations as catholic institutions which could serve the whole community. Wise found himself at odds with the radical and doctrinaire Reform of David Einhorn and other east-coast, German-speaking rabbis. Eventually the breach in the Reform movement was healed in the Pittsburgh conference of 1885, which produced a clear formulation of Reform doctrine and led to the formation of the Central Conference of American Rabbis, over which Wise presided until his death in 1900. The Pittsburgh conference also, by the same token, advanced the fragmentation of American Jewry into distinct religious factions. The Orthodox leaders, such as Sabato Morais, who had at first supported the Hebrew Union College, founded in 1886 a more

conservative rabbinical college, the Jewish Theological Seminary (Leeser's Maimonides College having collapsed in 1873). Even then, some Orthodox Jews regretted the creation of the new seminary, and argued that Reform influence should be combated from within the Hebrew Union College.

The Jewish Theological Seminary did not long survive as an Orthodox establishment. In 1902 it was reorganized with a new purpose: to train English-speaking rabbis of a conservative mold to serve the eastern European immigrants. Those responsible for this undertaking were primarily Reform Jews. Their aim was not to spread Reform Judaism among the immigrants but to help to acculturate and Americanize them. They recognized that Reform Judaism would have little appeal to them, but expected that the naturalized traditionalism of the Seminary would become the religion of the immigrants, while Reform would continue as that of the longer-settled Jews. The Seminary soon became, under the charismatic guidance of its president Solomon Schechter, an outstanding center of Jewish learning and the powerhouse of that uniquely American compromise, Conservative Judaism. In 1913 the leaders and graduates of the Seminary created the United Synagogue of America as the congregational arm of the new movement. The name speaks for the catholic aims of the enterprise, reminiscent of Wise's attempt to create a central "Hebrew Union." A proposal to call the new body the "Union of Conservative Congregations" was rejected as being too sectarian.

Meanwhile a different initiative in dealing with the immigrant problem had led to the establishment in 1898 of the Union of Orthodox Jewish Congregations. Most of the founders were associated with the Seminary, but the Union was soon taken over by the immigrants who were unhappy with the Conservative ethos. They also founded the *yeshivot* which were the acorns from which the decidedly American Orthodox seminaries were to grow, the New York Yeshivah (now Yeshivah University) and the Hebrew Theological College of Chicago. Their rabbinical graduates mainly belong to the Rabbinical Council of America, founded in 1923, and to be distinguished from the more traditionalist Union of Orthodox Rabbis of America and Canada (the *Aggudas ho-Rabbonim*), formed by Yiddish-speaking immigrant rabbis in 1902. Traditional eastern European Judaism was greatly strengthened by the immigrants of the 1930s and 1940s. One of them, Rabbi Aaron Kotler, set up a notable old-style *yeshivah* in Lakewood, New Jersey. Many of its graduates have set up *yeshivot* of their own, but few have become congregational rabbis: they prefer to cultivate talmudic learning for its own sake. Meanwhile, following the general trend of congregational associations, the Union of Sephardic Congregations was established in 1929.

The obvious divisions within the Orthodox-traditionalist camp illustrate one aspect of the internal divisions which exist within all the different trends. Here it is mainly a matter of the permissible degree of Americanization and cooperation with other religious Jews. (The Union of Orthodox Jewish Congregations and the Rabbinical Council belong, with the corresponding Conservative and Reform bodies, to the Synagogue Council of America; the *Aggudas ho-Rabbonim* rarely collaborates with any other group.) For Reform, after the Pittsburgh reunion, the main bone of contention was for a long time Zionism. Classical Reform was inherently anti-Zionist, even though it had many Zionists among its adherents. In 1922 Stephen Wise, one of the most outstanding and controversial figures in the history of American Judaism and a leading figure in the American Jewish Congress, founded the Jewish Institute of Religion to train Reform (and indeed Conservative and Orthodox) rabbis in a Zionist atmosphere. Most of the graduates of the Institute joined the Central Conference of American Rabbis, which gradually became more favorable to Zionism and in 1942 passed a resolution approving the establishment of a Jewish army in Palestine. Several dozen rabbis seceded at that time, deploring the "growing emphasis upon the racial and nationalistic aspect of Jewish thought," and founded the anti-Zionist American Council for Judaism. Once the Jewish state was a reality, such anti-Zionism seemed increasingly anachronistic and isolated. The Jewish

Jews play their full part, of course, in the democratic processes of American life, even while giving expression to certain political interests of their own.
Below A rabbi and his wife, delegates to the 1980 Democratic Convention.
Right Solidarity with Israel: an Israel Independence Day parade in New York.
Below right Solidarity with Soviet Jewry: an all-night vigil in Los Angeles.

Institute of Religion was merged with the Hebrew Union College and eventually a campus was established in Jerusalem. The Reform movement still has its radical and conservative wings, and conflict is apparent on such issues as rabbinic officiation at mixed marriages and active proselytism outside the Jewish fold. In matters of ritual Reform Judaism has moved discernibly towards a more traditional flavor, and this change too has occasioned some controversy.

Conservative Judaism was from the start an alliance between liberal traditionalists and traditionalist liberals, and even today the tension between the two wings can be felt. (It came noticeably into the open in the 1960s and 1970s over the issue of the ordination of women.) Conservatism represents an eminently practical compromise in matters of ritual and religious law, and this is the source of its strength and popularity, but it is weak on ideology. It has, however, given birth to one important ideological innovation in the form of the Reconstructionism of Mordecai Kaplan, who argued forcefully against all the prevailing expressions of Judaism and in favor of a new approach, which abandons the starting point of belief in a personal God and the divine election of Israel and sees

Judaism as a civilization in which organized religion is only one element.

Kaplan's emphasis on the ''organic community'' rather than the religious congregation as the basic unit in corporate Jewish life comes closer than any alternative formulation to furnishing a theoretical basis for the practical reality of Jewish existence, and in fact American congregations of all denominations have tended increasingly to conform to his description. The synagogue has become a community center, the locus for a wide range of activities, not all of them overtly religious. Religious observance as a regular feature of daily life is rare outside the rabbinate and the small traditionalist communities, but there is a widespread and strong attachment to rites of passage (circumcision, *bar* and *bat mitzvah*, religious marriage and burial) and to certain festivals (high holy days, Passover, Hanukkah) which focus on Jewish identity and its transmission from one generation to the next. There are signs of young people actively seeking a richer appreciation of traditional rituals and creating new forms of religious self-expression, but even this interest appears to derive from a sense of a distinctive Jewish identity coupled with an urge to rediscover lost roots.

Canada

It is tempting to compare Canada with the United States. There are certainly superficial similarities in the Jewish experience, especially in terms of patterns of immigration and settlement, and there are also close personal and institutional links between Canadian and American Jewry. But the comparison may be misleading. Canada's political history is very different from that of the United States, and there is a totally different relationship between the many and varied ethnic groups. Whereas American Jews think of themselves primarily as Americans, Canadian Jews have tended to see themselves as first and foremost Jews. Zionism has been much stronger in Canada, and anti-Zionism all but nonexistent. But Jews have made their contribution to Canada too, at all levels and most notably in the field of literature.

In 1867, when the four provinces of Ontario, Quebec, New Brunswick and Nova Scotia were united to form the Dominion of Canada, the Jewish population numbered about 1000. The largest community was in Montreal; its oldest synagogue was about to celebrate its centenary, and it traced its origins back to the British conquest in 1759. Many of the Jews in Quebec Province were of British extraction, and despite family ties with the Thirteen Colonies they had mainly been loyal to Britain during the crises of the American Revolution, the American invasion of 1812 and the 1837 rebellion. They had been granted full civil rights in 1832, well ahead of parallel developments in Britain. They were highly integrated in local society and had already made an important contribution to the life of the province. The Jews of Ontario were scattered through a number of towns and were mostly more recent settlers from the continent of Europe. Far to the west there were 100 Jews in the colony of British Columbia, who had arrived from California, England and Australia during the gold rush of 1858. Their synagogue building at Victoria, erected in 1863, is now the oldest in Canada.

But, as in the USA, it was the eastern European emigrants from 1881 onwards who laid the foundations for the present large Jewish community. Between 1881 and 1891 the Jewish population rose from 2400 to 6400 and by 1921 it was over 126 000 out of a total population of nearly nine million. Most of the immigrants settled in Montreal and Toronto, where they tended to concentrate in dense voluntary ghettos, but many traveled across the plains to the growing towns of the west. Winnipeg soon established itself as the third largest Jewish community, with 14 500 Jews by 1921. Meanwhile some agricultural settlements had been established, with help from the Jewish Colonization Association, in Manitoba, Saskatchewan and Alberta.

The 1931 census showed that there were 156 726 Jews in Canada, forming 1·5 percent of the total population (a proportion which has remained virtually constant ever since). There were obvious irregularities in the pattern of Jewish settlement compared to the general trends. The Jews were almost exclusively urban, in stark contrast to the general population, and well over half of them were concentrated in Montreal and Toronto. The provinces of Ontario and Quebec accounted together for

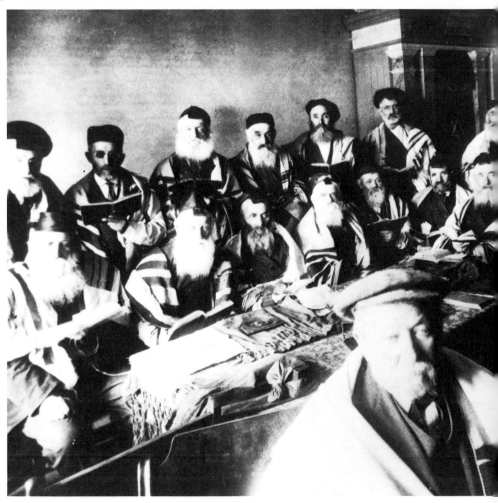

Left Jewish farm settlement began in the early 1890s, through the initiative of the Baron de Hirsch Fund and the Jewish Colonization Association. By 1930, 100 000 acres were under cultivation by Jewish farmers in western Canada.

The Holy Blossom Temple in Toronto (*below*) has its origins in the small-scale immigration of the 1840s. Then there were only a handful of Jews in Toronto: now it is a thriving community of over 100 000, with some 40 synagogues and ten Jewish schools, including the Associated Hebrew Schools where this

Hanukkah ceremony is being held (*left*).

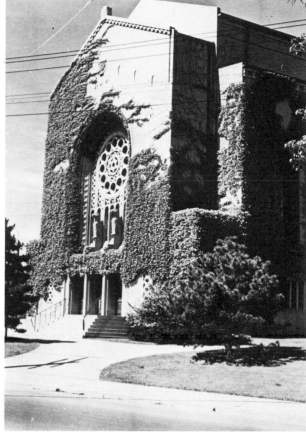

The Jewish presence in Winnipeg dates from 1882 and derives from the great eastern European immigration. By 1900 it had established its position as the third strongest community in Canada.
Above A religious service in the Old Folks' Home, c. 1922.
Top left A slogan in Yiddish and English at a May Day parade, 1932.

nearly 80 percent of the Jews, but only 60 percent of all Canadians. Twelve percent of the Jews lived in Manitoba, as against less than 7 percent of the total population. The immigrant character of the Jewish population was also apparent. Although by now 44 percent of the Jews were born in Canada, 47 percent were born in eastern Europe and 95 percent (in many places over 99 percent) named Yiddish as their mother tongue. On the other hand only some 3 percent said they could not speak English. By 1941 the picture had changed considerably. A majority of the Jews (51 percent) were Canadian-born and only 77 percent gave Yiddish as their mother tongue, the percentage in some places being 55 or less.

The 1930s were a time of immigration restrictions (fewer than 1000 Jews were admitted annually, and in some years emigration exceeded immigration) and, for the first time, of vocal antisemitism. Both trends were actively combated by the representative body, the Canadian Jewish Congress. But, apart from some 2000 "enemy alien" internees from Germany and Austria admitted at the beginning of the war and subsequently released (they included some distinguished academics, rabbis and creative artists), immigration was severely restricted until 1947. Then Canada agreed to accept a number of displaced persons, including over 1000 war orphans and groups of tailors and furriers brought in under special arrangements with the clothing industry. Throughout the 1950s immigration continued at a higher level. Several thousand Jews were among the Hungarian refugees accepted in 1956, and a new type of Jewish immigrant began to appear in the form of French-speaking Jews from North Africa. More recently Canada, like the USA (though on a smaller scale), has given a home to immigrants from the Soviet Union and Israel.

All the immigrant groups have established themselves well and responded to new opportunities. The only serious source of anxiety has been the francophone separatist movement in Quebec. A noticeable exodus of young Jews from the province has been reported, and the rejection of separatism in the 1980 referendum has not entirely quelled fears for the future.

Canadian Judaism conforms more closely to the British than to the American model, in that the large majority of synagogues are Orthodox and only a small minority (including most of those founded before the eastern European immigrations) are Conservative or Reform. But whereas in earlier times Canadian synagogues tended to look to Britain for rabbinic leadership and guidance, their closest links now are with the USA. The synagogal associations and rabbinic bodies follow the American pattern, and tend to be associated with their American equivalents.

Like Britain and unlike the USA, there is a single representative body, the Canadian Jewish Congress (founded 1919), which concerns itself with the welfare of the community and provides a unified voice for Canadian Jewry. The diverse Zionist organizations have worked harmoniously together, and cooperate in the Canadian Zionist Federation. As in the USA, fundraising is channeled through a United Jewish Appeal, which devotes most of its efforts to Israel but also benefits local causes.

A unique feature of Canadian Jewry is the strong emphasis on Jewish education. All communities of any size have at least one Jewish day school, and the schools are very successful in attracting pupils. The Associated Hebrew Schools in Toronto (whose origins go back to the beginning of the century) is one of the largest Jewish schools in the world, with nearly 3000 pupils in 1982.

LATIN AMERICA

Each of the countries of Latin America has its own distinctive history and character, but they all bear the marks of the long centuries of European colonial rule, from the arrival of the Spaniards and Portuguese early in the 16th century to the wars of independence in the early 19th century. Independence opened the countries to immigration and economic development, and brought about important changes in the social structure, notably the growth of cities and of a new commercial and industrial governing class. It is these modern developments that have shaped the Jewish communities of the region.

Jews first arrived from Europe in the West Indies with Christopher Columbus in 1492, the year of the expulsion from Spain. During the centuries of Spanish and Portuguese rule Judaism was officially banned in the American colonies, and for much of the time even descendants of Jews were forbidden entry. Nevertheless there was some immigration of New Christians who kept up their Judaism in secret, and they made a notable contribution to the development of the colonies. They may even have spread their religious beliefs among the natives, some of whom profess to be Jews to this day. The Catholic Inquisition, however, maintained a close watch on Judaizing tendencies, and numbers of alleged Judaizers were apprehended and tried.

It was only in the small English, Dutch and French possessions that Judaism could be practiced openly. From 1631 to 1654 there was a thriving Jewish community in Recife, the capital of Dutch Brazil, consisting of New Christians who had returned to Judaism and new immigrants from Holland. After the Portuguese reconquest these Sephardim dispersed to other places, laying the foundations for the communities of Surinam and Curaçao, Barbados and Jamaica, and even New York.

With independence the Inquisition was abolished in the Latin colonies and freedom of religion was gradually introduced, although Roman Catholicism has always maintained its dominance. The Jews were not specifically emancipated (they were too few to constitute a political issue), but rather benefited from legislation framed with Protestant minorities in mind.

Jewish immigration was slow to respond to the opportunities offered by the independent republics, and it was not until the last years of the 19th century that large waves of immigrants arrived, although Mexico received some Austrian and western European settlers under the emperor Maximilian (1864–67). Between 1880 and 1914 130000 Jews arrived, the large majority settling in Argentina. About 20 percent were Sephardim from North Africa, the Balkans and the Ottoman empire; the rest were Ashkenazim from central and eastern Europe. The immigrants were mostly attracted to the larger towns, but there was some settlement in rural areas, especially in Argentina (and to a lesser extent Brazil), where agricultural colonies were established under the auspices of the Jewish Colonization Association. The exploitation of undeveloped regions provided excellent opportunities for immigrants with experience of trade and manufacture, and gradual industrialization provided further openings, so that many Jews who started as pedlars or laborers were soon able to improve their social and economic status.

After World War I immigration continued at an average rate of about 10000 a year until 1940, when Jewish immigration was severely restricted. The majority continued to settle in Argentina and Brazil, but Uruguay also received large numbers: it is now one of the few countries in the world where Jews constitute more than one percent of the total population. The countries which attracted most Jewish immigration were typically those that had high European and urban populations and more developed economies. Since World War II there has been much less immigration and rather more emigration, either from one country to another within the region or to the USA and Israel. The Jews continued to improve their economic status, and they generally belong now to the relatively small middle class. They are prominent in commerce and manufacturing industry, and many have entered the liberal professions, but very few have made a mark in political life. In several countries nationalist sentiment, coupled with economic grievances and religious prejudice, has been hostile to the Jewish minority, and antisemitism, promoted by Nazi refugees from Europe and more recently by Arabs, has made itself felt in publications and occasionally in legislation or in acts of violence. On the whole, however, the Jewish communities have been well tolerated, even at times of national upheaval.

Each of the various indigenous and immigrant groups in Latin America has tended to maintain a strong sense of its own identity, and the Jews are no exception. In fact the different groups of Jewish immigrants have developed their own institutions which tended to persist despite attempts to form overall Jewish organizations. Early associations were primarily religious, centering on the synagogues, which provided a social focus for immigrants sharing a common origin. The religious organizations still reflect differences not only between Ashkenazim and Sephardim, but between Spanish- and Arabic-speaking Sephardim or between Yiddish- and German-speaking Ashkenazim, or even between settlers from specific regions or towns of Europe and the Middle East. Beginning in the 1950s the American Conservative movement has established synagogues in many countries, and more recently there has also been some growth in Reform Judaism. Alongside religious associations various kinds of secular organizations have been set up, beginning with ideological clubs (mainly Bundist, Zionist or Communist) founded by eastern European immigrants. These maintained social and

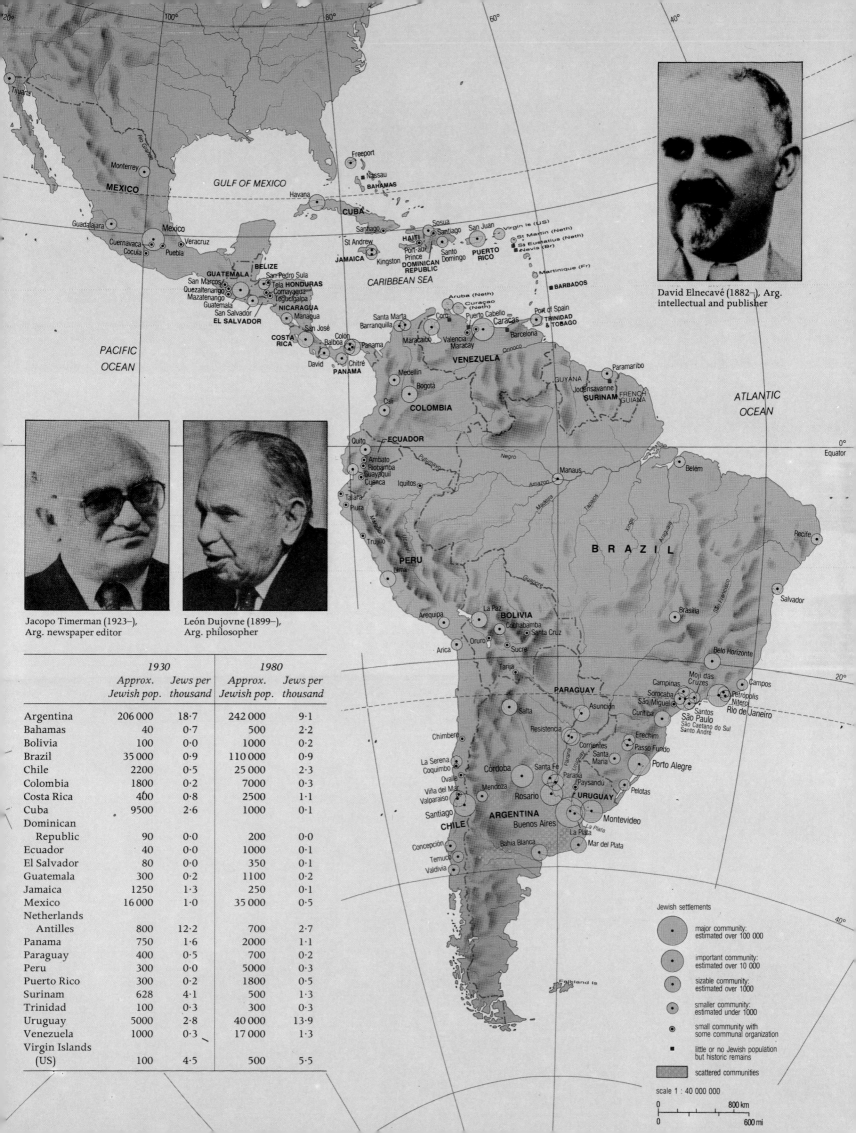

David Elnecavé (1882–), Arg. intellectual and publisher

Jacopo Timerman (1923–), Arg. newspaper editor

León Dujovne (1899–), Arg. philosopher

	1930		1980	
	Approx. Jewish pop.	Jews per thousand	Approx. Jewish pop.	Jews per thousand
Argentina	206 000	18·7	242 000	9·1
Bahamas	40	0·7	500	2·2
Bolivia	100	0·0	1000	0·2
Brazil	35 000	0·9	110 000	0·9
Chile	2200	0·5	25 000	2·3
Colombia	1800	0·2	7000	0·3
Costa Rica	400	0·8	2500	1·1
Cuba	9500	2·6	1000	0·1
Dominican Republic	90	0·0	200	0·0
Ecuador	40	0·0	1000	0·1
El Salvador	80	0·0	350	0·1
Guatemala	300	0·2	1100	0·2
Jamaica	1250	1·3	250	0·1
Mexico	16 000	1·0	35 000	0·5
Netherlands Antilles	800	12·2	700	2·7
Panama	750	1·6	2000	1·1
Paraguay	400	0·5	700	0·2
Peru	300	0·0	5000	0·3
Puerto Rico	300	0·2	1800	0·5
Surinam	628	4·1	500	1·3
Trinidad	100	0·3	300	0·3
Uruguay	5000	2·8	40 000	13·9
Venezuela	1000	0·3	17 000	1·3
Virgin Islands (US)	100	4·5	500	5·5

Jewish settlements

· major community: estimated over 100 000

· important community: estimated over 10 000

· sizable community: estimated over 1000

· smaller community: estimated under 1000

· small community with some communal organization

■ little or no Jewish population but historic remains

scattered communities

scale 1 : 40 000 000

0   800 km

0   600 mi

cultural activities, including schools and Yiddish newspapers. Numerous *Landsmannschaften* (associations of immigrants from a particular European community) also appeared. With the rise of a younger native-born generation a new type of association has grown up, based on sporting and cultural activities, and these have proved very popular as an expression of Jewish identity. The growth of antisemitism has encouraged the development of regional or national organizations to coordinate activities and make corporate representations to the government; they are affiliated to the World Jewish Congress. But the tendency towards centralization has not, as yet, diminished the colorful variety of Jewish communal organizations.

As the immigrant generation gives way to new generations born in the land, the maintenance of a distinct Jewish identity becomes increasingly problematical. The strong emphasis on Jewish culture and education, coupled with parental pressure on children to seek marriage partners within the community, does serve to bolster this identity, as does the persistence of antisemitic sentiment and the existence in some countries of other groups with their own social and cultural ties. But, as in other parts of the world, increasing social integration makes a separate identity difficult to sustain, even with the concerted efforts of the Zionist agencies. The earliest immigrant groups have long since disappeared through intermarriage and conversion, and a similar fate threatens many of the smaller contemporary communities. Political and economic difficulties have led to Jewish emigration from some countries. Nevertheless, despite the lack of precise statistics, it would appear that most of the larger communities (with the exception of Argentina) are numerically stable at present or even showing a modest growth, due mainly to immigration.

Argentina

It could be said that modern Argentina was created by the European population explosion of the late 19th century, which by its demand for cheap food encouraged the agricultural development of the pampas and at the same time provided the human labor necessary for this development. In the early 1850s the white population was little over a million, and Buenos Aires had only 90000 inhabitants. Between 1857, when the first railroad was built, and 1930 more than six million immigrants arrived, almost all of them from Europe, and after the economic and political crisis of the 1930s and World War II immigration on a large scale was resumed for a few years. The population is now 28 million, and Buenos Aires, with a population of nearly 10 million, is one of the largest cities in the world.

Jewish immigration, after slow beginnings, began in earnest in the late 1880s. Between 1881 and 1900 some 26000 arrived, and a further 88000 between 1901 and 1914. Immigration continued through the 1920s and 1930s, under increasingly severe restrictions. The 1947 census showed 250000 Jews in a total population of nearly 16 million, the 1960 census 276000 in a total of 20 million. (The reliability of the figures for Jews has been disputed, and some Jewish authorities claim a population of 400000–500000.)

Many of the immigrants were attracted to the pampas, particularly after Baron de Hirsch negotiated with the Russian and Argentinian governments an agreement providing for the emigration of Russian Jews to specifically Jewish colonization projects in 1892. Large numbers of such colonies were established, and by 1925 there were over 30000 Jews farming over a million and a half acres. But the projects were beset with difficulties, and few Jews now remain on the land. Two-thirds of the Jewish population live in the capital, and there are sizable communities in most of the main cities.

Although poverty has not been eradicated entirely, the Jews have made rapid economic progress. They have contributed greatly to the industrialization of the country and have been active in commerce and finance. They are generally in the middle and upper economic classes, but although a few have become provincial governors or even government ministers, they have played little real part in the government of the country, which in any case has been rather irregular in recent years.

The constitution of 1853 guaranteed freedom of religion for all residents of Argentina, although Roman Catholicism remains the country's official religion. Antisemitism was virtually unknown until the Russian Jews fell victim to an upsurge of anti-Bolshevik feeling in the ruling circles after 1917. In January 1919, following a general strike, Jews were beaten up and robbed in full view of the police, in scenes reminiscent of the milder excesses of the Russian pogroms. In the 1930s antisemitism, fomented by German Nazis, became a serious problem, which led to the setting up of DAIA (Delegación de Asociaciones Israelitas Argentinas), a representative political organization uniting both Ashkenazi and Sephardi Jews. Antisemitic agitation increased with the influx of Nazi refugees after the war, despite the helpful attitude of President Perón and the inclusion in the 1949 constitution of a clause explicitly outlawing racial discrimination. The kidnapping of the Nazi war criminal Adolf Eichmann in Argentina and his execution in Israel in 1961 provoked an escalation of antisemitic activity, which successive governments did nothing to quell in practice, despite repeated protestations of concern. After the military coup in March 1976 there were many

Jewish agricultural settlement in Argentina was begun during the great migration from eastern Europe. The first agricultural colony, Moisesville (*above*) was founded in 1889, under the auspices of the Alliance Israélite Universelle. Subsequently Baron de Hirsch and his ICA (Jewish Colonization Association) took the leading initiative, with the eventual aim of creating an autonomous Jewish region. The location of the colonies is shown on the map *below*.

Right Argentinian agriculture has been much enriched by the contribution of the agricultural cooperatives originally formed with the support of the ICA.

The Jewish gauchos (*above*) were the subject of the first book to be written in Spanish by an Argentine Jew, Alberto Gerchunoff. Although the ambitious aims of the ICA project were never realized, the settlements played an important role in the absorption of immigrants, and in the development of the cooperative movement.
Right An old photograph of a school outing. The school is named for I. L. Peretz, the famous Yiddish writer.

attacks on Jews and Jewish institutions, and Jews were represented disproportionately among the 20 000 or more people who "disappeared" (although it is a matter for debate how far this reflected official antisemitism). In 1981 the president, General Viola, gave assurances that his government would end the antisemitic incidents, and the following year his successor, General Galtieri, expressed similar sentiments after a cemetery was painted with swastikas, but no positive action was taken.

Although there are numerous synagogues, of every conceivable variety, the low level of religious observance has often caused comment. Against the trend in most countries, even the high holy day services do not succeed in attracting many congregants, and there are few rabbis in the country. A notable development was the opening in 1962 of the Latin American Rabbinic Seminary, associated with the Jewish Theological Seminary of America. Graduates of the seminary are serving congregations in several South American countries. Most Jews, however, appear to identify socially rather than religiously or even culturally. The once flourishing Yiddish press is all but defunct and Jewish schools are attracting fewer pupils and little financial support; the Jewish content of their curriculum is often negligible. If present trends continue, Argentinian Jewry is likely to be very much reduced in the next generation through intermarriage and assimilation, assuming that continued economic and political uncertainty does not lead to a mass exodus.

Brazil

After Argentina it was Brazil that received most Jewish immigration to Latin America, and here too agricultural colonies were established by the Jewish Colonization Association. Their demise was even more speedy and complete than in Argentina. Most of Brazil's Jewish population is divided between the two largest cities, Rio de Janeiro and São Paolo. The smaller community of Pôrto Alegre was established by former agricultural settlers from the nearby colonies of Philippson and Quatro Irmãos. The first synagogue in Brazil was actually founded far to the north, in Belém, by Moroccan immigrants in 1824, and other small Moroccan communities developed in the northern provinces in the course of the 19th century, but the large majority of Brazil's Jews are of Ashkenazi origin. The new federal capital, Brasilia, has begun to attract a small Jewish presence, beginning with the Israeli embassy. Jewish immigration continues at a modest rate.

Brazil traditionally has a relaxed and tolerant attitude to ethnic differences, and Jews have fitted in well. They have played a full part in the political life of the country at all levels, and are active in the arts and sciences, as well as in pioneering industrial development.

Antisemitism has been almost nonexistent, and Brazil has enjoyed good relations with Israel. As in Argentina, there is a wide range of synagogues (the largest being Conservative), and there are numerous Jewish sporting and social clubs.

Uruguay

The other countries in South America have much smaller Jewish communities. The largest is in Uruguay, a country unusual in the continent for its liberal traditions, high literacy and virtually all-white population. There is complete freedom of religion and no established church. The older immigrant groups have been largely assimilated, and the Jews are no exception, but a considerable proportion of them are first-generation immigrants who retain a strong sense of Jewish identity. A few Jews have been involved in politics but they are generally absent from the highest social levels, and from the military, which has effectively ruled the country since 1973. There has been some antisemitic activity, often associated with Nazi cells having connections with Argentina, but on the whole the Jews are well integrated and Uruguay has maintained excellent relations with Israel. A few agricultural projects initiated in the east of the country have not succeeded, and the large majority of the Jewish population is concentrated in the capital, which has a number of Jewish schools of different affiliations, and four separate religious communities, Ashkenazi, Sephardi, German-speaking and Hungarian.

Zionism has a long and important history in South America, and governments in the region have taken a sympathetic interest in Israel. Uruguay's large Jewish community has shown strong support for the Jewish state, witnessed by the enthusiastic welcome accorded to President Shazar during his visit in 1966 (*right, center*) and by the demonstration of support at the time of the Six Day War in 1967 (*right*).

Right São Paolo has a strong Jewish community of some 50 000 souls, with 20 synagogues representing a variety of different denominations.

Below Brazil has enjoyed friendly relations with Israel. In fact it was a Brazilian statesman, Oswaldo Aranha, who presided over the UN General Assembly which voted in 1947 for the partition of Palestine, and so for a Jewish state. A street in Tel Aviv has been named for him, while in Rio de Janeiro a square has been named for Israel's first president, Chaim Weizmann.

Left Brazil, like Argentina, was selected by the ICA for agricultural settlement, but the results were less successful. The colony at Quatro Irmaos was initiated in 1909, and struggled on through a painful series of setbacks until, after 50 years, it was eventually decided to wind it up.

religion from New Christians in the colonial period. In the 1930s there was an important influx of German refugees, and there is also a Hungarian element. Antisemitism has found fertile ground in Chile, which is riven by internal conflicts and has attracted both Nazi and Arab immigration. In the social and economic chaos under the Marxist government of Salvador Allende (1970–73) many Jews left the country, but some have returned under the more stable military regime of General Pinochet, whose strict censorship has had the incidental effect of stilling the voice of the formerly legal antisemitic periodicals. Assimilation has been strong—the intermarriage rate is assessed at about 30 percent. Nonetheless there is a large number of Jewish organizations, particularly in the capital, where more than 90 percent of Chile's Jews live.

Venezuela

In Venezuela the early constitutions (of 1819 and 1821), promulgated during the struggle for independence, established freedom of religion and this encouraged some Jewish immigration from Curaçao (where Simón Bolívar, the liberator, had found refuge in Jewish homes during the war). Organized communities were slow to develop and the settlers eventually abandoned Judaism, but they have left behind a number of old cemeteries, one of which has been restored as a national monument. Until 1958 a long series of liberal constitutions was punctuated by harsh dictatorships, which several times imposed restrictions on Jewish immigration, but Venezuela (the richest country in Latin America thanks to its oil revenues) has continued to attract Jews, both from Europe and the Middle East and from other South American countries.

Above The Ashkenazi Great Synagogue in Caracas. The city has experienced dramatic growth since the war, and its Jewish community too has expanded considerably. It now stands at about 10 000. Sephardim and Ashkenazim maintain separate synagogues, but they come together in communal and Zionist organizations, and in supporting the large Jewish day school.

Chile

Chile's tempestuous history has not provided comfortable conditions for a secure Jewish existence. The conservative constitution of 1833 established Roman Catholicism, and it was not until 1925 that full freedom of religious observance was allowed to non-Catholics. Early Jewish settlers tended to adopt the dominant religion, or else disguise their associations under evasive names. They included Ashkenazim from Argentina and Sephardim from Macedonia. In 1919 the first Congress of Chilean Jews brought together representatives of both groups, and also of the "Hijos de Sión," Judaizing Indians claiming to have received their

Other Countries in South America

Colombia, Ecuador, Peru, Bolivia and Paraguay have a similar history of Jewish settlement, on a much smaller scale. There was a notable influx of refugees from Nazi Europe, but many lingered only briefly before moving on to Argentina and other countries. Their Jewish populations are now insignificant, although a fair number of synagogues and communal organizations remain. The Guianas have never attracted much Jewish immigration, but there was some settlement in the 17th century. Surinam in fact claims the oldest permanent Jewish settlement in the western hemisphere (dating back to 1639); it still has a small community in Paramaribo, and the synagogue at Jodensavanne ("Jews' Savanna") has been restored as a tourist sight.

Mexico

In 1960 Mexico's census recorded 110750 Jews (*Israelitas*), but this figure includes adherents of some extreme Protestant sects whose members are not generally regarded as Jews except by themselves. In the absence of other dependable statistics it is estimated that there are some 35000 Jews of a more recognizable type, of whom some 20000 are of eastern European origin and the rest Sephardi, Syrian, German, Hungarian and American. Each of the ethnic groups maintains its own communal institutions, but there are some larger organizations, of which the most successful are those directed to the younger generation—a sports club with a membership of over 25000 and a comprehensive network of schools. The religious spectrum ranges from the highly traditionalist Aleppo community to the Conservative, but religious observance is generally lax. The Jews, who mostly arrived in the country between the two world wars, benefited from the economic prosperity of the 1940s and 1950s, but have suffered from lingering antisemitism. The government has traditionally enjoyed good relations with the Jewish community and with Israel. In 1982, however, Jews voiced anxiety because of the country's economic problems and a mood of hostility to Israel following the war in Lebanon.

One of the curiosities of Mexico is the presence of several different groups of Indians or *mestizos* calling themselves "Israelites" and practicing some Jewish rites. The *Israelitas* of Venta Prieta (*center and below*) have claimed to be descended from the Carvajal family, several of whom were burned at the stake by the Inquisition in 1596.

Curaçao. Congregation Mikveh Israel was founded in 1651, but the present synagogue (*left*) was completed in 1732. It is still the oldest synagogue in continuous use in the New World, and its 250th anniversary in 1982 was celebrated with a formal service (*far left*) attended by Dutch government officials.

Above The Emanuel synagogue in Curaçao, founded in 1864.

Left Out of a population of over 10 000 before the 1959 revolution, only about 1000 Jews remain in Cuba.

Central American Republics

The communities of the six Central American republics, which together number only a few thousand souls, have been linked since 1964 in the Federation of Jewish Communities of Central America. Following the pattern of settlement in South America, the largest concentration is in Costa Rica, with its high standard of living and mainly white population, while at the other extreme Honduras, Nicaragua and El Salvador, underdeveloped and largely *mestizo*, have attracted very few Jews. Political and military conflicts have also deterred settlement in these countries; the small community of Nicaragua departed after the left-wing coup in 1979. Costa Rica and Guatemala in particular have enjoyed cordial relations with Israel; their Jewish communities, despite local antisemitism, have experienced a certain stability. The community of Panama, which is predominantly Sephardi, is well integrated, and has made notable contributions to the culture and political life of the country. There is also a small presence of American Jews in the Canal Zone.

The Caribbean

The West Indies have a very varied and interesting Jewish history, going back to the 17th century, when refugees from the Portuguese reconquest of Dutch Brazil settled in a number of islands under Dutch, English or French rule, and even in Spanish Cuba. They played an important part in the trade of the region, and relics of their settlements can still be seen in Curaçao, Barbados and other places. The community of Curaçao traces an uninterrupted history back to 1651, and the Jews have been very prominent in the island's affairs. But most of the settlements were less permanent. The French ex-

Above This fountain for washing hands formerly graced the courtyard of the synagogue in Bridgetown, Barbados. In 1680, out of 405 householders in Bridgetown 54 were Jews. But the original Sephardi community declined sharply in the 19th century, and its last member died in 1934. In the following years a few refugees from Nazi Europe established a small Ashkenazi community which still exists.

Left A Jewish lady of Panama in her home. The central photograph on the wall behind her shows her brother-in-law, one of several Jewish governors of the Virgin Islands.

pelled the Jews from their colonies in 1683 and there were other upheavals later. The communities in any case tended to dwindle with the changing fortunes of the islands, and the ones which exist today are generally the result of fresh immigration in the past hundred years, from the troubles in Europe and more recently from the USA to its own possessions, Puerto Rico and the Virgin Islands, and to the Bahamas. Cuba, which had an American community with a Reform synagogue at the beginning of this century, soon received some immigrants from the Near East, and subsequently became a port of transit for large numbers of Jews from eastern Europe on their way to the USA. American immigration restrictions led to the buildup of a considerable Ashkenazi presence in the course of the 1920s, which was augmented by the arrival of thousands of refugees from Nazi Europe between 1933 and 1944. After the war there were well over 10 000 Jews widely dispersed over the island, although the majority lived in Havana. From meager beginnings they made very good economic progress, and most of them opted to emigrate after the 1959 revolution, mainly to the USA. The smaller numbers who had found refuge from Nazism in Haiti and the Dominican Republic have also now mostly left, and political uncertainty has recently reduced the once large and prosperous community of Jamaica to a mere handful.

EUROPE

The history of the Jews in modern Europe is totally dominated by the Nazi holocaust. In 1930 Europe (excluding Turkey, which is treated under Asia, and the present territories of the Soviet Union) contained over 6·5 million Jews: three million lived in Poland, nearly a million in Romania, and several hundred thousand each in Hungary, Czechoslovakia, Germany, France and Britain. Today there are barely 1·25 million, and only two countries, France and Britain, have more than 100 000 Jewish inhabitants (and many of these are non-European immigrants). The rest either perished in the death camps or emigrated to other parts of the world.

The devastation of World War II fell heavily on the Jews in eastern Europe. Of a prewar population of five million, only a million or so survived the deportations and bombings. Jewish losses were out of all proportion, owing to the Nazi policy of extermination and, too often, to the hostility or indifference of the local non-Jews. The war shattered the economy of the region and in most countries Jews were placed at a special disadvantage in the slow postwar recovery, especially where Communism dispossessed the last remnants of the middle class. Economic hardship, political upheavals and continuing antisemitism led to large-scale emigration, so that Hungary and Romania alone now have significant Jewish populations, and cities and regions which were once among the most densely populated of the Jewish world are almost devoid of Jewish inhabitants. The countries under Soviet influence also suffered from attempts at forcible integration, state control of religion and isolation from the main centers of Jewish life abroad.

The loss has been doubly tragic, because in addition to its large Jewish population the region contained before the war some of the most important cultural centers, and had a thriving religious and intellectual life which exerted a powerful influence far beyond its own borders. The *yeshivot* and rabbinic seminaries, the printing presses and journals, the Hasidic communities and Zionist groups which contributed so much to predestruction Jewry, have almost all been obliterated. Remnants of eastern and central European Jewish culture have been preserved or revived elsewhere, but the uprooted tree cannot easily bear fruit. In Jewish terms the region has become little more than a wilderness.

Only a few countries which were fortunate enough to escape occupation by the Nazis emerged with their Jewish populations unscathed; they were in fact augmented by refugees. More recently there has been an infusion of new blood, from North Africa and the Middle East, southern Africa and South America. This new immigration has transformed the Jewish community of France and created a new Jewish life in Spain. Britain, too, has received a varied influx. But in most European countries the Jewish population is small and decreasing, through emigration, assimilation and demographic decline.

J. Offenbach (1819–80), Fr. composer

Sir J. Epstein (1880–1959), UK sculptor

other Jewish settlements in the U K
estimated over 1000
1 Bushey
2 Chigwell
estimated under 1000
3 St Albans
4 Luton
5 St Annes
6 Preston

other Jewish settleme
the French Riviera
estimated under 1000
1 Fréjus
2 Grasse
3 Antibes
4 Menton

Sir Joshua Hassan (1915–), Gib. statesman

Bruno Kreisky (1911–), Austrian statesman

Sarah Bernhardt (1844–1923), Fr. actress

	1930		1980	
	Approx. Jewish pop.	Jews per thousand	Approx. Jewish pop.	Jews per thousand
Albania	200	0·2	200	0·1
Austria	250 000	40·0	8000	1·1
Belgium	45 000	5·6	33 000	3·4
Bulgaria	46 000	7·9	5000	0·6
Czechoslovakia	357 000	24·2	8000	0·5
Denmark	6000	1·7	7000	1·4
Finland	1800	0·5	1200	0·3
France	230 000	5·4	600 000	11·2
Germany, East	565 000	9·1	1000	0·1
Germany, West			33 500	0·6
Gibraltar	1100	50·0	550	18·3
Greece	73 000	11·7	5000	0·5
Hungary	445 000	51·1	100 000	9·3
Ireland	3700	1·2	2000	0·6
Italy	47 000	1·2	32 000	0·6
Luxembourg	2250	7·5	750	2·1
Netherlands	157 000	19·8	27 000	1·9
Norway	1500	0·5	900	0·2
Poland	3 000 000	96·0	5000	0·1
Portugal	1000	0·1	600	0·1
Romania	900 000	50·0	33 000	1·4
Spain	4000	0·2	12 000	0·3
Sweden	6500	1·0	15 000	1·8
Switzerland	18 000	4·5	21 000	3·3
United Kingdom	300 000	6·6	350 000	6·3
Yugoslavia	68 000	4·9	50 000	0·2

Jewish settlements

● major community: estimated over 100 000

● important community: estimated over 10 000

● sizable community: estimated over 1000

● smaller community: estimated under 1000

● small community with some communal organization

■ selected site of little or no Jewish population but historic remains

scale 1 : 12 000 000

0   300km

0   200 mi

Great Britain

Geography and history have set Britain somewhat apart from mainland Europe, and the Jewish experience here, too, has been rather special. The Jews were late in gaining admittance, but once admitted they have enjoyed basic liberties for much longer than in any other European country, and they have never had to face serious outbreaks of violence or widespread public hostility. The heterogeneous composition of British society (in both ethnic and religious terms) may be one factor: prejudice, although commonly voiced, is rarely institutionalized in discriminatory legislation or expressed through mob violence. The existence of established churches (which continues) has inevitably entailed restrictions on the rights of other religious groups, but most of these restrictions have gradually been removed since the beginning of the 19th century, and the few which remain have little or no practical effect.

Britain seems to provide an environment for its Jewish minority close to the ideal. Many practicing Jews can trace their ancestry to the original 17th- and 18th-century settlers, a striking testimony to the generous conditions in a country where religious diversity is tolerated and tradition appreciated. Intermarriage has led to some defection from the community, particularly among the upper social classes, but there is a growing tendency for non-Jewish marriage partners to become Jews. As one of the smallest and least conspicuous minorities the Jews have rarely attracted adverse public attention, and individual Jews have been prominent in politics, commerce, the arts and sciences—in fact every facet of national life.

Britain's former commanding position in world affairs endowed her Jewish leaders with an international role, for example in the protection of Jewish rights in the 19th century or in the early development of Zionism. Even today Anglo-Jewry has a voice in world Jewish affairs disproportionate to its numerical strength.

There are no official statistics on the Jewish population (the Jewish community has always opposed the inclusion of questions on religion or ethnic origin in the United Kingdom's decennial census). The most careful recent studies estimate the population in 1977 at 354000, representing a decrease of 56000 since 1965. The decrease was attributed to a low birthrate and to emigration. The majority, just over two-thirds, lived in the London area, the rest being scattered in nearly 100 provincial towns.

The foundations of the present community were laid by Sephardi and Ashkenazi immigrants, mainly from Holland and Germany, in the second half of the 17th century. By the mid-19th century there were some 30000 Jews. Massive immigration from Russia increased the total to well over 250000 by 1914. There was a further important influx of refugees from Nazism in the 1930s, and smaller numbers have continued to arrive since the end of the war, from eastern Europe, the Middle East and elsewhere.

The regularization of the status of the Jews has taken place for the most part unobtrusively over a

Four-fifths of British Jewry derives from the huge Russian immigration which began in the 1880s. The immigrants faced a hard struggle in the slums and sweatshops. Looked down on by the more established Jews, they were not even accepted by their fellow workers. Meeting with resistance in their attempts to set up Jewish branches within existing trade unions, they formed their own, such as the Jewish Master Bakers (*left*). Most Jewish immigrants worked in the clothing industry. In 1912 the whole industry was brought to a standstill by a strike of Jewish workers. This action put an end to the sweatshops and also led to improved relations with the British trade union movement, in which Jews subsequently played a full part.

Below The East End of London in 1900. It was here, not far from the medieval Jewry, that the immigrant Jews first settled, and in 1900 many of the streets were entirely Jewish—a kind of voluntary ghetto in fact. But already the wealthier Jews were moving out to the fashionable West End and into the suburbs, and the teeming Jewish life of the East End is now little more than a nostalgic memory.

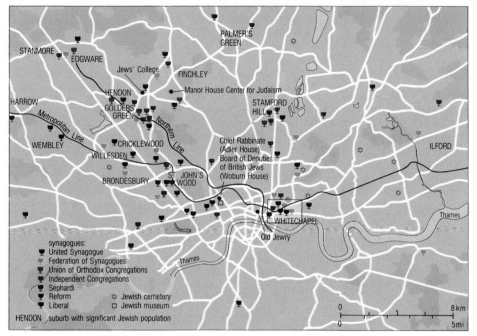

synagogues:
- United Synagogue
- Federation of Synagogues
- Union of Orthodox Congregations
- Independent Congregations
- Sephardi
- Reform   ✡ Jewish cemetery
- Liberal   ▢ Jewish museum

HENDON suburb with significant Jewish population

Top This Jewish policeman is one of a small but steady trickle of proselytes. Judaism does not go out of its way to seek converts.

Above The movement towards the newer suburbs can be traced through the spread of synagogues. By 1900 there were already a dozen synagogues outside the East End, mainly to the west and north, although some Jews were moving eastwards or south of the river. Subsequently there was a very marked tendency to settle in northern or northwestern London, notably in specific areas such as Stamford Hill, Golders Green or (later) Edgware, which still retain a strong Jewish flavor.

Left A hundred years ago London was the heart of a great empire, and so it was for the Jews too: the communities of Canada, South Africa, Australia and smaller centers like Jamaica or Hong Kong looked to Britain for religious guidance and support. The relationship has continued, in a drastically attenuated form, in the British Commonwealth. Here leaders of 13 Commonwealth communities are seen posing with the British Prime Minister, Margaret Thatcher, at a conference held in London in 1982.

long period of time. Permission to meet for worship was granted to a small group of Sephardim by Oliver Cromwell in 1656 and was maintained after the restoration of the monarchy in 1660. Religious tests were abolished gradually in the 19th century, often—in typically pragmatic British fashion—in response to specific cases. Thus in 1833 a Jew was first admitted to the Bar; another became sheriff of London in 1835 and lord mayor in 1855. In 1847 the first Jew was elected to parliament, but was prevented from taking his seat without taking the oath "on the true faith of a Christian." His loyal electors returned him year after year, until in 1858 a compromise was reached and he finally took his seat without the oath. His son was raised to the peerage (he was the first Lord Rothschild) in 1886. A Jew first joined the government in 1871, the cabinet in 1909. There are few bars now on the opportunities open to Jews (some doubt exists as to whether a Jew may be Lord Chancellor, that is Speaker of the House of Lords, and the monarch is bound to be an Anglican). The House of Commons elected in 1983 contained 28 Jewish members, including the Home Secretary and the Chancellor of the Exchequer; there were over 40 Jewish peers, 10 of them hereditary. Various Acts of Parliament accord special concessions to the Jews in recognition of their religious needs and traditions, including the unique privilege of marrying at home. But there is no regulation by the state of Jewish communal life.

The representative body of Anglo-Jewry, the Board of Deputies of British Jews, traces its history back to 1760 when the Sephardim appointed a delegation to present a loyal address to the new king. Its effective origin, however, was in 1836, when it received its first constitution. It then consisted of 22 deputies from the four main London synagogues. It now has well over 500 members, representing synagogues in London and the provinces, as well as some nonreligious organizations and Commonwealth communities. For a long time the Board was mainly active in protecting and extending Jewish political and civil rights, and it still scrutinizes new legislation and makes official representations as appropriate. But in the 1930s, when antisemitism briefly took an acute form in Britain with the growth of the British Union of Fascists, it coordinated the fight against Fascism, and communal defense has remained one of its main preoccupations. It strongly supported the outlawing of incitement to racial hatred, which was eventually made an indictable offense in 1965, and it keeps a close watch on incidents of violence against Jews or Jewish institutions. In 1943 the Zionists, by a concerted campaign, gained control of the Board, and it has retained an active interest in matters concerning Israel. But the real strength of the Board of Deputies lies in its representative constitution. It is the only forum in Anglo-Jewry which brings together delegates of every shade of religious and political opinion and, particularly in recent years, it has come to assert itself as, in some sense, the "governing body" of Anglo-Jewry. It is also taken seriously by the government, as presenting the united voice of British Jews. In 1982 the Board convened a conference of Jewish leaders from 13 countries of the British Commonwealth. This resulted in the establishment of a permanent council, based in London, to strengthen the contacts between the Commonwealth countries and to give support to the smaller communities, several of which are dwindling fast.

The Commonwealth dimension has old roots. The chief rabbi in London is officially designated Chief Rabbi of the Commonwealth, and before 1953 he was Chief Rabbi of the British Empire. After World War I the then chief rabbi undertook a grand pastoral tour of his diocese, taking in 42 different communities. Since then South Africa has left the Commonwealth, Canada has renounced the authority of the chief rabbi, and Australia has threatened to do the same. Within Britain, however, the chief rabbi still commands respect, principally because he tends to be regarded by non-Jews as the spokesman for religious Jewry.

In fact religious Anglo-Jewry is deeply divided, and very many devout Jews do not regard the chief rabbi as their spokesman. His support comes in the main from the United Synagogue (a confederation of Orthodox synagogues in London) and like-minded provincial congregations. The United Synagogue, which is the largest synagogal body in Britain with a membership of over 35 000 families, was established by Act of Parliament in 1870: it is the Jewish equivalent to the Church of England, with the chief rabbi as primate. The dissenting groups which do not recognize his authority stand both to the right and to the left: on the right the Union of Orthodox Hebrew Congregations (founded in 1926 by extreme

British and Jewish. In Britain, as elsewhere, the Jews are seeking to carve out for themselves an identity of their own. Every November Britain mourns the dead of two world wars; British Jewry shared the loss, but prefers to hold its own celebration at the same spot a week later (*left*), a forceful reminder that Jews have also fought and died for Britain, and at the same time a statement of distinctness. Within Anglo-Jewry there are also many divisions, ethnic, social and religious. One unique society is the community of Gateshead, in the northeast of England. Small but staunchly observant, the community originates in a group of immigrants from Lithuania. *Center right* The kosher shop: a focus for social life. Even the milk is kosher (*below*).

In the middle ages the Jews were the property of the king, and were entrusted with the vital economic role of banking. A reminder of this role are the medieval Jews' houses, built of stone for security, like this one at Lincoln (*right*). In more recent times, too, some Jews have been prominent financiers. Most famous of all are the Rothschilds, who in a dramatic gesture in 1875 loaned the government 4 million pounds to buy a controlling interest in the Suez Canal. Waddesdon Manor (*below*) is only one of a chain of magnificent country houses they built.

Above The wealth of the Rothschilds made a powerful impact on the public mind; it became legendary among the poverty-stricken Jews of Russia. Most Jews were far from rich, and many lived below the bread-line. But self-help charity was always a strong feature of the community and it was rare for a Jew to starve. Here Jews queue for a free food distribution in the East End of London.

Right A Zionist youth camp in Ireland. Zionism serves to encourage a greater awareness of Jewish identity and a knowledge of Hebrew.

170

Below In the 18th century Jews began to radiate out of London to provincial centers. The graceful Exeter synagogue of 1763 is a reminder of that age.

Center Scottish Jewry has its own distinctive flavor: the Jewish Lads' Brigade in Glasgow trains a traditional Scottish pipe band.

Orthodox from central Europe, now dominated by later Hasidic immigrants) and the Federation of Synagogues (originally an amalgamation of prayer-houses of the Russian immigrants, founded in 1887); to the left are the Reform Synagogues of Great Britain (whose origins go back to 1840) and the Union of Liberal and Progressive Synagogues (a more radical association dating back to 1902). Separate and parallel are the Sephardim, long-established descendants of European and West Indian immigrants now augmented by recent arrivals from further afield. Each of the groups has its own rabbis and spokesmen.

The differences between these various denominations are hardly doctrinal: they are more a question of origins and ethos. Loyalty to the different groups is strong, even if it is difficult to discern in practice the difference between the Federation and the United Synagogue or between the Reform and Liberal Synagogues. Mergers have been discussed, and there is a good deal of practical cooperation between the various bodies, but institutions once founded die hard.

The one doctrinal issue which continues to have a real impact is the question of the divine authority of Torah, the question which dominated the split between Reform and Orthodoxy in the 19th century. The issue was invoked by the chief rabbi in 1842, when he pronounced a ban on the first Reform Synagogue. This was the first and most enduring division to be introduced into Anglo-Jewry (the division between Sephardim and Ashkenazim was preexistent, and had by then largely been healed). It has grown stronger over the years, even though moderate reforms were accepted in the United Synagogue in the course of the 19th century. In the present century successive chief rabbis have laid stress on the dangers of the "Reformist heresy." (The reason is presumably not unconnected with the influx of traditionalists from Russia, to whom even the United Synagogue seemed to verge dangerously on Reform.) In the early 1960s a much-publicized rift in the United Synagogue on the question of doctrinal Orthodoxy almost (but not quite) led to the formation of an American-style Conservative movement. In the past decade anti-Reform agitation has once again been whipped up by Orthodox leaders. It has little effect: Anglo-Jewry is not particularly interested in theology.

The one permanent effect of the schism of the 1960s was to seal the doom of Jews' College, a rabbinic seminary founded on modernist Orthodox lines in 1855 and with an important tradition of Jewish scholarship. Condemned to undeviating doctrinal Orthodoxy, it has failed to attract the best talents and now leads a purely nominal existence. The demand for traditionalist rabbis is satisfied by the *yeshivah* in Gateshead, one of the finest institutes of traditional talmudic learning in the world. The Reform movement, greatly strengthened by refugee rabbis from Europe in the 1930s, set up its own seminary in 1956, named Leo Baeck College for the spiritual leader of German Jewry in the Nazi years. Eventually it gained the support of the Liberal wing as well. It has produced a whole generation of younger English rabbis in a modern mold.

Interestingly, Leo Baeck College has also attracted students from Europe, many of whom have returned to serve European congregations. This is one sign of a growing awareness of a new role for Britain in Europe, deriving from the destructions of the holocaust and to some extent also from the entry of Britain into the European Community. Another sign is the Conference of European Rabbis, an Orthodox forum based on London and presided over by the British chief rabbi. On the whole, however, Anglo-Jewry has been slow to respond to the challenges of the new Europe.

Irish Republic

The Jewish community of Ireland is estimated at under 2000, and is almost entirely concentrated in the capital, Dublin. Despite its small size, and signs of rapid numerical decline, the community maintains a Jewish school, various communal organizations, and separate traditionalist, Orthodox and Liberal congregations.

France

The experience of the Jews of France faithfully mirrors the conflicting urges which have dominated modern France as a whole—revolution and tradition, hospitality and xenophobia, nationalism and minority consciousness. The 19th century began with a serious attempt to normalize the status of the Jews and ended with an outrageous antisemitic scandal: both events disclose great heights of idealism and depths of bigotry. In the 1930s France accepted more refugees from Nazism than did any other country in the world, and was the only country to support them from public funds. Within a few years they were being handed over to the Nazis with apparent indifference and with more ready compliance than was strictly necessary. The same contrasting attitudes were visible in reactions to the antisemitic atrocities of the early 1980s—demonstrations of solidarity with Jews coupled with indifference or outright hostility. (When a bomb, intended to kill worshipers in a synagogue, killed instead four passersby, one of whom was an Israeli tourist, a prominent French politician referred to "four victims, three of them innocent French people.")

One factor in the complex of paradoxes is the varied composition of the French Jewish population itself. The old Sephardi and Ashkenazi communities were geographically separate and culturally quite distinct, and for a long time they barely acknowledged a common identity. (As recently as the early 1950s an antisemitic journal ascribed the mutual hostility of the political leaders René Mayer and Pierre Mendès-France to the ancient antagonism between Ashkenazi and Sephardi!) In the late 1930s half the Jews in France were unassimilated immigrants, and much of the antisemitism of the time was due to simple xenophobia: in both occupied France and Vichy France in the early 1940s the immigrants were the first to be thrown to the wolves while genuine efforts were made to preserve the "French" Jews. Today half the Jews are once again immigrants, this time from North Africa, and they tend to attract the prejudices directed against foreigners in general and against Arabs in particular. But the endurance of a certain authentic French antisemitism is not to be ruled out, despite the efforts of successive governments and of some leading churchmen to discourage it. France was one of the main seedbeds of classical antisemitism, and it is a heritage which is slow in dying.

Assimilation, being officially sanctioned, has always tended to take a civic and public form. French Jews were proud of their French citizenship and of their faithfulness to the French fatherland; they were deeply conscious of the Jewish contributions to French culture and politics. (These attitudes have always tended to exaggerate the rift between native and foreign Jews.) Such Jews were Frenchmen first and Jews second. They took little interest in purely Jewish culture, much less in Zionism, and their important philanthropic enterprises were humanitarian and indeed patriotic rather than particularistic. The schools run by the Alliance Israélite Universelle in North Africa and the Middle East were intended to give Jewish children a French

Below Eighty thousand Jews were deported to death through the detention camp at Drancy, near Paris, between 1942 and 1944. After the Liberation the survivors made this solemn pilgrimage to the site, where an annual act of commemoration is still held.

Center left Even the sufferings which the Jews shared with all Frenchmen during the nightmare years of Nazism have not exorcised the specter of antisemitism. "Unworthy to be a part of the new Europe": a neo-Nazi slogan scrawled on a monument to holocaust victims in a Paris suburb, in 1981.

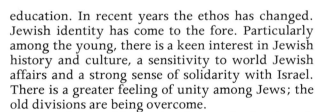

education. In recent years the ethos has changed. Jewish identity has come to the fore. Particularly among the young, there is a keen interest in Jewish history and culture, a sensitivity to world Jewish affairs and a strong sense of solidarity with Israel. There is a greater feeling of unity among Jews; the old divisions are being overcome.

An unforeseeable destiny has made the French community one of the largest in the modern Jewish world, and the only one on the continent of Europe with a really strong and buoyant Jewish life. So far its impact on the broader Jewish scene, in Europe or worldwide, has been negligible, but its potential is surely great.

The present Jewish population of France is estimated at 500000–700000, of whom more than half live in the Paris region. There is great uncertainty about statistics, as indeed, in a country of advanced assimilation, about the definition of Jewish identity.

At the time of the Revolution (1789) there were several thousand Jews in France, but only a few hundred of them lived in Paris. The rest were concentrated in three remote regions, and each group had its own history and culture. The most numerous group were the Yiddish-speaking Ashkenazim of Alsace-Lorraine, with their strong German connections. In the south the Jews of the Comtat Venaissin, around Avignon, had survived in ghettos under papal rule, with a south European medieval culture. The Sephardim of the southwest

Violence continues to haunt the Jews of France. Amid hundreds of recent incidents, two stand out. On 3 October 1980, during the Sabbath Eve service, a bomb exploded outside a packed synagogue in Paris. Clearly intended for the worshipers, it killed four passersby. Among the reactions was a demonstration—said to be the largest seen in Paris since 1945—which united all sectors of the Jewish community and numerous sympathizers (*top*). The banner *Renouveau Juif* is that of the Jewish Renewal movement, founded in 1979 as an outspoken expression of Jewish identity and support for Israel. The second incident was a gun attack on a well-known Jewish restaurant in the Paris "ghetto," the rue des Rosiers, on 9 August 1982. Six people were killed, many seriously injured. The French president, François Mitterrand, is seen paying his respects on the first anniversary of the outrage (*above*). With him is his secretary of state for public security, a post created in response to the shooting.

The Jewish population of France is now largely concentrated in Paris and a few other centers, but numerous provincial towns can boast old synagogues, a reminder of times past. At Carpentras (*above right*) the synagogue dates back to the 14th century and was restored in the 18th century; it has been declared a historic monument. It recalls the papal Jews of the Comtat Venaissin, who remained during the long centuries when Jews were banned from the territories of the king of France. The seven-branch candelabra are most unusual. In recent years immigration from North Africa has revived the fortunes of many such dwindling communities of southern France.

were well-established merchants of Portuguese origin who had gradually shrugged off the yoke of Christianity and adopted a high French culture. With the Revolution they all acquired the similar rights and obligations of citizens, and under Napoleon I they were organized in consistories, officially recognized communities under state control, in which the rabbis were charged with the duty of converting their flocks into loyal French citizens. In time this formula worked and the Jews became Frenchmen (of the "Israelite religion"—or not: many became Christians), even though some traces of their different origins remained. The Central Consistory was in Paris, which inevitably gained a dominant position in the demography of French Jewry as of France as a whole. With the separation of Church and State in 1905 the consistories (except in Alsace-Lorraine, then under German rule) became purely religious organizations, and the Central Consistory became the Union of Jewish Religious Associations in France and Algeria.

A continuous stream of immigrants from central and eastern Europe brought the Jewish population up to about 350 000 by 1939, of whom 200 000 were not of French nationality. Ties between French Jews and non-Jews had been strengthened during common service in World War I, in which 6500 Jews had lost their lives. A Jew (Léon Blum) had been prime minister and others had occupied cabinet posts. But foreign Jews, too, had enlisted and died for their adopted country in the Great War, and when war broke out again in September 1939 many of them volunteered for service.

The defeat of June 1940 was a disaster for France as a whole, but especially for the Jews, whose very existence soon became precarious. An official anti-semitic campaign was launched throughout the country immediately after the armistice, and in September the first of a series of anti-Jewish measures was taken by the Germans in the occupied zone. Many Jews fled south into the unoccupied zone, but there the Vichy government's anti-Jewish legislation was in some respects even more severe than that of the occupiers. In any case the Germans soon occupied the whole of the country, including eventually the southeast where the former Italian occupiers had sheltered large numbers of Jewish fugitives. Despite protests and desperate subter-fuges, tens of thousands of Jews were deported, and many were summarily killed in France itself. Those who survived were dispossessed, demoralized and bereaved. The tasks of postwar restoration and rehabilitation were enormous, not least because of the poisonous aftereffects of Nazi propaganda and the strains on personal relations imposed by war-time and the appropriation of Jewish property.

In fact the recovery was surprisingly good. The postwar governments took steps to stamp out antisemitism and to absorb numbers of eastern European survivors. The severe economic problems of rehabilitation were in large part shouldered by the Joint Distribution Committee. Restitution of property caused so many problems that many claims were simply abandoned in the face of resistance from collaborators, who formed associ-ations to protect their "rights." This issue did foment a certain antisemitic feeling, as did Catholic propaganda about the question of Israeli sovereign-ty over the holy places in Palestine. Jewish com-munal life was fragmented and insecure, and for a

Paris: A Meeting of Cultures

synagogues:
- ♀ Sephardi
- ♀ Ashkenazi
- ♀ Sephardi and Ashkenazi
- ▲ memorial
- □ Jewish library
- ○ historic site
- ■ Jewish restaurant

Below Paris began on the Île de la Cité, and it was here that the first Jewish community lived—the central street was known as "Jewry Street" until the Revolution. Later, after a brief exile, Jews resettled on both sides of the Seine. The district around the rue Pavée was known as the "Old Jewry" in the 13th

In 1807, when Napoleon convened the Great Sanhedrin which made Paris the administrative center of French Jewry, fewer than 3000 Jews were living permanently in the city. Gradually in the course of the 19th century numbers of Jews began to arrive, mainly from Alsace-Lorraine. This was a time of assimilation for the Jews of Paris, many of whom established themselves in bourgeois life. In religion a decorous Orthodoxy evolved. Splendid synagogues were built. The consecration of the chief consistorial synagogue in rue de la Victoire in 1874 was attended by three Barons de Rothschild and a prominent Jewish member of the government, Adolphe Crémieux. The architect, Aldrophe, was chief architect to the city of Paris, and the city shared the cost of the building with the consistory.

The early part of the 20th century was a period of immigration from eastern Europe. The city was particularly attractive to intellectuals, and of course to artists like Chaim Soutine, Marc Chagall and many other Jewish members of the School of Paris.

After the ravages of the Nazi occupation and the deportations, recovery was slow. It seemed that, like other former glittering centers of Jewish life in western and central Europe, Paris was doomed. Then, unexpectedly, there was a massive new influx from North Africa, bringing a Jewish life just as exotic as the eastern European ethos had seemed in its day.

Paris is now the largest and liveliest center of Jewish life in all Europe—and the keyword is variety.

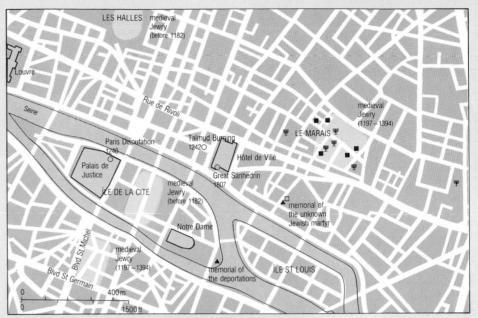

Above The synagogue of rue de la Victoire, the largest in Paris and seat of the chief rabbi of France, stands as a monument to the dignified, discreet Judaism of the late 19th century. The massive Romanesque building has restrained Moorish overtones, but there is little to indicate from the outside that it is a synagogue.

Far left Belleville was settled briefly by Polish Jews after World War I, but it is now largely populated by Arabs, both Jewish and Muslim, living together in apparent harmony. The shops and restaurants of the quarter offer delicious Tunisian and Moroccan flavors.

Left A *bet hamidrash* in the rue des Rosiers, the throbbing heart of the *Pletzel*, where traditional life is still kept up.

Right The arrival of the Jews from North Africa has revitalized many spects of Jewish life. In 1950 there were only five kosher butchers in the whole of Paris; now there are more than 70.

century; curiously it was here that Jews settled again, after a long absence, in the 18th and 19th centuries. It came to be known as the *Pletzel* ("Little Square"), and is still a center of Jewish life, although Arabic has almost ousted Yiddish.

Below The Jews are now dispersed all over Paris, and indeed in the suburbs, but the map shows well-defined concentrations, mainly on the Right Bank, extending towards Montmartre and Belleville, and to a lesser extent in the fashionable districts to the west.

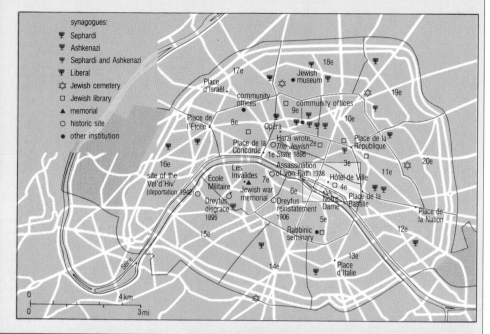

long time there was no central body to combat such manifestations of hostility. Under the pressures of the German occupation the major communal organizations had eventually come together to form a Representative Committee of the Jews of France (Crif): it included the Central Consistory, the Zionist Organization, the Jewish Communists, the Bund and a variety of welfare and action groups. After the liberation centrifugal force had once again taken over, and conflict between the different factions tended to neutralize the joint effort. Conflict between Zionists and Communists was especially open, though neither movement attracted much support from native French Jews. Eventually the Crif was somewhat revitalized, as was the Central Consistory, and a new cultural and welfare organization, the United Jewish Social Fund, was established. These three continue to be the main communal institutions of French Jewry.

In the mid-1950s a large influx of Jews from Algeria, Tunisia and Morocco, together with the growth of cordial relations between the French government and Israel, brought about a notable revitalization of Jewish life in France. French Jewry became more numerous and active, and it also became more self-confident. Support for Israel began to be openly expressed even by more conservative Jews: it was no longer in conflict with loyalty to France. The newfound confidence survived President de Gaulle's attacks on Zionism in 1968, the year which also saw an upsurge of dramatic militancy among French youth. Young Jews firmly asserted their Jewish identity and their solidarity with Israel, and their enthusiasm and openness gradually percolated through to their elders. A wave of terrorist attacks on Jewish property and communal institutions in Paris since 1979, involving hundreds of incidents and several deaths, has only served to reinforce the solidarity and commitment of French Jewry. Jewish issues are now widely ventilated in the press, and all the political parties openly woo the Jewish vote. The government of President François Mitterrand formed in June 1981 contained a number of Jewish members, one of whom was a vice-president of the Social Fund.

French Judaism has traditionally tended towards moderate Orthodoxy, and the consistorial system has gradually eradicated the divisions between Sephardim and Ashkenazim, although a formal reunion has never been achieved. Many congregations have grown up outside the Consistory, ranging from the Liberal to the extreme traditionalist. The synagogues have tended to maintain a purely religious function, and the level of Jewish culture and education has not been high outside the groups of recent immigrants. In recent years this situation has changed. With a more positive assertion of Jewish identity has come a greater demand for literature, education and cultural activity. To a limited extent this demand is being met by the synagogues, but it is also satisfied in a wide variety of other ways, ranging from schools and university courses to independent study circles and publishing projects.

There is a rabbinic seminary in Paris, one of only a handful still functioning on the continent of Europe, but there is still a relative shortage of rabbis, given the size of the Jewish population.

Netherlands

In the Netherlands the Nazis pursued a policy of ruthless extermination which, despite memorable resistance, was largely successful. Only some 25 000 Jews survived the deportations, out of a prewar population of over 150 000. A rapid economic recovery and the moral and material support of the government, the churches and the general population could not compensate for the sense of utter loss, and many Jews left the country, feeling that there was no future for the community. Those who remained succeeded in restoring a remarkably vital Jewish life, albeit on a pathetically reduced scale, aided by the sympathetic interest of the non-Jewish populace. There is a sensitive appreciation of the rich cultural heritage of Dutch Jewry: several of the old synagogues have been restored at public expense and some of them have returned to Jewish use. Half the population is in Amsterdam, which has a number of synagogues (Sephardi and Ashkenazi, traditionalist and Liberal) and a notable Jewish museum, but there are small communities in various other towns. Liberal Judaism, introduced originally by German refugees in the 1930s, is enjoying a certain success under the leadership of London-trained rabbis, but Orthodoxy is fading and the venerable Sephardi community was all but obliterated in the holocaust.

Belgium

Belgium has always been less welcoming to the Jews than the Netherlands, of which it was a part until 1830. Although they were granted freedom of worship under the constitution of 1831, popular sentiment has been against them and it has been difficult for Jews to acquire Belgian citizenship. Consequently large numbers of Jews, even those born in the country, have been aliens. Before the last war there were 80 000 Jews in Belgium and there are now fewer than half that number, almost all living in the two main cities, Brussels and Antwerp. The contrast between the two communities could not be more complete. Antwerp has a close-knit and intensely Jewish community, of eastern European origin, Yiddish-speaking and traditionalist in religion, inhabiting a distinct quarter and mainly involved in the diamond industry. The larger community of Brussels is more heterogeneous in origin and character, largely assimilated and with little interest in religion and traditional Jewish culture. Both communities have suffered from terrorist attacks in recent years. In July 1980 a group of schoolchildren in Antwerp was attacked; one was killed and 17 were injured. In October 1981 a bomb exploded outside the Sephardi synagogue in the city's diamond district, killing three people and wounding 90, many seriously. In Brussels gunmen opened fire on the Great Synagogue during the New Year service in September 1982.

Luxembourg

In Luxembourg Jews gained equal citizenship rights after the French Revolution (1789), and a small community was established in 1808. In 1890 there were 1000 Jews and by 1930 nearly 2000, extraordinarily dispersed through the towns of the Grand Duchy. Since the war there have been only a few hundred, most of them living in the capital.

The shadow of the holocaust still looms large over these countries with their glorious Jewish past and very uncertain future. The monument in Amsterdam's Weesperplein (*top*) was erected in 1947 by the city's Jews as a token of gratitude to all those who helped the Jews during the Nazi ordeal.
Above Ossip Zadkine's statue *The Destroyed City* in Rotterdam evokes the terror and agony of the ruthless German bombing in 1940. *Left* The Luxembourg City synagogue was built in 1953 to replace an earlier building destroyed by the Nazis.

Above German Economics Minister Ludwig Erhard speaking at the rededication of the Rashi Synagogue in Worms in 1961. Until its destruction by Nazis during *Kristallnacht* (9 November 1938) this was the oldest synagogue in Europe still in use, dating back in part to 1034.

Below The synagogue in Lengnau, one of only two places in Switzerland where Jews were allowed to live from the early 17th century to the mid-19th.

Germany

In Germany the Jews are numerically insignificant, but their presence has a symbolic value in the context of efforts to come to terms with the experience of Nazism. After a period of profound embarrassment and uncertainty, a mood of reconciliation and open discussion of the wounds of the past has come to prevail. The governments of both German republics have repeatedly condemned the Nazi treatment of Jews and taken measures to combat antisemitism. They have assisted the rehabilitation of the Jews in postwar Germany and the commemoration of the victims of the holocaust. Whereas the West German government has acknowledged a sense of responsibility towards the victims and paid out large sums of money by way of reparation, the East German government has refused to consider responsibility as a German problem, pointing out that German socialists, in common with Jews, were victims of Nazism. Churchmen have been at the forefront of the movement for reconciliation; there are now frequent demonstrations of Christian–Jewish friendship.

In West Germany the census of 1970 recorded 31 684 Jews (there were 27 million Roman Catholics and nearly 30 million Protestants). Registered members of the 66 Jewish communities numbered 28 173 at the beginning of 1981, an increase of 405 over the previous year. The increase was due mainly to immigration and to a very small extent to conversion, since the ratio of births (95) to deaths (456) was very negative. The largest community was in Berlin (6530 members), followed by Frankfurt (4897) and Munich (3920). The representative body, the Central Council of Jews in Germany, has expressed deep anxiety about the proliferation of anti-Jewish extremism, particularly from the political right. Neo-Nazi groups have been responsible for hundreds of antisemitic incidents in recent years, particularly the desecration of cemeteries, and for spreading anti-Jewish propaganda.

In East Germany there are only eight communities, with a registered membership of some 650, half of them in Berlin. They are all affiliated to the Federation of Jewish Communities in the German Democratic Republic. The average age is high and there are no rabbis. Their future appears tenuous in the extreme.

Switzerland

There are more than 20 000 Jews in Switzerland, but the total membership of the Jewish communities, which are affiliated to the Swiss Federation of Jewish Communities, is only 6000, dispersed in 22 towns. This reflects the priorities of the Jewish population, which is well integrated and has a high rate of intermarriage. The largest communities are in Zurich, Basle and Geneva, which also houses the world or European headquarters of a number of international Jewish organizations and relief agencies. Most of the synagogues in the country are Orthodox or traditionalist, but there are Liberal congregations in Zurich and in Geneva, which also has a Sephardi synagogue.

Left Bomb damage in Belgium, 1981. Between 1979 and 1982 there were hundreds of attacks on Jewish life and property throughout western Europe. Some of them were attributed to Arab terrorists, but the majority were due to native political extremists.

Right This commemorative ceremony at the Dachau concentration camp near Munich is another reminder of the gruesome past. The reminder is still needed in Germany where there are strong pressures to wipe away or shrug off the memory of the Nazi atrocities.

1933-1945

Austria

Vienna, once one of the intellectual capitals of the Jewish world, has been reduced to a sluggish backwater. In 1934 there were 178 000 Jews in the city, out of a total population of well under two million. Today there are barely a few thousand, many of them immigrants from eastern Europe and central Asia. There are small communities in the other main cities of Austria. Deeply rooted antisemitism makes life disagreeable for the Jews of Austria and occasionally erupts into acts of violence. Vienna was the scene of an Arab terrorist attack on the main synagogue in August 1981, when two people were killed. The then Austrian Chancellor, Bruno Kreisky, who was of Jewish origin, was strongly criticized for his outspoken support for Palestinian activists and for his subsequent remarks blaming the attack on Israel's intransigence in relations with the Palestinian Arabs.

Scandinavia

The Jews of Scandinavia number only a few thousand. Denmark and Sweden, which have a Jewish history going back 200 years and more, are among the very few European communities which have grown in this century, through immigration. Both countries provided homes for refugees from Poland in 1968. Sweden received large numbers of refugees before, during and after the last war, including virtually the whole of the Danish community, but many subsequently left. There are now some 5000 Jews in the country, half of them in the capital. Most of Denmark's Jews live in Copenhagen. The much smaller communities of Norway and Finland trace their beginnings back only to the 1850s. They are also mainly concentrated in the capital cities.

Left The original grave of one of the best-known Viennese Jews, Theodor Herzl. In 1949 his remains were exhumed and reburied in a national shrine in Israel.

Below Everywhere in Spain are traces of the medieval Jewish presence; in recent years many have been restored. This magnificent 12th-century synagogue, generally known under its Christian name of Santa María la Blanca, cannot fail to impress the visitor to Toledo, with its rows of columns and horseshoe arches evoking the Great Mosque at Cordoba.

Left "Cordoba to Maimonides," reads the dedication on this statue, erected in 1964 to one of the city's most famous sons.

Below in Portugal the Jews were forcibly baptized in 1497, but many kept their Judaism alive in total secrecy, marrying only among themselves and transmitting the prayers and rituals by word of mouth from generation to generation. Often it was the women who led the prayers and preserved the traditions. A few remote communities of New Christians managed to survive, believing themselves to be the last Jews left on earth, until they were "discovered" accidentally in 1917.

The revival of Jewish life in Spain after centuries of desolation seems almost a miracle. It dates substantially from the 1960s. Previously the Jews, like other religious minorities, maintained an apprehensive existence, exacerbated by the negative image of the Jew in official Spanish history.
Left Queen Sofia signs the visitors' book during a visit to the Madrid synagogue in 1976.
Center The community of Majorca was officially founded in 1971. It owes its existence to the popularity of the island as a holiday resort and place of retirement for foreigners.

Iberian Peninsula

Spain is another growing community. There were few Jews in the country before the proclamation of the republic in 1931 and their freedom was closely restricted. The provisional republican government announced a willingness to accept Jewish immigration, and the Madrid municipality granted a plot of land for a cemetery to the local Jewish community. Immigrants soon began to arrive, both Sephardim from Morocco and the Near East and Ashkenazim from central and eastern Europe. The Nationalist revolt which broke out in 1936 had a distinct anti-Jewish undercurrent, but General Franco offered a refuge in Spain to many fugitives from Nazism and eventually, in 1967, granted the Jewish communities full recognition as religious associations. There are now estimated to be some 12000 Jews in Spain, more than 3000 each in Madrid and Barcelona, and smaller communities in Malaga and a number of other places. Immigration continues, particularly from Morocco and South America, and there has been a marked revival of interest among the wider public in the cultural heritage of Spanish Jewry.

In Portugal the Jews were granted freedom of religious worship after the fall of the monarchy in 1910, but the community has remained small. In fact there are hardly more Jews in Portugal than in Gibraltar which, surprisingly, has a significant Jewish history going back to the 18th century and four venerable synagogues still in use within a few hundred meters of each other. Jews began to settle in Gibraltar soon after it was captured by the British in 1704, and by 1749, when their rights of settlement were formally recognized, they constituted a third of the total population. They have remained staunchly proud of their Jewish heritage and faithful to their religious traditions, while playing a full part in the life of the city.

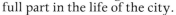

Italy

The Jewish presence in Italy has an uninterrupted history of 2000 years and more, and in modern times Jews have been active in all aspects of Italian life (several of the best-known Italian writers are of Jewish origin). Although under Nazi pressure the Fascist government introduced racial laws and many Jews were deported during the war, antisemitism was not very pronounced in Italy and a large part of the Jewish population survived. After the war Italy gave a temporary home to thousands of displaced persons (at one time they almost outnumbered the native Jews); most of them left in due course for Israel. More recently there was an influx of Jews from Libya, and many Soviet emigrants passed through Italy on their way to other countries.

Italy's present Jewish population is estimated at something over 30000, of whom almost half live in Rome, with a second important community in Milan. A central organization, the Union of Italian Jewish Communities, coordinates communal activities. Italian Jewry is traditionally well integrated and assimilated, although immigration has kept traditional forms of religion alive. Strenuous efforts to foster Jewish education and culture have met with little success. The growth of neo-Fascist activity has recently caused anxiety; there were several violent incidents in 1982, some of which seemed to be aimed particularly against Libyan immigrants. But the most barbaric outrage, an attack on worshipers leaving the main synagogue of Rome after a festival service in October 1982, in which a two-year-old child was killed and many people were injured, was blamed on Arab terrorists.

Right The wartime deportations of Jews from Rome and northern Italy were part of the trauma of defeat and German occupation in the autumn of 1943. Even if the numbers involved were not large compared with other countries occupied by the Nazis, the impact was severe. Within six weeks nearly 10000 Jews were deported to Auschwitz: few survived. The entire City Council of Rome attended this ceremony to mark the twentieth anniversary of the deportations from Rome in October 1963. The commemoration was held at the Portico of Octavia, in the main thoroughfare of what was once the ghetto.

Below The medieval synagogue of Sermoneta, south of Rome. It was abandoned when the Jews were expelled by order of the pope in 1555.

Below right The registration of a marriage in the Rome synagogue.

Right Garibaldi's entry into Rome in 1870 gave a new lease of life to the Jewish community, but led to the clearance of the overcrowded ghetto on the bank of the Tiber as part of a redevelopment scheme. In place of the five old synagogues the community opted for a single monumental building in keeping with the new-found liberty and self-respect. The new building was inaugurated in 1904, and occupies a commanding site overlooking the river. Eschewing the dominant Moorish revival styles, the architects aimed for a more genuinely Italian neoclassicism, with dominant Oriental features.

Few cities in the world can compare with Venice for its wealth of Jewish monuments, with its two ghettos and five remarkable synagogues clustering side by side. The word "ghetto" may be Venetian in origin; at any rate it was here in 1516 (*below*) that the Jews were first confined to a particular quarter and locked in at night. The Great German synagogue (*bottom*) in the New Ghetto was dedicated in 1528, but what is visible dates mainly from a late 17th-century renovation.

Hungary

Hungary is exceptional in still having a relatively numerous Jewish population and a thriving Jewish life, at least in the capital. In fact Budapest is one of the few cities in Europe that can boast a large number of active synagogues, several rabbis, cantors and Jewish butchers, and its own rabbinic seminary.

The 1930 census recorded 444 567 Jews in Hungary, or 5·11 percent of a total population of nearly 8·7 million. But in Budapest the proportion was much higher: 204 371 Jews out of a total of just over one million. About half of Hungarian Jewry was eradicated in the holocaust, mostly in the months following the German occupation in March 1944. After the war there were about 110 000 Jews left in Budapest and only some 30 000 in the rest of the country. More than 20 000 young Jews are estimated to have fled when the borders were briefly opened during the abortive uprising of 1956, but otherwise emigration has barely been possible. In 1975 the Jewish population was put at 100 000 out of a total of 10·5 million, four-fifths of them living in the capital.

There are traces of a Jewish presence in Roman antiquity, but the basis of Jewish settlement was laid in the 13th century, when King Béla IV invited

Hungarian Jewry is alone in having a religious establishment which still holds fast to the principles of European modernism. The Neologue movement, which began in the late 18th century, has withstood the trauma of the Nazi era and the painful transition to Communist rule, and is now exercising a renewed appeal among young Hungarian Jews. *Right* A funeral in Budapest. The coffin is being carried by rabbis who wear the distinctive Neologue clerical dress. *Below* Orthodoxy leads a much reduced existence, centering on this courtyard behind the beautiful and sadly dilapidated Kazinczy utca synagogue.

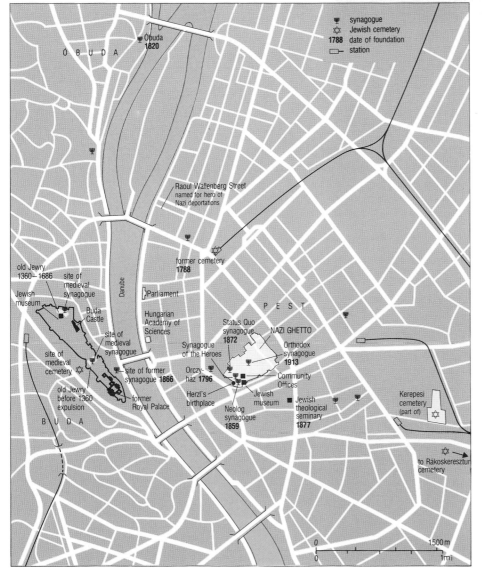

Above The main Jewish cemetery of Pest. In the background is the memorial to the Nazi deportations, inscribed with the names of those who perished.

Left Jewish Budapest. The medieval community was concentrated within the castle of Buda. Jews were permitted to settle in Pest after an imperial edict of 1783.

Top right The Dohány utca synagogue is one of the outstanding buildings of Budapest, and the largest synagogue building in Europe. Built in 1859 in Moorish style, it seats well over 3000 worshipers. The dome visible behind belongs to the Synagogue of the Heroes, a memorial to the dead of World War I, while the courtyard is laid out as a memorial to the victims of the Nazi terror who are buried there.

Center right The interior of the synagogue during a high holy day service. The bearded officiant is Dr László Salgó, Neologue chief rabbi and a member of the Hungarian Parliament.

Left An ordination ceremony at the Jewish Theological Seminary, founded in 1877. Its role in training rabbis and scholars has become even more essential in recent decades. The learned principal, Professor Alexander Scheiber, is seen here addressing the ordinand.

peoples with mercantile experience into the country to help restore the economy after the Mongol invasion. In modern times, too, Jews made a disproportionate contribution to the economic development of the country. In 1868, the year after emancipation, the government convened a General Jewish Congress with a view to regulating the structure of the community. The Jews were deeply divided at that time between Orthodoxy and the Neologue (moderate Reform) movement. In 1895 Judaism was officially recognized as a minority religion. The Orthodox, finding themselves considerably outnumbered in the Congress, formed their own separate organization, while a small number of congregations declined to join either grouping. The three separate religious structures survived until 1950 (the Orthodox population, located mainly in the provinces, suffering disproportionately from the wartime deportations). Then, in the course of moves aimed at bringing the various religious denominations under greater state control, they were merged in a single organization. The government had already, at the end of 1948, concluded an agreement with the Central Board of Hungarian Jews, granting official recognition, freedom of religious practice and financial support on the same basis as other religions; this agreement was renewed in 1968. The Zionist organizations were liquidated in 1949.

There are now some 30 synagogues and prayerhouses in Budapest, and another 70 outside the capital. They are all affiliated to the Central Board, but there are separate Neologue and Orthodox rabbinates. The Orthodox minority, however, has few rabbis. The Jewish Theological Seminary, founded in 1877, trains rabbis for Hungary and other eastern European countries.

Romania

It is estimated that there are some 30 000 Jews left in Romania, half of them living in Bucharest and the rest scattered in nearly 70 smaller communities. More than half the Jews are said to be over 60 years old, and only a small percentage aged under 20.

Before the war there were more than 800 000 Jews in Greater Romania, including the territories added after World War I. It was in these territories—particularly Bessarabia, the Bukovina and Transylvania—that the deportations were most disastrous. The Jewry of old Romania came through the ordeal if not unscathed (the pogroms in Bucharest and Jassy in 1941 when thousands of Jews were brutally murdered are still remembered with horror) then at least relatively intact. In 1948, even after a frantic emigration of survivors and returnees, there were still some 350 000 left—the largest Jewish population of any country in Europe with the exception of the Soviet Union and Britain. During the Stalinist period emigration was blocked and the Jewish communal and political organizations were either liquidated or brought under Communist control. Religious affairs were strictly regulated and religion, together with Zionism, was violently attacked by the Communist Jewish leadership. Under the government of Nicolae Ceausescu

Above Memories of the holocaust are strong in Prague. Here memorial prayers are being said for those who perished at Auschwitz.
Right The gothic Old-New Synagogue is the most important building inherited from the old Prague Jewry. It is owned by the Prague Jewish Religious Community and is used for regular worship.
Far right The Romanesque mortuary hall was erected at the beginning of the present century, and it was here that the first items of a Jewish museum were assembled before the war. It now houses a poignant collection of children's drawings and poems from the Terezín concentration camp.

Communist domination of the community structures was abolished and there was a gradual revival of religious, educational and social institutions coupled with the orderly removal of most of the Jewish population to Israel. This new policy was skillfully handled by a charismatic and politically prominent chief rabbi.

Romanian Jewry is mainly Ashkenazi and Orthodox, but there is a small Sephardi presence and there are some Neologue synagogues in Hungarian-speaking Transylvania. In 1949 the different congregations in each town were merged by government decree into a single community. Antisemitism, which was rife until the end of the monarchy, has been progressively eradicated under Communist rule.

Czechoslovakia

The number of professing Jews in Czechoslovakia is generally reckoned at about 8000, of whom half live in the Czech Socialist Republic (Bohemia and Moravia) and half in Slovakia.

The 1930 census registered 356 000 people of the Jewish faith, of whom 191 000 stated that they were of Jewish nationality. (This national status, recognized in the 1920 constitution, was abolished after the war.) After liberation there were some 45 000 Jews in the country (not including the area of Subcarpathian Ruthenia, which was annexed by the Soviet Union in 1945, and which contained over 100 000 Jews before 1939). Of these about two-thirds had emigrated by 1950 and a further, smaller, wave of emigration occurred after the Soviet intervention in 1968.

The first socialist constitution (1948) proclaimed freedom of religion and prohibited incitement to racial or religious hatred. Laws regulating religious institutions (1949) were strongly opposed by the Catholic Church but welcomed by the Jewish communities as guaranteeing equality and financial security. In the event religious properties (including synagogues) were sequestrated and in some instances donated to Christian communities while insufficient funds were made available to support the Jewish communities, many of which disappeared. Prominent Jews in the Party and government were removed in 1951, stigmatized as "agents of Western imperialism," and imprisoned. At the spectacular show trial in 1952 11 of the 14 defendants were Jews, among them Rudolf Slansky, a vice-premier and former secretary-general of the Communist Party. Some of the leading "liberal Communists" of 1968 were of Jewish origin. Soviet propaganda stressed this factor to exploit anti-semitic prejudice, and the Jewish leaders were eventually replaced.

Jewish religious services are now held regularly at two synagogues in Prague and in a number of other centers. There are some traditionalist communities in Slovakia, but Czech Judaism has traditionally tended towards Reform. The older generation of rabbis has passed away, and for several years there has been no religious leadership in Czechoslovakia, but there is now one young rabbi in Prague trained in Budapest.

Left The entrance to Kazimierz, the old ghetto of Krakow, 1937. Images of Jewish Poland inevitably highlight the unspeakable contrast between the richness of the past and the poverty of the present. Before the holocaust there were 17 000 different communities, ranging from great cities to tiny hamlets. Few could compare, in terms of historic experience or impressive monuments, with Krakow. There are few Jews left now, although services are still held in the magnificent Rema Synagogue, which has been carefully restored. The Old Synagogue, one of the oldest in Europe, has also been restored, and serves as a Jewish museum. But in fact the whole of Poland is a Jewish museum—or rather a poorly tended cemetery.

Bottom Hands raised in priestly blessing: a tombstone in Sientawa.

Below Crumbling stones in a field—all that remains of a once populous rural community.

Poland

In Poland the Jewish community is estimated at fewer than 6000, mostly elderly state pensioners. The Union of Religious Congregations claims 19 member congregations, the largest being in Warsaw and Wroclaw.

Before the war there were more than three million Jews in Poland. At the liberation barely 50 000 remained; several hundred of them were killed in subsequent outbreaks of anti-Jewish violence. In the following years some 200 000 returned, mostly from the Soviet Union, but the majority soon reemigrated, and by 1950 the population was reckoned to be between 60 000 and 70 000. Between 40 000 and 50 000 were allowed to emigrate when Wladyslaw Gomulka came to power in 1956, and most of the remainder left during a ferocious government-sponsored antisemitic campaign in 1968.

Below A rabbi. Warsaw, 1938. Before its destruction Warsaw was one of the Jewish cultural capitals of Europe, and had a really outstanding Jewish life. Books were treated with respect and veneration. Little remains now, even by way of monuments to the dead past.

Right Lvov also belongs to the story of Poland, even though it was under Austrian rule that its Jewry flourished and it is now in the Soviet Ukraine. Poles have always lived at the mercy of arbitrary frontiers.

Center right Hanukkah in a Polish *shtibl*. The lights hold out little hope for an aging and dwindling community.

Above The last kosher butcher in Poland, photographed in Krakow in 1978. He opened his shop once a week. The last kosher restaurant had been closed a decade earlier.

Below A remarkable discovery. In 1950 two sealed milk cans were unearthed in the former ghetto area of Warsaw. They contained documents relating to the ghetto, and had been soldered shut before the historic uprising in 1943.

As in other Communist countries the Jewish organizations were liquidated or brought under Communist control in the late 1940s. The various Zionist parties were suppressed and the Bund was merged with the United Workers Party. A decree of 1949, subsequently incorporated in the 1952 constitution, granted freedom of religion, and the Religious Union (incorporating 63 congregations) was formed and officially recognized. At the same time a Communist-dominated Jewish Cultural and Social Union was set up to promote a Jewish culture "national in form and socialist in content." The Communist government has generally striven to suppress antisemitism, which has long been endemic in Poland, but there have been serious lapses, notably in 1968 and again since 1980, both times in the context of national political and economic crises.

Polish Judaism is traditionalist, but there are no rabbis, no facilities for religious education, and few religious activities.

Other Balkan Countries

In the southern Balkans the Jewish presence has its roots in ancient times, but was substantially augmented under Ottoman rule by refugees from Spain and to a lesser extent from eastern Europe. Despite centuries of anti-Jewish indoctrination by the churches, the general population was highly supportive of the Jews during the Nazi period, and in Bulgaria the number of Jews actually increased slightly during the war. Nevertheless there were heavy losses elsewhere, of which the most calamitous was the elimination of the 60 000-strong community of Salonica. At the end of the war there were 49 000 Jews in Bulgaria, 11 000 in Yugoslavia and a similar number in Greece, and a couple of hundred in Albania. Between October 1948 and May 1949 some 40 000 Jews emigrated from Bulgaria, and another 4000 left in the summer of 1950. Several thousand emigrated from Yugoslavia and Greece in the same period, with the result that all three communities now number only a few thousand members.

Above A family in Salonica. In the 19th century Salonica was virtually a Jewish city. The non-Jewish minorities—Greek, Turkish and Albanian—closed their shops on Jewish holidays and many even spoke Judeo-Spanish. In 1930 there were 60 synagogues in Salonica: only two are used today.
Above right Little remains of the once splendid Jewry which flourished in Rhodes after the island was conquered by the Turks in the 16th century. But there is a functioning synagogue, one of only a dozen in the whole of Greece.
Center right The synagogue in Sofia, built in the Byzantine-Moorish style fashionable in the last century. The origins of Sofia Jewry are in Roman antiquity, but it was after the Spanish expulsion that it became a flourishing Jewish center, mainly Sephardi but with an Ashkenazi synagogue founded by refugees from Bavaria.
Below A view of old Dubrovnik. Few tourists take the trouble to visit the attractive little synagogue, hidden away in a sidestreet which was once the Jewry.
Bottom right This restored synagogue at Zenica in Bosnia is now a museum.

THE SOVIET UNION

Jewish settlements

- major community: estimated over 100 000
- important community: estimated over 10 000
- sizable community: estimated over 1000
- smaller community: estimated under 1000
- functioning synagogue
- little or no Jewish population but historic remains
- scattered communities

scale 1:16 500 000

0   400 km

0   300 mi

Murmansk

Ventspils
Liepaja
Skuodas
Mazeikiai
Telšiai
Kargzdai
Plunge
Kretinga
Klaipeda
Silute
Siauliai
KalinIngrad
Jelgava
Jonava
Tauragé
Kaunas (Kovno)
Kybartai
Marijampole
LITHUANIA
Vilkaviskis
Kalvarija
Lazdijai
RSFSR
Alytus
Trakai
Ukmerge
Panevezys
Vilnius (Vilna)
Grodno
BYELORUSSIA
Slonim
Brest
Pinsk
Pripyat
Jekabpils (Jakobstadt)
Rezekne
Daugavpils
LATVIA
Riga
Tartu
ESTONIA
Tallinn
Pskov
L. Chudskoye
Leningrad
L. Ladozhskoye
L. Onezhskoye
Petrozavodsk

Vitebsk
Minsk
Mogilev
Bobruysk
Gomel
Smolensk
Kalinin
Moscow
Yaroslavl
Kaluga
Bryansk
Tula
Oka
Gorky
Sovetsk
Kazan
Perm
Sukhona
Syktyvkar
Volga
Pechora

Vladimir
Volynsky
Lutsk
Dubno
Rovno
Kovel
Zhitomir
Kremenets
Ternopol
Brody
Lvov
Drogobych
Stry
Uzhgorod
Buchach
Ivano-Frankovsk
Kolomyya
Chernovtsy
Chortkov
Kamenets Podolskiy
Khmelnitsky
Vinnitsa
Berdichev
Kiev
Chernigov
Sumy
Kursk
Voronezh
Desna
Dnieper
UKRAINE

MOLDAVIA
Lipkany
Soroki
Orgeyev
Beltsi
Bendery
Khotin
Kishinev
Kagul
Bolgrad
Izmail

Odessa
Nikolayev
Kherson
Krivoy Rog
Poltava
Dnepropetrovsk
Cherkassy
Kirovograd
Kharkov
Donetsk
Voroshilovgrad
Zaporozhye
Melitopol
Belgorod
Yevpatoriya
Sevastopol
Simferopol
Yalta
Feodosiya
Kerch
Primorsk
Rostov
Krasnodar
Stavropol
BLACK SEA

Saratov
Volga
Don
Volgograd
Kuybyshev
Orenburg
Ural
Ufa
Sverdlovsk
Chelyabinsk
Astrakhan

RUSSIAN SOVIET FEDERAL SOCIALIST REPU

UNION OF SOVI

Omsk
Irtysh
Ishim

Nalchik
Ordzhonikidze
Grozny
Buynaksk
Makhachkala
Derbent
Khasavyurt
Kuba
Khachmas
Kirovabad
GEORGIA
see inset map
ARMENIA
Yerevan
AZERBAIJAN
Baku
Araks
Lenkoran
CASPIAN SEA

KAZAKHSTAN
Karaganda
L. Balkhash
ARAL SEA

Ashkhabad
TURKMENISTAN
Amu Darya
Bukhara
Samarkand
UZBEKISTAN
Syr Darya
Chimkent
Tashkent
Leninabad
Namangan
Kokand
Margilan
Andizhan
Fergana
KIRGIZIA
Frunze
Alma
Dushanbe
TADZHIKISTAN

190

David Oistrakh (1908–74) and Igor Oistrakh (1931–), violinists

B. Pasternak (1890–1960), author

S. Eisenstein (1898–1948), director

Boris Volynov (1934–), cosmonaut

M. M. Litvinov, politician

Y. L. Levin, chief rabbi, Moscow

	1930		1980	
	Approx. Jewish pop.	Jews per thousand	Approx. Jewish pop.	Jews per thousand
USSR	**2 672 000**	**18**	**1 811 000**	**7**
RSFSR	589 000	6	700 000	5
Ukraine	1 574 000	54	634 000	13
Byelorussia	407 000	82	135 000	14
Moldavia*	—	—	80 000	20
Lithuania*	155 000	56	15 000	4
Latvia*	96 000	52	28 000	11
Estonia*	4500	4	5000	3
Uzbekistan	38 000	7	100 000	6
Azerbaijan	31 000	14	35 000	6
Georgia	31 000	12	28 000	6
Tadzhikistan	—	—	15 000	4
Turkmenistan				
Kazakhstan			35 000	4
Kirgizia				
Armenia				

*Not in USSR in 1930: figures in first column relate to nearest census. Note that frontiers of some other republics have changed since 1930.

Jewish Emigration from the Soviet Union

1948–1970	24 000	1976	14 000
1971	14 000	1977	17 000
1972	31 000	1978	29 000
1973	34 000	1979	50 000
1974	20 000	1980	21 000
1975	13 000		

scale 1:5 500 000

0   100 km

0   80 mi

ABKHAZ ASSR
Sukhumi

Zugdidi
Tskhaltubo
Mikha Tskhakaya
Kutaisi
Oni
Kvaisi
Sachkhere
Poti
Abasha
Zestafoni
Tskhinvali
Surami
BLACK SEA
Vani
Khashuri
Gori
Kobuleti
Borzhomi
Kareli
Batumi
ADZHAR ASSR
Akhaltsikhe
GEORGIA
Tbilisi (Tiflis)

Right The Jews of the USSR belong to several different ethnic groups. This Bukharan Jew's forebears were of Persian origin, and his own mother tongue is a Jewish dialect of Tadzhik, a Persian language. In the 1920s and 1930s there was an emerging literature in Judeo-Tadzhik, but it was completely suppressed in the great purge beginning in 1938—the first Soviet Jewish culture to be so eradicated.

Despite huge wartime losses and considerable emigration during the 1970s, the Soviet Union still has the third largest Jewish population of any country in the world, at least three times as large as that of its closest rival, France. It is a population which suffers, however, from serious disadvantages. Like other religions in the Soviet Union, Judaism labors under severe constraints. There are no communal institutions apart from a few synagogues. There are barely any opportunities for cultural development and self-expression, and there is none of that fruitful broadening of horizons which comes from travel abroad, foreign immigration or participation in international gatherings. Zionism is prohibited, and there is no contact with Israel. Nor is there any sign of a creative dialogue between Judaism and socialism or Christianity. The Jews are artificially classified as a nation, but unlike other nations they have no territory of their own, and the classification is paradoxical in other respects too. Up to 1917 the Jews of Russia were among the most backward and oppressed Jewish communities to be found anywhere in the world. After the Revolution serious efforts were made to "normalize" their condition and to integrate them within Soviet society, but the measures employed were often clumsy and crude and were hampered by open or covert discrimination and even by officially sponsored antisemitism of the most primitive kind. From 1970 there appears to have been an increase in anti-Jewish discrimination and harassment, coupled with a sharp rise in emigration; since 1980 the former has become more severe while the latter has been virtually stopped. The problems of Soviet Jewry have come to occupy a prominent place in the concerns of Jews in Israel and the West, partly because of the large numbers involved and partly because of the sentimental attachment of many eastern Ashkenazim to the lands of their forefathers.

According to the 1979 census there were 1·81 million Jews in the Soviet Union, constituting about 0·8 percent of the total population. They ranked sixteenth in the list of "nations" of the Union, between the Kirgiz and the Chuvash. Earlier censuses reported over five million Jews in 1897, three million in 1939, and 2·15 million in 1970 (the frontiers of the country were different in each case).

These population figures have often been contested, and totals of between 2·5 and three million have been cited by Soviet officials and Western specialists. The census figures are based on a national definition of Jewish identity, and on respondents' own replies to the enumerators' question. Given the difficulties of definition (particularly in view of the high proportion of mixed marriages) and the possibility of a certain reluctance to specify Jewish nationality, a higher figure cannot be ruled out, but the census figures are the only ones with any claim to accuracy or consistency. They are particularly interesting in view of the lack of detailed official statistics from other large centers of Jewish population apart from Israel.

Above In the Sephardic synagogue, one of two synagogues functioning in Tiflis (Tbilisi), capital of the Georgian SSR. Georgian Jewry has retained its identity and a very strong religious tradition. A Georgian Jewish museum was opened in Tiflis in the 1930s, but was soon closed. Its rich collections testified to the deep roots of the Jews in Georgia.

Left The synagogue in Leningrad, completed in 1893. The city, then known as St Petersburg, was the capital of czarist Russia. The Jews, being confined to the Pale of Settlement, gravitated to the capital only slowly, but by the end of the century they had a solid and well-established community. Although it has since been outpaced by Moscow, it still has a very considerable Jewish population.

Top In the synagogue. The women's gallery in the grandiose Central Synagogue of Moscow, one of only two still open in the Soviet capital and a natural focus for communal identification. Worshipers still tend to be mainly elderly, but growing numbers of young Jews have been appearing in synagogue in recent years.

Overleaf A service in the synagogue of Minsk, capital of the Byelorussian SSR. The Jewish presence here dates back to the 15th century, when Minsk was the main trading center of Byelorussia; by the 19th century it was one of the largest communities of all Russia. The Great Synagogue was closed down in 1959. This small wooden prayerhouse was subsequently erected on the outskirts of the city.

Soviet Jews belong to several distinct ethnic communities, with different historical, religious and linguistic backgrounds. The large majority, almost 90 percent, are Ashkenazim of European origin whose ancestral spoken language is Yiddish. Their origin is in Poland, of which large parts were annexed to Russia in the late 18th and early 19th centuries. Under the czars they were prevented from spreading beyond the confines of the "Pale of Settlement," but since the 1920s there has been a considerable movement to the main urban centers of Russia and indeed throughout the Soviet Union. Further regions of eastern Europe (the Baltic republics, western Byelorussia, Moldavia and the western Ukraine, including northern Bukovina and Transcarpathia) were annexed by the Soviet Union during or after World War II and the Jews of these western regions still display significant cultural differences from those whose families have been in the Soviet state since its inception. Whereas the latter have become largely assimilated to Russian culture and society, the "western" Jews have retained a higher level of attachment to the Yiddish language and traditional religious observances.

The other Jewish groups originate further east. Jews have been established since ancient times in Georgia. Their native language is Georgian and they have maintained a strong religious culture and social cohesiveness. The 1897 census recorded nearly 19000 Jews in Georgia; in 1970 there were more than 55000, of whom 32000 were native Georgian speakers. Since then there has been considerable emigration to Israel.

A little further east, in Dagestan and Azerbaijan, live the "mountain Jews," who traditionally speak a Turkic language called Tat. They originally inhabited mountain villages but in recent decades have been moving into the cities of the region.

The most numerous of the eastern Jews are the Bukharans, who take their name from the old khanate of Bukhara. Their origins can be traced to the ancient Persian empire. Their native language is Tadzhik (a form of Persian), and their main centers are in Samarkand, Tashkent, Dushanbe and other towns of Uzbekistan and Tadzhikistan. Bukharans have been settling since the last century in Jerusalem, where they form a distinct ethnic community.

A fourth group, the Tatar-speaking Krimchaks of the Crimea, were virtually annihilated by the Nazis.

The Jews are dispersed throughout the 15 republics which make up the USSR. A considerable majority live in the two largest republics, the Russian Republic (RSFSR) and the Ukraine. Important concentrations are also found in Byelorussia, Uzbekistan and Moldavia.

They are almost exclusively an urban population. Ninety-eight percent of Jews inhabit urban areas (compared to some 60 percent of the total population), and about a quarter live in the three largest cities, Moscow, Leningrad and Kiev. They are also an aging population. The 1970 census showed that in the RSFSR only 15·1 percent of Jews were aged under 20 while 26.4 percent were over 60 (the corresponding figures for Russian nationals were 35·5 percent and 12 percent). The birthrate is very low—too low to maintain the present population, even without the losses due to intermarriage and emigration. In fact successive censuses show a steady and dramatic decline in the size of the Soviet Jewish population.

The Jews under czardom and Communism

Under the czars the Jews suffered from severe disadvantages. There were virtually no Jews in the Russian empire before the first partition of Poland in 1772. In the following decades hundreds of thousands came under Russian rule, but they were systematically confined to the Pale of Settlement and were treated with suspicion and contempt. Inferior status, antisemitism, poverty and overcrowding in the Pale and a lack of opportunity for self-improvement created a feeling of frustration and despair. The situation deteriorated still further in the period of reaction following the assassination of Alexander II in 1881. The government adopted an openly anti-Jewish policy, and there were savage waves of pogroms. Large numbers of Jews emigrated or were drawn into revolutionary movements.

The Revolution of February 1917 was welcomed with enthusiasm. One of the first acts of the provisional government was to abolish all legal restrictions on the Jews, who immediately awoke to an unprecedented frenzy of political and cultural activity. Zionist, socialist and religious parties attracted a mass following. For the first time there seemed to be no bar to Jewish advancement and a real hope of total freedom. At the same time Jews suffered terribly in the civil war, the continuing pogroms and the economic reorganization. Over 200000 were massacred in the Ukraine alone, and hundreds of thousands more were made homeless and destitute. Jews flooded out of the Pale into the big cities of Russia. Large numbers joined the Communist Party—in fact by 1927 they were the third largest national group among Party members.

The official Soviet attitude to the Jews is confused and contradictory. Socialist theory maintains a negative view of religion, but allows some scope to the encouragement of national cultures, as a temporary measure strictly subservient to socialist aims. But were the Jews a nation? Stalin, in his authoritative essay on *Marxism and the National Question* (1913), had answered in the negative. "A nation is a historically evolved, stable community of

language, territory, economic life, and psychological makeup manifested in a community of culture." But the Jews, he claimed, have nothing in common except "their religion, their common origin and certain relics of national character." They were heading inevitably towards assimilation, and demands for Jewish national autonomy were merely a reaction against this process. In practice, however, the Jews were implicitly recognized as a national entity. Early in 1918 a Commissariat for Jewish National Affairs (*Yevkom*) was established; it liquidated the existing autonomous Jewish institutions and appropriated their funds and property. At the same time Jewish Sections (*Yevsektsii*) were created within the Communist Party to carry out Party policy and propagate Communism among Jewish workers. The *Yevkom* was abolished in 1924 and the *Yevsektsii* in 1930, but the Jews continue to be treated as a nationality in all official publications. Since internal passports were introduced in 1933 children of Jewish parents have been identified as being of Jewish nationality in personal documents.

One of the obvious inconsistencies in classing the Jews as a nation was their lack of a national territory. The Communists were strongly opposed to Zionism, which has been ruthlessly suppressed since the 1920s. In the meantime a scheme was being formulated to settle Jews on the land in what might become a territory of their own. Mikhail Kalinin, the Soviet president, who was a member of Geserd (or Ozet: the "Society for the Settlement of Working Jews on the Land in the USSR"), said to the Society in 1926: "The Jewish people now faces the great task of preserving its nationality. For this purpose a large segment of the Jewish population must transform itself into a compact farming population, numbering at least several hundred thousand souls." Birobidzhan, a large, sparsely populated region in the far east, on the banks of the River Amur which divides the Soviet Union from Manchuria, was selected for this project. The objective was partly to settle a vulnerable border area, partly to distract attention from Zionism while relieving the economic plight of impoverished Jews with the help of financial contributions from Jews abroad. The project was well received but the practical results were disappointing. It was hard to persuade people to settle voluntarily in the far east, to undertake hard labor in a difficult terrain, with winter temperatures of minus 14°C. Few Jews took up the challenge, and within a few years those leaving outnumbered those arriving. In 1934, when the area was officially proclaimed the "Jewish Autonomous Oblast," Kalinin stated that if only 100000 Jews settled there the government would consider creating a Soviet Jewish republic. By the end of the following year the Jews of Birobidzhan numbered only 14000, 23 percent of the total population. This percentage was never surpassed. The region was closed to Jewish refugees during the war and in 1948 its Jewish institutions were suppressed. The 1970 census reported 11452 Jews, or 6·64 percent of the total population of 172449, in the Jewish Autonomous Oblast.

The nationality question is complicated by the existence of two opposing tendencies in Soviet theory. The Soviet Union is a multinational state, which recognizes the existence of more than 100 distinct nationalities. The equality of the different nationalities is asserted and protected, and the development of national cultures is sanctioned and even encouraged. At the same time the centralism of the Soviet state, the demands of socialist ideology and the dominant position of the Russians produce tensions in the political, economic and cultural spheres. The Declaration of Rights of Peoples issued shortly after the Bolshevik seizure of power in November 1917 proclaimed the "free development of national minorities and ethnic groups," and in the 1920s Jewish administrative and judicial institutions were set up in areas of concentrated Jewish population. In the 1926 census over 70 percent of all Jews specified Yiddish as their mother tongue, and a conscious attempt was made to establish Yiddish schools, theaters, newspapers and publishing houses, to serve as a tool in the Sovietization of the Jewish "popular masses." Most of these institutions were destroyed during World War II, and those that remained were closed down in 1948, at the beginning of the period of Stalinist persecution of Jewish culture. Since 1959 there has been a very slight relaxation: a few Yiddish books have been published, some theatrical activity is permitted and there are two regular publications, the monthly literary review *Sovietish Heymland* (established in 1961) and a newspaper published in Birobidzhan. There are no Yiddish schools or classes. Meanwhile the use of Yiddish has suffered a serious decline. In the 1979 census only 14 percent of all Jews specified Yiddish as their mother tongue. No other nationality of the Soviet Union recorded such a low percentage of speakers of the national language as their mother tongue. The proportion of Yiddish speakers was notably higher in the older age groups, and somewhat higher in rural than in urban areas. Significantly, a much larger percentage of Yiddish speakers was recorded in the western regions which came under Soviet rule as a result of the war. In Lithuania as many as 43 percent of the Jews gave Yiddish as their mother tongue.

The statistics on language are an indication of the extent of cultural assimilation, particularly among Jews whose families have lived in the Soviet Union since the beginning. Assimilation is in fact a long-term aim of Soviet policy, formulated by Stalin in a celebrated speech made in 1925: national cultures "must be given an opportunity to develop, expand and reveal all their potentialities in order to establish the conditions for their fusion into a single common culture with a single common language." Stalin's own antisemitism, which became visible during the campaigns against Jewish nationalism and "cosmopolitanism" in the Black Years 1948–53, allowed little scope for Jewish culture to develop or expand. Since his death there has been no respite in the pressure for assimilation. Khrushchev in 1956 explained to a parliamentary delegation of French socialists that the absence of Jewish schools was due to the advanced state of Jewish assimilation: "even if Jewish schools were established very few would attend them voluntarily." The party congress in 1961 called for the "effacement of national distinctions . . . including distinctions of language." This inevitably means greater pressure for Russification. In 1970 nearly 80 percent of all Jews specified Russian as their mother tongue, and a further 16 percent named it as their second language. By 1979 the figures were, respectively, 83 and 14 percent.

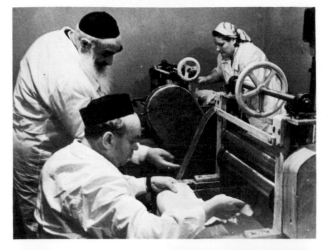

Left Baking *matzot* for Passover. Facilities for religious observance are limited and somewhat unpredictable. Restrictions on the baking of *matzot* were eased in 1965, but provisions are still not readily available in many places.

Right Jews protesting outside the Ministry of Internal Affairs, Moscow, in 1973. The signs read "I want to go to Israel" and "Visa for Israel or prison together." It was a time of mounting desperation and openness in voicing Jewish demands, including the right to emigrate to Israel. And the efforts were being crowned with success, despite the hardships in store for those daring to apply.

Above The issue of antisemitism in the USSR came to the fore in the trial of the writers Yuli Daniel (*left*) and Andrei Sinyavski in Moscow in 1966. Both men, charged with defaming Russia in books smuggled out of the country and published abroad, were alleged to have slandered Soviet society by claiming that it was not free of antisemitism. Daniel was sentenced to five years' imprisonment, Sinyavski to seven. Both had pleaded not guilty.

Above left Young musicians give a concert in 1973 in Birobidzhan, capital of the Jewish Autonomous Province (*oblast*) of the same name. On the wall behind them is a map of the province. Founded in the 1920s as a rational solution to the unique condition of the Jews as a people without a territory, Birobidzhan has never managed to attract much Jewish settlement, and its Yiddish schools and other institutions have been closed down. Well under 1 percent of Soviet Jewry lives there now: Birobidzhan has become a faded dream.

Left This old Jewish graveyard in the Ukraine is a poignant reminder of the Jews' deep roots in the land in eastern Europe. This was a rural settlement, like so many others in the region.

Multinational policy may have the effect of favoring some nationalities at the expense of others, through quotas based on the relative numerical strengths of the different populations. These arrangements tend to work to the disadvantage of the Jews. Jews have traditionally sought, and attained, a high level of education. In 1970 46·8 percent of the employed Jewish population in the RSFSR had a higher education, as against 6·5 percent of employed Russians. Since then very severe quotas have been introduced. Few Jews are admitted to institutes of higher education, particularly the better ones in the major cities. Some Jewish students have applied successfully to institutes in Siberia and the Asiatic republics, whose admission practices are freer, but the overall decline in Jewish student numbers has been dramatic and will inevitably soon have a marked effect on the character of the Jewish population as a whole. The Jews are not the only people to suffer from such discriminatory policies, but they have suffered more severely than others. In some areas the representation of Jews has been reduced far below even the small percentage due to them by virtue of their share in the total population. There are hardly any Jews at all in the central committee of the Communist Party, the Supreme Soviets of the USSR and its constituent republics, the military hierarchy or the diplomatic service. It is hard to avoid the suspicion that the operative factor is discrimination against Jews as such.

Antisemitism and Judaism in the Soviet Union
The question of antisemitism in the Soviet Union is a complicated one. Antisemitism was rife in prerevolutionary Russia; its roots may even go back in part to the struggle against so-called "Judaizing" ideas in the late 15th century. It existed at all levels of society and was actively encouraged by the Church and the government. The triumph of Bolshevism actually contributed to popular antisemitism, the prominent involvement of Jews in the movement nurturing fears of a Jewish takeover of Russia. The Bolsheviks themselves were deeply sensitive to the problem and consciously worked to eliminate antisemitism. Incitement to racial or national hatred was made a punishable offense in successive criminal codes and constitutions, including the 1977 All-Union Constitution which, echoing earlier formulations, outlaws "any advocacy of racial or national exclusiveness, hostility or contempt." But antisemitism is far from having been eradicated,

even at the official level, and crude caricatures of Jews and Judaism deriving from classical antisemitism have been perpetuated in officially sanctioned publications.

Antisemitic propaganda, together with practical discrimination against Jews, has become increasingly noticeable since the renewed anti-Zionist campaign which followed the Six Day War in 1967. A strong Jewish protest movement has grown up, not unconnected to the wider movement for human rights and to other minority pressure groups. The official response has been a marked increase in police moves against Jewish activities and against individual activists, many of whom have been condemned to harsh prison sentences or internal exile. At the same time there was, for a while, an unexpected increase in the number of Jews allowed to emigrate. Despite the heavy risks involved in political dissent, applying for an exit visa, or unofficial cultural activity, large numbers of Jews have rediscovered or reasserted their Jewish identity and there has been an extraordinary upsurge in interest in the Hebrew language and Jewish history.

Russian Judaism has hardly been touched by Western influences. Under the czars the Jews enjoyed a large measure of religious freedom, although there was a strong internal polemic against the allegedly harmful effects of traditional religion and rabbinic dominance. After the Revolution anti-religious activity was institutionalized in the work of the *Yevsektsii*. The traditional community organizations were dissolved in 1919, and nothing has taken their place. In the 1920s there were widely publicized "community trials" directed against Jewish observances and institutions, and against the religion in general. Jewish primary and secondary schools and synagogues were gradually closed, rabbis and other religious functionaries were arrested and deported and religious books and ritual objects were confiscated. The Hebrew language was declared to be reactionary, and was eventually banned in the late 1920s. Despite all these repressive measures, groups of Jews (especially some of the Hasidic sects) continued to practice and to teach the religion in secret, and World War II brought under Soviet rule large Jewish populations which still adhered to traditional Judaism. The oppression of Jewish culture during the "Black Years" was not specifically directed against the religion, but a vigorous anti-religious campaign was renewed in 1957, and many of the surviving synagogues were subsequently closed. There are now only some 60 synagogues in the Soviet Union, half of which are in the Caucasus and the Asiatic republics where the anti-religious campaigns were never waged as ruthlessly as in the west. There is no central religious organization or representative body. There are no facilities for the training of rabbis or cantors, although a handful of selected students have been sent to Hungary. The recent revival of Jewish consciousness has brought the synagogues to prominence as places of assembly, and large crowds tend to gather around them on Sabbaths and festivals, but this does not indicate a return to religion so much as a lack of other Jewish meeting places. In fact there has been a certain tendency for Jews in search of spiritual satisfaction to turn to Christianity. The future of Jewish religion in the Soviet Union seems extremely bleak.

ASIA

Apart from the Soviet Union there is only one Asian country of any real importance in the Jewish world, and that is Israel. Israel is in Asia but not of it, cut off by the desert and the hostility of the Arab states to the east. In any case the western coastlands of Asia are part of the Mediterranean world: they have always looked west rather than east, and this is also true of the Jews of the region—the Greek Jews under Roman rule, the Sephardim who found refuge in the Ottoman empire or the modern Israelis. But even in ancient times there were populous Jewish communities in Mesopotamia and Iran whose outlook on the world was very different. They maintained contacts with the west, notably in the heyday of Islam when the Babylonian Talmud was exported along the coast of North Africa and even into Europe, but they had deep roots in Asia and their trading links extended to India, and over the Silk Route to China. In modern times, too, the Sassoons of Baghdad maintained a trading empire with branches in Bombay and Calcutta, Canton and Hong Kong, Shanghai and Yokohama.

But the currents of Asian history have turned against the Jews. Economic and political changes have ousted the Far Eastern traders and caused massive emigration from the thronging centers of the Near East. The Nazi onslaught in Europe brought thousands of refugees trekking overland to Shanghai and other eastern havens, but they have left little permanent trace, moving on to more familiar climes as soon as conditions permitted. Worst of all was the Muslim fanaticism and Arab nationalism which have all but eliminated the Jewish presence in Arab lands since the creation of Israel, and recently disrupted the last remaining community of any size, in Iran.

No country of Asia is drawing Jewish immigration in any appreciable numbers at the present time, with the sole exception of Israel which has absorbed hundreds of thousands of Asian refugees in its short existence. Very few countries can offer the combination of political security, a welcome to strangers and economic opportunity which can attract foreign settlement.

Most of the Asian communities are dwindling at a clearly visible rate; some have been extinguished in recent years. East of the Indus India is now the only country with more than 1000 Jewish inhabitants.

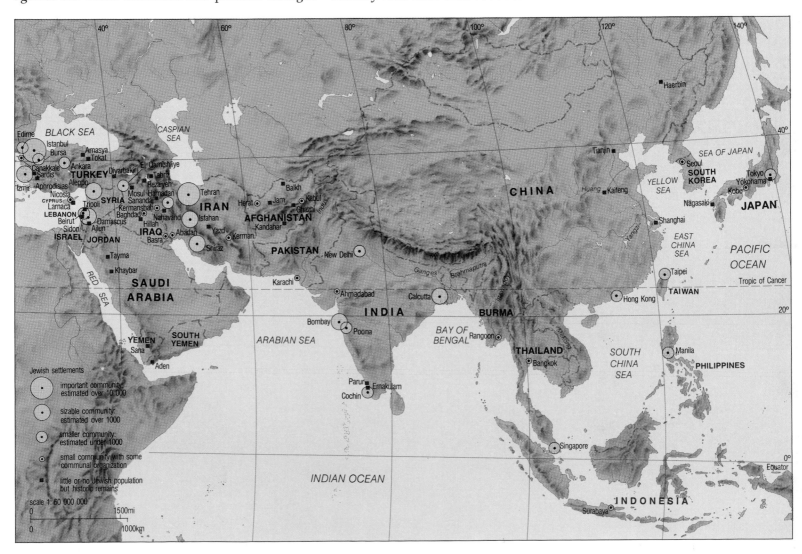

| | 1930 | | 1980 | |
	Approx. Jewish pop.	Jews per thousand	Approx. Jewish pop.	Jews per thousand
Aden	4000	78·4	—	—
Afghanistan	5000	0·6	100	0·0
Burma	2000	0·1	20	0·0
China	20 000	0·0	50	0·0
Cyprus	75	0·2	30	0·0
Hong Kong	250	0·0	250	0·0
India	24 000	0·1	4500	0·0
Indochina	1000	0·0	—	—
Indonesia	900	0·0	100	0·0
Iran	90 000	7·0	37 000	1·0
Iraq	73 000	25·5	200	0·0
Israel	175 000	169·1	3 283 000	837·1
Japan	2000	0·0	800	0·0
Lebanon	5000	5·3	200	0·1
Pakistan	—	—	250	0·0
Philippines	500	0·0	200	0·0
Singapore	500	1·0	450	0·2
Syria	21 000	7·0	4500	0·5
Taiwan	—	—	70	0·0
Thailand	—	—	250	0·0
Turkey	80 000	6·0	22 000	0·5
Yemen	58 000	24·2	1200	0·1

Chaim Weizmann (1874–1952), Israeli chemist and statesman

Golda Meir (1898–1978), Israeli statesman

S. Y. Agnon (1888–1970), Israeli author

Ruth Prawer Jhabvala (1927–), Indian author

Topol (1935–), Israeli actor

continuation southwards
scale 1:2 000 000

Jewish settlements

population over 100 000

50 000 to 100 000

10 000 to 50 000

5000 to 10 000

under 5000

kibbutz, moshav or moshav shitufi

LEBANON

Qiryat Shemona

GOLAN HEIGHTS

Nahariyya

Maalot-Tarshiha

Zefat (Safed)

Hazor HaGelilit

Akko (Acre)

Qiryat Motzkin

Qiryat Yam

Sakhnin

Teverya (Tiberias)

Hefa (Haifa)
Jewish pop 211 000

Qiryat Bialik

Qiryat Ata

Sea of Galilee

Nesher

Tirat Karmel

Nazerat (Nazareth)

Nazerat Illit

Qiryat Tivon

Migdal HaEmeq

Yoqneam Illit

Qishon

Afula

Bet Shean

Or Aqiva

Pardes Hanna-Karkur

Hadera

Netanya

Tulkarm

Raananna

Kefar Sava

Nablus (Shechem)

WEST BANK

Herzliyya

Bene Beraq

Ramat HaSharon

Qiryat Ono

Fari a

Jordan

Yaboq

Ramat Gan

Petah Tiqwa

Rosh HaAyin

Givatayim

Givat Shemuel

Tel Aviv-Yafo (Jaffa)
Jewish pop 321 000

Ganne Tiqwa

Yehud

Bat Yam

Or Yehuda

Holon

Azor

Rishon le Ziyyon

Lod (Lydda)

Nes Ziyyona

Ramla

JORDAN

Yavne

Rehovot

Ramallah

Gedera

El Ariha (Jericho)

Ashdod

Mevasseret Ziyyon

Bet Shemesh

Jerusalem
Jewish pop 298 000

Lakhish

Qiryat Malakhi

Ashqelon

Qiryat Gat

Hebron

Dead Sea

Sederot

Gaza

Netivot

GAZA STRIP

Khan Yunis

Ofaqim

Arad

Rafah

Besor

Beer Sheva
(Beer-sheba)

Dimona

Yeroham

Arava

Elat

34°

35°

35°

33°

32°

31°

30°

international boundary

armistice line, 1949

later cease-fire line

scale 1 : 1 250 000

0   30 km

0   20 mil

Israel

Israel is unique in the Jewish world, not only because its population is mainly Jewish but because it defines itself as a "Jewish state." This concept is novel and to a large extent experimental. The implications for the internal constitution of the state and for its relations with the rest of the Jewish world are far reaching and hard to define; they are complex and fraught with actual and potential conflicts. The establishment of the state in 1948 was the fulfillment of the Zionist dream and was hailed by Jews the world over as an epoch-making, possibly even Messianic, event. It was seen as the renewal of the ancient kingdom of Israel, the ending of 19 centuries of exile: the influx of Jews from all parts of the world was described in typically religious language as the "ingathering of exiles." It gave hope and new life to Jewish outcasts from many lands and fused them together into a new society. For the first time Jews had a country of their own, in which they could settle freely and govern their own affairs. Even the majority of Jews, who had no desire to settle in Israel, looked on with pride as the state established and maintained its existence in the face of implacable hostility from the neighboring Arab states. Israel became a focus of attention for the whole Jewish world, offering much-needed reassurance to a generation which had come through utter darkness, capturing the imagination of a younger generation in search of an explicit Jewish identity. But the problems of the state are many: internal disharmony, continuing border disputes with neighboring countries and uncertainty about the relationship between Israel and the Jewish diaspora (not to mention the chronic economic crisis which has tormented Israel since its creation). The tragic plight of the Palestinian Arab refugees has also soured the happiness of a dream come true, and added further discord both within Israel and abroad.

Israel has created a new type of Jewish identity—nationalist, self-confident and predominantly secular. The young Israeli (often nicknamed *sabra* after the juicy but prickly fruit of a common cactus) often seems to cultivate an image that is the opposite of the stereotype of the diaspora Jew: suntanned, sure of himself to the point of arrogance, unbowed by the burdens of Jewish religion and gentile antisemitism. The contrast is an archaic one, and its simplicity is belied by the complex reality of Israeli life. Israelis are drawn from many different backgrounds, and not all conform to the pioneering *macho* image. Psychological studies have revealed deep-seated anxieties underlying the brash exterior of the *sabra*, and the figure of the conquering Israeli soldier has recently begun to arouse misgivings, not least among young Israelis themselves.

Israelis are justifiably proud of their achievements in democracy and human rights, social welfare, agricultural development, education, technology, defense and a plethora of other spheres, while being the first to admit that much more remains to be done. Paradoxically, the most glaring failure has been in the area of Jewish religion, where Israel continues to be dependent on the heritage of the past and on developments originating abroad.

Modern Israel has produced no significant Jewish religious movement, no notable contribution to Jewish theology, no viable solution to any of the pressing problems confronting Judaism today. The prophetic vision that "Torah will come forth from Zion" remains unfulfilled, and in fact Israel is the one community in the Jewish world where the public image of religion is almost entirely negative.

The first census held in Palestine, in 1922, recorded 84000 Jews, 11 percent of the total population of 752000, while in 1931 there were 175000 Jews, 17 percent of the total of 1036000. By 1946 there were over 600000 Jews out of a total of some 1900000. In 1982, according to official estimates, there were 3354000 Jews in Israel, out of a total population of 4038000.

The Jews of Israel are essentially an immigrant population, even though the majority now were born in the country. They hail from every part of the world and speak a babel of native tongues. The state has consciously attempted to fuse them into a single, Hebrew-speaking society, a process in which schools and especially the army play important parts, but ethnic differences persist through the generations and there is still a strong awareness of national and linguistic divisions. The Western Jews who have always dominated the country politically and socially tend to look down on the Jews of African and Asian origin, but even within these two main groupings there are many subgroups and it remains common for Jews from a particular country or region to be concentrated in the same neighborhood or occupation.

In theory Israel is a secular democratic state. In practice there are features of Israel's life which are neither secular nor democratic. Many concern the *Kulturkampf* between religious and secularist activists. Some of the religious refuse to recognize the authority of the government or the state; others have compromised to the extent of forming religious political parties which, although very small, control considerable power on account of the system of coalition government. The secularists exert less power, whether because they are unwilling to abandon their main weapon, reason, or because they are loth to appear in the guise of persecutors of holy men. Clashes have occurred for various reasons, and to an outsider perhaps the most surprising cause is archaeology. But in Israel archaeology is virtually a national sport, and the uncovering of the heritage of the remote past is a source of pride and fascination. Few excavations have aroused as much excitement as those in the "City of David" to the south of the Temple Mount in Jerusalem. When the excavations had been proceeding successfully for several seasons, a rumor spread that they were disturbing ancient graves, perhaps even the tombs of King David and his family. It took police and border guards several hours to disperse the ultra-pious demonstrators who fought to prevent the archaeologists from desecrating the supposed tombs (*left*). The issue soon became a national crisis, which threatened to bring down the governing coalition. *Above* Secularists and archaeologists protesting against the religious interference in the digs. The placard shows a caricature of the Ashkenazi chief rabbi of Israel holding up two tablets of the law inscribed "Thou shalt not dig. Thou shalt not investigate. Thou shalt not know. For I am the Rabbinate who brought you out of the land of law."

In line with the worldwide trend, the Jews of Israel tend to gravitate to the towns, but Zionist policy has favored settlement on the land. A distinctive feature of the Israeli countryside is the kibbutz, a peculiarly Zionist form of collective settlement. The kibbutzim have played a role in the military as well as the political and economic life of the country totally disproportionate to number and size. Not all agricultural settlements are kibbutzim, however: there is also the cooperative settlement (*moshav*), which allows for a greater degree of private family life, as well as the mixed system called the *moshav shitufi*, which combines elements from the other two.

There have always been Jewish communities in the land of Israel. Before the present century their number was small, but there were several significant waves of immigration at various times, motivated usually by religious devotion. In the 1880s a new style of immigration began, of Russian Jews with a more secular ideology. The two groups, the "Old Yishuv" and the "New Yishuv," had little in common and hardly mixed. At the beginning of the 20th century the numbers in both groups were roughly equal, but the second and third waves of immigration (1903–14 and 1918–23) brought large numbers of eastern European newcomers, a significant proportion of whom were Labor Zionists sharing a vision of a classless Jewish nation wielding autonomous control of its own destiny. The area had meanwhile been conquered from Turkey by the British, committed by the Balfour Declaration of 1917 to "the establishment in Palestine of a national home for the Jewish people." This objective was written into the League of Nations Mandate for Palestine (dated 24 July 1922; formally implemented on 29 September 1923), which recognized a Jewish Agency for advising and cooperating with the administration on matters affecting the establishment of the Jewish National Home and the interests of the Jewish population. The Jewish Agency was not formally constituted until 1929. It was considered to represent Jewry worldwide; in effect it was an organ of the Zionist organization. The Jews of Palestine had an elected assembly, whose executive was the National Council. The Agency and the Council between them constituted a kind of shadow government, preparing the way for the formation of a national Jewish government after the end of British rule in 1948. Meanwhile there was a fourth wave of immigration from Poland in 1924–26, and a fifth wave, in 1933–39, from Nazi Germany and other European countries. The issue of Jewish immigration became the focus of a three-cornered conflict between Zionists, British and Arabs. In conditions of mounting chaos the United Nations voted on 29 November 1947 for a partition of the land between Jews and Arabs, a scheme which was accepted by the majority of the Zionists but rejected by the Arabs and the British. On 14 May 1948 the British withdrew and the Jewish National Council issued the Declaration of Independence. Immediately the newborn state was invaded by armies from five Arab states (Egypt, Transjordan, Iraq, Syria and Lebanon). The War of Independence left Israel in control of an area larger than that allocated to the Jews in the partition plan, and in a state of suspended war with all her neighbors. Full-scale fighting broke out again sub-

Above Immigrants arriving in Israel in 1949. The creation of the Jewish state and the immediate lifting of immigration restrictions brought miraculous relief to the tens of thousands of Jews pent up in the DP camps of Europe. They had lost their families, their homes, their belongings, in many cases even their will to live. At last they could look forward to a future as human beings and as Jews, "To be a free people in our own land," as the national anthem, *Hatikvah*, expressed it.

Right The land of Israel is a land with a past. At one point the Zionist movement was almost split apart over a painful decision—whether to press for a homeland in Israel which seemed unattainable or to settle for a territory elsewhere. The main stream insisted on the land which carried that name of the people of Israel, and where the early history of the people had been played out. The fact that this land was already occupied by Arabs, who also had a past in the land, was overlooked in the enthusiasm of the moment.

Israel may give the impression of being governed by the elderly, but it is in a real sense a land of and for the young. *Right* A close look at these youngsters will reveal their diverse origins, and also hints of diverse cultural influences. *Above* In the kibbutz, children are cared for communally, so that both parents can be free to work. *Opposite* Nahalal, an early attempt at a cooperative village (*moshav*), constructed in 1921 to the plans of Richard Kaufmann. The design is bold, symbolic and uncompromising.

sequently in 1956 (the Sinai Campaign), 1967 (the Six Day War), 1973 (the Yom Kippur War) and 1982 (the Lebanon Offensive). A positive step towards peace was the peace treaty with Egypt signed in 1979 as a result of President Anwar Sadat's historic visit to Jerusalem two years earlier. In the meantime Jewish immigration on an unprecedented scale has raised the Jewish share of the population from 30 percent to over 80 percent.

The character of the "Jewish state"

The Declaration of Independence proclaimed the establishment of a "Jewish state," but the precise character of such a state had never been formally defined. Jews, both within the state and abroad, held widely differing and conflicting views of the matter. For many, the "Jewish" ingredient was purely national: Israel was to be a modern state whose raison d'être was the need to "normalize" Jewish national existence. For others the term "Jewish" inevitably implied a religious commitment. The conflict has still not been resolved. Theoretically, Israel is a secular, democratic state, in which religious freedom is guaranteed for all and non-Jews enjoy equal civil rights with Jews. The reality often appears to fall short of this ideal. Various elements of the population have, over the years, voiced legitimate grievances, and serious and much-publicized conflicts of interest have broken out, sometimes into violence and public commotion. The main focus of concern has been the place of traditional Jewish law (*halakhah*) in the state, and the jurisdiction of the rabbinic courts: a complex of problems with far-reaching ramifications. But serious questions have also been raised about the rights of the non-Jewish minorities and about the status of different elements within the Jewish population. The present situation represents a reluctant and unstable compromise between various interest groups, none of which is entirely happy with the prevailing arrangements.

The relations between religion and state are a thorny issue. There is no established religion, but the concept of the "Jewish state," coupled with the large Jewish majority, ensures that Judaism will occupy a position of primacy and that the various other religions will be allotted a secondary role. The majority of Jews in Israel would not classify themselves as religious, and many of them are militant secularists, but most accept a measure of religious observance in public life, for instance the legal enforcement of Sabbath rest in many spheres. This is in part a concession to the religious minority, in part an acceptance that even a secular Jewish state should embody some basic features of the distinctive Jewish way of life, and partly perhaps an assertion of a bond with Jews abroad, who expect to see certain familiar Jewish institutions in a Jewish state. But secularists are sensitive to any encroachment of religion on the public domain and strongly resent religious interference in their private lives. Many religious Jews, for their part, feel that there should be greater religious content in the life of the Jewish state, a feeling given concrete expression by the religious political parties.

The National Religious Party (NRP) was formed in 1956 by a merger of two factions in Mizrachi, the religious wing of the Zionist movement. It commanded 10–12 seats in the 120-seat Knesset (parliament) until the elections to the Tenth Knesset in 1981, when its support shrank from 9 percent to under 5 percent of the vote and its representation from 12 to 6 seats. The Agudat Israel, founded in Poland in 1912, is more lukewarm in its commitment to Zionism (in fact it held aloof from Zionist politics until 1947). With its "workers' branch," Poalei Agudat Israel, it had five or six seats in earlier parliaments and in 1981 secured four seats.

The system of proportional representation allows considerable influence to small parties if they are prepared to join the governing coalition. The NRP has participated in every government since the creation of the state and has been able to command important ministries. In 1977, when Labor lost power for the first time, the Agudah also joined the Likud coalition and the religious parties succeeded in wresting considerable concessions from the Likud as the price of their allegiance. NRP ministers held responsibility for home affairs, the police, religious affairs, education and culture; the Agudah was barred by its policy-making authority, the "Council of Torah Sages," from accepting any ministry but received other important appointments. The government also agreed to a number of specific measures aimed at enforcing *halakhah* or benefiting the religious sector of Israeli Jewry. In addition to their political activities, at parliamentary and local level, the religious parties have developed agricultural settlements, economic enterprise and educational institutions. (The NRP actually sponsors a university, Bar Ilan.)

The rationale for the existence of religious parties is the perceived clash of interests between religious and secular Jews. In fact many religious Jews support other political parties, while some ultra-religious Jews eschew Israeli politics altogether. Moreover, the activities of the religious parties are in part directed against a sector of the religious community, that is the non-Orthodox, since the Mizrachi was founded in 1902 by eastern European traditionalists and the Agudah by central European Orthodox Jews, both of which groups have remained resolutely opposed to religious reforms. (An Aguda member once hurled a Reform prayer book to the ground during a Knesset debate and was seen to spit on it.) This religious conservatism may explain why the religious parties have not publicly called for the transformation of Israel into a "theocratic state" governed by *halakhah*: such a change would inevitably lead to large-scale reform of the *halakhah*, which in its present form is unsuited to the needs of the modern state. They therefore confine their efforts on the whole to ensuring that observant Jews are not placed at a disadvantage, to maintaining and extending the privileges of their own institutions, and to enforcing certain basic principles of *halakhah* in the public domain.

In the area of legislation the first success of the religious parties was to block the enactment of a full written constitution for the state. Their most far-reaching achievement, however, has been the extension of the jurisdiction of the rabbinic courts and the prevention of the introduction of civil marriage and divorce. The Mandate had in effect perpetuated the Ottoman *millet* system, under which each religious community, through its own courts, had virtual autonomy in matters of personal status. The provisions only applied to Palestinian nationals and membership of a religious community was a voluntary act. A law passed in 1953 extended the jurisdiction of rabbinic courts in matters of marriage and divorce to all Jews resident in Israel, whether citizens or foreign nationals, whether religious or atheist. Consequently in Israel Jews may only marry other Jews (as defined by the rabbinic authorities); certain kinds of union are forbidden (for example a hereditary priest may not marry a

divorcée); and even secular Jews are obliged to have a religious marriage ceremony. Marriages (including mixed and civil marriages) contracted abroad are, however, recognized, and many Israeli couples have exploited this loophole and traveled abroad to marry. All moves to introduce civil marriage in Israel have been blocked by the religious parties.

Another area on which the religious parties have kept a watchful eye is that of religious education. This is the issue which led to the dissolution of the first Knesset, in 1951, and it has proved a delicate topic ever since. Education in Israel is compulsory and (in the public system) free. The Mizrachi schools, employing only religious teachers and placing an emphasis on religious subjects, were brought into the state system in 1953, but the party insisted that they should remain separate from the secular schools and maintain their religious content (which was, however, limited to 25 percent of class time). The Aguda schools, which taught religious subjects to the virtual exclusion of everything else, opted out of the state system but were granted a recognized status which allowed them to receive financial assistance from the state in return for the introduction of an approved secular curriculum. A small number of independent religious schools remained entirely outside the state educational system, with Yiddish as the language of instruction and hardly any attention being paid to secular subjects. All the state primary schools taught "values of Jewish culture," under a syllabus laid down by the Ministry of Education, including study of the Bible and of Jewish history, but the effectiveness of these courses when taught by nonreligious or even anti-religious teachers has been frequently questioned. After the election of 1977 the NRP for the first time took over the Ministry of Education and the new minister devoted careful attention to enriching the religious content of the syllabus in secular schools by producing modern, attractively designed courses. This new development may have far-reaching effects in overcoming a serious deficiency in Israeli education, even though it will not in itself do anything to remedy the rift in Israeli society arising from the social segregation of "religious" and "nonreligious" schoolchildren.

Other controversial matters on which the religious parties have taken a strong line include Sabbath observance, pig-farming, pornography, abortion, post-mortem examinations and military service for women and student rabbis. They jealously protect the financial interests of their various enterprises and are active at local-government level in promoting religious interests.

Religious politics are also involved in a fundamental constitutional question, the definition of Jewish identity within the state. The Law of Return, passed by the Knesset in 1950, gave formal legal expression to Zionist doctrine by conferring on every Jew the right to emigrate to Israel. The Nationality Law of 1952 granted Israeli citizenship automatically to any Jewish immigrant. For administrative purposes a register of Jewish nationals is kept by the Ministry of Home Affairs, and nationality (as distinct both from citizenship and from religion) is entered on each resident's official papers. The law did not at first define the term "Jewish." The Rabbinical Courts Law of 1953 in effect introduced a criterion of Jewish identity, since the Jewish courts, which have sole jurisdiction over all Jews in matters of marriage and divorce, are entitled (indeed are obliged under their own constitution) to apply the talmudic definition of a Jew, that is anyone either born to a Jewish mother or converted according to specific procedures. The definition is at odds with the national conception of the Jewish state, which would tend to confer Jewish status on anyone considering himself a Jew or suffering discrimination as a Jew, regardless of whether or not he would conform to the narrower talmudic criteria. The early immigrants to Israel included many people who had been victims of the Nazi race laws, but who were not "halakhically" Jewish. The talmudic definition would also exclude many Soviet emigrants from mixed families, as well as people converted by non-Orthodox rabbinic courts abroad, whose procedures are not recognized as valid by the rabbinic authorities in Israel. It would seem paradoxical and inequitable if persons seeking refuge from anti-Jewish discrimination or considered to be Jews by a large sector of world Jewry were refused access to Israel under the Law of Return or discriminated

Above left A kibbutz funeral procession. The kibbutz is a closely knit community, almost an extended family.

Above Bat mitzvah ceremony at Masada: a breathtaking location for this solemn affirmation of Jewish commitment. The Western Wall in Jerusalem has become a popular location for open-air *bat mitzvah* services. Masada, another national shrine, is a logical extension of this idea, and more attractive perhaps to anyone sensitive about the treatment of women in traditional Judaism.

Right Dawn celebration of Jerusalem Day. The reunification of Jerusalem during the Six-Day War in 1967 was an event which stirred every Israeli heart. Previously Israeli Jerusalem had been confined to the western suburbs. The Old City, the heart of Jerusalem, could be glimpsed but not entered. Then everything changed overnight. The Old City itself still seemed strange and unapproachable, thronged with alien faces, but within it stood the wall which had always symbolized age-old Jewish aspirations. At that time the Jerusalem poet Yehuda Amihai wrote:
"I have come back to this city where far-off places like people have names and routes have numbers—not those of bus routes but AD 70, 1917, five hundred BC, 'forty-eight. These are the routes we truly travel."

Overleaf Jerusalem, seen from the east. In the foreground is the Jewish cemetery on the Mount of Olives, where for centuries Jews came to be buried in the expectation of a swift and easy resurrection at the coming of the Messiah. In the center stands the Dome of the Rock. This earliest surviving masterpiece of Islam resembles a jeweled reliquary enclosing the hilltop on which Abraham is supposed to have offered his son as a sacrifice to the one God. This is the point, surely, where the three monotheistic faiths are united in contemplation of their common origins.

against within the Jewish state. Equally, it would be inconceivable to compel or persuade the rabbinic courts to authorize mixed marriages. The idea of formally separating "national" Jewish status from religious Jewish identity has met with strong opposition from some secular Zionists as well as from the religious establishment, and would require the introduction of civil marriage, to which the religious parties are resolutely opposed. The result is a situation of wary compromise, which has caused hardship to individuals and periodic public outcry. In a *cause célèbre* in 1958 a Carmelite monk of Jewish birth and undisputed Zionist convictions was refused citizenship under the Law of Return and registration as a Jewish national. The ruling of the Home Affairs Ministry was upheld by the Supreme Court, even though under the *halakhah* the applicant's claim to be considered a Jew was probably valid. The question of registration had already sparked off a government crisis earlier the same year, and after continued agitation in Israel and abroad and a further controversial decision by the Supreme Court in 1968 the Knesset eventually, in 1970, defined the word "Jew," for the purposes of the Law of Return, as "a person born to a Jewish mother, or who has been converted to Judaism, and is not a member of another religion." This formula was acceptable to majority opinion in Israel and abroad, but not to extreme secularists, nor to the religious parties which wanted the words "in accordance with *halakhah*" to be added after "converted to Judaism." In 1977, as part of the price of NRP and Aguda participation in the coalition, the prime minister undertook to "make every endeavor" to mobilize a parliamentary majority for the amendment of the Law of Return in this direction. The commitment caused a storm of protest, not least from the non-Orthodox religious bodies in America, where the majority of religious Jews belong to Reform or Conservative synagogues.

All recognized religious institutions in Israel fall under the authority of the Ministry for Religious Affairs. The Ministry (which has been headed almost without interruption by a nominee of the NRP) provides financial assistance for religious institutions and activities and is responsible for the religious courts of the various communities. The Jewish religious establishment consists of chief rabbis, state rabbis, religious councils and rabbinic courts. Under a system inherited from the British and ultimately from the Ottomans there are two chief rabbis of Israel, one Ashkenazi and one Sephardi, and local chief rabbis in the towns (the four main cities have a dual chief rabbinate). The election of the chief rabbis has caused repeated problems, and the dual chief rabbinate has led to serious and absurd conflicts. The district rabbis and other local rabbis with official positions are appointed, with the approval of the chief rabbinate, by local religious councils, which also pay their stipends. The religious councils, another heritage from the period of the Mandate, are effectively part of the structure of local government. They are appointed jointly by the Ministry of Religious Affairs, the local authority and the local rabbinate, and are totally under the influence of the NRP. Their considerable funds derive from the Ministry, the local authority and fees for services (such as supervision of kosher food). The rabbinic courts (*Batei Din*) each consist of

three judges (*Dayanim*) who are appointed formally by the president of the state with the approval of both chief rabbis. The positions are well paid and highly sought after. There are 24 *Batei Din*, eight of them in Tel Aviv and three in Jerusalem. There is a rabbinic court of appeal (the Supreme *Bet Din*), headed by the two national chief rabbis. Both the chief rabbis of Israel elected in March 1983 had been longstanding members of the Supreme *Bet Din*.

The chief rabbis, the Dayanim and other officially appointed rabbis are state functionaries and their authority derives from the state rather than from the consent of the Jewish community or from their inherent powers of spiritual leadership. A few chief rabbis have commanded widespread respect on account of their personal qualities, but they constitute the exception; by contrast other holders of religious appointments have earned public ridicule and have contributed to the very obvious alienation of most young Israeli Jews from religion. The image of the rabbinate tends to be a negative one, particularly among secular Jews. The rabbis are perceived as part of a state apparatus which often arouses feelings of impatience or downright hostility. This is not merely a matter of anticlerical prejudice. The state rabbis rarely involve themselves in pastoral care and religious instruction, as the rabbis of diaspora communities do, and so are not treated with that blend of respect and affection commanded by many diaspora rabbis or Christian clergymen or by some religious figures in Israel who are outside the state system. Technically the very concept of a hierarchy of rabbis is alien to Jewish tradition and law, and there is no halakhic basis for the essentially secular political device of a chief rabbi or Supreme *Bet Din*. The authority of the chief rabbis is not recognized by the more extreme Orthodox groups (the Old Yishuv and the Aguda) or by the non-Orthodox movements (Conservative and Reform).

Synagogues in Israel also differ from those in the diaspora, which are normally built, maintained and run by their members and often cater for a wide range of religious, educational and social activities. Orthodox synagogues in Israel do not offer membership rights. They are not social centers but usually small, architecturally nondescript prayer halls, used only for religious services. They are funded by the government through the local religious councils.

It is otherwise with the Reform and Conservative synagogues. They are not recognized by the Ministry of Religious Affairs and are not entitled to government funds. The growth of non-Orthodox Judaism in Israel has been slow and arduous. Neither movement was involved in the early development of Zionism and it was only during the Nazi crisis in Europe that significant numbers of Reform and Conservative Jews arrived in the country. The first Reform synagogue was opened in Haifa in 1935, the first Conservative synagogue in Jerusalem in 1937. They were small and unobtrusive and made little impact. The movements gradually grew in numbers, largely through American immigration. The main rabbinic seminaries of America, the (Reform) Hebrew Union College and the (Conservative) Jewish Theological Seminary, have opened branches in Jerusalem, incorporating synagogues which attract increasing numbers of Israelis and foreign visitors, and synagogues have been estab-

Jerusalem: The Holy City

Jerusalem is the meeting place of centuries and peoples, hopes and dreams. It is a city of contrasts and conflicts, a symbol of antiquity and renewal, which can be an enigma even for people who have lived there all their lives. The sacred city of three faiths, its holy places are associated with the names of Adam and Abraham, David and Solomon, Jesus and Muhammad. For Jews it has a sanctity which can hardly be expressed in territorial terms: it is an abstraction, a painful yearning, an intimation of perfection and fulfillment which are always beyond reach. For centuries Jews traveled there in their old age from distant lands to die and be buried close to the place where redemption would first be proclaimed. But Jerusalem is also the capital of a modern state, with its government buildings and public monuments, some of which, like Yad Vashem, express the unique relationship between Jerusalem and the whole Jewish people. And everywhere the past imposes on the present, in this city where (as a Jerusalem poet has written) "even the dead have voting rights."

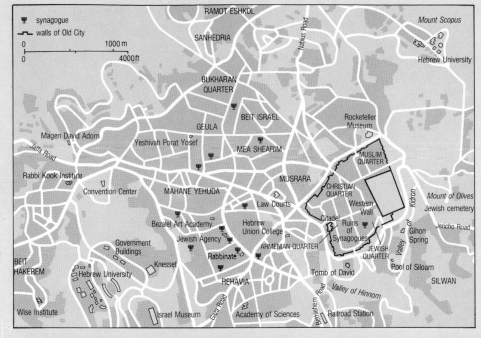

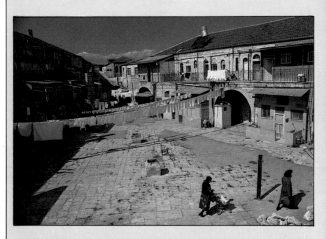

Left The Knesset (Parliament
Building) by night. In the
foreground stands the Shrine of
the Book, in which the Dead Sea
Scrolls are displayed.
Far left, center The Hungarian
Buildings, an area of Jerusalem
developed in the 19th century,
preserve the flavor of an east
European *shtetl*.
Far left, below A windmill
dominates Yemin Moshe, one of
the earliest of the Jewish
developments outside the walls.
It is named for Sir Moses
Montefiore, who built this
quarter to relieve the unhealthy
congestion of the Old City.
Top Jerusalem is a fascinating
blend of old and new. The
spacious walled precinct in the
foreground, marking the site of
Solomon's temple, is the Noble
Sanctuary of the Muslims, with
its two splendid mosques.
The excavations immediately to
the left have brought to light
fascinating remains of David's
city. Just above, on the other
side of the Tyropoeon Valley,
rises the newly restored Jewish
quarter of the Old City, to the
right of which can be seen the
Holy Sepulcher, the heart of the
Christian quarter. In the
background, outside the city
walls, the modern buildings of
the new city begin.
Above A view of Mea Shearim.

lished in the main towns. There is even a Reform
kibbutz, Yahel, founded in 1976. The growth of
non-Orthodox Judaism has been met by fierce
opposition from the Orthodox establishment, which
has vigorously campaigned against the movements
and even tried to suppress their activities by
threatening to revoke the licenses of catering
establishments serving their communities. At one
point it was suggested that Reform and Conservative Judaism should accept the status of non-Jewish
religions, and so qualify for recognition and state
aid on the same basis as Christianity and Islam. In
1976 the minister for religious affairs canceled the
appointment of a Reform rabbi to the Jerusalem
Religious Council, and in 1980 the two chief rabbis
of Jerusalem issued a joint pronouncement that a
worshiper hearing the *shofar* sounded in a Conservative synagogue at the New Year would be
considered not to have heard the *shofar* (which is a
religious obligation). Such actions receive wide
publicity, and if anything have tended to gain
sympathy and support for the two movements,
which are now growing fast and have begun to
encounter some success in their demands for state
help. In 1981, after a 10-year battle with the
authorities, the Tel Aviv Reform community finally
received permission from the municipality to erect
the city's first purpose-built Reform synagogue and
community center. (The first synagogue building of
this kind in Israel had been opened the previous
year in Haifa.)

The movements would like to be treated on the
same basis as Orthodoxy, either through official
recognition, with financial aid from the state and
the right of their rabbis to solemnize marriages and
sit on religious councils, or alternatively through
the disestablishment of the official rabbinate. The
annual convention of the (Reform) Central
Conference of American Rabbis, meeting in
Jerusalem in 1981, issued a strong call for disestablishment: "Stripped of arbitrary power, all
rabbis would need to rely on moral suasion and
inspired teaching to reach Israel's vast majority of
unaffiliated Jews ... The present state of the
established rabbinate has atrophied any spiritual
impact Judaism should be making on the society."
Leaders of both movements expressed strong concern after the 1981 elections at the concessions
demanded by the religious parties, particularly the
amendment of the Law of Return to exclude Reform
and Conservative converts. At present there are
some 15 synagogues affiliated to the (Reform) Israel
Movement for Progressive Judaism, a constituent of
the World Union for Progressive Judaism which has
its headquarters in Jerusalem, and some 30 synagogues affiliated to the (Conservative) United
Synagogue of Israel, which belongs to the World
Council of Synagogues.

At the other extreme the most traditionalist
Jewish groups have also remained outside the state
system—in this case by their own choice. The Jews
of the Old Yishuv for the most part held aloof from
Zionism and opposed the creation of the Jewish
state. Their ranks were swollen after World War II
by obsessively traditionalist immigrants from Hungary. They live in segregation in their own closely
knit communities, mainly concentrated in the Mea
Shearim quarter of Jerusalem. There they maintain
the life-style of the old ghetto and attempt to

preserve the system of internal autonomy which developed under non-Jewish rule. They have their own schools and *yeshivot* and keep up a high standard of traditional Jewish learning. Their numbers are small, and they would remain an antique curiosity were it not for a streak of religious zealotry which has often led to much-publicized clashes with the secular powers. Such incidents are often associated with the extreme anti-Zionist *Neturei Karta* ("Guardians of the City"), but in fact they have come to involve a much wider sector of the traditionalist population in different parts of the country, who have taken the law into their own hands to safeguard the Sabbath rest and other religious observances. In 1966 a well-known artist was killed when his motorcycle hit a cable illegally blocking a road in Jerusalem on the Sabbath, and there was a similar death in Bnei Brak in 1977. On other occasions ambulances answering emergency calls have been pelted with stones, buses have been attacked by rioters complaining of obscene advertisements, and there have been violent demonstrations against sporting, social and cultural centers open to both sexes.

The authorities have tended to handle such incidents cautiously, partly perhaps out of respect for religious sensibilities and partly because of the danger of dissidence spreading more widely within the religious establishment. This danger became a reality as a result of disturbances in August 1981 over archaeological excavations in Jerusalem on a site alleged to contain old Jewish graves. After a long-drawn-out battle between police and demonstrators, tombs of Zionist notables were daubed with swastikas and offensive slogans. The Eda Haredit, an umbrella organization of all the traditionalist groups, denounced the desecration of the tombs, but called for an end to the excavations, a demand which gained the support of the Ashkenazi chief rabbi of Israel. This official support placed the minister for education and culture, a member of the NRP, in an awkward position. He asked the chief rabbi for a ruling on the permissibility of the excavations. When both chief rabbis and the Supreme Rabbinical Council ruled that the digs must stop he issued an injunction to halt them. The apparently trivial issue of the excavations blew up into a full-scale political and constitutional crisis, in which the governing coalition was threatened and the NRP was brought into direct conflict with the chief rabbinate. The Supreme Court and the attorney general independently denied the right of the rabbinate to dictate to government ministers, to which the Rabbinical Council replied with a declaration that "the *halakhah* is eternal and not subordinate to any secular authority." This incident highlights the instability of the constitutional compromise and the tensions which exist not only between religious and secular elements but within the religious sector itself

Eastern and western communities in Israel

Another area of tensions and conflicts is the relationship between "eastern" and "western" Jewish communities, brought together into a single nation under the Zionist aegis. The blanket terms "eastern" and "western" are inherently misleading, since both comprise many different communities, of diverse and to some extent overlapping

geographical and cultural backgrounds. But there is a real problem of intercommunal relations, and the widely used term "eastern communities" (referring basically to Jews from Arab lands including, paradoxically, the Arab west, the Maghrib) indicates the common perception of the root of the problem, at least from a "western" perspective. The traditional terms "Ashkenazi" and "Sephardi" are also employed (in a uniquely Israeli sense) to define the two sides.

The Sephardi and Ashkenazi communities maintained their separate identities for a long time under Ottoman rule, with the Sephardim exercising a certain dominance. Their chief rabbi was the one recognized by the government, and they treated the western Zionist newcomers with a certain lofty condescension. The Zionists, for their part, came under the influence of eastern ways, even to the point of adopting the Sephardi pronunciation of Hebrew. But under British rule it was the westerners who were closer to the ruling power, and as western immigration increased the Sephardim became an insignificant and overlooked minority. After 1948 the demographic pattern was reversed again, and eastern Jews or their children are now the majority of the Jewish population. The establishment, however, remained solidly western. Few easterners reached top positions in politics, the professions or the army. Eastern immigrants were crowded into urban slums; they were economically and educationally disadvantaged compared with westerners. In the schools and the army young easterners were taught to neglect and despise their own heritage, and were educated in western culture

Israel is involved in a constant, conscious striving after normality—an elusive goal when the present is haunted by so many specters from the past. The names of the Nazi camps, inscribed on the martyrs' memorial of Yad Vashem (*top*), are a reminder of the nightmarish events leading up to the founding of the state, and of the six million victims who were posthumously declared citizens of Israel. The worshipers gathered for penitential prayers on the beach at Tel Aviv (*above*) give a visible expression to the power of traditional religion and its deep roots in the soil of the

as the road to "absorption." Resentment bubbled up in the 1960s, and exploded into violent and direct political action in the early 1970s. The Labor government began to take remedial action, but it was little and late, and Labor's surprise defeat in the 1977 elections has been blamed in part on the defection of eastern voters who, as the poorer section of the community, were badly hit by high inflation. A year later Itzhak Navon became the first Sephardi president of Israel. His selection indicates official recognition of one dimension of the problem, but the difficulties continue and easterners register their protests through demonstrations and even through ethnic political parties, one of which gained three seats in the 1981 elections.

The non-Jewish citizens of Israel
Relations between the Jewish majority and the non-Jewish (mainly Arab) minority are bedeviled by the political and military conflict between Zionists and Arab nationalists. A minority of Jews espouse openly anti-Arab policies, but the majority are committed to the Zionist idea and have difficulty in considering non-Jews as fully fledged Israelis. The Israeli Arabs thus suffer from some of the nationalist prejudices of which Jews themselves have been victims in other countries, prejudices which are reinforced by the more concrete fear that the Arabs may constitute a security risk. Most Arabs do not serve in the armed forces, although in other respects they enjoy full civil rights. Arab-language schools are state financed, but the dual educational system underlines and perpetuates the social and cultural barriers.

The state accords full freedom of worship to all religions, and recognized religious communities enjoy internal autonomy on the same basis as the Jewish community. Conversionist activity, however, is strongly discouraged. The state also protects the holy places of all religions and guarantees access to them. A few violent incidents, provoked by fanatics of different religions, have been sternly prosecuted. But in a country where religion is prominently in evidence, and which includes among its citizens an unusually large number of different denominations, very little has been done to raise the level of interreligious understanding. Jewish schoolchildren are not taught about other religions, and there have so far been few formal opportunities for Israelis to meet across confessional

holy land. The Jewish soldier reciting his prayers in the Arab city of Gaza during its capture in the 1967 war (*top right*) recalls the long and arduous struggle of the Jews for citizen rights and freedom of worship and the power to control their own destiny. The same image cannot fail to evoke also the conflicting claims of two long-suffering peoples to this narrow strip of territory.

barriers. Some fine pioneering ventures have met with a very limited and cautious response.

Israel and the diaspora
The link between Israel and world Jewry is solid and formal, yet in many respects intangible and even controversial. Under the British Mandate the role of world Jewry in building the Jewish National Home was recognized in the official status accorded to the Zionist Organization and from 1930 to its successor, the Jewish Agency (which nominally incorporated non-Zionist representation). Zionist policy, involving important decisions affecting the lives of Jews in Palestine, was largely determined outside the country. The result was constant conflict. In 1947, when Jewish independence became an imminent reality, the Palestinian Jewish leadership strongly asserted its right to determine its own destiny. After independence the government wished to preserve the useful link with the diaspora while ensuring its own autonomy and indeed extending its influence within Jewish communities abroad. In 1952 the Knesset enacted a law formally regulating the relationship:

The state of Israel regards itself as the creation of the entire Jewish people, and its gates are open, in accordance with its laws, to every Jew wishing to immigrate into it . . . The state of Israel recognizes the World Zionist Organization as the authorized agency which will continue to operate in the state of Israel for the development and settlement of the country, the absorption of immigrants from the diaspora, and the coordination of the activities in Israel of Jewish institutions and organizations active in those fields. The mission of gathering in the exiles which is the central task of the state of Israel and the Zionist movement in our days requires constant efforts by the Jewish people in the diaspora. The state of Israel therefore, expects the cooperation of all Jews, as individuals and groups, in building up the state and assisting the immigration into it of the masses of the people, and regards the unity of all sections of Jewry as necessary for this purpose . . .

This formula, which imposes demands on the Jewish people as a whole and allots a formal, if limited, role within the state to an international Jewish organization, has continued to govern Israel–diaspora relations ever since. Instead of Israel being a "colony" of the Jewish people, the Jewish people has become a "reservoir" for the Jewish state. Jews are called on to give their loyalty, their financial support and ultimately their persons to the state, which claims the right to intervene in their affairs by promoting Zionist activities and fundraising, or (as in the case of the Soviet Union) by campaigning for a change in government policy, for the recognition of the right of Jews to emigrate to Israel.

The relationship has, on the whole, been a stable and successful one. Jews the world over have derived satisfaction and pride from the existence of Israel and have shared in its anxieties and its triumphs. The Zionist agencies, which maintain offices in the principal diaspora centers, have contributed to raising the level of Jewish consciousness and have undertaken educational activities aimed especially at disseminating knowledge of Israel and the Hebrew language. Jews have res-

Iran

There are no reliable statistics on the Jews of Iran. In 1950 it was estimated that there were around 100 000 Jews in a total population of 16·5 million, with 40 000 living in Tehran, 15 000 in Shiraz, 10 000 in Isfahan and the rest scattered through more than 100 small towns and villages. The vast majority were poor and backward, living in overcrowded ghettos, undernourished and disease-ridden. A minority (some 10 percent) belonged to the middle class, and there were a few wealthy individuals. The standard of education and Jewish knowledge was low, although the Alliance Israélite Universelle maintained some 20 schools in the large towns, with an enrollment of 7000 pupils. The Jews had been granted civil rights in the constitution of 1906 and under the system of religious representation they had one deputy in the parliament, but there were few opportunities for advancement for Jews because of the hostility of the dominant Shiite religious leaders.

Since the Islamic revolution of 1979 the status of the Jews, in common with that of other minorities, has deteriorated sharply. Hundreds of Jews have been arrested and imprisoned, and several were executed for alleged economic crimes or for being "Zionist spies." The majority have now fled the country.

Afghanistan

In the 1930s there were an estimated 5000 Jews in Afghanistan. Following the assassination of Nadir Shah in 1933 they were subjected to a series of repressive measures: they were expelled from the small towns and villages and "ghettoized" in Kabul, Herat and Balkh. They were deprived of their citizenship, banned from commercial activity and forbidden to leave the country. But many did flee illegally and most of the rest left in the late 1960s when emigration was once more permitted. There are now only a few families in Herat and Kabul.

Left Like the Kurds and Yemenis, the Persian Jews have preserved their own traditions untouched by Sephardi influences. How very Persian they were in their homeland can be gauged from this cemetery at Pir Bakran, where the Jews of Isfahan used to bury their dead.

Below left To the world of Persian Jewry belong also the Jews of Bukhara and of Afghanistan.

Below right Japanese Jews are as yet only a tiny element among the Jews of Japan, who are mainly business and professional people from the USA and elsewhere, with some Russian Jews who arrived from China after the last war.

Right The Bene Israel are well integrated into Indian life, and some members of the community have even risen to positions of prominence in local government and the armed forces.

Below Simhat Torah in Cochin. According to a local saying, "if you have never seen Simhat Torah in Cochin you have never seen happiness in your life."

India

When India was partitioned in 1947 it was estimated that there were more than 25 000 Jews in the subcontinent, forming three distinct groups: the Bene Israel (the largest group, with over 17 000 members), the Baghdadis (6000) and the Cochin Jews (2000). Of these the second were relatively recent arrivals, having come from Iraq since the end of the 18th century. Wealthy merchants and industrialists, they identified with British society and held aloof from the other two groups, the "native Jews." These had an ancient history in India — indeed they claimed to have come from Israel in biblical times. Their actual origins have given rise to much speculation, but it seems clear that they led a completely separate existence, with no contact until the 18th century. The Bene Israel were scattered in villages on the Konkan coast until in the 18th and 19th centuries they began to move into Bombay, where they prospered. The Cochin Jewish communities had grown up on the Malabar coast in the south, under the protection of the local Hindu ruler. Both groups were subdivided into subgroups, "White" and "Black" in the case of the Bene Israel, "White," "Brown" and "Black" in the case of the Cochin Jews. Until recent times the different groups and subgroups did not intermarry.

Since independence the numbers of all the groups have declined considerably through emigration. In Cochin only a few families remain, while Bombay has some 3000 Jews, and the whole of India probably only 5000.

Far East

The tiny communities of the Far East are mainly relics of trading enterprises set up in the last century. In their time they flourished, but little remains now of their former splendor apart from some imposing buildings and a few surviving families or individuals. But Singapore, Taiwan and Japan have attracted a little immigration, and new synagogues have recently been built in Hong Kong and Manila.

AUSTRALASIA

The origins of Jewish settlement in Australia reach back to the early 19th century. The first communal organizations were founded in Sydney in 1817 and in Melbourne in 1839. By 1850 both towns had permanent synagogue buildings and there were others in Adelaide, Hobart and Launceston. The gold rush of that period brought a notable influx, and by the end of the century congregations had been founded in Brisbane, Fremantle, Perth and Kalgoorlie. The settlers were speedily assimilated, however, and several of these early communities became defunct. Immigration was resumed during the 1930s and became more abundant after the war. In 1933 there were 27000 Jews, in 1971 60000. Half of them lived in Melbourne, where the largely eastern European community has kept up its sense of identity and its attachment to Yiddish language and culture. But the tendency to assimilation continues to have a negative effect on the strength of the Jewish community, and despite the immigration of several thousand Jews from the Soviet Union, Israel and South Africa in the intervening period, only 62000 Australians declared themselves as Jews in the census of 1981.

Australia's Jews have played a distinguished part in public life and have been well represented in the state and federal parliaments and the judicature. The first Australian to command an army, Sir John Monash, was a Jew, as was the first native-born governor-general, Sir Isaac Isaacs, in the 1930s. A second Jewish governor-general, Sir Zelman Cowen, served from 1978 to 1982.

The diverse origins of Australian Jewry are reflected in the character of the religious congregations, which range from Hasidic at one extreme to Liberal at the other. There is a notable emphasis on Jewish day schools, of which in 1980 there were eight in Melbourne and three in Sydney, accounting between them for a very large proportion of the Jewish schoolchildren of Australia. It is tempting to compare Melbourne to Montreal or Johannesburg: all three have a strongly eastern European, originally Yiddish-speaking background, where the old arguments survive even if they are carried out in English, and in all three the strength of the day-school movement reflects partly dissatisfaction with the ethnic or religious character of the alternative education but more a desire to perpetuate a sense of Jewish identity by making sure that social bonds within the community are developed from an early age. The Australian day schools have a good record in general subjects, but there are difficulties in reaching a high standard of specifically Jewish education, and perhaps after all it is not that that counts. With an intermarriage rate of 20 percent (reaching 50 percent in some smaller communities) serious doubts have been raised about the long-term future of Australian Jewry.

The case of New Zealand is very similar to that of Australia in many ways, only on a much smaller scale. The origins of the community reach back to individual settlers who arrived before the establishment of British sovereignty in 1840, and organized communities began to be founded soon afterwards. The Jews helped to lay the foundations for the commercial and industrial prosperity of the country, and here too they have a fine record of public service. (In 1873 Sir Julius Vogel became the first professing Jewish prime minister in the British empire.) But the community has difficulty maintaining its numbers and is urgently seeking fresh immigration to compensate for "natural wastage." The Jewish population has remained fairly constant in recent years at between 4000 and 5000, but without steady immigration it is likely to decline rapidly.

Above Gen. Sir John Monash (1865–1931), Australian engineer and soldier.

Below left The Great Synagogue, Sydney, is the parent congregation of Australian Jewry. The present building was consecrated in 1878, but the origin of the congregation dates back as far as 1828. The architecture recalls the grander English synagogues of the era, and English Orthodoxy continues to dominate in Sydney.

Left The earliest Jewish settlers in Australia were criminals transported from Britain. One of the most famous convicts was Ikey Solomons, who is thought to have served as the model for the Jewish criminal Fagin in Dickens's *Oliver Twist*.

Below The largest communities in New Zealand are in Wellington and Auckland. The first synagogue in Wellington was erected in 1870; a new community center, incorporating an Orthodox synagogue, was inaugurated in 1977.

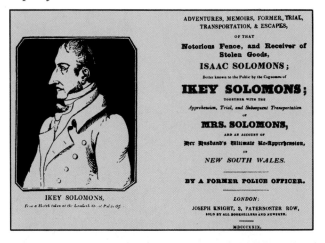

IKEY SOLOMONS,
From a Sketch taken at the Lambeth Street Police Office

ADVENTURES, MEMOIRS, FORMER, TRIAL, TRANSPORTATION, & ESCAPES, OF THAT Notorious Fence, and Receiver of Stolen Goods, ISAAC SOLOMONS; Better known to the Public by the Cognomen of **IKEY SOLOMONS;** TOGETHER WITH THE *Apprehension, Trial, and Subsequent Transportation* OF **MRS. SOLOMONS,** AND AN ACCOUNT OF Her Husband's Ultimate Re-Apprehension, IN NEW SOUTH WALES. BY A FORMER POLICE OFFICER.

LONDON: JOSEPH KNIGHT, 3, PATERNOSTER ROW, SOLD BY ALL BOOKSELLERS AND NEWSMEN.

MDCCCXXIX.

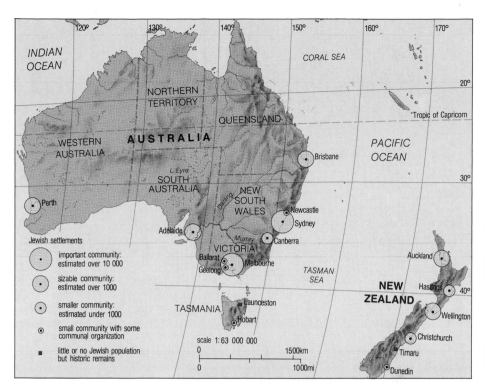

	1930		1980	
	Approx. Jewish pop.	*Jews per thousand*	*Approx. Jewish pop.*	*Jews per thousand*
Australia	24 000	3·6	70 000	4·9
New Zealand	2800	1·8	4000	1·3

Above Sir Julius Vogel (1835–99), N.Z. statesman.

Above Sir Zelman Cowen (*left*), Governor-General of Australia, 1978–82.

Left Immigration is a valuable bulwark for a population which is shrinking through defection and through emigration. In recent years the main immigration has come from the Soviet Union, South Africa and Israel. Here the 2000th Russian Jewish immigrant is being welcomed at Sydney airport by representatives of the Jewish Welfare Society.

Below Pupils at a Sydney Jewish dayschool learn to celebrate Simhat Torah. There are 15 Jewish dayschools in Australia, and it is estimated that they cater for 75 percent of all children receiving some Jewish education. This is obviously a vital safeguard for the future of a community which is very open to erosion.

AFRICA

ATLANTIC OCEAN

Canary Islands (Sp)

MOROCCO

ALGERIA

Africa, like Asia, has a Mediterranean seacoast divided from the rest of the continent by desert, and it is here, on the narrow coastal strip, that Jewish life was concentrated from remote antiquity until relatively recent times. Egypt is associated with the very origins of the people of Israel. In Ptolemaic times there were Jews in Libya; under Roman rule they made their appearance in the western parts of North Africa. Under the Arabs the region was for a long time the home of a flourishing Jewish culture, and there were periodic incursions of refugees from Spain and elsewhere throughout the middle ages and more recently. In the 1930s, despite recent waves of emigration, there were well over 400 000 Jews in the countries of North Africa, of whom three-quarters lived under French rule. Since then Arab nationalism has provoked a massive exodus, and there are now barely 20 000 Jews in the whole region, 90 percent of them in Morocco.

South of the Sahara the history of the Jews belongs to the history of European colonization. Jewish navigators contributed to the success of the early Portuguese voyages of exploration, and Jewish merchants in Holland were involved with the Dutch East India Company which pioneered white settlement in the Cape. Jews from Britain participated in the exploration and economic exploitation of southern Africa in the 19th century, and when the mass migrations of eastern European Jews began in the 1880s the region attracted a large influx, particularly from the Baltic republics, while Jews from Rhodes settled (appropriately) in Rhodesia. With the movement to black majority rule and the subsequent decline of the white presence the smaller communities have shrunk dramatically or disappeared, but South Africa, with its prosperous and proudly distinctive Jewish population, still ranks as one of the larger centers of the Jewish world.

Sir Roy Welensky (1907–), Rhod. politician

Helen Suzman, S.A. politician

| | 1930 | | 1980 | |
	Approx. Jewish pop.	Jews per thousand	Approx. Jewish pop.	Jews per thousand
Algeria	110 000	16·5	300	0·0
Egypt	66 000	4·8	250	0·0
Ethiopia	51 000	6·8	32 000	1·1
Kenya	300	0·1	450	0·0
Libya	24 500	34·4	0	0·0
Morocco	143 000	23·8	18 000	1·0
South Africa	85 000	9·4	108 000	3·7
Tunisia	70 000	29·9	2500	0·8
Zaïre	200	0·0	200	0·0
Zambia	400	0·3	300	0·1
Zimbabwe	2000	2·0	1500	0·2

MEDITERRANEAN SEA

Bizerte
Tunis
Naro
Nabeul
Sousse
ras
Kef
Kairouan
ala
Mahdia
Sbeitla
UNISIA
Sfax
aafsa
Gabès
Djerba
Kébili
Zarzis
Medenine
Ben Gardane
Tataouine
Tripoli
Lebda
Zuwarah
Misurata
Nalut
Giado
Gharyan
Meslatah
Sirte
Yahudia

Cyrene
Barce
Benghazi
Tobruk

Damyat
Alexandria
El Mahalla el Kubra
Damanhur
Cairo
Memphis
Helwân
El Faiyûm

LIBYA

EGYPT

Nile
Akhmîm
Qift
Qus
Thebes

Aswan

RED SEA

Tropic of Cancer

L. Nasser

Jewish settlements

- major community:
  estimated over 100 000
- important community:
  estimated over 10 000
- sizable community:
  estimated over 1000
- smaller community:
  estimated under 1000
- small community with some
  communal organization
- little or no Jewish population
  but historic remains

scale 1:12 000 000

0   400km
0   300mi

MOROCCO
TUNISIA
ALGERIA
LIBYA
EGYPT
Tropic of Cancer

Asmera
Gonder
Ambovar
Addis Abeba
ETHIOPIA

KENYA
Nairobi
ZAÏRE
0°
Equator
Kinshasa
Lubumbashi
ZAMBIA
Lusaka
Harare
(Salisbury)
Gatooma
ZIMBABWE
NAMIBIA
Que Que
Gwelo
Windhoek
Bulawayo
Réunion
(Fr)
St Denis
Tropic of Capricorn
SOUTH
AFRICA

WITWATERSRAND
1 Randfontein
2 Krugersdorp
3 Roodepoort
4 Germiston
5 Kempton Park
6 Boksburg
7 Benoni
8 Brakpan
9 Springs

Tropic of Capricorn

Limpopo

Pietersburg

Rustenburg
Pretoria
Middelburg
Lichtenburg
Johannesburg
Carletonville
Bethal
SWAZILAND
Potchefstroom
Nigel
Klerksdorp
Vereeniging

Kroonstad
Vryheid
Bethlehem

Upington
Orange
Kimberley
Bloemfontein
Caledon
LESOTHO
Pietermaritzburg
Durban

SOUTH   AFRICA

Vaal

Doring

Queenstown

Sondags
Grahamstown
East London

Bellville
Wellington
Worcester
Oudtshoorn
Paarl
George
Uitenhage
Cape Town
Stellenbosch
Port Elizabeth

scale 1:14 000 000

0   400km
0   300mi

219

Morocco

According to the 1947 census there were 203 800 Jews in French Morocco, forming 2·3 percent of the total population and 38·5 percent of non-Muslims. A further 25 000 Jews lived in Spanish Morocco and the International Zone of Tangier. The Moroccan Jews were predominantly an urban population, and there was a steady movement to the cities from the smaller towns and villages. The largest concentration was in Casablanca, which had 50 000 Jewish inhabitants in 1945 and 80 000 by 1951. There were 18 000 Jews in 1947 in Marrakesh, and sizable communities of 10 000 or more in Fez, Meknes, Rabat and Tangier. Despite 35 years of French influence the Jews were almost completely excluded from political life, and were despised and hated by the Muslim majority. Soon after the establishment of Israel in May 1948 a mass exodus began, hastened by the outbreak of savage anti-Jewish riots in a couple of places. Ten years later, in the course of the strengthening of relations between Morocco (now independent) and the Arab League, anti-Jewish policies were implemented and at the same time emigration was halted, although Jews continued to flee the country illegally at considerable risk. After the accession of King Hassan II in 1961 the right to emigrate was restored and the harassment of the Jewish community was ended. There are now fewer than 20 000 Jews left in Morocco, of whom three-quarters live in Casablanca. This is the largest Jewish population of any Arab country, and the king has repeatedly expressed his desire to see the Jewish community live in security and prosperity.

Algeria

Under French rule the Jews of Algeria, particularly in the northern districts which were administratively part of France and where the Jewish population was largely concentrated, enjoyed considerable freedom. The Crémieux Decree of 1870 made them French citizens, and they came to play an important role in local political life. French culture took a strong hold among them, although they also enjoyed better relations with the Muslim population than prevailed in Morocco. The creation of Israel made little impact here; it was the struggle for independence from France which brought about the liquidation of this ancient community. Caught in a conflict of loyalties to France and to Algeria the Jews found themselves in an impossible position, and they joined the precipitate mass exodus which preceded independence in 1962. One hundred and fifteen thousand Algerian Jews arrived in France within the space of a few months, causing at first acute embarrassment and difficulties for the French Jewish communities which they have since notably reinvigorated. Of the few thousand who remained most have since departed, and there are now only a few hundred Jews in Algiers and a handful elsewhere.

Morocco now has the largest Jewish population of any Arab country, but it is only a sad remnant of the numerous communities which existed all over the country before the establishment of Israel. These old photographs convey something of the flavor of Moroccan Jewish life. *Above* A street scene in Marrakesh. In 1930 there were more Jews in Marrakesh than in the whole of Morocco today. *Left* In the synagogue at Asni, in the mountains not far from Marrakesh.

Below left This old picture postcard features the synagogue in Algiers. It was the raid on the Great Synagogue on Christmas Eve 1960 that heralded the final breakdown of reasonable conditions for Jewish existence in Algeria, and the mass emigration of Algerian Jewry.

Below On the island of Djerba in Tunisia Jewish life continues, despite emigration, much as it has done for centuries. *Right* Of many synagogues on the island the gem is the Ghriba. According to tradition a door from the Jerusalem temple was built into its walls.

Left The Maimouna festival is peculiar to Jews from North Africa. Held at the end of Passover, its theme is renewal, fertility, good fortune. In Israel it enjoys great popularity as a way for North African Jews to express their own identity.

Bottom Religious devotion and study have always been a strong feature of North African Judaism, as has an attachment to the *Kabbalah*. This man is intent on his private prayers in the Ghriba Synagogue, Djerba.

Tunisia

In the early 1950s the Jewish population of Tunisia was calculated at 105 000, including many who had French nationality. Sixty percent lived in and around the city of Tunis, and there were other important communities in the northern towns where the European presence was strongest, but there were also communities living in the south of the country in more traditional conditions, as well as hundreds of scattered families. In all the Jews constituted nearly a third of the non-Muslim population. They had their own distinct political status, and their own representatives in the national and municipal councils.

On independence in March 1956 they acquired equal civil rights and a Jew was briefly a member of the first Tunisian cabinet, but despite an orderly transition large-scale emigration soon ensued and by 1962 there were only some 30 000 Jews in the country. The present Jewish population is variously estimated at between 3500 and 7000; it is mainly concentrated in Tunis, with smaller communities in Sfax and Sousse and on the island of Djerba.

Libya

The 1931 census recorded 24 500 Jews in Libya, the majority of whom lived in Tripoli, one of the most dynamic centers of Jewish life in the whole of North Africa. There were smaller centers in Cyrenaica and in the south of the territory, where Jewish cave-dwellers had excited the interest of occasional travelers. Victimized by the Fascists during World War II, the Jews suffered under indifferent British rule from Muslim attacks in Tripoli in 1945 and again after the establishment of Israel in 1948. An emigration movement began, which became a spate the following year after the decision to grant the country independence. By the end of 1951, when Libya became an independent monarchy, only a few thousand remained, mostly foreign nationals. Many of these left after the Middle East war of 1967, and the rest after the overthrow of the monarchy in 1969.

Egypt

In Egypt the census of 1917 reported nearly 60 000 Jews, of whom more than half were foreigners, mainly recent immigrants from Europe and Palestine. They played an important part in the economic and political life of the country. In 1937 the privileges enjoyed by foreigners were annulled and 10 years later legislation limiting the activities of non-Egyptian nationals seriously damaged the economic basis of the Jewish community (only 15 percent were Egyptians; 20 percent were foreign nationals and the rest were stateless). The war with Israel in 1948 brought mob violence and official harassment, and thousands of Jews left. The harassment became more severe after Gamal Abdel Nasser seized power in 1954; following the Suez campaign of 1956 thousands more Jews had their possessions confiscated and were forced to leave the country. Expulsions and emigration continued until by 1979, when an uneasy peace was concluded between Egypt and Israel, there were only a few hundred Jews remaining in Cairo and Alexandria. The reestablishment of links with Israel has restored the self-confidence of this tiny community, which in 1982 joined the World Jewish Congress.

Above The imposing modern synagogue of Alexandria is a reminder of an earlier generation. In 1900 it was the largest community in Egypt, with 10 000 members. By 1917 the Jewish population had more than doubled. Many of the Jews were wealthy immigrants, who made an important contribution to the development of modern Egypt. But the Alexandria of that period has ceased to exist.

Above left The Karaite synagogue in Cairo. Karaites have lived in Cairo for centuries; 40 years ago, after the annihilation of their brethren in the Crimea, the Cairo community was the largest in the world. Now most have left, and the impressive synagogue is too large for the 40 or so who remain. Karaites remove their shoes before entering the synagogue, and unlike Rabbinites they kneel and prostrate themselves during prayer.

Left An old postcard showing a coppersmith in Port Said. There were Jewish coppersmiths in Egypt in ancient times: they had their own section in the great synagogue of Alexandria.

Far left A Jewish scribe, one of the victims of anti-Jewish violence in Tripoli in 1945. Unable to rely on the protection of the British army, the Jews organized their own self-defense, but conditions for Jewish life became impossible, and by 1951 most of the Jews of Libya had emigrated.

Left The establishment of peace between Egypt and Israel in 1977, after almost 30 year of war, inaugurated a new era for the few remaining Egyptian Jews. Here the Israeli delegation is seen visiting the synagogue at Alexandria.

Below The Falashas or Beta Israel of Ethiopia have traditionally been a primarily agricultural people, living for the most part in scattered villages. Their liturgical language is Ge'ez (ancient Ethiopic), and their religion combines biblical and native African elements. For centuries they lived in isolation from the Jewish world; more recently contacts have been reestablished and many Falashas have emigrated to Israel.

Ethiopia

Ethiopia had, until the military coup of 1974, small communities of Adeni Jews in Addis Abeba and Asmera. There are also several thousand Falashas, native Jews living mainly scattered in a large number of villages in Gondar province in the northwest of the country, near the border with Sudan. A poor and isolated community, the Falashas have often suffered from the prejudices of their neighbors, the arbitrary dictates of their rulers, and the ministrations of Christian missionaries from Europe. Their Jewish status has been much disputed, and these arguments have prevented them from receiving the wholehearted support and material aid from international Jewish welfare agencies which have benefited other remote and underprivileged communities. Some educational and relief work has been undertaken, however, and in 1975, two years after the Sephardi chief rabbi of Israel had finally decided that they were indeed Jews, the Israeli parliament declared them eligible for Israeli citizenship under the Law of Return. In 1984 more than 15000 Falashas were rescued from famine-stricken Ethiopia and secretly airlifted to Israel in the dramatic "Operation Moses."

South Africa

In 1910, when the former self-governing colonies of the Cape of Good Hope, Natal, the Transvaal and the Orange River Colony were united to form the Union of South Africa, there were some 46000 Jews in the population. Most of them were recent immigrants. The earliest congregations in the Cape had been established in Cape Town and Grahamstown in the 1840s, by settlers from Britain and Germany. A few individuals had ventured into the undeveloped inland areas. The opening up of the diamond fields around Kimberley and the gold mines of the Witwatersrand had transformed the patterns of white settlement and boosted European immigration just at the time when the oppressed and impoverished Jews of eastern Europe were looking for new opportunities overseas. Jewish immigration

from Britain and western Europe had continued, but it was soon swamped by eastern Europeans, the majority of whom came from Lithuania. Between 1880 and 1910 some 40000 Jewish immigrants arrived, and the outlines of the present-day network of communities had been established, with important centers in Johannesburg and Pretoria in the Transvaal, Bloemfontein in the Orange Free State, Durban in Natal and Cape Town and Port Elizabeth in the Cape. There were strings of smaller congregations spread out across the Witwatersrand and along the south coast, and isolated Jewish traders were to be found in almost every village.

South African censuses provide reliable and revealing information about the development of the Jewish population. In 1926 nearly 72000 South Africans declared themselves to be of Jewish religion, or 4·28 percent of a total white population of 1·68 million. But 93 percent of the Jews lived in urban areas, as against 58 percent of the whole population, and in Johannesburg, which had nearly 25000 Jews, they were 15 percent of the white population. There were 11000 Jews in Cape Town, and more than 1000 each in Durban, Pretoria, Port Elizabeth, Bloemfontein and Benoni.

In 1960, the year of the referendum which narrowly decided for republican status, there were nearly 115000 Jews (3·62 percent of the whites), of whom 113000 lived in urban areas. There were 57800 in Johannesburg, 22700 in Cape Town and 3000 or more in Durban, Pretoria and Port Elizabeth. The only significant difference was that by now the large majority were South African-born, whereas in 1926 the majority were still immigrants. This reflects the virtual halting of Jewish immigration since the outbreak of World War II. Indeed there had been a certain amount of emigration, particularly to Israel and Britain. Since 1960 a small-scale two-way migration has continued, with some immigration from Central Africa and more especially from Israel (in 1982 the number of permanent Israeli settlers was estimated to be between 15000 and 30000).

The clearly multiethnic character of South African society has created a Jewish community which is well integrated in the white sector of the population yet strongly maintains its own distinct identity. The Yiddish of the eastern European immigrants has gradually yielded to English as the first language, although in line with the general trend the use of Afrikaans has increased in recent years. (There have been some Afrikaans Jewish writers, but it is in English that Jewish South Africans have made their major contributions to South African culture.) The strong Calvinist ethos of the early Dutch settlers allowed little scope for other religious expression, but a more tolerant attitude was introduced in the Cape at the beginning of the 19th century with the constitutional reforms in Holland and the initiation of British supremacy. In the Transvaal religious tests for public office and for education in government schools were maintained until the former republic came under British rule in 1902. From that time on all Jewish citizens have enjoyed complete civil equality and religious freedom.

Antisemitism surfaced in certain quarters in the Nazi period, and was expressed for a time in the official policy of the National Party, but in 1948, when the party won the general election, the

"Jewish question" was formally dropped from its program and it has subsequently adhered to a policy of equality and nondiscrimination for all sections of the white population. Antisemitism has continued to be propagated among right-wing Afrikaner groups, but in general the government has acted sternly to suppress extremism.

Jews have played a full part in the civic and political life of the country at all levels. Many have served as mayors or represented various political parties in the provincial councils and national parliament. Jews have also participated in the economic development of South Africa, in trade, mining and other industries, and to a much smaller extent in farming. Individual Jews have been particularly prominent in the development of the mining industry, on which South Africa's wealth is based, and in large-scale commercial enterprises. Others have distinguished themselves in the legal and academic professions, in medicine and in cultural life.

South African Judaism reflects the largely Lithuanian origins of the community and also the traditional British connections. The Lithuanian legacy is visible still in a respect for traditional Jewish scholarship and in the predominance of Orthodox congregations, together with the absence of the more obscurantist forms of Polish traditionalism. There is little interest in religion as such, however, and the many synagogues function more as an expression of formal identification with Judaism than of spiritual vitality. Reform Judaism was introduced in the 1930s and claims a strong following, but it has always encountered vigorous opposition from the Orthodox sector and conflicts have often threatened to divide even the non-religious communal institutions. In 1980 a Sephardi synagogue was opened in Cape Town (a result of immigration from Zimbabwe and Zaïre), and in 1982 a Conservative congregation was established in Johannesburg.

South African Jewry has developed a multiplicity of communal organizations, representing a wide variety of objectives, but with a characteristically strong emphasis on philanthropic action and on education. There is an extensive network of Jewish day schools (the first was opened in Johannesburg in 1948), in which Jewish studies are integrated in a full secular curriculum. These are estimated to cater for a third of all Jewish schoolchildren.

The representative body of the whole community is the South African Board of Deputies, named for its British counterpart and performing similar functions. The South African Zionist Federation also occupies a strong central position in the structure of communal organizations. Both bodies represent a large number of diverse elements and they work closely together. Zionism has traditionally been very strong in South Africa. It commands impressive financial support and personal involvement, and there are close links between South African Jewry and Israel, where immigrants from South Africa have made an important contribution to the life of the country. (By contrast Israeli immigrants in South Africa, as in other countries, have contributed little to Jewish communal life.) The Zionist cause has received strong sympathy and support from the South African public and from successive governments. Jan Smuts was a member of the

The Jews of South Africa are very largely descendants of settlers from eastern Europe, particularly Lithuania, who arrived in the last decades of the 19th century, just as the opening of the Transvaal goldmines was attracting a sudden surge of immigration to this previously undeveloped region. The story of the Jewish communities of Johannesburg and its satellites is intimately tied up with the history of these towns themselves. Jews were among the earliest settlers, and they have continued to make a full contribution to economic, civic and cultural life.

Left Members of a Jewish family pose outside their home and family photographic business in Germiston, c. 1920. Here the Jewish community traces its origins to the foundation of the town, in 1896.

Center left A Jewish foodstore in Johannesburg, where Jewish life also dates back to the very foundation of the city, in 1886.

Below Jewish symbols are prominent on the ceremonial robes of this Zulu religious sect.

British cabinet which issued the Balfour Declaration and a lifelong pro-Zionist. One of the last political acts of his government, in May 1948, was to grant *de facto* recognition to the newly proclaimed state of Israel. The Nationalist government continued the friendly policy, and recognized Israel *de jure* on her admission to the United Nations in 1949. The two countries have enjoyed cordial relations ever since, despite Israeli endorsement of international condemnation of South Africa's racial policies, which has on occasion given rise to tensions between the South African government and the country's Jewish minority.

The Jews of South Africa have traditionally trodden a cautious path in the matter of the racial question. Instinctively moderate in politics, they have explicitly declined to express a united voice on questions not directly related to their own rights and freedoms, although individual Jews have taken a prominent role in the opposition to apartheid, and the Reform sector in particular has undertaken some welfare work in the black community. In 1980, however, the Board of Deputies took a more outspoken line, with a resolution urging all concerned, "in particular all members of our own community, to cooperate in securing the immediate

amelioration and ultimate removal of all unjust discrimination based on race, creed, or color."

Given the racial divisions existing in South Africa, it is hardly surprising that Judaism has made little impact among the black population. A black Jewish community in Soweto, under the leadership of an African rabbi who was moved to adopt Judaism after witnessing the religious faith of holocaust survivors in Poland, is regarded as something of a curiosity, while the claims by a tribe in northern Transvaal, the Lemba, to be of Jewish origin have been met with skepticism.

The future of South African Jewry is evidently bound up with the future of the white population as a whole. Unlike so many others, this staunch community is threatened not by assimilation but by the specter of the possible disruption of the economic and political conditions on which its existence is based, a fate which has already overtaken most of the other communities of the continent.

Other African Countries

The communities of Central Africa were never very large and most of them have now completely disappeared. In Rhodesia there was a small Jewish influx, mainly from South Africa, in the 1880s and congregations were soon formed in Bulawayo (1894), Salisbury (1895) and Gwelo (1901). Immigration steadily increased the Jewish population and by 1953, when the Federation of Rhodesia and Nyasaland was established, congregations had also been founded in Que Que and Gatooma, as well as in Lusaka and in a number of centers in the copperbelt of Northern Rhodesia. (Nyasaland never received more than a handful of Jewish immigrants.) These communities all flourished during the lifetime of the Federation, which for several years was led by a Jewish prime minister, Sir Roy Welensky. After it was dissolved in 1963 the communities of Northern Rhodesia (Zambia) began to decline and only a few families now remain in Lusaka. Southern Rhodesian Jewry numbered some 7000 in the 1960s, with a strong network of communal institutions, but the economic boycott and unsettled political future led to considerable emigration in the 1970s, and by the time the independent republic of Zimbabwe was proclaimed in 1980 fewer than 2000 Jews remained. In Zaïre few traces now remain of the eight communities which existed before independence, with a combined membership of 2500 souls.

Jewish settlement in Kenya dates back to 1903, when the British government offered the Zionist Organization a territory for autonomous Jewish settlement—a proposal which was rejected, but not without causing a profound split in the ranks of the Zionist movement. A few Jews settled in the territory and there was a subsequent small influx of refugees from Nazism. The present Nairobi community is very small and consists largely of Israelis.

A few other African capitals have exiguous groups of Jewish diplomats or businessmen who meet socially or to celebrate the major festivals together, but they have no permanent basis.

Left A garden party in aid of Israel. The Zionist movement has enjoyed extraordinary success in South Africa, providing an important focus for identification with the Jewish community and sponsoring many important projects in Israel. The links with Israel are strengthened by large-scale migration in both directions.

Right A Hasidic radio station, Johannesburg. The gamut of religious expressions in South Africa runs from Hasidism to Reform, but the dominant mode has always been Orthodoxy of a British flavor, coupled with a strong respect for traditional religious learning.

GLOSSARY

Note: The abbreviations CE (Common Era) and BCE (Before the Common Era), used throughout the Atlas, correspond to AD and BC, which have Christological connotations to which Jews do not subscribe. Heb. = Hebrew.

ark of the covenant   See **aron ha-kodesh.**

aron ha-kodesh (Heb. ''holy ark'')   Originally referring to the biblical ark of the covenant—the chest containing the two stone tablets given by God to Moses at Sinai—the term is now used for the shrine containing the scrolls of the **Torah** in the synagogue.

Ashkenazim (from *Ashkenaz*, a biblical name (Gen. 10:3) identified with Germany)   Jews of German or Polish extraction.

atonement, day of   See **Yom Kippur.**

bar mitzvah (Aramaic and Heb. ''son of the commandment'')   In common usage, the ceremony of admission of a boy to the adult worshiping community, normally at the age of 13. Strictly speaking the term applies to the boy himself, or indeed to any adult male Jew, subject to the full rigor of the commandments.

bat mitzvah (Heb. ''daughter of the commandment'')   The female equivalent of **bar mitzvah**: women become technically adult at the age of 12.

bet hamidrash (Heb. ''study-house'')   A room or building devoted to the study of the **Torah**. Because of the high status accorded to study in rabbinic Judaism the *bet hamidrash* is traditionally considered more holy than a **synagogue.**

blood libel   An accusation that Jews use human blood in preparing *matzot* (see **matzah**). It is particularly associated with medieval Christendom (the first occurrence here being at Norwich in 1144), but it has ancient Egyptian roots, and has also been known in modern times, spreading from Europe to the Muslim Ottoman empire and even to America. The blood libel has often been used as a pretext for physical assaults on Jews.

brit milah (Heb. ''covenant of circumcision'')   Removal of the foreskin, regarded as a symbolic sign of the covenant between God and Israel. The operation is performed by a **mohel** on male babies at the age of one week and also on male proselytes.

Conservative Judaism   Religious movement which developed in the USA in the early 20th century, and has spread more recently to Israel, Britain and elsewhere. Essentially a movement of cautious modernism, it accommodates a broad range of beliefs and practices and rejects both rigid traditionalism and radical reform.

conversos   A Spanish term used to designate the Jews converted to Christianity as a result of persecution in the 14th and 15th centuries.

diaspora (Greek ''dispersion'')   Collective term for the Jewish communities outside the land of Israel. The diaspora has a distinct status from Israel in Jewish law and ritual going back to antiquity. In modern times the concept of diaspora has played a prominent part in Zionist thinking.

emancipation   Release from civil disabilities. The emancipation of the Jews was a political issue closely connected with the struggle for religious freedom and the separation of Church and State.

ethnarch (Greek ''ruler of the nation'')   A title used by the Hasmonean kings and later by the hereditary rulers of the Jews under Roman rule (also called ''patriarchs'').

etrog (Heb. ''citron'')   One of the four species associated with the festival of **Sukkot**, the citron is commonly found as a symbol on tombstones and other ancient Jewish remains. See **lulav.**

exilarch   Hereditary head of Babylonian Jewry.

gaon (Heb. ''eminence'')   A title applied specifically to the heads of the major talmudic schools in the Middle East in the 6th to 12th centuries. It is used more generally of any outstanding scholar.

genizah (Heb. ''storage'')   A storage place for unwanted texts and objects which are considered too holy to be destroyed. The most famous *genizah* is that in the synagogue of old Cairo, but in the middle ages virtually every synagogue had one (see pp. 18–19).

ghetto   A walled reservation in which Jews were compelled to live in some European cities before the emancipation. The term is derived from a quarter of Venice designated for this purpose in 1516. It is now applied loosely to any urban district inhabited by a minority community, even voluntarily.

gnosticism (from Greek *gnosis* ''(esoteric) knowledge'')   A complex religious movement, spilling over the borders of institutional Judaism and Christianity, which exercised an important role in the development of Jewish and Christian orthodoxy in the early centuries, and influenced the evolution of **Kabbalah** in the middle ages.

haftarah (Heb. ''conclusion'')   Reading from the prophetic books of the Bible which follows the reading of the **Torah** in the Sabbath or festival morning service.

Haggadah (Heb. ''narration'')   The set ritual for the recitation of the exodus from Egypt and its enduring meaning at the family meal on **Passover** Eve.

halakhah (Heb. ''regulation'')   The portion of Jewish religion and thought dealing with rules for living, whether legal or ethical.

hametz (Heb. ''leaven'')   Technically dough made from flour and water and left to stand until it has soured. Biblical law forbids its use during **Passover** or in the Temple meal offering. The eradication of *hametz*, in whatever form, from the home is an essential part of the preparation for Passover.

Hanukkah (Heb. ''dedication'')   A winter festival commemorating the rededication of the Jerusalem temple by Judah Maccabee on 25 Kislev, 165 BCE. It lasts eight days and is observed by lighting lamps or candles.

Hasidism (from Heb. *hasid*, ''pious'')   A movement of religious revivalism which began in 18th-century Poland. Its devotees are called Hasidim. The term itself has a much older history: a Hasidic movement existed in the Hasmonean period, and another flourished in Germany in the 13th century.

havdalah (Heb. ''differentiation'')   Prayer recited at the conclusion of Sabbaths and festivals, to mark the difference between sacred and profane.

havurah (Heb.)   A small religious fellowship.

herem (Heb. ''anathema'')   The most solemn and extreme form of ban, or exclusion of an individual from the community. As a result of the breakup of the medieval community structure the *herem* has become virtually inoperative, and is rarely invoked today.

high holy days   New Year and **Yom Kippur**, the most solemn festivals in the Jewish year.

holocaust (Greek ''whole burned offering'')   Originally denoting a sacrifice wholly consumed by fire, the term is now used to refer to the mass murder of some six million Jews by the Nazis and their collaborators.

host libel   A medieval Christian slander alleging that Jews desecrated the host or consecrated wafer which was identified with the body of Christ. The libel was often accompanied or followed by physical violence against Jews.

huppah (Heb. ''canopy'')   The canopy (symbolizing the bridal chamber) under which the marriage ceremony takes place. By extension, the term can mean simply ''wedding.''

Israel   An alternative name of the biblical patriarch Jacob, Israel denotes in Hebrew the whole Jewish people or an individual Jew (or ''Israelite''). This is the sense in which it is still used theologically by Jews and Christians alike (the Christian Church being the ''New Israel''). The name of the modern state of Israel is derived from the older phrase ''land of Israel.''

Kabbalah (Heb. ''tradition'')   A theosophical system which reached one peak of creativity in 13th-century Spain with the composition of the *Zohar* and another in 16th-century Safed (Zefat in modern Israel) in the school of Isaac Luria. Essentially esoteric, *kabbalah* has had a considerable influence, notably in Renaissance Christianity, **Hasidism** and the popular Judaism of North Africa and the Yemen.

Karaism (from Heb. *kara* ''read (scripture)'')   A religious movement rejecting rabbinic tradition and basing its teaching on Scripture alone.

kehilla (Heb. ''congregation'')   In a traditional sense, the self-governing Jewish community of the medieval system.

ketubbah (Heb. ''document'')   A legal document recording a marriage and the obligations undertaken by the bridegroom towards the bride.

kibbutz (Heb.)   A collective settlement in Israel.

kiddush (Heb. ''sanctification'')   A prayer chanted, in home or **synagogue**, over a cup of wine on Sabbaths and festivals.

kosher (adj.) or *kasher* (Heb. ''fit'')   ''Ritually acceptable'': the term is most commonly applied to food which conforms to the dietary regulations or to butchers and foodstores selling such items.

Kristallnacht (German)   The ''night of broken glass'' (9–10 November 1938) when hundreds of German synagogues were destroyed in a concerted Nazi attack on Jewish property.

Ladino   A name applied to the Spanish language of Sephardi Jews.

Liberal Judaism   A term virtually synonymous with **Reform Judaism**, and used particularly in western Europe. In Britain it denotes the more radical wing of the reform movement.

Lubavitch Hasidism   Also known as Habad Hasidism. A branch of **Hasidism** characterized by a belief in intellectual striving as an important element in religious devotion and by the attention devoted to the *Tanya*, a work by Shneour Zalman of Lyady (in Russia), founder of the Lubavitch dynasty. The seat of the Lubavitcher *Rebbe* is currently in New York, but the sect maintains active missions in many parts of the world.

lulav (Heb.)   Strictly denoting a palm branch, the term is commonly extended to refer to the bundle consisting of one palm branch, two willow twigs and three sprigs of myrtle which, together with the *etrog*, make up the ''four species'' used in the ritual of the festival of **Sukkot.**

marranos (Spanish ''swine'')   Derogatory term applied to Spanish and Portuguese Jews forcibly converted to Christianity, and to their descendants, many of whom kept up Jewish beliefs and rituals in secret.

matzah (pl. *matzot*) (Heb.)   Unleavened bread particularly associated with the feast of the **Passover.**

melammed (Heb.)   A teacher of children.

mellah (Arabic)   Jewish quarter in Moroccan towns.

menorah (Heb. ''candelabrum'')   The seven-branched lampstand which stood in the Jerusalem temple, and became one of the most familiar Jewish symbols. Its form is often copied in the eight-branched lampstand or candlestick used at **Hanukkah.**

mezuzah (Heb. ''doorpost'')   A small parchment scroll inscribed with two biblical texts, enclosed in a case, and fixed to the doorposts of Jewish homes.

misnagdim (Heb. ''opponents'')   Opponents of the Hasidic movement in eastern Europe.

Mizrachi   Religious wing of the Zionist organization.

mohel   The person who performs the operation of **brit milah.**

moshav (Heb.)   A cooperative settlement in Israel.

Neologue Movement   Religious movement of moderate reform in Hungary.

Orthodox Judaism   The most conservative of the modernist trends in Judaism. The term (which is borrowed from Christianity) is applied by extension to strictly traditionalist forms of Judaism (also known as "ultra-orthodox").

parokhet (pl. *parokhot*) (Heb.)   A curtain which hangs in front of the ark in Ashkenazi synagogues.

Passover (Heb. *pesah*)   Spring festival commemorating the liberation of the Hebrew slaves and the exodus from Egypt. The festival lasts a full week and begins with an elaborate ritual meal (*seder*) at which the story of the exodus is narrated and the theme of liberation discussed.

peot (Heb. "corners")   Sidelocks which are allowed to grow by traditionalist Jews of Polish or Yemenite origin.

Pesah   See **Passover**.

pogrom (Russian)   A sudden, unprovoked raid. Originally applied to the attacks on Jewish settlements which were widespread in the last decades of czarist rule in Russia, the term has come to be applied to any violent assault on a Jewish community.

Purim (Heb. "lots")   A festival commemorating the deliverance of the Jews of the Persian empire from the genocidal plot of Haman, as narrated in the biblical book of Esther. Local communities and even families have instituted their own *purim* to celebrate rescue from impending disasters.

rabbi (Heb.)   Originally the title of a sage qualified to give decisions in Jewish law; in modernist Judaism the term tends to denote a minister of the Jewish religion.

Reconstructionism   Religious movement originating in the USA, and combining a naturalist theology with a conception of Judaism as a civilization which bears a religious validity of its own.

Reform Judaism   Religious movement, originating in 19th-century Germany, which aims to adapt Jewish tradition to the conditions of modern life. In Britain the term denotes the more traditional wing of the movement, in contrast to the more radical Liberal branch.

Sabbataeanism   A messianic movement, named for Shabbetai Zvi, which swept across Europe and the near east in the 17th century and eventually petered out in local sectarian feuds and witchhunts.

sanhedrin (from Greek *synhedrion*, "council")   Name of various deliberative and judicial bodies in antiquity, which was revived for the rabbinical assembly convened in Paris in 1807 to endorse the Napoleonic reforms.

Second Temple Period   The great formative period of Jewish religion and culture between the Babylonian exile in the 6th century BCE and the destruction of the Second Temple in 70 CE.

Seder   See **Passover**.

Sephardim (from Heb. *Sepharad* "Spain")   Jews of Spanish and Portuguese origin, as opposed to **Ashkenazim**. In Israel the term is commonly applied to all non-Ashkenazi Jews.

shofar (Heb.)   A ram's horn which is blown during the New Year service and at the conclusion of **Yom Kippur**. In Israel it is also sounded on solemn public occasions and to announce the advent of Sabbath in religious communities.

shtetl (Yiddish "small town")   A Jewish settlement in eastern Europe; the term is now applied to the whole lost world of eastern European Jewry.

shtibl (Yiddish "little house")   A small prayerhouse of Ashkenazi Jews, particularly Hasidim.

shield of David (Heb. *magen David*)   A hexagram or six-pointed star, which since the 17th century has become a characteristic Jewish symbol or badge. It is particularly associated with the Zionist organization, and was also adopted by the Nazis for the yellow Jewish badge of shame.

Simhat Torah (Heb. "joy of Torah")   Festival marking the end of the annual cycle of Torah-readings. Of late medieval origin, it has become firmly established as a joyful celebration, with scrolls of the **Torah** paraded in the synagogue and even through the streets.

Sukkot (Heb. "booths" or "tabernacles")   The autumn festival celebrated with the building of a *sukkah*, a hut adorned with greenery and fruit, and in the synagogue with the waving of the "four species" (see **lulav**, **etrog**).

synagogue (from Greek *synagōgē*, "assembly")   A hall or building for congregational worship, nowadays often including facilities for other communal activities such as education and social gatherings. The term may also denote the congregation in an abstract sense, but the phrase "the Synagogue" as a synonym for "Jewry" or "Judaism" (by analogy with "the Church") is confined to Christian usage.

tallit (Heb.)   A tasseled stole worn (traditionally by adult male Jews only) during morning prayers and on certain other religious occasions. It is usually made of white wool striped with black, or white silk striped with blue.

Talmud (Heb. "teaching")   A corpus of literature, written in Hebrew and Aramaic, recording debates and discussions of the ancient rabbis on a wide range of subjects, and existing in two distinct compilations, the Palestinian Talmud and the Babylonian Talmud. The Talmud became the cornerstone of rabbinic Judaism, and its authority has come under attack from Karaites, Christians and Reform Jews. It is still the basis of instruction in *yeshivot*.

tebah (Heb. "chest")   Sephardi name for the raised dais in the synagogue, on which the reading desk is situated. Ashkenazim call it *almemar* or *bimah*.

tefillin (Heb.)   Phylacteries consisting of biblical texts inscribed on parchment and enclosed in two small leather boxes with leather straps attached. They are worn during weekday morning prayers, one being placed on the forehead and the other on the upper arm.

temple   A synagogue. This use of the term is confined to **Reform Judaism**.

Torah (Heb. "instruction")   In a general sense, revealed or traditional Jewish teaching, sometimes divided into "written Torah" (contained in the Bible) and "oral Torah" (contained in the **Talmud** and other non-biblical compilations). More specifically, the five books of Moses (the Pentateuch), or the scroll on which they are written for synagogue use. The misleading translation "Law," which has ancient origins, has established itself in English usage. The phrase "Torah-true" is used by some traditionalist Jews to describe their own form of Judaism, in contradistinction to other religious and secularist trends.

yeshivah (pl. *yeshivot*) (Heb.)   An academy of learning, particularly associated with the study of the **Talmud**, although some *yeshivot* have had a much broader curriculum. The term is also applied today to a religious Jewish highschool.

Yiddish   A medieval German dialect which became the vernacular of Ashkenazim in eastern Europe, from where it has spread to many parts of the world.

Yom Kippur (Heb. "Day of Atonement")   The most solemn fast in the Jewish calendar, and the climax of the penitential season which begins in late summer.

zaddik (Heb. "righteous")   A Hasidic leader (also called *rebbe*), owing his authority to charismatic powers or dynastic succession.

Zionism   Movement, originating in 19th-century Europe, aiming to bring about the return of the Jews to the land of Israel.

Zohar (Heb. "splendor")   The classical text of **Kabbalah**. An anonymous compilation of diverse elements, its central core is a mystical commentary on the **Torah**, written in Aramaic by Moses de León in the late 13th century.

LIST OF ILLUSTRATIONS

While every attempt has been made to trace copyright owners, anyone having a query in this regard is invited to apply to Equinox.

BIBLIOGRAPHY

The literature on the Jews is enormous, and any brief bibliography must inevitably be very selective. The notes which follow make no pretense of being complete or comprehensive. They are intended for the reader of this Atlas who wishes to follow up some of the themes suggested in the preceding pages. The selection is limited to complete books which are available in English, and preference has been given, where possible, to recent works. Many of the books listed contain their own suggestions for further reading; those with a particularly useful bibliography are marked (bibl.).

For general reference the *Encyclopaedia Judaica* (16 vols.; Jerusalem 1971–72) is an invaluable storehouse of information, with an excellent computerized index in volume 1. It will often provide a quick and satisfactory answer to a query, but its coverage is very uneven and the whole work is fraught with errors and idiosyncracies. A series of accompanying Year Books provides some helpful supplements and updatings. For more enduring subjects the older *Jewish Encyclopedia* (12 vols.; New York and London 1906–07) is still a useful reference work.

Part I: The Historical Background

The Jews and their History
On Jewish historiography see S. W. Baron, *History and Jewish Historians* (Philadelphia, Pa. 1964). For Josephus and his achievement the latest treatment is T. Rajak, *Josephus* (London 1983). The first full-scale modern history of the Jews was written at the beginning of the 18th century by the French Protestant Jacques Basnage (*Histoire des juifs . . .*, 7 vols., La Haye 1706–11; one vol. English trans. by T. Taylor, *A History of the Jews . . .*, London 1707); it was imitated (and quarried) by other Christian authors in the 18th and 19th centuries. The first such effort by a Jewish writer, I. M. Jost (*Geschichte der Israeliten seit der Zeit der Maccabäer bis auf unsere Tage*, 10 vols., Berlin 1820–47), was soon superseded by the impressive history of H. Graetz (*Geschichte der Juden von der ältesten Zeiten bis auf die Gegenwart*, 11 vols., Leipzig 1855–76; English trans. by B. Löwy et al., 6 vols., Philadelphia, Pa. 1891–98, and reprints), which is still valuable, though very dated. The English version lacks the notes and appendixes which are a vital feature of the German original. S. M. Dubnow's attempt to improve on Graetz was not very successful; it is available in an indifferent English translation by M. Spiegel (*History of the Jews*, 5 vols., New Brunswick, N.J. 1967). S. W. Baron's *Social and Religious History of the Jews* (2nd edn, New York and Philadelphia, Pa. 1952–; 18 vols. to date) is a masterly synthesis, drawing on a vast range of sources and rich in interpretative judgments, but focusing almost exclusively on the interests indicated in the title. Of the more compact histories the most readable and reliable are those by C. Roth (*A Short History of the Jewish People*, rev. edn, London 1948; further rev., enlarged and illustrated edn, London 1969), J. Parkes (*A History of the Jewish People*, London 1962) and S. Grayzel (*History of the Jews*, 2nd edn, Philadelphia, Pa. 1968). There are some interesting reflections on Jewish attitudes to history and the impact of the past on the present in L. Kochan, *The Jew and his History* (London 1977) and Y. H. Yerushalmi, *Zakhor: Jewish History and Jewish Memory* (Washington, D.C. 1983).

The Jews in the Ancient World
The encounter between Jews and Greeks is presented succinctly in A. D. Momigliano, *Alien Wisdom* (Cambridge 1975). For a more extensive treatment see V. Tcherikover (trans. S. Applebaum), *Hellenistic Civilization and the Jews*

(2nd edn; Philadelphia, Pa. and Jerusalem 1961). There is an excellent account of the early Roman period in E. Schürer (English trans. rev. and edited by G. Vermes and F. Millar), *The History of the Jewish People in the Age of Jesus Christ (175 B.C.–A.D. 135)* (2 vols.; Edinburgh 1973, 1979). For Palestine, the story is continued down to the Arab conquest in M. Avi-Yonah, *The Jews of Palestine* (Oxford 1976). The history of the Roman diaspora has yet to be written, and indeed for the most part the evidence is still scanty, but for Rome see H. J. Leon, *The Jews of Ancient Rome* (Philadelphia, Pa. 1960). The scarcity of literary evidence highlights the work of the archaeologists. Sardis is an important case: G. M. A. Hanfmann, *Sardis from Prehistoric to Roman Times* (Cambridge, Mass. 1983). Dura is another: C. H. Kraeling, *The Synagogue* (New Haven, Conn. 1956; repr. New York 1979). Virtually the only history of the eastern disaspora available in English is J. Neusner, *A History of the Jews in Babylonia* (5 vols.; Leiden 1965–70).

Christianity and the Jews
For the early history of relations between Jews and Christians the most comprehensive book is still J. Parkes, *The Conflict of the Church and the Synagogue* (London 1934), which traces the story from the beginning of Christianity to the 7th century. There is no continuous treatment of the succeeding period in English, but for the west see J. Parkes, *The Jew in the Medieval Community* (London 1938), and E. A. Synan, *The Popes and the Jews in the Middle Ages* (New York 1965), and for the east A. Sharf, *Byzantine Jewry* (London 1971). J. Trachtenberg, *The Devil and the Jews* (2nd edn; New York 1966), is a study of the more lurid side of Christian anti-Judaism, while J. R. Marcus, *The Jew in the Medieval World* (Cincinnati, OH 1938), is a very useful collection of original documents in translation. Among various books dealing with individual countries, special mention should be made of Y. Baer (trans. L. Schoffman), *A History of the Jews in Christian Spain* (2 vols.; Philadelphia, Pa. 1961–66). For the Italian Renaissance see C. Roth, *The Jews in the Renaissance* (Philadelphia, Pa. 1959), and M. A. Shulvass (trans. E. I. Kose), *The Jews in the World of the Renaissance* (Leiden and Chicago, Ill. 1973).

Islam and the Jews
The best study of the "Pact of Umar" is A. S. Tritton, *The Caliphs and their Non-Muslim Subjects* (London 1930; repr. London 1970). For an excellent general survey of the Jewish experience under Arab rule see N. A. Stillman, *The Jews of Arab Lands* (Philadelphia, Pa. 1979)—lucid, reliable, and with a wealth of documents in English translation. The Cairo Genizah discoveries have begun to generate a considerable literature on Jewish life in the Arab middle ages. S. D. Goitein, *A Mediterranean Society* (4 vols., Berkeley and Los Angeles, Calif. 1967–), is essential reading on this subject. Goitein's short book, *Jews and Arabs* (3rd edn; New York 1974), is also of value. Another important study is W. J. Fischel, *Jews in the Economic and Political Life of Medieval Islam* (London 1937). For Spain we have a detailed study by E. Ashtor (trans. A. and J. M. Klein), *The Jews of Moslem Spain* (2 vols.; Philadelphia, Pa. 1973).

On the Periphery
For China, see W. C. White, *Chinese Jews* (2nd edn; Toronto 1966), D. D. Leslie, *The Survival of the Chinese Jews* (Leiden 1972), M. Pollak, *Mandarins, Jews and Missionaries* (Philadelphia, Pa. 1980). There is no reliable recent treatment in English of the history of the Jews of India, but see H. S. Kehimkar, *The History of the Bene Israel of India* (Tel Aviv 1937). On the Falashas of Ethiopia see D.

Kessler, *The Falashas* (London 1982), and on the Khazars D. M. Dunlop, *The History of the Jewish Khazars* (Princeton, N.J. 1954).

The Sephardi Diaspora
Curiously enough there is no book in English devoted to the expulsion from Spain and the resettlement of Jews in the Ottoman empire. For the subsequent Ottoman experience see B. Braude and B. Lewis, *Christians and Jews in the Ottoman Empire* (2 vols.; New York 1982). On the Portuguese dispersion see C. Roth, *A History of the Marranos* (Philadelphia, Pa. 1932). His biographical work, *The House of Nasi* (2 vols.; Philadelphia, Pa. 1948), paints a vivid picture of the period of the expulsions.

The Ashkenazi Diaspora
S. M. Dubnow (trans. I. Friedländer), *History of the Jews in Russia and Poland* (3 vols.; Philadelphia, Pa. 1916–20), has not really been superseded. For an account of Polish Jewish culture in its heyday see M. A. Shulvass, *Jewish Culture in Eastern Europe: the Classical Period* (New York 1975). The origins of Ashkenazi Jewry are studied in some detail in I. A. Agus, *The Heroic Age of Franco-German Jewry* (New York, 1969), and for the reemigration of Polish Jews westwards in the 17th and 18th centuries see M. A. Shulvass, *From East to West* (Detroit, Mich. 1971).

Into the Modern World
J. Katz, *Out of the Ghetto* (Cambridge, Mass. 1973), is a fine evocation of the historical background, which may be supplemented by a number of biographical studies: C. Roth, *A Life of Menasseh Ben Israel, Rabbi, Printer and Diplomat* (Philadelphia, Pa. 1934), A. Altmann, *Moses Mendelssohn* (London 1973), I. Berlin, *The Life and Opinions of Moses Hess* (Cambridge 1959). R. Mahler, *A History of Modern Jewry, 1780–1815* (London and New York 1971), is a detailed study of 35 crucial years. For developments in France see also S. Schwartzfuchs, *Napoleon, the Jews and the Sanhedrin* (Madison, N.J. 1980), and more generally on the emancipation J. Jehouda, *The Five Stages of Jewish Emancipation* (New Brunswick, N.J. 1966), and A. G. Duker and M. Ben Horin (eds.), *Emancipation and Counter-Emancipation* (New York 1974), a reader with a useful bibliography.

The Last Hundred Years
For a general account see S. Grayzel, *A History of the Contemporary Jews* (Philadelphia, Pa. 1960), I. Elbogen, *A Century of Jewish Life* (Philadelphia, Pa. 1966), H. Sachar, *The Course of Modern Jewish History* (London 1958). For an introduction to the subject of antisemitism see J. Parkes, *Antisemitism* (London 1963), and for more specialized studies U. Tal (trans. N. Jacobs), *Christians and Jews in Germany* (Ithaca, N.Y. and London 1975), and S. Wilson, *Ideology and Experience: Anti-Semitism in France at the Time of the Dreyfus Affair* (Rutherford, N.J. 1982) (bibl.). There is no overall account of the great migrations, but for the experience of immigrant Jews in New York see M. Rischin, *The Promised City* (Cambridge, Mass. 1962), and I. Howe, *World of Our Fathers* (Boston, Mass. 1976; British edn entitled *The Immigrant Jews of New York*, London 1976). There are two recent biographical studies of that remarkable figure, Baron Maurice de Hirsch: K. Grunwald, *Turkenhirsch* (New York 1966), and S. J. Lee, *Moses of the New World* (New York 1970). On Jewish involvement with socialism see N. Levin, *Jewish Socialist Movements, 1871–1917* (London 1978), R. Wistrich, *Socialism and the Jews* (New York 1982), and J. Frankel, *Prophecy and Politics* (Cambridge 1982). A convenient introduction to the history of Zionism is W. Laqueur, *A History of Zionism* (New York and London 1972), and for more detail on the

early years see the two books by D. Vital, *The Origins of Zionism* (Oxford 1975) and *Zionism: the Formative Years* (Oxford 1982). For the subsequent story see L. Stein, *The Balfour Declaration* (London 1961), C. Sykes, *Cross Roads to Israel* (London 1965), Y. Bauer, *From Diplomacy to Resistance* (Philadelphia, Pa. 1970), and the very personal account by M. Begin (trans. S. Katz), *The Revolt* (London 1951). The moment of the establishment of the Jewish state is vividly captured by Z. Sharef in *Three Days* (trans. J. L. Meltzer; London 1962). Anyone interested in gaining an insight through original documents into the struggle for Israel should consult the collections by W. Laqueur, *The Israel/Arab Reader* (London 1969), and W. Khalidi, *From Haven to Conquest* (Beirut 1971). And for detailed descriptions of the major Israeli wars see D. Kurzman, *Genesis, 1948* (London 1972), D. Kimche and D. Bawly, *The Sandstorm: The Arab–Israeli War of 1967* (London 1968), and C. Herzog, *The War of Atonement* (London 1975).

There are many general and detailed books about the Nazi holocaust. It is best to begin with one of the more general accounts: L. S. Dawidowicz, *The War against the Jews, 1933–45* (London 1977), G. Reitlinger, *The Final Solution* (London 1953), or N. Levin, *The Holocaust* (New York 1965). There is a detailed *Atlas of the Holocaust* by M. Gilbert (London 1982).

Part II: The Cultural Background

Jewish Identity

One approach to the question "Who are the Jews?" is that of A. E. Mourant *et al.*, *The Genetics of the Jews* (Oxford 1978). Another is found in the collection of responses to Ben-Gurion's question on the registration of children of mixed marriages: B. Litwin (compiler) and S. B. Hoenig (ed.), *Jewish Identity* (New York 1965). And yet another in works such as A. Leon, *The Jewish Question: a Marxist Interpretation* (Mexico City 1950), or I. Deutscher, *The Non-Jewish Jew* (Oxford 1968). S. N. Herman, *Jewish Identity* (Beverly Hills, Calif. and London 1977), is a technical study by a social psychologist. On the crisis of Jewish identity in Germany see, for the Enlightenment period, M. A. Meyer, *The Origins of the Modern Jew* (Detroit, Mich. 1967), and for a more recent period P. Gay, *Freud, Jews and Other Germans* (Oxford 1979). The problem is well illustrated in the collection of documents by P. R. Mendes-Flohr and J. Reinharz, *The Jew in the Modern World* (New York and Oxford 1980). On the challenge of Israel see S. N. Herman, *Israelis and Jews* (New York 1970), and D. V. Segré, *A Crisis of Identity—Israel and Zionism* (Oxford 1980). On Jewish identity in the Soviet Union: A. Voronel and V. Yakhot (ed.), *Jewishness Rediscovered* (New York 1974). And for a theological approach, see D. Marmur, *Beyond Survival* (London 1982).

Jewish Life

For an introduction to medieval Jewish life see I. Abrahams, *Jewish Life in the Middle Ages* (2nd edn; London 1932), and on the eastern European *shtetl* M. Zborowski and E. Herzog, *Life is with People* (New York 1962). For a concise survey of contemporary dilemmas and developments see S. Sharot, *Judaism: a Sociology* (Newton Abbot 1976). There are many books on the family and everyday life, of which the following may be mentioned: G. S. Rosenthal (ed.), *The Jewish Family in a Changing World* (New York 1970), B. Schlesinger, *The Jewish Family* (Toronto 1971) (bibl.), H. Schauss, *The Lifetime of a Jew* (New York 1950), J. Fried, *Jews and Divorce* (New York 1968), S. E. Freedman, *The Book of Kashruth* (New York 1970), and for those interested in trying it themselves J. Grossinger, *The Art of Jewish Cooking* (New York 1958). Death, of course, is also an aspect of life; see M. Lamm, *The Jewish Way in Death and Mourning* (New York 1969).

Jewish Religion

The classic work in English on Jewish theology is K. Kohler, *Jewish Theology* (New York 1918). For a modern, nonpartisan survey see L. Jacobs, *A Jewish Theology* (London 1974) (bibl.). L. Baeck (trans. V. Grubenweiser and L. Pearl, rev. I. Howe), *The Essence of Judaism* (New York 1948), is a valuable study, if somewhat dated; for a more modern interpretation see W. Herberg, *Judaism and Modern Man* (Philadelphia, Pa. 1951). The comparison between Judaism, Christianity and Islam is explored historically (for the early centuries) by F. E. Peters, *Children of Abraham* (Princeton, N.J. 1982), and theologically by I. Maybaum, *Trialogue between Jew, Christian and Muslim* (London 1973) and *Happiness outside the State* (Stocksfield, Northumberland 1980).

A basic introduction to the history of Judaism is B. J. Bamberger, *The Story of Judaism* (3rd edn; New York 1970). For a lucid and original account of early Judaism in the Persian and Greek periods see M. E. Stone, *Scriptures, Sects and Visions* (Philadelphia, Pa. 1980). The most comprehensive and reliable introduction to the Roman period is still G. F. Moore, *Judaism in the First Centuries of the Christian Era* (3 vols.; Cambridge, Mass. 1927–30). On philosophy see J. Guttmann, *Philosophies of Judaism* (Philadelphia, Pa. 1964), and on the mystical tradition two books by G. G. Scholem: *Major Trends in Jewish Mysticism* (3rd edn; New York 1954, London 1955) and *On the Kabbalah and its Symbolism* (trans. R. Mannheim; New York 1965); on folk religion J. Trachtenberg, *Jewish Magic and Superstition* (New York 1939), and on messianism A. H. Silver, *A History of Messianic Speculation in Israel* (New York 1927). On Shabbetai Zvi there is a major study by G. G. Scholem (trans. R. J. Z. Werblowsky), *Sabbatai Sevi* (2 vols; Princeton, N.J. 1973). Among the many books on Hasidism those by M. Buber deserve mention, for example *Origin and Meaning of Hasidism* (trans. M. Friedman, New York 1960), as does L. Jacobs, *Hasidic Prayer* (London 1973).

The development of the modernist movements in the 19th century is treated in some detail by D. Philipson, *The Reform Movement in Judaism* (2nd edn; New York 1931); there is a briefer and more up-to-date account in J. L. Blau, *Modern Varieties of Judaism* (New York 1966). On the early development of Orthodoxy see H. Schwab (trans. I. R. Birnbaum), *The History of Orthodox Jewry in Germany* (London 1951). On Conservatism see M. Sklare, *Conservative Judaism* (New York 1955), and M. Davis, *The Emergence of Conservative Judaism* (Philadelphia, Pa. 1963), and on Judaism in America N. Glazer, *American Judaism* (Chicago, Ill. 1957). M. M. Kaplan, *Judaism as a Civilization* (New York 1934), in addition to being one of the foundation documents of Reconstructionism, presents a thoroughgoing if sternly critical account of the other main trends. For a rare glimpse of an interesting new development see L. Lilker, *Kibbutz Judaism* (Darby, Pa. 1982).

Finally, for an introduction to Jewish worship see A. Z. Idelsohn, *Jewish Liturgy and its Development* (New York 1932), and J. J. Petuchowski, *Understanding Jewish Prayer* (New York 1972).

Language and Literature

Hebrew: For a historical account of the language see E. Y. Kutscher, *A History of the Hebrew Language* (Jerusalem and Leiden 1982), and on Ben Yehuda and the modern revival of Hebrew, J. Fellman, *The Revival of a Classical Tongue* (The Hague and Paris 1973) (bibl.). There is a do-it-yourself guide to the alphabet by J. S. Greenspan, *Hebrew Calligraphy* (New York 1981). For an introduction to Hebrew literature see E. Silberschlag, *From Renaissance to Renaissance* (2 vols.; New York 1973–77); S. Halkin, *Modern Hebrew Literature* (New York 1950) or *Major Trends in Modern Hebrew Literature* (New York 1970). T. Carmi (ed.), *The Penguin Book of Hebrew Verse* (Harmondsworth 1981), is an anthology by a leading Hebrew poet which excellently conveys the depth and breadth of Hebrew poetry over a history of some 3000 years.

Yiddish: For a general account see M. Weinreich, *History of the Yiddish Language* (Chicago, Ill. 1980), and S. Liptzin, *History of Yiddish Literature* (New York 1972). C. Sinclair, *The Brothers Singer* (New York 1982), is a splendid book about an amazing family of Yiddish writers.

Jewish Literature: M. Waxman, *A History of Jewish Literature* (5 vols.; New York 1960), is more of a reference book than a readable history; it is packed with information about Jewish writers and their work in various languages, and for Hebrew writing it usefully supplements the books by Silberschlag and Halkin mentioned above, which concentrate on the modern period. It is not easy nowadays to define the scope of "Jewish literature," and many Jewish writers are themselves caught up in a crisis of identity, which is explored in A. Gottmann, *The Jewish Writer in America* (New York 1971). The same theme has been studied more recently, and over a wider range of writers and languages, in M. Baumgarten, *City Scriptures* (Cambridge, Mass. 1983). There is an excellent anthology of Jewish poetry translated from many languages: H. Schwartz and A. Rudolf (eds.), *Voices within the Ark* (New York 1981).

The Impact of the Holocaust

The literature on the holocaust is vast. Most of it is concerned with uncovering and describing the events, and paying tribute to the victims, but even historical studies tend to contain, at least implicitly, some reflections on how the past should influence the present. Y. Bauer, *The Holocaust in Historical Perspective* (London 1978), is an important contribution by a historian who has made himself a specialist in this subject. There are interesting historical reflections, too, in G. M. Kren and L. Rappaport, *The Holocaust and the Crisis of Human Behaviour* (London and New York 1981), a joint study by a historian and a psychologist, E. Fleischner (ed.), *Auschwitz: Beginning of a New Era?* (New York 1977), and in H. Arendt, *Eichmann in Jerusalem* (New York 1963), a book which aroused a fierce controversy when it first appeared because of its remarks about Jewish passivity in the face of the "Final Solution." R. R. Brenner, *The Faith and Doubt of Holocaust Survivors* (New York and London 1980), is a quantitative survey of actual reactions, which provides a factual basis for study of the effects of the holocaust on those who went through it and survived.

In the theological domain the most influential works are R. Rubenstein, *After Auschwitz* (Indianapolis, Ind. 1966), I. Maybaum, *The Face of God after Auschwitz* (Amsterdam 1965), and E. Berkovits, *Faith after the Holocaust* (New York 1973). For the impact of the holocaust on Jewish thought see also A. A. Cohen (ed.), *Arguments and Doctrines* (Philadelphia, Pa. 1970), and S. T. Katz, *Post-Holocaust Dialogues* (New York 1983). And for its impact on Christian attitudes to Judaism see A. R. Eckardt, *Elder and Younger Brothers* (New York 1967), A. T. Davies, *Antisemitism and the Christian Mind* (New York 1969).

One approach to the holocaust is through art: J. Blatter and S. Milton, *Art of the Holocaust* (London 1982). Another approach is through literature: A. H. Friedlander (ed.), *Out of the Whirlwind* (New York 1968), is an anthology of writing produced during the holocaust. But there is also a great deal of post-holocaust fiction which grapples with the wider implications of the events, such as the novels of E. Wiesel, for example *Night* (trans. S. Rodway; New York 1960). For an Israeli approach see A. Oz (trans. N. de Lange), *Touch the Water, Touch the Wind* (New York 1974). This Jewish experience has also entered the common vocabulary of a wider literature—an outstanding specimen is D. M. Thomas, *The White Hotel* (London and New York 1981).

Zionism

Some books on the history of Zionism have already been mentioned in the bibliography to Part One; and see also "Israel" in Part Three, below. Some further historical studies, which focus on the roots of Zionism and its wider implications for the Jewish world, are M. Gilbert, *Exile and Return* (London 1978), S. Avineri, *The Making of Modern Zionism* (New York 1981), and B. Halpern, *The Idea of the Jewish State* (2nd edn; Cambridge, Mass. 1969). A. Hertzberg, *The Zionist Idea* (New York 1960), contains an excellent presentation of the subject as well as an illuminating selection of readings.

The founders of Zionism can be approached through their lives and writings—an approach which also reveals a great deal about the general historical background of the movement and its psychological roots. The most stimulating and readable biography of Herzl is A. Elon, *Herzl* (London 1975). His novel *Old-New Land* has been translated by L. Levensohn (New York 1960), and his diaries (edited by R. Patai) are translated by H. Zohn (5 vols.; New York and London 1960). For the life of Ahad Ha'am see L. Simon, *Ahad Ha'am* (Philadelphia, Pa. 1960), and for selected translations from his writings H. Kohn (ed.), *Nationalism and the Jewish Ethic* (New York 1962). Among numerous volumes of personal memoirs the following are particularly revealing: C. Weizmann, *Trial and Error* (New York and London 1949; illustrated edn, London 1950), Viscount Samuel, *Memoirs* (London 1945), S. Wise, *Autobiography* (New York 1951), S. Brodetsky, *Memoirs* (London 1960), M. Pearlman, *Ben Gurion Looks Back* (London 1965), N. Goldmann (trans. H. Sebba), *Memories* (New York 1969).

Part III: The Jewish World Today

The Shape of the Jewish World

The first serious sociological and statistical study of the Jewish world in English was A. Ruppin, *The Jews in the Modern World* (London 1934). It is still worth reading, though the approach clearly shows the marks of its time, and of course it describes a world which no longer exists. There is no comparable study of the contemporary Jewish world, but some very thorough work on Jewish population statistics and demographic trends is being done by the Division of Jewish Demography and Statistics of the Institute of Contemporary Jewry in Jerusalem, which periodically publishes analyses and bibliographic surveys. For recent assessments of world Jewish population trends see R. Bachi, *Population Trends of World Jewry* (Jerusalem 1976), and U. O. Schmelz, *World Jewish Population: Estimates and Projections* (Jerusalem 1981). The *American Jewish Year Book*, published annually by the American Jewish Committee (New York) and the Jewish Publication Society of America (Philadelphia, Pa.), carries updated population statistics as well as informative articles about various communities of the Jewish world. The World Jewish Congress has sponsored a small series of useful surveys of the different Jewish communities of the world. The first of these, S. Federbush (ed.), *World Jewry Today* (New York and London 1959), contains an exhaustive list of the communities with estimated numbers, a brief history and lists of national and local institutions and publications. An updated edition would be very valuable; unfortunately the last edition, entitled *Jewish Communities of the World* (London 1971), is rather brief and noticeably out-of-date.

North America

United States: For the latest statistical information see the *American Jewish Year Book*, mentioned immediately above. And for a general history of the Jewish experience in America see R. Learsi, *The Jews in America* (2nd edn; New York 1972), or H. L. Feingold, *Zion in America* (New York 1974) (bibl.). For the early period there is a fascinating reader edited by J. L. Blau and S. W. Baron: *The Jews of the United States 1790–1840: a Documentary History* (3 vols.; New York and Philadelphia, Pa. 1963). For a biographical approach to the success story of the earlier immigrants and their contribution to American life see the very readable books by S. Birmingham, *Our Crowd: the Great Jewish Families of New York* (New York 1967) and *The Grandees: America's Sephardic Elite* (New York 1971). The history of the American Jewish Committee is set out in N. W. Cohen, *Not Free to Desist* (Philadelphia, Pa. 1972). Studies of American Jewish society and life are in generous supply. For recent surveys see M. Sklare (ed.), *Understanding American Jewry* (New York 1982), and B. Martin (ed.), *Movements and Issues in American Judaism: an Analysis and Sourcebook of Developments since 1945* (Westport, Conn. 1978) (bibl.). J. L. Blau, *Judaism in America* (Chicago, Ill. 1976), is a concise historical survey. D. Sidorski (ed.), *The Future of the Jewish Community in America* (New York 1973), is a very interesting collective profile of the community, and N. Mirsky, *Unorthodox Judaism* (Columbus, OH 1978), is a good introduction to the uncertainties and paradoxes of contemporary American Jewish life. For studies of specific groups see S. Poll, *The Hasidic Community of Williamsburg* (New York 1962), H. M. Brotz, *The Black Jews of Harlem* (New York 1970), and S. C. Heilman, *Synagogue Life* (Chicago, Ill. 1976), a sociological study of an Orthodox community.

Canada: S. E. Rosenberg, *The Jewish Community of Canada* (2 vols.; Toronto and Montreal 1970–71), is a splendidly illustrated portrait of the community and its history. For a historical account of Jewish immigration and achievements see J. Kage, *With Faith and Thanksgiving* (Montreal 1962), and S. Belkin, *Through Narrow Gates* (Montreal 1966), and for statistics and demographic surveys see the various publications of the Canadian Jewish Congress. There is a good taste of Canadian Jewish life in the novels of Mordecai Richler (for example, *The Apprenticeship of Duddy Kravitz*, London 1959; *St Urbain's Horseman*, London 1971), and in N. Levine, *Canada Made Me* (London 1959).

Latin America

For obvious reasons the English reader is less well served for Latin America than for North America, but several useful studies have emerged in recent years: J. Beller, *Jews in Latin America* (New York 1969), M. H. Sable, *Latin American Jewry: a Research Guide* (Cincinnati, OH 1978), J. L. Elkin, *Jews of the Latin American Republics* (Chapel Hill, N.C. 1980) (bibl.). For the colonial period see S. B. Liebman, *The Jews in New Spain* (Coral Gables, Fla. 1970), and A. Wiznitzer, *Jews in Colonial Brazil* (New York 1960). For Argentina we have a general survey, R. Weisbrot, *The Jews of Argentina from the Inquisition to Perón* (Philadelphia, Pa. 1979), as well as a detailed study of an agricultural colony, M. D. Winsberg, *Colonia Baron Hirsch* (Gainesville, Fla. 1964), and a translation (by P. de Pereda) of the classic work by A. Gerchunoff, *The Jewish Gauchos of the Pampas* (New York 1955; rev. edn London 1959). For Mexico see I. T. Lerner, *Mexican Jewry in the Land of the Aztecs* (3rd edn; Mexico 1973), and for Surinam, R. Cohen (ed.), *The Jewish National in Surinam* (Amsterdam 1982). I. S. and S. A. Emmanuel, *History of the Jews of the Netherlands Antilles* (2 vols.; Cincinnati, OH 1970), contains everything one could want to know about this fascinating community.

Europe

Great Britain: For a good general history see C. Roth, *A History of the Jews in England* (3rd edn; Oxford 1964), which however takes the story only as far as 1858. The period of political emancipation has recently been reexamined by M. C. N. Salbstein, *The Emancipation of the Jews in Britain* (London 1983). On the period of mass immigration before World War I see L. P. Gartner, *The Jewish Immigrant in England* (2nd edn; London 1973) (bibl.), and on more specific questions B. Gainer, *The Alien Invasion: the Origins of the Aliens Act of 1905* (London 1972), and W. J. Fishman, *East End Radicals* (London 1975). J. Gould and S. Esh (eds.), *Jewish Life in Modern Britain* (London 1964), presents the fruits of an interesting symposium held in 1962. A similar conference was convened 15 years later, and the results, published in S. L. and V. D. Lipman (eds.), *Jewish Life in Britain 1962–77* (Munich 1981), make for an informative comparison. See also H. Pollins, *Economic History of the Jews in England* (London 1982), V. D. Lipman, *Social History of the Jews in England 1850–1950* (London 1954), and for a very readable account of the main institutions of Anglo-Jewry C. Bermant, *Troubled Eden* (London 1969). For the other island, see L. Hyman, *The Jews of Ireland from the Earliest Times to the Year 1910* (London and Jerusalem 1972).

France: Works on the periods of Napoleon and the Dreyfus affair have already been mentioned under Part One; on the development of French Jewish institutions in the 19th century there is a very solid book by P. Cohen Albert, *The Modernization of French Jewry* (Hanover, N.H. 1977). The crucial post-Dreyfus period is covered in P. Hyman, *From Dreyfus to Vichy* (New York 1979) (bibl.), and there is a valuable study on the Jews of Paris in the 1930s by D. H. Weinberg, *A Community on Trial* (Chicago, Ill., and London 1977). For World War II see M. R. Marrus and R. O. Paxton, *Vichy France and the Jews* (New York 1981), and for an account of the contemporary community, D. Schnapper (trans. A. Goldhammer), *Jewish Identities in France* (Chicago, Ill. 1983).

Germany: For a readable survey of German Jewish history see M. Lowenthal, *The Jews of Germany* (Philadelphia, Pa. 1936 and London 1939), which ends in the twilight years before the great destruction. Another passionate study from the same period, J. R. Marcus, *The Rise and Destiny of the German Jew*, has been reissued with a "Post Mortem" by the author (New York 1973). The latest work on the last phase of predestruction German Jewish history is D. L. Niewyk, *The Jews in Weimar Germany* (Baton Rouge, La. 1980) (bibl.). There are two highly evocative books about Germany after the destruction, in which the survivors (Jews and gentiles) speak with their own voices: L. Katcher, *Post Mortem* (London 1968), and K. Gershon, *Postscript* (London 1969).

Austria: For a general account see J. Frankel (ed.), *The Jews of Austria* (2nd edn; London 1970) (bibl.), and on postwar immigration F. Wilder-Okladek, *The Return Movement of Jews to Austria* (The Hague 1969).

Denmark: L. Yahil (trans. M. Gradel), *The Rescue of Danish Jewry* (Philadelphia, Pa. 1969), includes an outline history of the Jews in Denmark. There are interesting glimpses of Danish Jewish life in the memoirs of Chief Rabbi M. Melchior, *A Rabbi Remembers* (London 1968).

Spain: F. Torroba Bernaldo de Quirós, *The Spanish Jews* (Madrid n.d.), is discursive and highly fanciful, but is rich in detail and brings the story down to the present day. On the struggle for religious freedom see C. C. Aronsfeld, *The Ghosts of 1492* (New York 1979).

Italy: For a general history see C. Roth, *The History of the Jews in Italy* (Philadelphia, Pa. 1946), and on the more recent period H. S. Hughes, *Prisoners of Hope* (Englewood Cliffs, N.J. 1983). For a political study of the Fascist period see M. Michaelis, *Mussolini and the Jews* (Oxford 1978).

Eastern Europe: For the interwar period see B. Vago and G. L. Mosse, *Jews and Non-Jews in Eastern Europe 1918–1945* (New Brunswick, N.J., and Jerusalem 1974), and E. Mendelsohn, *The Jews of East Central Europe between the World Wars* (Bloomington, Ind. 1983), and on the postwar situation P. Meyer *et al.*, *The Jews in the Soviet Satellites* (Syracuse, N.Y. 1953). See also P. Lendvai, *Antisemitism in Eastern Europe* (London 1971).

Hungary: R. L. Braham (ed.), *Hungarian-Jewish Studies* (New York 1966), is a useful collection of essays which can serve as an introduction to Hungarian Jewish history. W. O. McCagg Jr, *Jewish Nobles and Geniuses in Modern Hungary* (Boulder, Colo. 1972), is, despite its title, mainly concerned with the 19th century. It gives a fascinating impression of the extraordinary Jewish contributions to Hungarian life. On the Nazi deportations and their background see N. Katzburg, *Hungary and the Jews, 1920–1943* (Tel Aviv 1981).

Romania: Two books deserve a mention, both rather elderly: S. W. Baron, *The Jews in Roumania* (Philadelphia, Pa. 1930), and I. Cohen, *The Jews in Rumania* (London 1938).

Czechoslovakia: There is a valuable collection of historical studies entitled *The Jews of Czechoslovakia* (Philadelphia, Pa. and New York 1968). *The Prague Ghetto*, with text by J. Lion and photographs by J. Lukas (trans. J. Layton; London n.d.), is a wonderfully vivid evocation of that remarkable museum-piece of the Jewish world.

Poland: For the history of Polish Jewry between the two World Wars see H. M. Rabinowicz, *The Legacy of Polish Jewry* (New York 1965) (bibl.); C. S. Heller, *On the Edge of Destruction* (New York 1977); and J. Marcus, *Social and Political History of the Jews in Poland, 1919–1939* (Berlin 1983) (bibl.). For the period of World War II see A. Melezin, *Particulars about the Demographic Processes among the Jewish Population of the Towns: Lodz, Cracow, Lublin, during the Occupation Period 1939–45* (Lodz 1946), and the outstanding work by a participant in the Warsaw Ghetto uprising, Y. Gutman, *The Jews of Warsaw, 1939–1943* (trans. I. Friedman; Brighton 1983). On the exodus of Jews in 1968 see J. Banas (trans. T. Szafar, ed. L. Kochan), *The Scapegoats* (London 1979). There are several outstanding photographic essays on Polish Jewish life: L. Dobroszycki and B. Kirshenblatt-Gimblett, *Image before My Eyes: a Photographic History of Jewish Life in Poland, 1864–1939* (New York 1977); E. Vinecour (text) and C. Fishman (photos), *Polish Jews: the Final Chapter* (New York 1977); M. Fuks *et al.*, *Polish Jewry: History and Culture* (Warsaw 1982).

Small Balkan Communities: On Bulgaria see V. Tamir, *Bulgaria and her Jews* (New York 1979); on Yugoslavia J. P. Freidenreich, *The Jews of Yugoslavia* (Philadelphia, Pa. 1979) (bibl.). There is no general book on the Jews of Greece, but interesting historical detail in local studies such as P. Argenti, *The Religious Minorities of Chios* (Cambridge 1971), and M. D. Angel, *The Jews of Rhodes* (New York 1978).

Soviet Union

For a general survey of Russian Jewish history see S. W. Baron, *The Russian Jew under Tsars and Soviets* (2nd edn; New York 1976), and for an important collection of authoritative essays on the Soviet period L. Kochan (ed.), *The Jews in Soviet Russia since 1917* (3rd edn; Oxford 1978). The *Yevsektsii* are studied in Z. Y. Gitelman, *Jewish Nationality and Soviet Politics* (Princeton, N.J. 1972). On the agonies of the Stalin period see Y. A. Gilboa (trans. Y. Schachter), *The Black Years of Soviet Jewry, 1939–1953* (Boston, Mass. 1971), as well as personal memoirs of the victims, such as I. Emiot, *The Birobidzhan Affair: a Yiddish Writer in Siberia* (trans. M. Rosenfeld; Philadelphia, Pa. 1982), N. Mandelstam, *Hope against Hope* (trans. M. Hayward; London 1971) and *Hope Abandoned* (trans. M. Hayward; London 1974), or E. S. Ginzburg, *Into the Whirlwind* (trans. P. Stevenson and M. Harari; London 1967) and *Within the Whirlwind* (trans. I. Boland; London 1981). The emigration movement of the 1970s is viewed from the outside in C. Shindler, *Exit Visa* (London 1978), and from the inside in M. Azbel, *Refusenik* (London 1981). There is a detailed account of the contemporary situation, including copious statistical tables, in T. E. Sawyer, *The Jewish Minority in the Soviet Union* (Boulder, Colo. and Folkestone 1979). On specific aspects of Jewish life see E. Schulman, *A History of Jewish Education in the Soviet Union* (New York 1971), and J. Rothenberg, *The Jewish Religion in the Soviet Union* (New York 1971).

Asia

Israel: For up-to-date statistical information, see *Statistical Abstracts of Israel*, published annually by the Central Bureau of Statistics in Jerusalem. Two books trace the history of Israel from the beginning of the Zionist movement until the Yom Kippur War: H. M. Sachar, *A History of Israel* (Oxford 1977), and N. Lucas, *The Modern History of Israel* (London 1974); of the two the first is more readable, the second more critical, and both have excellent bibliographies. W. Frankel, *Israel Observed* (London 1980), is an extremely useful and interesting account of the various institutions of the state. For a lively evocation of the flavor of Israeli society and its historical background see A. Elon, *The Israelis: Founders and Sons* (London 1971), and for a more stolid sociological description S. N. Eisenstadt, *Israeli Society* (London 1967). For detailed information on the political and legal institutions see L. Fein, *Politics in Israel* (Boston, Mass. 1967), Y. Freudenheim, *Government in Israel* (New York 1967), and H. E. Baker, *The Legal System of Israel* (Jerusalem 1968). H. R. Penniman (ed.), *Israel at the Polls* (New York 1979), is a remarkable study of the Knesset elections of 1977. There are various accounts of Jewish immigration to Israel: see R. Patai, *Israel between East and West* (Philadelphia, Pa. 1953), M. Sicron, *Immigration to Israel 1948–1953* (Jerusalem 1957), H. M. Sachar, *Aliyah* (Cleveland, OH 1961). There is an excellent study of the population of Israel, with numerous tables and projections for the future, by D. Friedlander and C. Goldscheider, *The Population of Israel* (New York 1979).

On the problems of Jewish religion in the Jewish state see E. Marmorstein, *Heaven at Bay* (Oxford 1969), E. Birnbaum, *The Politics of Compromise* (Rutherford, N.J. 1970), S. Z. Abramov, *Perpetual Dilemma* (New York 1976). On non-Jewish minorities S. Jiryis, *The Arabs in Israel 1948–1966* (Beirut 1968), J. M. Landau, *The Arabs in Israel* (Oxford 1969), S. P. Colbi, *Christianity in the Holy Land Past and Present* (Tel Aviv 1969), and W. Zander, *Israel and the Holy Places of Christendom* (London 1971). And on Israel in the wider context of the Jewish world, M. Davis (ed.), *World Jewry and the State of Israel* (New York 1977).

Other Countries of Asia: On the Middle East in general, see J. Lestschinsky, *Jews in Moslem Lands* (New York 1946), S. Landshut, *Jewish Communities in the Muslim Countries of the Middle East* (London 1950), and H. J. Cohen (trans. Z. and L. Alizi), *The Jews of the Middle East 1860–1972* (Jerusalem 1973). D. S. Sassoon, *A History of the*

Jews in Baghdad (Letchworth 1949), contains a chapter on Baghdadi Jews in the Far East, for which see also C. Roth, *The Sassoon Dynasty* (London 1941). See also H. Dicker, *Wanderers and Settlers in the Far East* (New York 1962), which concentrates on China and Japan. L. D. Loeb, *Outcaste: Jewish Life in Southern Iran* (New York 1977), is an anthropologist's study of Jews in modern Shiraz. On the Bene Israel of Bombay see S. Strizower, *The Children of Israel* (Oxford 1971).

Africa
On the Jews in North Africa see A. Chouraqui (trans. M. M. Bernet), *Between East and West* (Philadelphia, Pa. 1968), and for a more solidly historical account H. Z. Hirschberg, *A History of the Jews in North Africa* (2 vols.; Leiden 1972–81). J. M. Landau, *Jews in Nineteenth-Century Egypt* (New York and London 1969), is an excellent account, more than half of which is devoted to documents. On South Africa see G. Saron and L. Hotz (eds.), *The Jews in South Africa* (Cape Town 1955), which is mainly devoted to the period before 1910, M. Gitlin, *The Vision Amazing* (Johannesburg 1950), and G. Shimoni, *Jews and Zionism: the South African Experience 1910–1967* (Cape Town 1980).

Australasia
On the history of Jews in Australia see C. A. Price, *Jewish Settlers in Australia* (Canberra 1964), and I. Getzler, *Neither Toleration Nor Favour: the Australian Chapter of Jewish Emancipation* (Melbourne 1970), and on Australian Jewish society P. Y. Medding, *From Assimilation to Group Survival* (Melbourne 1968) (bibl.), and P. Y. Medding (ed.), *Jews in Australian Society* (Melbourne 1973). For New Zealand see L. M. Goldman, *The History of the Jews in New Zealand* (Wellington 1958).

GAZETTEER

Places of significance to Jewish history are listed below. Name-form variants – where appropriate – and the present country of location are included in each entry.

Aalborg (Denmark) 57°03′N 9°56′E, 166
Aarhus (Denmark) 56°10′N 10°13′E, 166
Aachen (W Germany) 50°46′N 6°06′E, 167
Abadan (Iran) 30°20′N 48°15′E, 198
Abasha (USSR) 42°02′N 144°17′E, 191
Aberdeen (UK) 57°10′N 2°04′W, 166
Abila (Jordan) 32°43′N 35°48′E, 24, 32
Abila (Syria) 33°38′N 36°10′E, 26
Accaron (Ekron) (Israel) 31°45′N 34°52′E, 24
Acrabeta (Aqraba) (Jordan) 32°08′N 35°21′E, 24, 32
Adana (Turkey) 37°00′N 35°19′E, 30
Addis Abeba (Ethiopia) 9°03′N 38°42′E, 219
Adelaide (Australia) 34°56′S 138°36′E, 217
Aden (S Yemen) 12°47′N 45°03′E, 40, 44, 57, 60, 198
Adiabene (region) 26
Adida (Hadid) (Israel) 31°58′N 34°55′E, 24
Adora (Dura) (Jordan) 31°31′N 35°01′E, 24, 32
Adramyttium (Turkey) 39°34′N 27°01′E, 25, 29
Adrianople *see* Edirne
Aegina *see* Aiyina
Afula (Israel) 32°36′N 35°17′E, 199
Agadir (Morocco) 30°30′N 9°40′W, 218
Agathe *see* Agde
Agde (Agathe) (France) 43°19′N 3°29′E, 30, 34
Agen (France) 44°12′N 0°38′E, 166
Agrigento (Italy) 37°19′N 13°35′E, 30
Agrippias *see* Anthedon
Ahmadabad (India) 23°03′N 72°40′E, 198
Aiguebelle (France) 45°33′N 6°18′E, 36
Ain Sefra (Algeria) 32°45′N 0°35′W, 218
Ait Daoud (Morocco) 31°03′N 9°38′W, 218
Aix-en-Provence (France) 43°31′N 5°27′E, 166
Aix-les-Bains (France) 45°41′N 5°55′E, 167
Aiyina (Aegina) (Greece) 37°45′N 23°26′E, 17, 29, 166
Ajaccio (Corsica, France) 41°55′N 8°43′E, 166
Ajlun (Jordan) 32°20′N 35°45′E, 198
Akbara (Israel) 32°56′N 35°30′E, 98
Akhaltsikhe (USSR) 41°37′N 42°59′E, 191
Akhmîm (Egypt) 26°35′N 31°48′E, 218
Akka (Morocco) 29°22′N 8°14′W, 218
Akko (Acre, Ptolemais) (Israel) 32°55′N 35°04′E, 24, 25, 32, 199
Akron (USA) 41°04′N 81°31′W, 138
Alameda County (USA), 138
Alba Iulia (Romania) 46°04′N 23°33′E, 166
Albany (Georgia, USA) 31°37′N 84°10′W, 138
Albany (New York, USA) 42°40′N 73°49′W, 10, 102,140
Albuquerque (USA) 35°05′N 106°38′W, 138
Alderney (isl) (Channel Islands) 49°43′N 2°12′W, 70
Aleppo (Syria) 36°14′N 37°10′E, 10, 20, 22, 30, 38, 40, 44, 57, 64, 99, 198
Alessandria (Italy) 44°55′N 8°37′E, 166
Alexandria (Egypt) 31°13′N 29°55′E, 17, 23, 25, 29, 30, 34, 40, 44, 66, 218
Alexandria (Louisiana, USA) 31°19′N 92°29′W, 138
Alexandria (Virginia, USA) 38°49′N 77°06′W, 138
Alexandrium (Surtaba) (Jordan) 32°06′N 35°28′E, 24, 32
Alexandrow (Aleksandrow Kujawski) (Poland) 52°52′N 18°40′E, 101
Algiers (Algeria) 36°50′N 3°00′E, 10, 47, 57, 60, 66, 74, 218
Alicante (Spain) 38°21′N 0°29′W, 166
Aliquippa (USA) 40°38′N 80°16′W, 138
Alkmaar (Netherlands) 52°38′N 4°44′E, 167
Allentown (USA) 40°37′N 75°30′W, 140
Alma-Ata (USSR) 43°19′N 76°55′E, 190
Almelo (Netherlands) 52°21′N 6°40′E, 167
Almería (Spain) 36°50′N 2°26′W, 166
Altona (W Germany) 53°35′N 9°57′E, 47, 166
Altoona (USA) 40°32′N 78°23′W, 138
Alytus (USSR) 54°24′N 24°03′E, 190
Alzey (W Germany) 49°44′N 8°07′E, 102
Amadia (Iraq) 37°06′N 43°29′E, 40
Amarillo (USA) 35°14′N 101°50′W, 138
Amastris (Turkey) 41°44′N 32°24′E, 29
Amasya (Turkey) 40°37′N 35°50′E, 47, 198
Ambato (Ecuador) 1°18′S 78°39′W, 159
Amberg (W Germany) 49°26′N 11°52′E, 166
Ambovar (Ethiopia) 12°38′N 30°05′E, 219
Amenia (USA) 41°51′N 73°33′W, 140
Amersfoort (Netherlands) 52°09′N 5°23′E, 167
Amherst (USA) 42°23′N 72°31′W, 140
Amida *see* Diyarbakir
Amiens (France) 49°54′N 2°18′E, 166
Amisus (Samsun) (Turkey) 41°17′N 36°22′E, 26, 29
Amizmiz (Morocco) 31°14′N 8°14′W, 218
Amman (Philadelphia, Rabbath-bene-ammon) (Jordan) 31°57′N 35°56′E, 22, 24, 32
Ammathus (Jordan) 32°12′N 35°34′E, 24, 32
Ammon (region), 22
Amsterdam (Netherlands) 52°21′N 4°54′E, 10, 17, 47, 50, 57, 60, 64, 66, 100, 121, 137, 167
Amsterdam (USA) 42°56′N 74°12′W, 138
Anchorage (USA) 61°10′N 150°00′W, 10, 138
Ancona (Italy) 43°37′N 13°31′E, 47, 166
Ancyra *see* Ankara
Andizhan (USSR) 40°45′N 72°22′E, 190
Angarsk (USSR) 52°31′N 103°55′E, 190
Angers (France) 47°29′N 0°32′W, 166
Angoulême (France) 45°40′N 0°10′E, 166
Ankara (Ancyra) (Turkey) 39°55′N 32°50′E, 10, 29, 64, 198
Annapolis (USA) 38°59′N 76°30′W, 138
Ann Arbor (USA) 42°18′N 83°43′W, 138
Annecy (France) 45°54′N 6°07′E, 166
Anniston (USA) 33°38′N 85°50′W, 138
Annopol (USSR) 50°28′N 27°08′E, 101
Anthedon (Agrippias) (Egypt) 31°32′N 34°27′E, 24, 32
Antibes (France) 43°35′N 7°07′E, 166
Antinoopolis (Egypt) 27°49′N 30°53′E, 29
Antioch (Antiochia, Antakya) (Turkey) 36°12′N 36°10′E, 23, 25, 26, 29, 30, 34, 38
Antiochia (Syria) 33°13′N 35°40′E, 24
Antiochia (Turkey) 38°18′N 31°09′E, 25, 29
Antipatris (Pegae) (Israel) 32°06′N 34°56′E, 24, 32
Antwerp (Belgium) 51°13′N 4°25′E, 10, 36, 47, 50, 121, 167
Apamea (Syria) 35°31′N 36°23′E, 34
Apamea (Birecik) (Turkey) 37°03′N 37°59′E, 17, 25, 29
Apamea (Dinar) (Turkey) 40°24′N 28°46′E, 25, 29
Apeldoorn (Netherlands) 52°13′N 5°57′E, 167
Apherema (Taiyiba) (Jordan) 31°57′N 35°18′E, 24
Aphrodisias (Turkey) 37°43′N 28°50′E, 29, 30, 198
Apollonia (Israel) 32°13′N 34°49′E, 24, 32
Appleton (USA) 44°17′N 88°24′W, 138
Aquileia (Italy) 45°47′N 13°22′E, 29, 34
Arad (Israel) 31°16′N 35°09′E, 199
Arad (Romania) 46°10′N 21°19′E, 166
Aramathea (Israel) 32°02′N 35°01′E, 24
Aram-Damascus (region), 22
Aram-Zobah (region), 22
Arbela (Arbil) (Iraq) 36°12′N 44°01′E, 26, 29
Arbela (Israel) 32°45′N 35°30′E, 24, 32
Arcachon (France) 44°40′N 1°11′W, 166
Archelais (Jordan) 31°52′N 35°28′E, 26, 32
Arelate *see* Arles
Arequipa (Peru) 16°25′S 71°32′W, 159
Argos (Greece) 37°38′N 22°43′E, 25
Arica (Chile) 18°30′S 70°20′W, 159
Aristobulias (Jordan) 31°27′N 35°15′E, 24
Arles (Arelate) (France) 43°41′N 4°38′E, 30, 34, 38
Arlon (Belgium) 49°41′N 5°49′E, 167
Armenia (region), 25, 26
Arnhem (Netherlands) 52°00′N 5°53′E, 167
Arta (Greece) 39°10′N 20°59′E, 47
Artaxata (Artashat) (USSR) 39°58′N 44°34′E, 26
Aruba (isl) 12°30′N 70°00′W, 10, 57, 159
Ascalon *see* Ashqelon
Ashdod (Azotus) (Israel) 31°48′N 34°38′E, 24, 25, 32, 199
Asheville (USA) 35°35′N 82°35′W, 138
Ashkhabad (USSR) 37°58′N 58°24′E, 190
Ashqelon (Ascalon) (Israel) 31°40′N 34°35′E, 24, 25, 32, 199
Asia *see* Etsion Gaber
Asilah (Morocco) 35°32′N 6°04′W, 218
Asmera (Ethiopia) 15°20′N 38°58′E, 219
Asochis (Israel) 32°47′N 35°15′E, 24
Assen (Netherlands) 53°00′N 6°34′E, 166
Assens (Denmark) 56°41′N 10°05′E, 166
Asshur (Ash Sharqat) (Iraq) 35°30′N 43°14′E, 20, 26
Assyria (region), 20
Asti (Italy) 44°54′N 8°13′E, 166
Astrakhan (USSR) 46°22′N 48°04′E, 60, 190
Asunción (Paraguay) 25°15′S 57°40′W, 159
Aswan (Egypt) 24°05′N 32°56′E, 218
Athens (Athenae) (Greece) 38°00′N 23°44′E, 25, 29, 30, 64, 137, 166
Athens (USA) 33°57′N 83°24′W, 138
Athol (USA) 42°36′N 72°14′W, 140
Atil (USSR) 46°05′N 48°06′E, 38
Atlanta (USA) 33°45′N 84°23′W, 10, 138
Atlantic City (USA) 39°23′N 74°27′W, 10, 140
Attleboro (USA) 41°57′N 71°16′W, 140
Auburn (Maine, USA) 44°04′N 70°15′W, 138
Auburn (New York, USA) 42°57′N 76°34′W, 138
Auckland (New Zealand) 36°55′S 174°47′E, 10, 60, 217
Augsburg (W Germany) 48°21′N 10°54′E, 36, 50, 99, 102, 120, 121, 166
Augusta (Georgia, USA) 33°29′N 82°00′W, 102, 138
Augusta (Maine, USA) 44°17′N 69°48′W, 138
Augusta Treverorum *see* Trier
Aumale (Sour el Ghozlane) (Algeria) 36°10′N 3°41′E, 218
Auranitis (region), 26, 32
Aurora (USA) 41°45′N 88°20′W, 138
Auschwitz-Birkenau (Oswiecim) (Poland) 50°02′N 19°11′E, 70
Austin (Minnesota, USA) 43°40′N 92°58′W, 138
Austin (Texas, USA) 30°18′N 97°47′W, 138
Avigdor (Argentina) 30°52′S 59°03′W, 160
Avignon (France) 43°56′N 4°48′E, 44, 166
Avila (Spain) 40°39′N 4°42′W, 17, 166
Axum (Ethiopia) 14°10′N 38°45′E, 29, 30
Azemmour (Morocco) 33°20′N 8°25′W, 47
Azor (Israel) 32°01′N 34°48′E, 199
Azotus *see* Ashdod

Babi Yar (USSR) 49°49′N 30°10′E, 70
Babylon (Iraq) 32°33′N 44°25′E, 20, 23, 25, 26
Babylonia (region), 20, 23, 25, 26, 98
Bacau (Romania) 46°33′N 26°58′E, 166
Badajoz (Spain) 38°53′N 6°58′W, 166
Baden (Switzerland) 47°28′N 8°19′E, 167
Baden-Baden (W Germany) 48°45′N 8°15′E, 167
Bad Homburg (W Germany) 50°13′N 8°37′E, 167
Badis (Morocco) 35°13′N 3°54′W, 218
Bad Kreuznach (W Germany) 49°51′N 7°52′E, 167
Bad Nauheim (W Germany) 50°21′N 8°44′E, 167
Baghdad (Iraq) 33°20′N 44°26′E, 38, 40, 44, 57, 60, 64, 66, 99, 198
Bahía Blanca (Argentina) 38°45′S 62°15′W, 159
Bahrain (isl) 26°00′N 50°35′E, 60
Baia (Italy) 40°38′N 14°38′E, 29
Baja (Hungary) 46°11′N 18°58′E, 166
Baku (USSR) 40°22′N 49°53′E, 10, 64, 190
Balanowka (USSR) 48°20′N 29°52′E, 70
Balboa (Panama) 8°57′N 79°33′W, 159
Balkh (Afghanistan) 36°48′N 66°49′E, 38, 44, 60, 198
Ballarat (Australia) 37°36′S 143°58′E, 217
Baltimore (USA) 39°18′N 76°38′W, 10, 66, 102, 137, 140
Bamberg (W Germany) 49°54′N 10°54′E, 36, 166
Bangkok (Thailand) 13°44′N 100°30′E, 198
Bangor (UK) 53°00′N 2°55′W, 166
Bangor (USA) 44°49′N 68°47′W, 138
Bar (USSR) 49°05′N 27°40′E, 70
Bar am (Israel) 33°04′N 35°26′E, 17
Barbados (isl) 13°00′N 59°30′W, 57, 159
Barce (Libya) 32°30′N 20°50′E, 218
Barcelona (Spain) 41°25′N 2°10′E, 10, 36, 38, 40, 99, 166
Barcelona (Venezuela) 10°08′N 64°43′W, 159
Bardejov (Czechoslovakia) 49°18′N 21°15′E, 166
Bari (Barium) (Italy) 41°07′N 16°52′E, 29, 38, 99
Barium *see* Bari
Barka (Libya) 32°30′N 20°40′E, 40
Bar-le-Duc (France) 48°46′N 5°10′E, 167
Baron Hirsch (Argentina) 37°30′S 64°45′W, 160
Barranquilla (Colombia) 11°10′N 74°50′W, 159
Barrow in Furness (UK) 54°07′N 3°14′W, 166
Basle (Switzerland) 47°33′N 7°36′E, 36, 120, 121, 167
Basra (Iraq) 30°30′N 47°50′E, 30, 38, 40, 44, 60, 99, 198
Bastia (Corsica, France) 42°41′N 9°26′E, 166
Batanaea (region), 26, 32
Batavia (USA) 43°00′N 78°11′W, 138
Bathyra (Syria) 33°11′N 36°28′E, 32
Baton Rouge (USA) 30°30′N 91°10′W, 138
Battle Creek (USA) 42°20′N 85°10′W, 138
Batumi (USSR) 41°37′N 41°36′E, 191
Bat Yam (Israel) 32°01′N 34°45′E, 137, 199
Bauduen (France) 43°30′N 6°22′E, 36
Bay City (USA) 43°35′N 83°52′W, 138
Bayonne (France) 43°30′N 1°28′W, 47, 57, 166
Bayonne (USA) 40°39′N 74°08′W, 140
Bayreuth (W Germany) 49°27′N 11°35′E, 166
Baytown (USA) 29°43′N 94°59′W, 138
Beacon (USA) 41°31′N 73°59′W, 140
Beaumont (USA) 30°04′N 94°06′W, 138
Beer Sheva (Beer-sheba) (Israel) 31°15′N 34°47′E, 22, 24, 32, 137, 199
Beirut (Berytus) (Lebanon) 33°52′N 35°30′E, 10, 60, 98, 198
Beit Laphet (Iran) 32°13′N 48°49′E, 29
Beja (Portugal) 38°01′N 7°52′W, 38, 166
Béja (Tunisia) 36°43′N 9°13′E, 218
Beka (Israel) 32°58′N 35°20′E, 98
Belém (Brazil) 1°27′S 48°29′W, 10, 66, 159
Belfast (UK) 54°35′N 5°55′W, 166
Belfort (France) 47°38′N 6°52′E, 167
Belgorod (USSR) 46°10′N 30°19′E, 190
Belgrade (Yugoslavia) 44°50′N 20°30′E, 64, 166
Belleville (Canada) 44°10′N 77°22′W, 138
Bellingham (USA) 48°45′N 122°29′W, 138
Bellville (S Africa) 33°55′S 18°38′E, 219
Belo Horizonte (Brazil) 2°37′S 67°30′W, 159
Beloit (USA) 42°31′N 89°04′W, 138
Belovár (Hungary) 45°50′N 16°50′E, 102
Beltsy (USSR) 47°44′N 27°41′E, 190
Belz (USSR) 50°23′N 24°01′E, 50, 101
Belzec (Poland) 50°21′N 23°28′E, 50, 70
Bendery (USSR) 46°50′N 29°29′E, 190
Bene Beraq (Israel) 32°05′N 34°52′E, 98, 137, 199
Ben Gardane (Tunisia) 33°13′N 11°13′E, 218
Benghazi (Berenice) (Libya) 32°07′N 20°05′E, 25, 29, 30, 64, 218
Bennington (USA) 42°54′N 73°12′W, 138
Benoni (S Africa) 26°12′S 28°18′E, 219
Benton Harbor (USA) 42°07′N 86°27′W, 138
Berdichev (USSR) 49°54′N 28°39′E, 101, 120, 190
Berenice *see* Benghazi
Bergen-Belsen (W Germany) 52°40′N 9°57′E, 70
Bergen County (USA), 140
Berlin (Germany) 52°32′N 13°25′E, 17, 36, 50, 57, 60, 64, 66, 72, 102, 120, 121, 166
Bernburg (E Germany) 51°49′N 11°43′E, 102
Berne (Switzerland) 46°57′N 7°26′E, 36, 167
Beroea (Greece) 40°32′N 22°11′E, 25
Beror Hayil (Israel) 31°34′N 34°39′E, 98
Berwick (USA) 41°04′N 76°13′W, 140
Berytus *see* Beirut
Besalú (Spain) 42°12′N 2°42′E, 166
Besançon (France) 47°14′N 6°02′E, 167
Besara *see* Beth Shearim
Bessarabia (region), 101
Bethal (S Africa) 26°27′S 29°28′E, 219
Beth-el (Beitin) (Jordan) 31°56′N 35°15′E, 22
Bethlehem (S Africa) 28°15′S 28°19′E, 219
Bethlehem (USA) 40°36′N 75°22′W, 140
Bethleptepha (Israel) 31°41′N 35°02′E, 32
Bethsaida *see* Julias
Beth Shean *see* Bet Shean
Beth Shearim (Besara) (Israel) 32°42′N 35°08′E, 17, 32, 98
Beth Ther (Battir) (Jordan) 31°44′N 35°08′E, 98
Beth-zur (Jordan) 31°34′N 35°07′E, 24
Bet Shean (Scythopolis, Beth Shean) (Israel) 32°30′N 35°30′E, 24, 25, 30, 32, 34, 98, 199
Bet Shemesh (Israel) 31°45′N 34°59′E, 199
Beverly (USA) 42°35′N 70°52′W, 140
Béziers (France) 43°21′N 3°13′E, 99, 166
Bialykamien (USSR) 49°58′N 25°00′E, 120
Bialystok (Poland) 53°09′N 23°10′E, 70, 101, 166
Biel (Switzerland) 47°09′N 7°16′E, 167
Bielefeld (W Germany) 52°02′N 8°32′E, 167
Bielnitz (Poland) 49°50′N 19°02′E, 102
Bilgoraj (Poland) 50°31′N 22°41′E, 120
Billings (USA) 45°47′N 108°30′W, 138
Biloxi (USA) 30°24′N 88°55W, 138
Bingen (W Germany) 49°58′N 7°55′E, 102
Birkenfeld (W Germany) 49°38′N 7°10′E, 102
Birlad (Romania) 46°14′N 27°40′E, 166
Birmingham (UK) 52°30′N 1°50′W, 64, 166
Birmingham (USA) 33°30′N 86°55′W, 138
Birobidzhan (USSR) 48°49′N 132°54′E, 10, 66, 190
Birzai (USSR) 56°10′N 24°48′E, 100, 190
Bischheim (France) 48°36′N 7°50′E, 167
Bischwiller (France) 48°46′N 7°53′E, 167
Bisenz (Czechoslovakia) 48°22′N 17°36′E, 102
Biskra (Algeria) 34°50′N 5°41′E, 218
Bistrita (Romania) 47°08′N 24°30′E, 166
Bitche (France) 49°03′N 7°26′E, 167
Bitola (Monastir) (Yugoslavia) 41°01′N 21°21′E, 166
Bizerte (Tunisia) 37°18′N 9°52′E, 218
Blackpool (UK) 53°50′N 3°03′W, 166
Blida (Algeria) 36°30′N 2°50′E, 218
Bloemfontein (S Africa) 29°07′S 26°14′E, 219
Bloomington (Illinois, USA) 40°29′N 89°00′W, 138
Bloomington (Indiana, USA) 39°10′N 86°31′W, 138
Bluefield (USA) 37°14′N 81°17′W, 138
Bobruysk (USSR) 53°08′N 29°10′E, 190
Boca Raton (USA) 26°22′N 80°05′W, 10, 138
Bochum (W Germany) 51°28′N 7°11′E, 167
Bogdanovka (USSR) 48°03′N 30°50′E, 70
Bogotá (Colombia) 4°38′N 74°05′W, 137, 159
Boise (USA) 43°38′N 116°12′W, 138
Bojan (USSR) 48°12′N 25°53′E, 101
Boksburg (S Africa) 26°13′S 28°15′E, 219
Bolgrad (USSR) 45°42′N 28°35′E, 190
Bologna (Italy) 44°30′N 11°20′E, 121, 166
Bombay (India) 18°56′N 72°51′E, 10, 60, 137, 198
Bône (Annaba) (Algeria) 36°55′N 7°47′E, 218
Bonn (W Germany) 50°44′N 7°06′E, 99, 102, 167
Bordeaux (Burdigala) (France) 44°50′N 0°34′W, 30, 38, 47, 57, 64, 166
Boreum (Libya) 31°38′N 20°01′E, 34
Borzhomi (USSR) 41°49′N 43°23′E, 191
Boston (USA) 42°20′N 71°05′W, 10, 57, 66, 102, 137, 140
Botosani (Romania) 47°44′N 26°41′E, 101, 166
Bougie (Algeria) 36°49′N 5°03′E, 218
Boulay (France) 49°11′N 6°30′E, 166
Boulogne (France) 50°43′N 1°37′E, 166
Bourges (France) 47°05′N 2°23′E, 36
Bournemouth (UK) 50°43′N 1°54′W, 166
Bou Saada (Algeria) 35°10′N 4°09′E, 218
Bradford (UK) 53°48′N 1°45′W, 166
Bragança (Portugal) 41°47′N 6°46′W, 166
Brakpan (S Africa) 26°15′S 28°22′E, 219
Brandon (Canada) 49°50′N 99°57′W, 138
Brantford (Canada) 47°36′N 98°58′W, 138
Brasília (Brazil) 15°46′S 47°57′W, 10, 159
Brasov (Romania) 45°39′N 25°35′E, 166
Bratislava (Pressburg) (Czechoslovakia) 48°10′N 17°10′E, 102, 166
Bratslav (USSR) 48°49′N 28°51′E, 101
Braunschweig (W Germany) 52°15′N 10°30′E, 167
Breda (Netherlands) 51°35′N 4°46′E, 167
Bremen (W Germany) 53°05′N 8°48′E, 64, 166
Bremgarten (Switzerland) 47°21′N 8°21′E, 167
Brescia (Brixia) (Italy) 45°33′N 10°13′E, 29, 121
Breslau *see* Wroclaw
Brest-Litovsk (USSR) 52°08′N 23°40′E, 50, 64, 100, 101, 190
Brevard County (USA), 138
Bridgeport (USA) 41°12′N 73°12′W, 10, 140
Bridgeton (USA) 39°26′N 75°14′W, 140
Brighton (UK) 50°50′N 0°10′W, 10, 166
Brisbane (Australia) 27°30′S 153°00′E, 60, 217
Bristol (UK) 51°27′N 2°35′W, 47, 166
Bristol (USA) 41°41′N 72°57′W, 140
Brixia *see* Brescia
Brno (Czechoslovakia) 49°13′N 16°40′E, 70, 166
Brody (USSR) 50°05′N 25°08′E, 50, 70, 190
Brookline (USA) 42°18′N 71°08′W, 102
Brownsville (USA) 25°54′N 97°30′W, 138
Bruges (Belgium) 51°13′N 3°14′E, 166

GAZETTEER

Brunswick (USA) 31°09′N 81°30′W, 102, 138
Brussels (Belgium) 50°50′N 4°21′E, 10, 36, 64, 137, 167
Bryansk (USSR) 53°15′N 34°09′E, 190
Buchach (Buczacz) (USSR) 49°09′N 25°20′E, 101, 190
Bucharest (Romania) 44°25′N 26°07′E, 10, 60, 64, 66, 72, 74, 102, 137, 166
Buchau (W Germany) 48°05′N 9°39′E, 102
Buchenwald (E Germany) 51°03′N 11°15′E, 70
Bucks County (USA), 140
Buczacz *see* Buchach
Budapest (Buda, Pest) (Hungary) 47°30′N 19°03′E, 10, 17, 44, 60, 64, 66, 72, 102, 137, 166
Buenos Aires (Argentina) 34°40′S 58°30′W, 10, 47, 60, 62, 66, 137, 159
Buffalo (USA) 42°52′N 78°55′W, 102, 138
Buis-les-Barronnies (France) 44°16′N 5°16′E, 36
Bukhara (USSR) 39°47′N 64°26′E, 44, 57, 60, 190
Bukovina (region), 101
Bulawayo (Zimbabwe) 20°10′S 28°43′E, 10, 219
Burdigala *see* Bordeaux
Burgas (Bulgaria) 42°30′N 27°29′E, 166
Burgos (Spain) 42°21′N 3°41′W, 36, 166
Burlington (USA) 44°28′N 73°14′W, 138
Bursa (Turkey) 40°12′N 29°04′E, 44, 47, 198
Bury St Edmunds (UK) 52°15′N 0°43′E, 36
Bushey (UK) 51°39′N 0°22′W, 166
Busra (Bostra) (Syria) 32°30′N 36°29′E, 34
Bussum (Netherlands) 52°17′N 5°10′E, 167
Buynaksk (USSR) 42°48′N 47°07′E, 190
Byblos (Jubail) (Lebanon) 34°08′N 35°38′E, 20, 98
Byelorussia (White Russia) (region), 50, 64, 101
Bytom (Poland) 50°21′N 18°51′E, 166

Cáceres (Spain) 39°29′N 6°23′W, 166
Cadasa (Israel) 33°02′N 35°26′E, 32
Caen (France) 49°11′N 0°22′W, 166
Caesarea (Strato's Tower) (Israel) 32°30′N 34°54′E, 24, 26, 29, 30, 32, 98
Caesarea (Kayseri) (Turkey) 38°42′N 35°28′E, 25, 26, 29
Caesarea Philippi (Banias) (Syria) 33°14′N 35°42′E, 26, 32
Cagliari (Caralis) (Sardinia, Italy) 39°13′N 9°08′E, 34
Cairo (Fustat) (Egypt) 30°03′N 31°15′E, 10, 17, 38, 40, 44, 57, 60, 64, 66, 74, 99, 100, 121, 218
Calais (USA) 45°11′N 67°16′W, 138
Calcutta (Fort St George) (India) 22°30′N 88°20′E, 10, 47, 57, 60, 198
Calgary (Canada) 51°05′N 114°05′W, 138
Cali (Colombia) 3°24′N 76°30′W, 159
Callinicum (Nicephorium, Raqqa) (Syria) 35°57′N 39°03′E, 26, 29, 34
Calumet Region (USA), 138
Cambridge (UK) 52°12′N 0°07′E, 17, 166
Camden (USA) 39°52′N 75°07′W, 140
Campinas (Brazil) 22°54′S 47°06′W, 159
Campos (Brazil) 21°46′S 41°21′W, 159
Canakkale (Turkey) 40°09′N 26°25′E, 198
Canatha (Syria) 32°43′N 36°31′E, 32
Canberra (Australia) 35°18′S 149°08′E, 217
Candia (Iraklion) (Greece) 35°20′N 25°08′E, 47
Cannes (France) 43°33′N 7°00′E, 166
Canton (USA) 40°48′N 81°23′W, 138
Capercotnei (Israel) 32°12′N 35°17′E, 24
Cape Town (S Africa) 33°56′S 18°28′E, 10, 60, 62, 219
Cappadocia (region), 26
Capua (Italy) 41°06′N 14°13′E, 29
Caracas (Venezuela) 10°35′N 66°56′W, 10, 66, 137, 159
Carana (Erzurum) (Turkey) 39°58′N 41°09′E, 26
Cardiff (UK) 51°30′N 3°13′W, 166
Carei (Romania) 47°40′N 22°28′E, 166
Carletonville (S Africa) 26°22′S 27°25′E, 219
Carpentras (France) 44°03′N 5°03′E, 17, 166
Cartagena (Colombia) 10°24′N 75°33′W, 47
Carthage (Carthago) (Tunisia) 36°54′N 10°16′E, 29, 30, 34
Casablanca (Morocco) 33°39′N 7°35′W, 10, 66, 137, 218
Casale Monferrato (Italy) 45°08′N 8°27′E, 17, 166
Casalmaggiore (Italy) 44°58′N 10°25′E, 121
Calatayud (Spain) 41°21′N 1°39′W, 38
Catana (Catania) (Sicily, Italy) 37°31′N 15°06′E, 29
Catskill (USA) 42°14′N 73°52′W, 140
Cavaillon (France) 43°50′N 5°02′E, 166
Cayenne (French Guiana) 4°55′N 52°18′W, 47
Cedar Rapids (USA) 41°59′N 91°39′W, 138
Cervera (Spain) 41°40′N 1°16′E, 36
Ceske Budejovice (Czechoslovakia) 48°58′N 14°29′E, 166
Cetis *see* Cilicia
Ceuta (Spain) 35°53′N 5°19′W, 218
Chalcedon (Kadikoy) (Turkey) 40°59′N 29°02′E, 29
Chalcis (Lebanon) 33°47′N 35°53′E, 26
Châlons-sur-Marne (France) 48°58′N 4°22′E, 167
Châlon-sur-Saône (France) 46°47′N 4°51′E, 167
Chambersburg (USA) 39°57′N 77°40′W, 138
Chambéry (France) 45°34′N 5°55′E, 36, 167
Champaign (USA) 40°07′N 88°14′W, 138
Chapel Hill (USA) 35°55′N 79°04′W, 138
Charleroi (Belgium) 50°25′N 4°27′E, 167
Charleston (South Carolina, USA) 32°48′N 79°58′W, 47, 57, 102, 138
Charleston (West Virginia, USA) 38°23′N 81°40′W, 138
Charleville (France) 49°46′N 4°43′E, 167
Charlotte (USA) 35°03′N 80°50′W, 138
Charlottesville (USA) 38°02′N 78°29′W, 138
Châteauroux (France) 46°49′N 1°41′E, 166
Châtel (France) 46°17′N 6°50′E, 36
Chatellerault (France) 46°49′N 0°33′E, 166
Chatham (Canada) 42°24′N 82°11′W, 138
Chattanooga (USA) 35°02′N 85°18′W, 138
Chaves (Portugal) 41°44′N 7°28′W, 166
Chelm (Poland) 51°08′N 23°29′E, 50, 166
Chelmno (Kulm) (Poland) 53°20′N 18°25′E, 70, 102
Chelyabinsk (USSR) 55°12′N 61°25′E, 10, 190
Cherchell (Algeria) 36°36′N 2°11′E, 218
Cherkassy (USSR) 49°27′N 32°04′E, 190
Chernigov (USSR) 51°30′N 31°18′E, 50, 190
Chernobyl (USSR) 51°17′N 30°15′E, 101
Chernovtsy (Czernowitz) (USSR) 48°19′N 25°52′E, 60, 64, 66, 101, 120, 190
Cherson *see* Sevastopol
Chester (USA) 39°50′N 75°23′W, 140
Cheyenne (USA) 41°08′N 104°50′W, 138
Chicago (USA) 41°50′N 87°45′W, 10, 66, 102, 137, 138
Chigwell (UK) 51°37′N 0°05′E, 166
Chimbero (Chile) 26°55′S 69°56′W, 159
Chimkent (USSR) 42°16′N 69°05′E, 190
Chinon (France) 47°10′N 0°15′E, 36, 99
Chita (USSR) 52°03′N 113°35′E, 60, 190
Chitré (Panama) 7°59′N 80°25′W, 159
Chortkov (Czortkow) (USSR) 49°01′N 25°42′E, 101, 190
Christchurch (New Zealand) 43°33′S 172°40′E, 60, 217
Christiania *see* Oslo
Ciechanowiec (Poland) 52°41′N 22°30′E, 50
Cilicia (Cetis) (region), 26
Cincinnati (USA) 39°10′N 84°30′W, 10, 17, 102, 138
Clara (Argentina) 31°50′S 58°48′W, 160
Claremont (USA) 43°23′N 72°21′W, 138
Clarksburg (USA) 39°16′N 80°22′W, 138
Clarksdale (USA) 34°12′N 90°33′W, 138
Clermont-Ferrand (Avernum) (France) 45°47′N 3°05′E, 34, 166
Cleveland (Mississippi, USA) 33°43′N 90°46′W, 138
Cleveland (Ohio, USA) 41°30′N 81°41′W, 10, 66, 102, 137, 138
Clifton (USA) 40°53′N 74°08′W, 140
Cluj (Kolozsvár) (Romania) 46°47′N 23°37′E, 102, 166
Coatesville (USA) 39°59′N 75°50′W, 140
Cochabamba (Bolivia) 17°26′S 66°10′W, 159
Cochin (India) 9°56′N 76°15′E, 10, 17, 47, 60, 198
Cocula (Mexico) 20°22′N 103°50′W, 159
Cohen Oungre (Argentina) 31°13′S 59°20′W, 160
Coimbra (Portugal) 40°12′N 8°25′W, 166
Colchester (USA) 41°35′N 72°19′W, 140
Colmar (France) 48°05′N 7°21′E, 167
Cologne (Colonia Agrippina) (W Germany) 50°56′N 6°57′E, 30, 36, 38, 40, 50, 64, 121, 167
Coloma (USA) 38°07′N 120°36′W, 102
Colombo (Sri Lanka) 6°55′N 79°52′E, 60
Colón (Panama) 9°21′N 79°54′W, 159
Colonia Agrippina *see* Cologne
Colorado Springs (USA) 38°50′N 104°50′W, 138
Columbia (Mississippi, USA) 31°14′N 89°51′W, 138
Columbia (South Carolina, USA) 34°00′N 81°00′W, 102, 138
Columbus (Georgia, USA) 32°28′N 84°59′W, 138
Columbus (Ohio, USA) 39°59′N 83°03′W, 138
Comayagua (Honduras) 14°30′N 87°39′W, 159
Commagene (region), 26
Concepción (Chile) 36°50′S 73°03′W, 47, 159
Concord (USA) 43°13′N 71°34′W, 138
Concordia (Italy) 45°45′N 12°50′E, 29
Constance *see* Konstanz
Constanta (Romania) 44°12′N 28°40′E, 166
Constantine (Algeria) 36°22′N 6°40′E, 218
Constantinople *see* Istanbul
Contra Costa County (USA), 138
Copenhagen (Denmark) 55°43′N 12°34′E, 10, 47, 57, 64, 121, 137, 166
Coquimbo (Chile) 29°57′S 71°25′W, 159
Cordele (USA) 31°59′N 83°49′W, 138
Córdoba (Argentina) 31°25′S 64°11′W, 10, 47, 159
Córdoba (Corduba) (Spain) 37°53′N 4°46′W, 17, 29, 30, 36, 38, 99, 166
Corinth (Corinthus) (Greece) 37°56′N 22°55′E, 25, 29, 30, 38
Cork (Irish Republic) 51°54′N 8°28′W, 166
Corning (USA) 42°10′N 77°04′W, 140
Cornwall (Canada) 45°02′N 74°45′W, 138
Coro (Venezuela) 11°27′N 69°41′W, 159
Corpus Christi (USA) 27°47′N 97°26′W, 138
Corrientes (Argentina) 27°30′S 58°48′W, 159
Corte (France) 42°18′N 9°08′E, 166
Cortland (USA) 42°36′N 76°10′W, 140
Corvallis (USA) 44°35′N 123°16′W, 138
Cos (Greece) 36°53′N 27°19′E, 25
Coucy (France) 49°32′N 3°20′E, 99
Council Bluffs (USA) 41°14′N 95°54′W, 138
Courland (region), 50
Coventry (UK) 52°25′N 1°30′W, 166
Craiova (Romania) 44°18′N 23°47′E, 166
Cracow *see* Krakow
Cremona (Italy) 45°08′N 10°01′E, 99, 100, 120
Ctesiphon (Iraq) 33°06′N 44°36′E, 29, 30
Cuenca (Ecuador) 2°54′S 79°00′W, 159
Cuenca (Spain) 40°04′N 2°07′W, 36
Cuernavaca (Mexico) 18°57′N 99°15′W, 159
Cumberland (USA) 39°40′N 78°47′W, 138
Curaçao (isl) (Netherlands Antilles) 12°10′N 69°00′W, 10, 57, 60, 66, 137, 159
Curitiba (Brazil) 25°25′S 49°25′W, 159
Cypros (Jordan) 31°49′N 35°26′E, 32
Cyrenaica (region), 23, 25, 29, 30
Cyrene (Libya) 32°48′N 21°54′E, 23, 25, 29, 30, 218
Cyzicus (Turkey) 40°25′N 27°54′E, 25
Czeladz (Poland) 50°29′N 19°41′E, 72
Czestochowa (Poland) 50°49′N 19°07′E, 70, 166
Czernowitz *see* Chernovtsy
Czortkow *see* Chortkov

Dachau (W Germany) 48°15′N 11°26′E, 70
Dallas (USA) 32°47′N 96°48′W, 10, 138
Dalton (USA) 34°46′N 84°59′W, 138
Damanhur (Egypt) 31°03′N 30°28′E, 218
Damascus (Syria) 33°30′N 36°19′E, 10, 17, 20, 22, 23, 26, 29, 30, 34, 38, 40, 44, 47, 57, 60, 64, 99, 121, 137, 198
Dampierre (France) 47°31′N 6°55′E, 99
Danbury (USA) 41°24′N 73°26′W, 140
Danville (Illinois, USA) 40°09′N 87°37′W, 138
Danville (Virginia, USA) 36°34′N 79°25′W, 102, 138
Danzig *see* Gdansk
Daphne (Turkey) 36°04′N 36°10′E, 34
Darlington (UK) 54°31′N 1°34′W, 166
Darmstadt (W Germany) 49°52′N 8°39′E, 167
Daugavpils (Dvinsk) (USSR) 55°52′N 26°31′E, 190
David (Panama) 8°26′N 82°26′W, 159
Davos (Switzerland) 46°48′N 9°52′E, 166
Dayton (USA) 39°45′N 84°10′W, 138
Daytona Beach (USA) 29°11′N 81°01′W, 138
Debdou (Morocco) 33°59′N 3°05′W, 218
Debrecen (Hungary) 47°30′N 21°37′E, 102, 166
Decatur (USA) 39°51′N 88°57′W, 138
Delemont (Switzerland) 47°22′N 7°21′E, 167
Delft (Netherlands) 52°01′N 4°21′E, 167
Delos (Greece) 37°24′N 25°20′E, 17, 166
Delphi (Greece) 38°29′N 22°30′E, 25
Denver (USA) 39°45′N 105°00′W, 10, 102, 138
Derazhno (USSR) 49°18′N 27°28′E, 100
Derbent (USSR) 42°03′N 48°18′E, 40, 44, 60, 190
Dertosa *see* Tortosa
Des Moines (USA) 41°35′N 93°35′W, 138
Dessau (E Germany) 51°51′N 12°15′E, 121
Detroit (USA) 42°23′N 83°05′W, 10, 66, 102, 137, 138
Deventer (Netherlands) 52°15′N 6°10′E, 36, 50, 167
Diessenhofen (Switzerland) 47°42′N 8°46′E, 167
Dijon (France) 47°20′N 5°02′E, 167
Dimona (Israel) 31°04′N 35°01′E, 199
Dium (Syria) 32°39′N 36°21′E, 24, 32
Dixon (USA) 41°50′N 89°29′W, 138
Diyarbakir (Amida) (Turkey) 37°55′N 40°14′E, 26, 30, 34, 198
Djerba (isl) (Tunisia) 33°56′N 11°00′E, 218
Djidjelli (Algeria) 36°50′N 5°43′E, 218
Dnepropetrovsk (Yekaterinoslav) (USSR) 48°29′N 35°00′E, 10, 66, 190
Docus (Dok) (Jordan) 31°51′N 35°26′E, 24
Doetinchem (Netherlands) 51°58′N 6°17′E, 167
Dolina (USSR) 49°00′N 23°59′E, 101
Donaldsonville (USA) 30°05′N 91°00′E, 102
Donetsk (USSR) 48°00′N 37°50′E, 10, 190
Dora (Argentina) 29°14′S 62°53′W, 160
Dora (Israel) 32°37′N 34°55′E, 24
Dordrecht (Netherlands) 51°48′N 4°40′E, 167
Dorohoi (Romania) 47°57′N 26°31′E, 166
Dortmund (W Germany) 51°32′N 7°27′E, 36, 167
Dothan (USA) 31°12′N 85°25′W, 138
Douai (France) 50°22′N 3°05′E, 166
Douglas (Isle of Man) 54°09′N 4°29′W, 166
Dover (USA) 43°12′N 70°55′W, 138
Draguignan (France) 43°32′N 6°28′E, 166
Drancy (France) 48°56′N 2°26′E, 70
Dresden (E Germany) 51°03′N 13°45′E, 50, 102, 166
Dreux (France) 48°44′N 1°23′E, 166
Drogobych (USSR) 49°10′N 23°30′E, 190
Dublin (Irish Republic) 53°20′N 6°15′W, 10, 40, 47, 64, 137, 166
Dubno (USSR) 50°28′N 25°40′E, 190
Dubrovnik (Ragusa) (Yugoslavia) 42°40′N 18°07′E, 44, 47, 166
Dubuque (USA) 42°31′N 90°41′W, 138
Duisburg (W Germany) 57°18′N 5°40′W, 167
Duluth (USA) 46°45′N 92°10′W, 138
Dumyat (Egypt) 31°26′N 31°48′E, 218
Dundee (UK) 56°28′N 3°00′W, 166
Dunedin (New Zealand) 45°52′S 170°30′E, 60, 217
Dunkerque (France) 51°02′N 2°23′E, 166
Dura (Syria) 34°46′N 40°46′E, 17, 25, 26
Durban (S Africa) 29°53′S 31°00′E, 219
Durham (USA) 36°00′N 78°54′W, 138
Dushanbe (USSR) 38°38′N 68°51′E, 190
Düsseldorf (W Germany) 51°13′N 6°47′E, 167
Dyhernfurth (Poland) 50°29′N 17°58′E, 121
Dynow (Poland) 49°50′N 22°11′E, 101
Dzerzhinsk (USSR) 53°40′N 27°01′E, 101

Eastbourne (UK) 50°46′N 0°17′E, 166
East London (S Africa) 33°00′S 27°54′E, 219
Easton (USA) 40°41′N 75°13′W, 102, 140
Eau Claire (USA) 44°50′N 91°30′W, 138
Ecbatana *see* Hamadan
Echmiadzin (Valarshapat) (USSR) 40°11′N 44°17′E, 34
Edessa (Urfa) (Turkey) 37°08′N 38°45′E, 25, 26, 29, 30, 34
Edinburgh (UK) 55°57′N 3°13′W, 64, 166
Edineti (Yedyntsy) (USSR) 48°12′N 27°19′E, 70
Edirne (Adrianople) (Turkey) 41°40′N 26°34′E, 44, 47, 99, 100, 121, 198
Edmonton (Canada) 53°34′N 113°25′W, 138
Edom (region), 22
Eger (Cheb) (Czechoslovakia) 49°59′N 12°23′E, 36, 166
Eglaim (Jordan) 31°12′N 35°45′E, 24
Eindhoven (Netherlands) 51°26′N 5°30′E, 167
Eisenstadt (Austria) 47°50′N 16°32′E, 166
El Ariha *see* Jericho
Elat (Elath) (Israel) 29°33′N 34°57′E, 22, 199
Elath *see* Elat
Elbeuf (France) 49°17′N 1°01′E, 166
El Centro (USA) 34°47′N 115°33′W, 138
Elephantine (isl) (Egypt) 24°05′N 32°54′E, 17
El Faiyum (Egypt) 29°19′N 30°50′E, 218
Elgin (USA) 42°03′N 88°19′W, 138
El Golea (Algeria) 30°35′N 2°51′E, 218
El Jadida (Mazagan) (Morocco) 33°19′N 8°35′W, 218
El Kef (Tunisia), 36°10′N 8°40′E, 218
Ellenville (USA) 41°43′N 74°23′W, 140
El Mahalla el Kubra (Egypt) 30°59′N 31°10′E, 218
Elmira (USA) 42°06′N 76°50′W, 140
El Paso (USA) 31°45′N 106°29′W, 138
El Qamishliye (Kameshli) (Syria) 37°03′N 41°15′E, 198
Elsinore (USA) 33°40′N 117°19′W, 138
Elusa (Israel) 31°06′N 34°39′E, 24, 32
Elvira (Illiberis) (Spain) 37°17′N 3°53′W, 34
El Yahûdiya (Egypt) 30°45′N 30°35′E, 17
Elyria (USA) 41°22′N 82°06′W, 138
Emden (W Germany) 53°23′N 7°13′E, 47, 166
Emerita Augusta *see* Mérida
Emesa (Homs) (Syria) 34°44′N 36°43′E, 25, 26, 29
Emmatha *see* Hammath Gader
Emmaus (Imwas) (Jordan) 31°50′N 34°59′E, 24, 32, 98
En-gedi (Israel) 31°28′N 35°23′E, 24, 32
Enkhuizen (Netherlands) 52°42′N 5°17′E, 167
Enschede (Netherlands) 52°13′N 6°55′E, 167
Ensisheim (France) 47°51′N 7°20′E, 36
Épernay (France) 49°02′N 3°58′E, 166
Ephesus (Turkey) 37°55′N 27°19′E, 23, 25, 29, 30, 34, 38, 198
Épinal (France) 48°10′N 6°28′E, 167
Erechim (Brazil) 27°35′S 52°15′W, 159
Erfurt (E Germany) 50°58′N 11°02′E, 36, 50, 166
Erie (USA) 42°07′N 80°05′W, 138
Ernakulam (India) 10°00′N 76°16′E, 198
Esbus (Hisban) (Jordan) 31°48′N 35°48′E, 24, 32
Esch-sur-Alzette (Luxembourg) 49°30′N 5°59′E, 167
Eschwege (W Germany) 51°11′N 10°03′E, 102
Essen (W Germany) 51°27′N 6°57′E, 167
Essex County (USA), 140
Etsion Gaber (Asia) (Jordan) 29°33′N 34°58′E, 98
Estonia (region), 64, 70, 190
Esztergom (Hungary) 47°46′N 18°24′E, 166
Eugene (USA) 44°03′N 123°04′W, 138
Euhemereia (Egypt) 29°23′N 30°27′E, 29
Eureka (USA) 40°49′N 124°10′W, 138
Evansville (USA) 38°00′N 87°33′W, 138
Évian (France) 46°24′N 6°35′E, 166
Évora (Portugal) 39°31′N 8°59′W, 166
Évreux (France) 49°03′N 1°11′E, 166

Faaborg (Denmark) 55°35′N 8°45′E, 166
Fadak (Saudi Arabia) 25°31′N 39°12′E, 30
Fairbanks (USA) 64°50′N 147°50′W, 138
Falaise (France) 48°54′N 0°11′W, 99
Fall River (USA) 41°42′N 71°08′W, 140
Falmouth (UK) 50°08′N 5°04′W, 166
Famagusta (Cyprus) 35°07′N 33°57′E, 30
Fano (Italy) 43°51′N 13°01′E, 121
Fargo (USA) 46°52′N 96°48′W, 138
Faro (Portugal) 37°01′N 7°56′W, 121, 166
Fayetteville (Arkansas, USA) 36°03′N 94°10′W, 138
Fayetteville (North Carolina, USA) 35°03′N 78°53′W, 138
Feodosiya (Kaffa) (USSR) 45°03′N 35°23′E, 47, 190
Fergana (USSR) 40°23′N 71°19′E, 190
Ferrara (Italy) 44°50′N 11°38′E, 47, 121, 166
Fez (Morocco) 34°05′N 5°00′W, 38, 40, 44, 47, 57, 99 121, 218
Fitchburg (USA) 42°35′N 71°50′W, 140
Fitzgerald (USA) 31°43′N 83°16′W, 138
Fiume *see* Rijeka
Flemington (USA) 40°31′N 74°52′W, 140
Flint (USA) 43°03′N 83°40′W, 138
Florence (Italy) 43°47′N 11°15′E, 47, 121, 166
Florence (Alabama, USA) 34°48′N 87°40′W, 138
Florence (South Carolina, USA) 34°12′N 79°44′W, 138
Flossenbürg (W Germany) 49°42′N 12°20′E, 70
Focsani (Romania) 45°41′N 27°12′E, 166
Fond du Lac (USA) 43°48′N 88°27′W, 138
Fontainebleau (France) 48°24′N 2°42′E, 166
Fontana (USA) 40°17′N 76°30′W, 138
Forcalquier (France) 43°56′N 5°46′E, 36
Forest City (USA) 35°12′N 91°57′W, 138
Fort Dodge (USA) 42°31′N 94°10′W, 138
Fort Lauderdale (USA) 26°08′N 80°08′W, 10, 137, 138
Fort Myers (USA) 26°39′N 81°51′W, 138
Fort Pierce (USA) 27°28′N 80°20′W, 138
Fort St George *see* Calcutta
Fort Smith (USA) 35°22′N 94°27′W, 138
Fort Wayne (USA) 41°05′N 85°08′W, 102, 138
Forth Worth (USA) 32°45′N 97°20′W, 138
Framingham (USA) 42°18′N 71°25′W, 140
Frankfurt am Main (W Germany) 50°06′N 8°41′E, 17, 36, 50, 57, 66, 102, 121, 167
Frankfurt an der Oder (E Germany) 52°20′N 14°32′E, 50, 102, 121
Fredericia (Denmark) 55°34′N 9°47′E, 166
Frederick (USA) 39°25′N 77°25′W, 138
Fredericton (Canada) 45°57′N 66°40′W, 138
Freeport (Bahamas) 26°30′N 78°47′W, 159
Freiburg (W Germany) 48°00′N 7°52′E, 120, 121, 167
Frejus (France) 43°26′N 6°44′E, 166
Fresno (USA) 36°41′N 119°47′W, 138
Fribourg (Switzerland) 46°50′N 7°10′E, 167
Friedberg (W Germany) 50°20′N 8°45′E, 167
Frunze (USSR) 40°07′N 71°44′E, 190
Fulda (W Germany) 50°33′N 9°41′E, 36
Fürth (W Germany) 49°28′N 11°00′E, 121, 166

Gabalis (Jordan) 31°03′N 35°36′E, 24
Gabès (Tunisia) 33°52′N 10°06′E, 60, 99, 218
Gadara (Jordan) 32°39′N 35°41′E, 24, 32
Gadsden (USA) 34°00′N 86°00′W, 138
Gainesville (USA) 29°40′N 82°20′W, 138
Galaaditis (region), 24
Galati (Romania) 45°27′N 28°02′E, 166
Galicia (region), 62, 101
Galilee (region), 24, 26, 32, 98
Galveston (USA) 29°17′N 94°48′W, 138
Gamala (Syria) 32°48′N 35°51′E, 24, 32
Gamzu (Israel) 31°55′N 34°54′E, 98
Gangra (Turkey) 40°35′N 33°37′E, 30
Ganne Tiqwa (Israel) 32°05′N 34°51′E, 199
Garaba (Israel) 32°51′N 35°20′E, 24, 32, 98
Gardner (USA) 42°33′N 71°59′W, 140
Gargzdai (USSR) 55°42′N 21°21′E, 190
Gastonia (USA) 35°14′N 81°12′W, 138
Gata (Spain) 40°15′N 6°35′W, 47
Gateshead (UK) 54°58′N 1°35′W, 166
Gath (Israel) 31°46′N 34°44′E, 22
Gatooma (Kadoma) (Zimbabwe) 18°16′S 29°55′E, 219
Gaulanitis (region), 24, 26
Gaza (Gaza Strip) 31°30′N 34°28′E, 20, 22, 24, 30, 32, 199
Gazara (Israel) 31°53′N 34°57′E, 24
Gdansk (Danzig) (Poland) 54°22′N 18°41′E, 62, 64, 166
Geba (Israel) 32°43′N 35°05′E, 24, 32
Gedera (Israel) 31°48′N 34°46′E, 199
Gedor (Salt) (Jordan) 32°03′N 35°44′E, 24, 32
Geelong (Australia) 38°10′S 144°26′E, 217
Gelnhausen (W Germany) 50°12′N 9°13′E, 167
Geneva (Switzerland) 46°13′N 6°09′E, 121, 167
Geneva (USA) 42°52′N 76°59′W, 138
Gennesaret *see* Ginnosar
Genoa (Genua) (Italy) 44°24′N 8°56′E, 29, 34, 47, 121, 166
George (S Africa) 33°57′S 22°28′E, 219
Gerar (Israel) 31°24′N 34°40′E, 24
Gerasa (Jarash) (Jordan) 32°17′N 35°53′E, 24, 32
Gerizim (mt) (Jordan) 32°12′N 35°16′E, 24
Germiston (S Africa) 26°15′S 28°10′E, 219
Gerona (Spain) 41°59′N 2°49′E, 17, 36, 166
Ghardaia (Algeria) 32°20′N 3°40′E, 218
Gharyan (Libya) 32°12′N 13°02′E, 218
Ghazni (Afghanistan) 33°33′N 68°28′E, 40, 44, 198
Ghent (Belgium) 51°02′N 3°42′E, 166
Giado (Libya) 31°58′N 12°01′E, 218
Gibraltar 36°09′N 5°21′W, 10, 60, 66, 137, 166
Giessen (W Germany) 50°35′N 8°42′E, 167
Gigen (Bulgaria) 43°39′N 24°30′E, 166
Ginnegar (Israel) 32°40′N 35°15′E, 98
Ginnosar (Gennesaret) (Israel) 32°51′N 35°31′E, 32, 98
Gischala (Jish, Gush Halav) (Israel) 33°01′N 35°27′E, 24, 32
Givatayim (Israel) 32°05′N 34°48′E, 199
Givat Shemuel (Israel) 32°05′N 34°51′E, 199
Glace Bay (Canada) 46°11′N 59°58′W, 138
Glasgow (UK) 55°53′N 4°15′W, 10, 62, 64, 166
Glens Falls (USA) 43°17′N 73°41′W, 138
Gliwice (Poland) 50°20′N 18°40′E, 166
Glogau (Poland) 51°40′N 16°06′E, 102
Gloucester (USA) 42°37′N 70°41′W, 140
Gloversville (USA) 43°03′N 74°19′W, 138
Glückstadt (W Germany) 53°47′N 9°26′E, 47
Goa (India) 15°31′N 73°56′E, 47
Goldsboro (USA) 35°23′N 78°00′W, 138
Golgoi (Cyprus) 35°07′N 33°40′E, 29
Gomel (USSR) 52°25′N 31°00′E, 10, 50, 190
Gonder (Ethiopia) 12°39′N 37°29′E, 219
Gophna (Jifna) (Jordan) 31°57′N 35°14′E, 32
Gora Kalwarija (Poland) 51°59′N 21°11′E, 101
Gori (USSR) 41°59′N 44°05′E, 191
Gorizia (Italy) 45°57′N 13°37′E, 166
Gorkiy (USSR) 56°20′N 44°00′E, 10, 190
Gorokhov (USSR) 50°30′N 24°46′E, 50
Goslar (W Germany) 51°55′N 10°25′E, 36
Göteborg (Sweden) 57°45′N 12°00′E, 10, 166
Göttingen (W Germany) 51°32′N 9°57′E, 166
Goulimime (Morocco) 28°56′N 10°04′W, 218
Grahamstown (S Africa) 33°18′S 26°32′E, 219
Granada (Spain) 37°10′N 3°35′W, 38, 99, 166
Grand Forks (USA) 47°57′N 97°05′W, 138
Grand Rapids (USA) 42°57′N 86°40′W, 138
Grasse (France) 43°40′N 6°56′E, 166
Graz (Austria) 47°05′N 15°22′E, 166
Great Barrington (USA) 42°12′N 73°22′W, 140
Great Yarmouth (UK) 52°37′N 1°44′E, 166
Green Bay (USA) 44°32′N 88°00′W, 138
Greenfield (USA) 42°36′N 72°37′W, 140
Greenville (Mississippi, USA) 33°23′N 91°03′W, 138
Greenville (South Carolina, USA) 34°52′N 82°25′W, 138
Greenwich (USA) 41°02′N 73°37′W, 140

Mata Mehasia (Iraq) 32°40′N 44°21′E, 98
Maui (isl) (Hawaii, USA) 20°45′N 156°20′W, 138
Mauricia (Brazil) 10°16′S 36°33′W, 47
Mauthausen (Austria) 48°15′N 14°31′E, 70
Mazatenango (Guatemala) 14°31′N 91°30′W, 159
Mechelen (Belgium) 51°02′N 4°29′E, 70, 167
Médéa (Algeria) 36°15′N 2°48′E, 218
Medeba (Jordan) 31°44′N 35°48′E, 24, 32
Medellín (Colombia) 6°15′N 75°36′W, 159
Media (region), 20, 23, 25
Medicine Hat (Canada) 50°03′N 110°41′W, 138
Mediolanum *see* Milan
Medzhibozh (USSR) 49°29′N 27°28′E, 101
Megiddo (Israel) 32°35′N 35°11′E, 20, 22
Meiningen (E Germany) 50°34′N 10°25′E, 102
Meknès (Morocco) 33°53′N 5°37′W, 218
Melbourne (Australia) 37°45′S 144°58′E, 10, 60, 66, 137, 217
Melfi (Italy) 41°00′N 15°33′E, 40
Melilla (Spain) 35°17′N 2°57′W, 218
Melitene *see* Malatya
Melitopol (USSR) 46°51′N 35°22′E, 190
Melville (Canada) 50°57′N 102°49′W, 138
Memel (Klaipeda) (USSR) 55°43′N 21°07′E, 190
Memphis (Noph) (Egypt) 29°52′N 31°12′E, 20, 25, 218
Memphis (USA) 35°10′N 90°00′W, 138
Mendoza (Argentina) 32°48′S 68°52′W, 159
Menton (France) 43°47′N 7°30′E, 166
Merano (Italy) 46°41′N 11°10′E, 166
Mérida (Emerita Augusta) (Spain) 38°55′N 6°20′W, 29, 30, 38, 166
Meriden (USA) 41°32′N 72°48′W, 140
Meridian (USA) 32°21′N 88°42′W, 138
Meroë (Sudan) 18°30′N 31°49′E, 25, 29
Merthyr Tydfil (UK) 51°46′N 3°23′W, 166
Merv (Mary) (USSR) 37°42′N 61°54′E, 38
Meslatah (Libya) 32°10′N 14°31′E, 218
Messene (region), 98
Messina (Italy) 38°13′N 15°33′E, 36, 47
Metz (Mettis) (France) 49°07′N 6°11′E, 30, 36, 57, 102, 167
Mevasseret Ziyyon (Israel) 31°48′N 35°10′E, 199
Mexico City (Mexico) 19°25′N 99°10′W, 10, 47, 60, 137, 159
Mezhirech (USSR) 49°37′N 31°25′E, 101
Miami (USA) 25°45′N 80°15′W, 10, 137, 138
Michalovce (Czechoslovakia) 48°45′N 21°55′E, 166
Michigan City (USA) 41°43′N 86°54′W, 138
Middelburg (Netherlands) 51°30′N 3°36′E, 167
Middelburg (S Africa) 25°47′S 29°28′E, 219
Middlesbrough (UK) 54°35′N 1°14′W, 166
Middlesex County (USA), 140
Middletown (Connecticut, USA) 41°34′N 72°39′W, 140
Middletown (New York, USA) 41°26′N 74°26′W, 138
Middletown (Ohio, USA) 39°31′N 84°13′W, 138
Miedzyrzec (Poland) 52°00′N 22°48′E, 166
Migdal HaEmeq (Israel) 32°40′N 35°13′E, 199
Mikha Tschakaya (USSR) 42°16′N 41°59′E, 191
Milan (Mediolanum) (Italy) 45°28′N 9°12′E, 10, 29, 34, 64, 121, 166
Miletus (Turkey) 37°30′N 27°18′E, 25, 29
Miliana (Algeria) 36°20′N 2°15′E, 218
Millville (USA) 39°24′N 75°02′W, 140
Milwaukee (USA) 43°03′N 87°56′W, 10, 102, 138
Minden (W Germany) 52°18′N 8°54′E, 102, 167
Minneapolis (USA) 45°00′N 93°15′W, 10, 138
Minorca (isl) (Spain) 40°00′N 4°00′E, 34
Minsk (USSR) 53°51′N 27°30′E, 10, 50, 60, 64, 66, 70, 100, 101, 102, 120, 190
Mir (USSR) 53°28′N 27°11′E, 102
Mirabel (France) 44°10′N 1°25′E, 36
Miranda do Corvo (Portugal) 40°05′N 8°20′W, 166
Miranda do Douro (Portugal) 41°30′N 6°16′W, 166
Miskolc (Hungary) 48°07′N 20°47′E, 72, 166
Mistras (Greece) 37°04′N 22°22′E, 47, 166
Misurata (Libya) 32°24′N 15°04′E, 218
Mittelbaudora (E Germany) 51°35′N 11°01′E, 70
Mlawa (Poland) 53°08′N 20°20′E, 120
Moab (Moabitis) (region), 22, 24
Mobile (USA) 30°40′N 88°05′W, 102, 138
Modena (Italy) 44°39′N 10°55′E, 166
Modesto (USA) 37°37′N 121°00′W, 138
Mogador (Morocco) 31°30′N 9°48′W, 218
Mogilev (USSR) 53°54′N 30°20′E, 10, 50, 190
Moisesville (Argentina) 30°45′S 61°25′W, 160
Moji das Cruzes (Brazil) 23°33′S 46°14′W, 159
Monastir *see* Bitola
Mönchengladbach (W Germany) 51°12′N 6°25′E, 167
Moncton (Canada) 46°04′N 64°50′W, 138
Monmouth County (USA), 140
Monroe (Louisiana, USA) 32°31′N 92°06′W, 138
Monroe (New York, USA) 41°20′N 74°12′W, 140
Monsey (USA) 41°07′N 74°04′W, 102
Montalbán (Spain) 40°50′N 0°48′W, 121
Montauban (France) 44°01′N 1°20′E, 166
Monte Carlo (Monaco) 43°44′N 7°25′E, 166
Montefiore (Argentina) 29°50′S 62°02′W, 160
Montmélian (France) 45°30′N 6°04′E, 36
Monterey (USA) 36°35′N 121°55′W, 138
Monterrey (Mexico) 25°40′N 100°20′W, 10, 159
Montevideo (Uruguay) 34°55′S 56°10′W, 10, 137, 159
Montgomery (USA) 32°22′N 86°20′W, 102, 138
Montgomery County (USA), 140
Monticello (USA) 41°39′N 74°41′W, 140
Montpellier (France) 43°36′N 3°53′E, 47, 99, 166
Montreal (Canada) 45°30′N 73°36′W, 10, 57, 60, 62, 66, 74, 102, 137, 138
Montreux (Switzerland) 46°27′N 6°55′E, 167
Moodus (USA) 41°30′N 72°27′W, 140
Moose Jaw (Canada) 50°23′N 105°35′W, 138
Morgantown (USA) 39°38′N 79°57′W, 138
Morristown (USA) 40°48′N 74°29′W, 102
Morris County (USA), 140
Moscow (USSR) 55°45′N 37°42′E, 10, 17, 60, 64, 66, 137, 190
Mostaganem (Algeria) 35°54′N 0°05′E, 218
Mostar (Yugoslavia) 43°20′N 17°50′E, 166
Mosul (Iraq) 36°21′N 43°08′E, 29, 38, 40, 47, 198
Mountaindale (USA) 41°42′N 74°32′W, 140
Mount Clemens (USA) 42°35′N 82°55′W, 138
Mount Holly (USA) 40°00′N 74°47′W, 140
Mount Pleasant (USA) 43°36′N 84°46′W, 138
M′Sila (Algeria) 35°40′N 4°31′E, 218
Mszczonow (Poland) 51°59′N 20°32′E, 101
Mülheim (W Germany) 51°25′N 6°50′E, 36, 167
Mulhouse (France) 47°45′N 7°21′E, 167
Muncie (USA) 40°11′N 85°22′W, 138
Munich (W Germany) 48°08′N 11°35′E, 17, 36, 50, 64, 72, 166
Munkacs (Mukachevo) (USSR) 48°26′N 22°45′E, 101
Münster (W Germany) 51°58′N 7°37′E, 36, 167
Münsterberg (Ziebice) (Poland) 50°37′N 17°01′E, 102
Murcia (Spain) 37°59′N 1°08′W, 166
Murmansk (USSR) 68°59′N 33°08′E, 10, 190
Mursa *see* Osijek
Muscatine (USA) 41°25′N 91°03′W, 138
Muskegon (USA) 43°13′N 86°15′W, 138
Muskogee (USA) 35°45′N 95°21′W, 138

Nabataea (region), 26
Nabeul (Tunisia) 36°30′N 10°44′E, 218
Nadvornaya (USSR) 48°37′N 24°30′E, 101
Navpaktos (Lepanto) (Greece) 38°28′N 21°50′E, 47, 166
Nagasaki (Japan) 32°45′N 129°52′E, 60, 198
Nagykanizsa (Hungary) 46°27′N 17°00′E, 166
Nahariyya (Israel) 33°01′N 35°05′E, 199
Nahavand (Iran) 34°13′N 48°21′E, 99, 198
Nairobi (Kenya) 1°17′S 36°50′E, 10, 66, 219
Najran (Saudi Arabia) 17°33′N 44°16′E, 29, 30
Nakhchevan (USSR) 39°12′N 45°24′E, 29
Nakskov (Denmark) 54°50′N 11°10′E, 166
Nalchik (USSR) 43°31′N 43°38′E, 190
Nalut (Libya) 31°53′N 10°59′E, 218
Namangan (USSR) 40°59′N 71°41′E, 190
Namur (Belgium) 50°28′N 4°52′E, 167
Nancy (France) 48°42′N 6°12′E, 167
Nantes (France) 47°14′N 1°35′W, 36, 47, 166
Naples (Italy) 40°50′N 14°15′E, 38, 40, 44, 47, 64, 121, 166
Narbata (Israel) 32°28′N 35°01′E, 24, 32
Narbonne (Narbo) (France) 43°11′N 3°00′E, 30, 99
Narcisse Leven (Argentina) 38°12′S 63°40′W, 160
Nares (Iraq) 32°28′N 44°25′E, 98
Naro (Tunisia) 36°47′N 10°17′E, 17, 218
Nashua (USA) 42°44′N 71°28′W, 140
Nashville (USA) 36°10′N 86°50′W, 138
Nassau (Bahamas) 25°03′N 77°20′W, 159
Natchez (USA) 31°32′N 91°24′W, 102, 138
Natzweiler (France) 48°22′N 7°26′E, 70
Naveh (Syria) 32°51′N 36°09′E, 32, 98
Nazerat (Nazareth) (Israel) 32°41′N 35°16′E, 199
Nazerat Illit (Israel) 32°42′N 35°19′E, 199
Nedroma (Algeria) 35°00′N 1°44′W, 218
Nefta (Tunisia) 33°53′N 7°50′E, 218
Nehardea (Iraq) 32°59′N 44°12′E, 25, 30, 98
Nemirov (USSR) 48°58′N 28°50′E, 101
Nesher (Israel) 32°46′N 35°03′E, 199
Nesukhoyshe (USSR) 51°11′N 24°58′E, 101
Nes Ziyyona (Israel) 31°56′N 34°46′E, 199
Netanya (Israel) 32°20′N 34°51′E, 137, 199
Neuengamme (W Germany) 53°32′N 10°13′E, 70
Nevis (isl) 17°11′N 62°35′W, 159
Newark (USA) 40°14′N 74°12′W, 66, 102, 140
New Bedford (USA) 41°38′N 70°55′W, 140
Newburgh (USA) 41°30′N 74°00′W, 140
Newburyport (USA) 42°47′N 70°53′W, 140
Newcastle (Australia) 32°55′S 151°46′E, 217
Newcastle-upon-Tyne (UK) 54°59′N 1°35′W, 62, 166
New Castle (USA) 41°00′N 80°22′W, 138
New Delhi (India) 28°37′N 77°13′E, 10, 198
New Haven (USA) 41°18′N 72°55′W, 10, 102, 140
New Kensington (USA) 40°34′N 79°46′W, 138
New London (USA) 41°21′N 72°06′W, 140
New Orleans (USA) 30°00′N 90°03′W, 10, 102, 138
New Paltz (USA) 41°45′N 74°05′W, 140
Newport (UK) 51°35′N 3°00′W, 166
Newport (USA) 41°30′N 71°19′W, 47, 102
Newport News (USA) 36°59′N 76°26′W, 138
New Square (USA) 41°08′N 74°02′W, 102
New York (USA) 40°40′N 73°50′W, 10, 17, 47, 57, 60, 62, 66, 102, 137, 140
Niagara Falls (USA) 43°06′N 79°04′W, 138
Nicaea (Iznik) (Turkey) 40°27′N 29°43′E, 29
Nice (France) 43°42′N 7°16′E, 10, 47, 166
Nicephorium *see* Callinicum
Nicomedia (Izmit) (Turkey) 40°47′N 29°55′E, 29, 30, 99
Nicopolis (Turkey) 40°04′N 38°34′E, 26
Nicopolis *see* Nikopol
Nicosia (Cyprus) 35°11′N 33°23′E, 198
Niederhagen (W Germany) 52°14′N 10°07′E, 70
Nigel (S Africa) 26°25′S 28°28′E, 219
Nijmegen (Netherlands) 51°50′N 5°52′E, 167
Nikolayev (Olbia) (USSR) 46°57′N 32°00′E, 190
Nikolsburg (Mikulov) (Czechoslovakia) 48°58′N 16°40′E, 100
Nikopol (Nicopolis) (Bulgaria) 43°41′N 24°55′E, 38, 47, 166
Nîmes (France) 43°50′N 4°21′E, 166
Nineveh (Ninus) (Iraq) 36°24′N 43°08′E, 20, 26, 29
Ningbo (China) 29°54′N 121°33′E, 44
Ninus *see* Nineveh
Nippur (Iraq) 32°10′N 45°11′E, 20, 23, 25, 29
Nishapur (Iran) 36°13′N 58°49′E, 38
Nisibis (Nusaybin) (Turkey) 37°05′N 41°11′E, 25, 26, 29, 34
Niterói (Brazil) 22°54′S 43°06′W, 159
Nitra (Czechoslovakia) 48°20′N 18°05′E, 70, 166
Noë (France) 43°26′N 0°51′E, 70
Noph *see* Memphis
Nördlingen (W Germany) 48°51′N 10°31′E, 36
Norfolk (USA) 36°54′N 76°18′W, 10, 102, 138
Norristown (USA) 40°07′N 75°20′W, 140
Northampton (USA) 42°19′N 72°38′W, 140
North Bay (Canada) 46°20′N 79°28′W, 138
North Hudson County (USA), 140
North Jersey (USA) 40°50′N 74°16′E, 140
Norwalk (USA) 41°07′N 73°25′W, 140
Norwich (UK) 52°38′N 1°18′E, 36, 166
Norwich (Connecticut, USA) 41°32′N 72°05′W, 140
Norwich (New York, USA) 42°33′N 75°33′W, 140
Nottingham (UK) 52°58′N 1°10′W, 166
Novi Sad (Yugoslavia) 45°15′N 19°51′E, 166
Novosibirsk (USSR) 55°04′N 83°05′E, 190
Nowy Sacz (Poland) 49°39′N 20°40′E, 101
Nuremberg (W Germany) 49°27′N 11°05′E, 36, 40, 44, 99, 102, 121, 166
Nyiregyhaza (Hungary) 47°57′N 21°43′E, 166
Nyons (France) 44°22′N 5°08′E, 36

Oak Ridge (USA) 36°02′N 84°12′W, 138
Oberhausen (W Germany) 51°27′N 6°50′E, 167
Obernai (France) 48°28′N 7°30′E, 167
Ocean County (USA), 140
Odense (Denmark) 55°24′N 10°25′E, 166
Odessa (USA) 31°50′N 102°23′W, 138
Odessa (USSR) 46°30′N 30°46′E, 10, 60, 62, 64, 66, 70, 137, 190
Oea *see* Tripoli
Oels (Olesnica) (Poland) 51°12′N 17°21′E, 121
Oescus (Romania) 43°44′N 24°27′E, 29
Offenbach (W Germany) 50°06′N 8°46′E, 102, 167
Ogden (USA) 41°14′N 111°59′W, 138
Okhara (Iraq) 33°58′N 44°32′E, 40
Oklahoma City (USA) 35°28′N 97°33′W, 138
Olbia *see* Nikolayev
Oldenburg (W Germany) 53°08′N 8°13′E, 102
Olyka (USSR) 50°44′N 25°50′E, 101
Omaha (USA) 41°15′N 96°00′W, 138
Omsk (USSR) 55°00′N 73°22′E, 60, 66, 190
On (Heliopolis) (Egypt) 30°08′N 31°18′E, 20
Oneonta (USA) 42°28′N 75°04′W, 140
Oni (USSR) 42°34′N 43°26′E, 191
Opatow (Poland) 50°49′N 21°25′E, 101
Opole (Lublin) (Poland) 51°08′N 22°00′E, 50, 101
Opole (Oppeln) (Poland) 50°40′N 17°56′E, 102
Oporto (Portugal) 41°09′N 8°37′W, 166
Oppeln *see* Opole
Oradea (Romania) 47°03′N 21°55′E, 166
Oran (Algeria) 35°45′N 0°38′W, 44, 218
Orange (France) 44°08′N 4°48′E, 36
Orangeburg County (USA), 138
Orange County (USA), 138
Or Aqiva (Israel) 32°31′N 34°55′E, 199
Orda (Israel) 31°23′N 34°24′E, 24
Ordzhonikidze (USSR) 43°02′N 44°43′E, 190
Orenburg (USSR) 51°50′N 55°00′E, 190
Orgeyev (USSR) 47°24′N 28°50′E, 190
Oria (Italy) 40°30′N 17°38′E, 38, 99, 166
Orlando (USA) 28°33′N 81°21′W, 10, 138
Orléans (Aureliani) (France) 47°54′N 1°54′E, 34, 99, 166
Oronaim (Jordan) 31°05′N 35°37′E, 24
Oroshaza (Hungary) 46°33′N 20°40′E, 166
Ortona (Italy) 42°21′N 14°24′E, 121
Oruro (Bolivia) 17°59′S 67°08′W, 159
Or Yehuda (Israel) 32°02′N 34°50′E, 199
Oshawa (Canada) 43°53′N 78°51′W, 138
Oshkosh (USA) 44°01′N 88°32′W, 138
Osijek (Mursa) (Yugoslavia) 45°33′N 18°42′E, 29, 166
Oslo (Christiania) (Norway) 59°56′N 10°45′E, 10, 64, 166
Osnabrück (W Germany) 52°17′N 8°03′E, 167
Ostend (Belgium) 51°13′N 2°55′E, 47, 166
Ostia (Italy) 41°46′N 12°18′E, 17
Ostrava (Mährisch-Ostrau) (Czechoslovakia) 49°50′N 18°15′E, 102, 166
Ostrog (USSR) 50°20′N 26°29′E, 100, 190
Otranto (Italy) 40°08′N 18°30′E, 38, 40, 99
Ottawa (Canada) 45°25′N 75°43′W, 138
Ottumwa (USA) 41°02′N 92°26′W, 138
Ouargla (Algeria) 32°00′N 5°16′E, 218
Oudtshoorn (S Africa) 33°35′S 22°12′E, 219
Oujda (Morocco) 34°41′N 1°45′W, 218
Ovalle (Chile) 30°33′S 71°16′W, 159
Ovruch (USSR) 51°20′N 28°50′E, 101
Oxford (UK) 51°46′N 1°15′W, 17, 121, 166
Oxford (USA) 39°47′N 75°58′W, 140
Oxyrhynchus (Egypt) 28°33′N 30°38′E, 17, 29, 30

Paarl (S Africa) 33°45′S 18°58′E, 219
Paderborn (W Germany) 51°43′N 8°44′E, 167
Padua (Italy) 45°24′N 11°53′E, 36, 50, 99, 100, 102, 166
Paducah (USA) 37°03′N 88°36′W, 138
Parkersburg (USA) 39°17′N 81°33′W, 138
Palermo (Panormus) (Sicily, Italy) 38°08′N 13°23′E, 30, 34, 40, 47, 64, 166
Palma (Majorca, Spain) 39°35′N 2°39′E, 17, 36, 166
Palm Beach County (USA), 138
Palm Springs (USA) 33°49′N 116°34′W, 138
Palmyra *see* Tadmor
Pamphylia (region), 98
Panama (Panama) 8°57′N 79°30′W, 60, 137, 159
Pancevo (Yugoslavia) 44°52′N 20°40′E, 166
Panevezys (USSR) 55°44′N 24°24′E, 190
Panormus *see* Palermo
Panticapaeum (USSR) 45°07′N 36°40′E, 25, 29, 30
Papa (Hungary) 47°20′N 17°29′E, 166
Papunia (Iraq) 33°20′N 44°00′E, 98
Paraíba (Brazil) 22°08′S 43°18′W, 47
Paralia (region), 24
Paramaribo (Surinam) 5°52′N 55°14′W, 10, 47, 159
Paraná (Argentina) 31°45′S 60°30′W, 159
Parczew (Poland) 51°39′N 22°53′E, 72
Pardes Hanna-Karkur (Israel) 32°29′N 34°58′E, 199
Paris (Lutetia, Parisii) (France) 48°52′N 2°20′E, 10, 17, 30, 34, 36, 40, 50, 60, 64, 66, 72, 74, 99, 121, 137, 166
Parksville (USA) 41°51′N 74°45′W, 140
Parma (Italy) 44°48′N 10°19′E, 17, 36, 166
Parur (India) 10°10′N 76°13′E, 198
Passaic (USA) 40°52′N 74°08′W, 140
Passau (W Germany) 48°35′N 13°28′E, 36, 38
Passo Fundo (Brazil) 28°16′S 52°20′W, 159
Patara (Turkey) 36°12′N 29°10′E, 29
Paterson (USA) 40°55′N 74°10′W, 102
Patras (Patrae) (Greece) 38°14′N 21°44′E, 25, 29, 44, 47, 166
Pau (France) 43°18′N 0°22′W, 166
Pavia (Italy) 45°12′N 9°09′E, 36, 99, 100
Pawling (USA) 41°34′N 73°37′W, 140
Paysandú (Uruguay) 32°21′S 58°05′W, 159
Peabody (USA) 42°33′N 70°58′W, 140
Pecs (Hungary) 46°04′N 18°15′E, 166
Pegae *see* Antipatris
Pella (Jordan) 32°27′N 35°37′E, 24, 32
Pelotas (Brazil) 31°45′S 52°20′W, 159
Penamacor (Portugal) 40°10′N 7°10′W, 166
Pensacola (USA) 30°26′N 87°12′W, 138
Peoria (USA) 40°43′N 89°38′W, 138
Peraea (region), 24, 26, 32
Pereyaslav (USSR) 50°05′N 31°29′E, 120
Pergamum (Bergama) (Turkey) 39°08′N 27°10′E, 25, 29, 30
Perge (Turkey) 36°59′N 30°46′E, 25
Périgueux (France) 45°12′N 0°44′E, 166
Perm (USSR) 58°01′N 56°10′E, 190
Perpignan (France) 42°42′N 2°54′E, 166
Perth (Australia) 31°58′S 115°49′E, 10, 60, 217
Perugia (Italy) 43°07′N 12°23′E, 166
Pesaro (Italy) 43°54′N 12°54′E, 17, 47, 121
Pessinus (Turkey) 39°17′N 31°32′E, 29
Pest *see* Budapest
Petah Tiqwa (Israel) 32°05′N 34°53′E, 137, 199
Petaluma (USA) 38°13′N 122°39′W, 138
Peterborough (Canada) 44°19′N 78°20′W, 138
Peterborough (UK) 52°35′N 0°15′W, 166
Petersburg (USA) 37°14′N 77°24′W, 138
Petrograd *see* Leningrad
Petrópolis (Brazil) 22°30′S 43°06′W, 159
Petrozavodsk (USSR) 61°46′N 34°19′E, 190
Phaena (Syria) 33°10′N 36°28′E, 32, 98
Phanagoria (USSR) 45°07′N 36°41′E, 30
Phasaelis (Jordan) 32°02′N 35°25′E, 32
Phaselis (Turkey) 36°39′N 30°31′E, 25, 29
Philadelphia (USA) 40°00′N 75°10′W, 10, 17, 47, 66, 102, 137, 140
Philadelphia *see* Amman
Philippi (Greece) 41°05′N 24°16′E, 25
Philoteria (Bet Yerah) (Israel) 32°43′N 35°35′E, 24
Phoenix (USA) 33°30′N 112°03′W, 10, 138
Phoenixville (USA) 40°07′N 75°31′W, 140
Piatra-Neamt (Romania) 46°53′N 26°23′E, 166
Pictavium *see* Poitiers
Pietermaritzburg (S Africa) 29°36′S 30°24′E, 219
Pietersburg (S Africa) 23°54′S 29°23′E, 219
Pilica (Poland) 50°28′N 19°40′E, 50
Pinczow (Poland) 50°30′N 20°30′E, 50, 101
Pine Bluff (USA) 34°13′N 92°00′W, 138
Pinsk (USSR) 52°08′N 26°01′E, 50, 57, 60, 100, 101, 190
Piotrkow (Poland) 51°27′N 19°40′E, 166
Piove di Sacco (Italy) 45°17′N 12°02′E, 121
Pisa (Italy) 43°43′N 10°24′E, 47, 166
Pittsburgh (USA) 40°26′N 80°00′W, 10, 66, 102, 138
Pittsfield (USA) 42°27′N 73°15′W, 140
Piura (Peru) 5°15′S 80°38′W, 159
Plaszow (Poland) 49°23′N 21°32′E, 70
Plattsburg (USA) 44°42′N 73°29′W, 138
Pleven (Bulgaria) 43°25′N 24°40′E, 47, 166
Ploiesti (Romania) 44°57′N 26°01′E, 166
Plovdiv (Bulgaria) 42°08′N 24°45′E, 166
Plymouth (UK) 50°23′N 4°10′W, 166
Plymouth (USA) 41°58′N 70°40′W, 140
Plzen (Pilsen) (Czechoslovakia) 49°45′N 13°25′E, 166
Podhajce (USSR) 49°19′N 25°10′E, 101
Podolia (region) 50, 101
Poitiers (Pictavium) (France) 46°35′N 0°20′E, 30, 166
Polonnoye (USSR) 50°10′N 27°30′E, 101
Polotsk (USSR) 55°30′N 28°43′E, 101
Poltava (USSR) 49°35′N 34°35′E, 190
Pomona Valley (USA) 34°04′N 117°45′W, 138
Ponary (USSR) 54°39′N 25°18′E, 70
Pontus (region), 26
Poona (India) 18°34′N 73°58′E, 198
Port Arthur (Canada) 48°27′N 89°12′W, 138
Port Arthur (USA) 29°55′N 93°56′W, 138
Port-au-Prince (Haiti) 18°33′N 72°20′W, 159
Port Charlotte (USA) 26°59′N 82°06′W, 138
Port Elizabeth (S Africa) 33°58′S 25°36′E, 219
Port Jervis (USA) 41°22′N 74°40′W, 138
Portland (Maine, USA) 43°41′N 70°18′W, 138
Portland (Oregon, USA) 45°32′N 122°40′W, 138
Pôrto Alegre (Brazil) 30°03′S, 51°10′W, 10, 159
Port of Spain (Trinidad & Tobago) 10°38′N 61°31′W, 159
Porto Vecchio (Corsica, France) 41°35′N 9°16′E, 166
Portsmouth (UK) 50°48′N 1°05′W, 166
Portsmouth (New Hampshire, USA) 43°03′N 70°47′W, 138
Portsmouth (Ohio, USA) 38°45′N 82°59′W, 138
Portsmouth (Virginia, USA) 36°50′N 76°20′W, 138
Posen *see* Poznan
Potchefstroom (S Africa) 26°42′S 27°06′E, 219
Poti (USSR) 42°11′N 41°41′E, 191
Potosí (Bolivia) 19°34′S 65°45′W, 47
Potsdam (E Germany) 52°24′N 13°04′E, 102
Pottstown (USA) 40°15′N 75°38′W, 140
Pottsville (USA) 40°42′N 76°13′W, 140
Poughkeepsie (USA) 41°43′N 73°56′W, 140
Poznan (Posen) (Poland) 52°25′N 16°53′E, 50, 57, 64, 99, 100
Prague (Czechoslovakia) 50°05′N 14°25′E, 17, 36, 44, 50, 57, 60, 64, 66, 99, 100, 102, 121, 166
Pressburg *see* Bratislava
Preston (UK) 53°46′N 2°42′W, 166
Pretoria (S Africa) 25°45′S 28°12′E, 219
Priene (Turkey) 37°38′N 27°17′E, 17
Primorsk (USSR) 60°18′N 28°35′E, 190
Prince Albert (Canada) 53°13′N 105°45′W, 138
Princeton (New Jersey, USA) 40°12′N 74°40′W, 140
Princeton (West Virginia, USA) 37°23′N 81°06′W, 138
Prostejov (Prossnitz) (Czechoslovakia) 49°30′N 17°10′E, 102, 121, 166
Providence (USA) 41°50′N 71°25′W, 138
Przemysl (Poland) 49°48′N 22°48′E, 166
Przemyslany (USSR) 49°40′N 24°33′E, 101
Przeworsk (Poland) 50°04′N 22°30′E, 50
Przysucha (Poland) 51°22′N 20°38′E, 101, 166
Pskov (USSR) 57°48′N 28°26′E, 190
Ptolemais *see* Akko
Puebla (Mexico) 19°03′N 98°10′W, 159
Pueblo (USA) 38°17′N 104°38′W, 138
Puerto Cabello (Venezuela) 10°29′N 68°02′W, 159
Pumbeditha (Iraq) 33°15′N 43°49′E, 25, 29, 30, 38, 40, 98, 99
Pum Nahara (Iraq) 32°35′N 45°16′E, 98
Puteoli (Pozzuoli) (Italy) 40°49′N 14°07′E, 25
Putnam (USA) 41°55′N 71°54′W, 140

Qalat Ahmad (Algeria) 36°00′N 5°06′E, 218
Qift (Egypt) 26°00′N 32°50′E, 218
Qiryat Ata (Israel) 32°48′N 35°06′E, 199
Qiryat Bialik (Israel) 32°50′N 35°05′E, 199
Qiryat Gat (Israel) 31°37′N 34°47′E, 199
Qiryat Malakhi (Israel) 31°44′N 34°45′E, 199
Qiryat Motzkin (Israel) 32°49′N 35°03′E, 199
Qiryat Ono (Israel) 32°04′N 34°51′E, 199
Qiryat Shemona (Israel) 33°13′N 35°35′E, 199
Qiryat Tivon (Tibeon) (Israel) 32°43′N 35°08′E, 98, 199
Qiryat Yam (Israel) 32°51′N 35°04′E, 199
Qom (Iran) 34°39′N 50°57′E, 38, 199
Quebec (Canada) 46°50′N 71°15′W, 138
Queenstown (S Africa) 31°54′S 26°53′E, 219
Que Que (Kwekwe) (Zimbabwe) 18°55′S 29°51′E, 219
Quezaltenango (Guatemala) 14°50′N 91°30′W, 159
Quincy (USA) 39°55′N 91°22′W, 138
Quito (Ecuador) 0°14′S 78°30′W, 159
Qumran (Jordan) 31°44′N 35°27′E, 10, 17
Qus (Egypt) 25°53′N 32°48′E, 218

Raananna (Israel) 32°11′N 34°52′E, 199
Rabat (Morocco) 34°02′N 6°51′W, 218
Rabbath-bene-ammon *see* Amman
Rachmanow (USSR) 50°00′N 25°59′E, 50
Racine (USA) 42°42′N 87°50′W, 138
Radauti (Romania) 47°49′N 25°58′E, 166
Radom (Poland) 51°26′N 21°10′E, 50, 60, 101, 166
Radomsko (Poland) 51°04′N 19°25′E, 166
Radun (USSR) 54°03′N 25°00′E, 102
Radzymin (Poland) 52°25′N 21°10′E, 101, 120
Radzyn (Poland) 51°49′N 22°38′E, 101
Rafah (Raphia) (Gaza Strip) 31°18′N 34°15′E, 24, 32, 199
Ragusa *see* Dubrovnik
Raleigh (USA) 35°46′N 78°39′W, 138

237

INDEX

Page numbers in *italics* refer to illustrations or their captions.

TYPVS CHOROGRA: PHICVS, CELEBRIVM LOCORVM IN REGNO IVDAE ET ISRAHEL.

arte factus
à
Tilemanno Stella Sigenensi.

EXPLICATIONES CHARAC: TERVM POSITIONIS:

⊙ *Metropoles et vrbes insigniores.*

◉ *Minus insignes.*

○ *Pagi, vici et villæ.*

◎ *Ciuitates sacerdotales et refugij.*

φ *Vrbes Philistinorum, quę alias quinque regiæ, vel reguli vocari solent. Ios. 13.*

✳ *Loca pertinentia ad tribum Ephraim.*

✛ *Loca pertinentia ad tribum Simeon.*

Hæc loca per notas peculiares à ceteris discernere coacti sumus, quia per vicinas tribus dispersa, certis limitibus circum scribi non potuerunt.

Mare MAGNVM, siue MARIS ME...

Michmethath.

SAMA

Bethchoron.

EPHR. Galgulis.

Diospolis.et Lidda.

Antipatris.

Ioppe. Arimathea.

IOSEPH. Remmon.

Aorab.

ACHOR vallis Ierich.

Serrona. Iabneel.

Azotus.

DAN BENIAMIN

THAMNITICA PRAEFECTVRA. Gathrimmon. Caphar Saral.

Ascalon.

Eleutheropolis.

Amor:

Enachim. ræi.

Gath. Lachis.

Gaza. Phi: listin. Eltholad. SIMEON. Debir. Sephala, vel Repha im vallis.

IVDAEA

Chebron.

Gerar.

Ziph. Charmel.

Enam.

Daroma Interior

Maon. Ether.

Ain.

Arath. VEL IDVMAEA.

Daroma Exterior.

EDOM et Pharam,

Raphia.

Rechoboth.

Acrabim.